GO!

with Microsoft®

Windows 10
Introductory

Shelley Gaskin and Heddy Pritchard

Pearson

330 Hudson Street, NY, NY 10013

Vice President, Career Skills: Andrew Gilfillan
Executive Portfolio Manager: Jenifer Niles
Managing Producer: Laura Burgess
Program Manager: Emily Biberger
Development Editor: Joyce Nielsen
Director of Product Marketing: Maggie Moylan
Director of Field Marketing: Leigh Ann Sims
Field Marketing Managers: Molly Schmidt and Joanna Conley
Marketing Coordinator: Susan Osterlitz
Operations Specialist: Maura Garcia
Senior Art Director: Mary Siener
Cover Photos: GaudiLab, Rawpixel.com, Pressmaster, Eugenio Marongiu, Boggy, Gajus, Rocketclips, Inc

Associate Director of Design: Blair Brown
Media Project Manager, Production: John Cassar
Full-Service Project Management: iEnergizer Aptara®, Ltd.
Composition: iEnergizer Aptara®, Ltd.
Printer/Binder: LSC Communications Kendallville
Cover Printer: LSC Communications Kendallville
Text Font: Times LT Pro
Cover Image Credits: Eugenio Marongiu/Fotolia, pressmaster/Fotolia (*top row, left to right*); Boggy/Fotolia, Gajus/Fotolia, Rawpixel.com/Fotolia (*middle row, left to right*); Rocketclips, Inc./Shutterstock, GaudiLab/Fotolia (*bottom row, left to right*)

Credits and acknowledgments borrowed from other sources and reproduced, with permission, in this textbook appear on the appropriate page within text. Microsoft and/or its respective suppliers make no representations about the suitability of the information contained in the documents and related graphics published as part of the services for any purpose. All such documents and related graphics are provided "as is" without warranty of any kind.

Microsoft and/or its respective suppliers make no representations about the suitability of the information contained in the documents and related graphics published as part of the services for any purpose. All such documents and related graphics are provided "as is" without warranty of any kind. Microsoft and/or its respective suppliers hereby disclaim all warranties and conditions with regard to this information, including all warranties and conditions of merchantability, whether express, implied or statutory, fitness for a particular purpose, title and non-infringement. In no event shall Microsoft and/or its respective suppliers be liable for any special, indirect or consequential damages or any damages whatsoever resulting from loss of use, data or profits, whether in an action of contract, negligence or other tortious action, arising out of or in connection with the use or performance of information available from the services. The documents and related graphics contained herein could include technical inaccuracies or typographical errors. Changes are periodically added to the information herein. Microsoft and/or its respective suppliers may make improvements and/or changes in the product(s) and/or the program(s) described herein at any time. Partial screen shots may be viewed in full within the software version specified.

Microsoft® and Windows® are registered trademarks of the Microsoft Corporation in the U.S.A. and other countries. This book is not sponsored or endorsed by or affiliated with the Microsoft Corporation.

Library of Congress Control Number on File

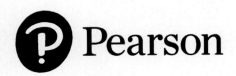

ISBN 13: 978-0-13-383982-1
ISBN 10   0-13-383982-6

Contents

Chapter 2 Use Backup and Recovery Tools and Discover Windows Apps 95

Chapter 3 Advanced File Management and Advanced Searching 147

Chapter 5 Monitoring and Tracking System Performance 273

About the Authors

Shelley Gaskin, Series Editor, is a professor in the Business and Computer Technology Division at Pasadena City College in Pasadena, California. She holds a bachelor's degree in Business Administration from Robert Morris College (Pennsylvania), a master's degree in Business from Northern Illinois University, and a doctorate in Adult and Community Education from Ball State University (Indiana). Before joining Pasadena City College, she spent 12 years in the computer industry, where she was a systems analyst, sales representative, and director of Customer Education with Unisys Corporation. She also worked for Ernst & Young on the development of large systems applications for their clients. She has written and developed training materials for custom systems applications in both the public and private sector, and has also written and edited numerous computer application textbooks.

This book is dedicated to my students, who inspire me every day.

Heddy Pritchard is an adjunct professor in the School of Engineering and Technology (EnTec) at Miami Dade College and in the School of Office Careers/Computer Science/Computer Science-Industrial at Broward College. She holds a bachelor's degree in Computer Information Systems from Florida Atlantic University and a master's degree in Computer Information Systems from Nova Southeastern University (Florida). She has been a programmer/analyst for 26+ years and involved in the development of numerous applications.

This book is dedicated to students who want to improve their lives with the use of computers.

GO! with Windows 10 Getting Started

GO! with Windows 10 is the right solution for you and your students in the modern fast-moving, mobile environment. The GO! Series content focuses on the real-world job skills students need to succeed in the workforce. They learn the new exciting Windows 10 by working step-by-step through practical job-related projects that put the core functionality of Windows 10 in context. And as has always been true of the GO! Series, students learn the important concepts when they need them, and they never get lost in instruction, because the GO! Series uses Microsoft procedural syntax. Students learn how and learn why—at the teachable moment.

Highlights

Easy-to-follow chapter opener includes a detailed introduction to the A & B instructional projects with clearly defined chapter Objectives and Learning Outcomes.

GO! for Job Success Discussions relate to the projects in the chapter and cover important career topics such as Managing Your Computer Files, Mobile Devices, 3D Printing, Cyber Hacking, and Wearable Technology.

GO! Learn It Online Section at the end of the chapter indicates where various student learning activities can be found, including multiple choice and matching activities.

In-Text Boxed Content: Another Way, Notes, More Knowledge, Alerts, and By Touch instructions are included in line with the instruction and not in the margins, so that students are more likely to read this information.

Visual Chapter Summary focuses on the four key concepts to remember from each chapter.

Review and Assessment Guide summarizes the end-of-chapter assessments for a quick overview of the different types and levels of assignments and assessments for each chapter.

Convenient End-of-Chapter Key Term Glossary with Definitions for each chapter makes reviewing easier.

Student Materials

Student Data Files – All student data files are available to all on: www.pearsonhighered.com/go.

Available in MyITLab.

Instructor Materials

Student Assignment Tracker – Lists all the assignments for the chapter. Just add the course information, due dates, and points. Providing these to students ensures they will know what is due and when.

Scripted Lectures – A script to guide your classroom lecture of each instructional project.

Annotated Solution Files – Coupled with the scorecards, these create a grading and scoring system that makes grading easy and efficient.

PowerPoint Lectures – PowerPoint presentations for each chapter.

Audio PowerPoints – Audio versions of the PowerPoint presentations for each chapter.

Scoring Rubrics – Can be used either by students to check their work or by you as a quick check-off for the items that need to be corrected.

Syllabus Templates – For 8-week, 12-week, and 16-week courses.

Test Bank – Includes a variety of test questions for each chapter.

Getting Started with Windows 10

PROJECT 1A

OUTCOMES
Sign in and out of Windows 10, identify the features of an operating system, create a folder and save a file, use Windows apps, and customize your Start menu.

PROJECT 1B

OUTCOMES
Start programs, search for and manage files and folders, copy and move files and folders, and use the Recycle Bin.

OBJECTIVES

1. Explore the Windows 10 Environment
2. Use File Explorer and Desktop Apps to Create a New Folder and Save a File
3. Identify the Functions of the Windows 10 Operating System
4. Discover Windows 10 Features
5. Sign Out of Windows 10, Turn Off Your Computer, and Manage User Accounts
6. Manage Your Windows 10 System

OBJECTIVES

7. Download and Extract Files and Folders
8. Use File Explorer to Display Locations, Folders, and Files
9. Start Programs and Open Data Files
10. Create, Rename, and Copy Files and Folders
11. Use OneDrive as Cloud Storage

Dragonstock/Fotolia

In This Chapter

In this chapter, you will use Microsoft Windows 10, which is software that manages your computer's hardware, software, communications, and data files. You will use the taskbar and Start menu features to get your work done with ease and use Windows apps to get your latest personal information and to find news and entertainment. You will sign in to your computer, explore the features of Windows 10, create folders and save files, use Windows apps, manage multiple windows, sign out of your computer, and examine user accounts.

The projects in this chapter relate to the **Bell Orchid Hotels**, headquartered in Boston, and which own and operate resorts and business-oriented hotels. Resort properties are located in popular destinations, including Honolulu, Orlando, San Diego, and Santa Barbara. The resorts offer deluxe accommodations and a wide array of dining options. Other Bell Orchid hotels are located in major business centers and offer the latest technology in their meeting facilities. Bell Orchid offers extensive educational opportunities for employees. The company plans to open new properties and update existing properties over the next decade.

PROJECT ACTIVITIES

In Activities 1.01 through 1.20, you will participate in training along with Steven Ramos and Barbara Hewitt, both of whom work for the Information Technology Department at the Boston headquarters office of the Bell Orchid Hotels. After completing this part of the training, you will be able to sign in and sign out of your computer, create folders and save files, use Windows apps, and manage your user account. As you progress through the Project, you will insert screenshots of windows that you create into a PowerPoint presentation similar to Figure 1.1.

 ## PROJECT FILES

For Project 1A, you will need the following file:

A new blank PowerPoint presentation into which you will insert screenshots of windows you create.

You will save your results in a PowerPoint file as:

Lastname_Firstname_1A_Know_Windows

PROJECT RESULTS

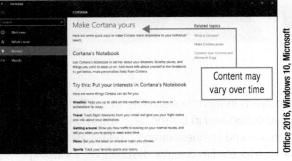

FIGURE 1.1 Project 1A Getting to Know Windows 10

A ***program*** is a set of instructions that a computer uses to accomplish a task. A computer program that helps you perform a task for a specific purpose is referred to as an ***application***. For example, there are applications to create a document using word processing software, to play a game, to view the latest weather report, or to manage information.

An ***operating system*** is a specific type of computer program that manages the other programs on a computing device such as a desktop computer, a laptop computer, a smartphone, a tablet computer, or a game console. You need an operating system to:

- use application programs
- coordinate the use of your computer hardware such as a keyboard, mouse, touchpad, touchscreen, game controller, or printer
- organize data that you store on your computer and access data that you store on your own computer and in other locations

Windows 10 is an operating system developed by Microsoft Corporation that works with mobile computing devices and also with traditional desktop and laptop PCs.

Activity 1.01 | Identifying Apps and Platforms

The term ***desktop app*** commonly refers to a computer program that is installed on the hard drive of your personal computer—usually referred to as a PC—and requires a computer operating system like Microsoft Windows or Apple macOS to run. The programs in the full-featured versions of Microsoft Office such as Word and Excel are popular desktop apps. Adobe's Photoshop photo editing software and Adobe's Premiere Pro video editing software are also popular desktop apps. Desktop apps typically have hundreds of features that take time to learn and use efficiently.

The shortened version of the term *application* is ***app***, and this is typically a smaller application designed for a single purpose. Apps can run from the device operating system on a PC, a tablet computer, a game console, or a smartphone. You might already be familiar with apps that run on mobile devices like an Apple iPhone, an Apple iPad, an Android phone, an Android tablet, a Windows phone, or a Windows tablet. Examples include games like Monument Valley and Words with Friends; social networking and messaging apps like Instagram, Facebook, and WhatsApp; information apps like The Weather Channel and NFL Mobile; apps provided by your bank to enable you to conduct transactions; and services like Skype or Google Search.

Windows apps are apps that run not only on a Windows phone and a Windows tablet, but also on your Windows desktop PC. Most popular apps have versions for each major ***mobile device platform***—the hardware and software environment for smaller-screen devices such as tablets and smartphones. For example, the NFL Mobile app is available for Apple mobile devices, Windows mobile devices, and Android devices.

Increasingly, an operating system environment is referred to simply as a ***platform***, which refers to an underlying computer system on which application programs can run. An ***application developer***, which is anyone who writes a computer application, must write his or her application for one or more platforms, the most popular of which are the iOS platform, the Android platform, and the Windows platform.

Example of apps available from the Windows Store (your screen will differ)

Office 2016, Windows 10, Microsoft Corporation.

FIGURE 1.2

Some Windows apps are also referred to as ***universal apps*** because anyone that wants to develop an app for the Windows 10 platform can use a common code base to deliver the app to any Windows device—a desktop or laptop PC, a Windows phone, a Windows tablet, or an Xbox game console.

App developers can also use this code base to develop apps for Microsoft's new ***HoloLens*** see-through holographic computer and for devices on the ***Internet of Things***, which refers to a growing network of physical objects that will have sensors connected to the Internet. Home automation devices like lights and appliances that you can control over the Internet are among the first objects connected to the ***IoT***—the common acronym for the Internet of Things.

Bildagentur Zoonar GmbH/Shutterstock

FIGURE 1.3

To check how well you understand apps and platforms, take a moment to think about the answers to the following questions:

Self-Check | Answer These Questions to Check Your Understanding

1 A set of instructions that a computer uses to accomplish a task is a _____.

2 A specific type of computer program that manages the other programs on a computer is an _____ _____.

3 Computer programs installed on the hard drive of a computer, such as Microsoft Excel and Adobe Photoshop, and that typically have hundreds of features and take time to learn and use efficiently, are referred to as _____ apps.

4 The hardware and software environment for smaller-screen devices such as laptops, tablets, and smartphones is referred to as a mobile device _____.

5 The growing network of physical objects that have sensors connected to the Internet is called the _____ _____ _____.

Activity 1.02 | Recognizing User Accounts in Windows 10

On a single computer, Windows 10 can have multiple user accounts. This is useful because you can share a computer with other people in your family or organization and each person can have his or her own information and settings—none of which others can see. Each user on a single computer is referred to as a *user account*.

ALERT!   **Variations in Screen Organization, Colors, and Functionality Are Common in Windows 10**

Individuals and organizations can determine how Windows 10 displays; therefore, the colors and the organization of various elements on the screen can vary. Your college or organization may customize Windows 10 to display a college picture or company logo, or restrict access to certain features. The basic functions and structure of Windows 10 are not changed by such variations. You can be confident that the skills you will practice in this instruction apply to Windows 10 regardless of available functionality or differences between the figures shown and your screen.

NOTE   **Comparing Your Screen with the Figures in This Textbook**

Your screen will more closely match the figures shown in this textbook if you set your screen resolution to 1280 × 768. At other resolutions, your screen will closely resemble, but not match, the figures shown. To view or change your screen's resolution, on the desktop, right-click in a blank area, click *Display settings*, click *Advanced display settings*, and then click the *Resolution arrow*.

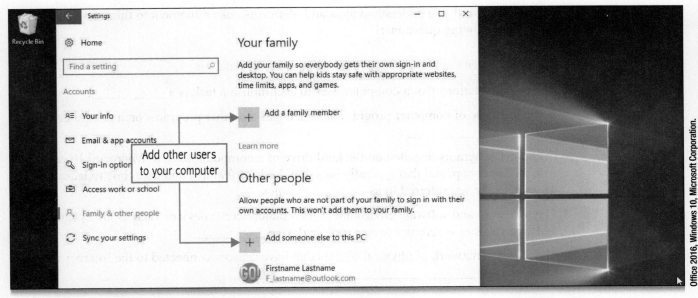

Office 2016, Windows 10, Microsoft Corporation.

FIGURE 1.4

With Windows 10, you can create a *Microsoft account*, and then use that account to sign in to *any* Windows 10 computer on which you have, or create, a user account. By signing in with a Microsoft account you can:

- download apps from the Windows Store
- get your online content—email, social network updates, updated news—automatically displayed in an app when you sign in

Optionally, you can create a local account for use only on a specific PC. On your own Windows 10 computer, you must establish and then sign in with either a local account or a Microsoft account. Regardless of which one you select, you must provide an email address to associate with the user account name. If you create and then sign in with a local account, you can still connect to the Internet, but you will not have the advantage of having your personal arrangement of apps displayed on your Start menu every time you sign in to that PC. You can use any email address to create a local account—similar to other online services where an email address is your user ID. You can also use any email address to create a Microsoft account.

To enjoy and get the full benefit from Windows 10, Microsoft Office, Skype, and free OneDrive cloud storage, if you have not already done so, create a Microsoft account by going to www.microsoft.com/en-us/account. There you can create an account using any email address and, if you want to do so, get more information about Microsoft accounts.

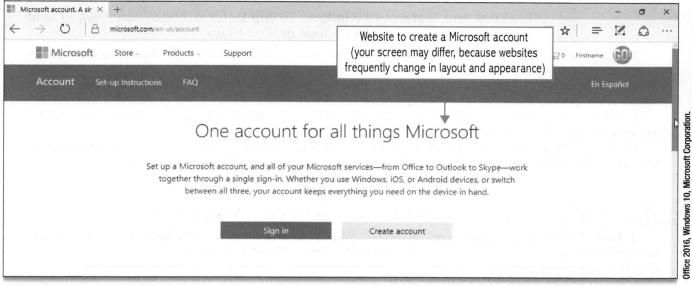

FIGURE 1.5

By signing in with a Microsoft account, your computer becomes your connected device where *you*—not your files—are the center of activity. At your college or place of employment, sign-in requirements will vary, because those computers are controlled by the organization's IT (Information Technology) professionals who are responsible for maintaining a secure computing environment for the entire organization.

To check how well you can identify operating system functions, take a moment to think about the answers to the following questions:

Self-Check | Answer These Questions to Check Your Understanding

1 On a single Windows 10 computer, multiple people can have a user account with their own information and _____.

2 On your own Windows 10 computer, it is recommended that you create a Microsoft account—if you do not have one—and then use that account to sign in because you will have your personal arrangement of _____ displayed on the Start menu every time you sign in to that PC.

3 To use your own Windows 10 computer, you must establish and then sign in with either a _____ account or a Microsoft account.

4 You can use any _____ address to set up a Microsoft account.

5 Sign-in requirements vary in organizations and colleges, because those computers are _____ by the organization's IT (Information Technology) professionals.

Activity 1.03 | Turning On Your Computer, Signing In, and Exploring the Windows 10 Environment

Before you begin any computer activity, you must, if necessary, turn on your computer. This process is commonly referred to as ***booting the computer***. Because Windows 10 does not require you to completely shut down your computer except to install or repair a hardware device, in most instances moving the mouse or pressing a key will wake your computer in a few seconds. So most of the time you will skip the lengthier boot process.

In this Activity, you will turn on your computer and sign in to Windows 10. Within an organization, the sign-in process may differ from that of your own computer.

1 If necessary, turn on your computer, and then compare your screen with Figure 1.6.

The Windows 10 *lock screen* displays a background—this might be a default picture from Microsoft or a picture that you selected if you have personalized your system already. You can also choose to have a slide show of your own photos display on the lock screen.

Your lock screen displays the time, day, and date. In Windows 10 Settings, you can select Personalization where you can choose *lock screen apps* to display, such as your calendar and mail. A lock screen app runs in the background and shows you quick status and notifications, even when your screen is locked. A lock screen app may also display a *badge*, which is an *icon*—small images that can represent commands, files, applications, or other windows—that shows status information such as your Internet connection or battery time remaining or summary information; for example, how many unread emails are in a mail app or the number of new posts in a social media app.

For example, one lock screen app that you can add is Mail so that you can use email without having to sign in to your computer.

Your organization might have a custom sign-in screen with a logo or sign-in instructions, which will differ from the one shown. If you are using Windows 10 Pro, in the Accounts section of Settings, there is a feature named Access work or school, from which you may be able to connect to your work or school system based on established policies.

Windows 10 lock screen
(your image will vary)

3:20

Thursday, September 3

FIGURE 1.6

2 Determine whether you are working with a mouse and keyboard system or with a touchscreen system. If you are working with a touchscreen, determine whether you will use a stylus pen or the touch of your fingers.

Windows 10 is optimized for touchscreen computers and also works with a mouse and keyboard in the way you are probably most accustomed. If your device has a touchscreen, you can use the following gestures with your fingers in place of mouse and keyboard commands:

NOTE	If You Are Using a Touchscreen
	Tap an item to click it.
	Press and hold for a few seconds to right-click; release when the information or commands display.
	Touch the screen with two or more fingers and then zoom in or zoom out; stretch out or pinch in.
	Slide your finger on the screen to scroll—slide left to scroll right and slide right to scroll left.
	Slide to rearrange—similar to dragging with a mouse.
	Swipe to select—slide an item a short distance with a quick movement—to select an item and bring up commands, if any.

3 Press Enter to display the Windows 10 sign-in screen.

BY TOUCH On the lock screen, swipe upward to display the sign-in screen. Tap your user image if necessary to display the Password box.

4 If you are the displayed user, type your password (if you have established one) and press Enter. If you are not the displayed user, click your user image if it displays or click the Switch user arrow → and then click your user image. Type your password.

BY TOUCH Tap the Password box to display the onscreen keyboard, type your password using the onscreen keyboard, and then at the right, tap the arrow.

The Windows 10 desktop displays with a default desktop background, a background you have selected, or perhaps a background set by your college or workplace.

5 In the lower left corner of your screen, move the mouse pointer over—*point to*—**Start** 🪟 and then *click*—press the left button on your mouse pointing device—to display the **Start menu**. Compare your screen with Figure 1.7, and then take a moment to study the table in Figure 1.8.

The *mouse pointer* is any symbol that displays on your screen in response to moving your mouse.

The Windows 10 *Start menu* displays a list of installed programs on the left and a customizable group of square and rectangular boxes—referred to as *tiles*—on the right. You can customize the arrangement of tiles from which you can access apps, websites, programs, folders, and tools for using your computer by simply clicking or tapping them.

Think of the right side of the Start menu as your connected *dashboard*—a one-screen view of links to information and programs that matter to *you*—through which you can connect with the people, activities, places, and apps that you care about.

Some tiles are referred to as *live tiles*, because they are constantly updated with fresh information relevant to you—the number of new email messages you have, new sports scores that you are interested in, or new updates to social networks such as Facebook or Twitter. Live tiles are at the center of your Windows 10 experience.

As you progress in your study of Windows 10, you will learn to customize the Start menu and add, delete, and organize tiles into meaningful groups. Your Start menu will not look like anyone else's; you will customize it to suit your own information needs.

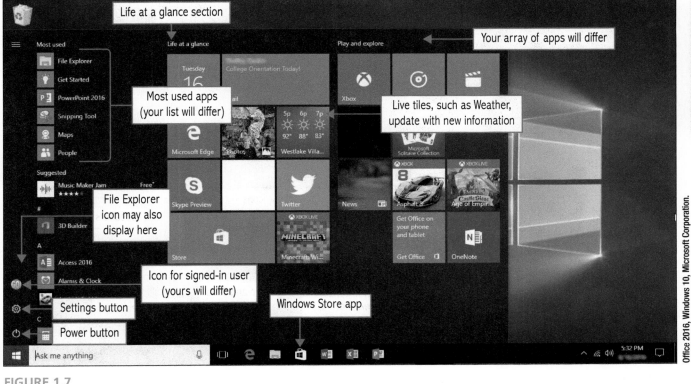

FIGURE 1.7

Office 2016, Windows 10, Microsoft Corporation.

PARTS OF THE WINDOWS 10 START MENU	
Life at a glance section	Apps pinned to the Start menu that relate to your own information; for example, your Mail, your Calendar, and your contacts (People); you can change this heading or delete it.
Most used	Displays a list of the apps that you use the most; updates as you use Windows 10.
Play and explore section	Apps pinned to the Start menu that relate to games or news apps that you have installed; you can change this heading or delete it.
Power button	Enables you to set your computer to Sleep, Shut down, or Restart.
Settings button	Displays the Settings window to change Windows 10 settings.
Signed-in user	Displays the icon or picture of the signed-in user.
Windows Store app	Opens the Windows Store to locate and download more apps.

FIGURE 1.8

Office 2016, Windows 10, Microsoft Corporation.

6 ▶ Click **Start** ⊞ again to close the Start menu. Compare your screen with Figure 1.9, and then take a moment to study the parts of the Windows desktop as shown in the table in Figure 1.10.

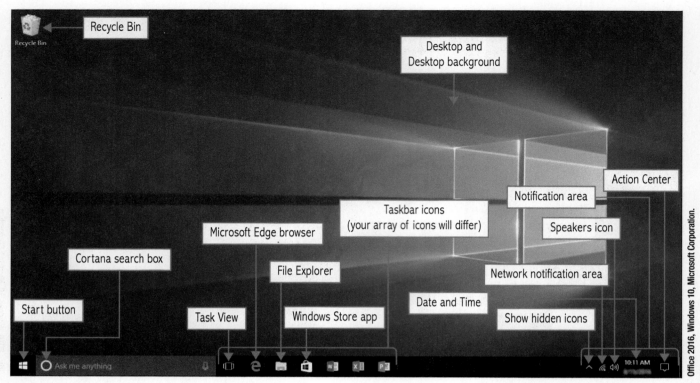

FIGURE 1.9

Office 2016, Windows 10, Microsoft Corporation.

PARTS OF THE WINDOWS 10 DESKTOP	
Action Center	Displays the Action Center in a vertical pane on the right of your screen where you can see app notifications—such as new mail or new alerts from Microsoft or from social networks like Facebook—at the top and access commonly used settings at the bottom.
Desktop	Serves as a surface for your work, like the top of an actual desk. Here you can arrange icons— small pictures that represent a file, folder, program, or other object.
Desktop background	Displays the colors and graphics of your desktop; you can change the desktop background to look the way you want it, such as using a picture or a solid color. Also referred to as **wallpaper**.
File Explorer	Launches the File Explorer program, which displays the contents of folders and files on your computer and on connected locations, and also enables you to perform tasks related to your files and folders such as copying, moving, and renaming. If your File Explorer icon does not display, click the Start button, point to the File Explorer icon, right-click, point to More, and then click Pin to taskbar.
Microsoft Edge browser	Launches Microsoft Edge, the web browser program developed by Microsoft that is included with Windows 10.
Network notification icon	Displays the status of your network.
Notification area	Displays notification icons and the system clock and calendar; sometimes referred to as the **system tray**.
Recycle Bin	Contains files and folders that you delete. When you delete a file or folder from a location on your hard disk drive, it is not actually deleted; it stays in the Recycle Bin if you want it back, until you take an action to empty the Recycle Bin.
Search box	If **Cortana**—Microsoft's intelligent personal assistant—is disabled, this will indicate *Search the web and Windows*. Assuming Cortana is enabled, this will indicate *Ask me anything*.

FIGURE 1.10 *(continued)*

PARTS OF THE WINDOWS 10 DESKTOP (*continued*)	
Show hidden icons	Displays additional icons related to your notifications.
Speakers icon	Displays the status of your computer's speakers (if any).
Start button	Displays the Start menu.
Task View	Displays your desktop background with a small image of all open programs and apps. Click once to open, click again to close.
Taskbar	Contains buttons to launch programs and buttons for all open programs; by default, it is located at the bottom of the desktop, but you can move it. You can customize the number and arrangement of buttons.
Windows Store	Opens the Windows Store where you can select and download Windows apps.

FIGURE 1.10

> **NOTE** **This Activity Is Optional**
>
> Complete this Activity if you are able to do so. Some college labs may not enable these features. If you cannot practice in your college lab, practice this on another computer if possible.

Activity 1.04 | Changing Your Desktop Background and Lock Screen Image

As a way to personalize your computer, you can change the desktop background to a personal photo. You can also change your lock screen image to a personal photo.

1 Click **Start** 🔳, just above the Start button click **Settings** ⚙, click **Personalization**, and then on the left, click **Background**.

2 On the right, under **Choose your picture**, click **Browse**, and then select a personal photo from the **Pictures** folder on your PC, select one of Microsoft's stock images—or navigate to some other location where you have stored a personal photo.

3 Click the picture, and then at the bottom of the Open dialog box, click **Choose picture**.

4 On the left, click **Lock screen**, on the right, click the **Background arrow**, and then click **Picture**.

5 Click **Browse**, and then select a personal photo from the **Pictures** folder on your PC—or navigate to some other location where you have stored a personal photo.

6 Click the picture, and then at the bottom of the Open dialog box, click **Choose picture**.

7 Close all open windows.

> **NOTE** **This Activity Is Optional**
>
> Complete this Activity if you are able to do so. Some college labs may not enable these features. If you cannot practice in your college lab, practice this on another computer if possible.

Activity 1.05 | Creating a PIN to Use in Place of Passwords

You can create a *PIN*—a personal identification number—to use in place of a password. Having a PIN makes it easier to sign in to Windows, apps, and services because it is short.

1 Click **Start** 🔳, just above the Start button click **Settings** ⚙, click **Accounts**, and then on the left click **Sign-in options**.

2 On the right, scroll down if necessary, and then under **PIN**, click **Add**. If necessary, enter the password for your Microsoft account and click **Sign in**.

3 In the **New PIN** box, type **1234**—or a PIN of your choice so long as you can remember it. In the **Confirm PIN** box, retype your PIN.

4 Click **OK**, and notice that you can use this PIN to sign in to Windows, apps, and services.

5 **Close** ⊠ the **Settings** window.

Objective 2	Use File Explorer and Desktop Apps to Create a New Folder and Save a File

Activity 1.06 | Pinning a Program and Adding a Toolbar to the Taskbar

Snipping Tool is a program within Windows 10 that captures an image of all or part of your computer's screen. A *snip*, as the captured image is called, can be annotated, saved, copied, or shared via email.

1 In the lower left corner of the taskbar, to the right of **Start** ⊞, click in the **Search box**.

By default, Cortana is enabled. In a college lab or business, it is possible that Cortana is disabled, but you can still search.

Search relies on *Bing*, Microsoft's search engine, which enables you to conduct a search on your PC, your apps, and the web.

2 With your insertion point in the search box, type **snipping** and then compare your screen with Figure 1.11.

🔄 BY TOUCH   On a touchscreen, tap in the Search box to display the onscreen keyboard, and then begin to type *snipping*.

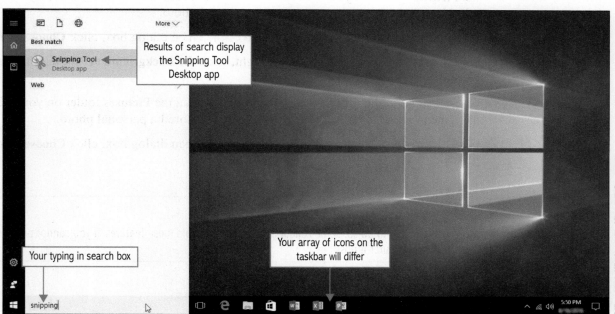

FIGURE 1.11

Office 2016, Windows 10, Microsoft Corporation.

3 With **Snipping Tool** shaded and displayed at the top of the search results, press ⌷Enter⌷ one time.

The Snipping Tool *dialog box*—a small window that displays options for completing a task—displays on the desktop, and on the taskbar, the Snipping Tool program button displays underlined and framed in a lighter shade to indicate that the program is open.

4 On the taskbar, point to the **Snipping Tool** button 🖼 and then *right-click*—click the right mouse button one time. On the displayed **Jump List**, click **Pin to taskbar**.

A *Jump List* displays destinations and tasks from a program's taskbar icon when you right-click the icon.

5 Point to the upper right corner of the **Snipping Tool** dialog box, and then click **Close** ⌷×⌷.

Because you will use Snipping Tool frequently while completing the Projects in this instruction, it is recommended that you leave Snipping Tool pinned to your taskbar.

6 Point to an empty area of the taskbar, and then right-click to display a list that contains *Toolbars*—if your taskbar is crowded, you might have to try several times to find an empty area.

7 Point to **Toolbars**, click **Links**, and then on the taskbar, notice the text *Links*.

8 On the taskbar, to the right of **Links**, click >> and then notice the links to websites you have visited.

These taskbar toolbars are available if you want to use them; however, it is now more common to add tiles to the Start menu for frequently used sites. There are some additional toolbars you might want to explore.

9 To remove the taskbar toolbar, right-click again in a blank area of the taskbar, point to **Toolbars**, and then click **Links** again to remove it from the taskbar.

Activity 1.07 | Creating a New Folder to Store a File

A *file* is a collection of information stored on a computer under a single name. Examples of a file include a Word document, an Excel workbook, a picture, a song, or a program. A *folder* is a container in which you can store files. Windows 10 organizes and keeps track of your electronic files by letting you create and label electronic folders into which you can place your files.

In this Activity, you will create a new folder and save it in a location of your choice. You might decide to use a *removable storage device*, such as a USB flash drive, which is commonly used to transfer information from one computer to another. Such devices are also useful when you want to work with your files on different computers. For example, you probably have files that you work with at your college, at home, and possibly at your workplace.

A *drive* is an area of storage that is formatted with a file system compatible with your operating system and is identified by a drive letter. For example, your computer's *hard disk drive*—the primary storage device located inside your computer where some of your files and programs are typically stored—is usually designated as drive C. Removable storage devices that you insert into your computer will be designated with a drive letter—the letter designation varies from one computer to another.

As you progress in your study of Windows 10, you will also learn to use *cloud storage*—storage space on an Internet site that can also display as a drive on your computer. When you create a Microsoft account, free cloud storage called *OneDrive* is provided to you. If you are signed in with your Microsoft account, you can access OneDrive from File Explorer.

Increasingly, the use of removable storage devices for file storage is becoming less common, because having your files stored in the cloud where you can retrieve them from any device is more convenient and efficient.

ALERT!

The steps in this Activity use the example of storing on a USB flash drive. If you want to store your file in a different location, such as the Documents folder on your computer's hard drive or a folder on your OneDrive, you can still complete the steps, but your screens will not match exactly those shown.

---

1 ▸ Be sure your Windows desktop is still displayed. If you want to do so, insert your USB flash drive. If necessary, close any messages.

Plugging in a device results in a chime sound—if sound is enabled. You might see a message in the taskbar or on the screen that the device software is being installed.

2 ▸ On your taskbar, check to see if the **File Explorer icon** ▯ displays. If it does, move to step 3. If not, in the search box type **file explorer** and then under **Best Match**, point to **File Explorer Desktop app**, right-click, and then click **Pin to taskbar**.

In an enterprise environment such as a college or business, File Explorer is not pinned to the taskbar by default, so you might have to pin it there each time you use the computer. Windows 10 Home, the version of Windows that comes on most consumer PCs, typically has File Explorer pinned by default.

3 ▸ On the taskbar, click **File Explorer** ▯. If necessary, in the upper right corner of the **File Explorer** window, click **Expand the Ribbon** ⌄ .

The *ribbon* is a user interface in Windows 10 that groups commands for performing related tasks on tabs across the upper portion of a window. Commands for common tasks include copying and moving, creating new folders, emailing and zipping items, and changing the view.

Use the *navigation pane*—the area on the left side of the File Explorer window—to get to locations—your OneDrive, folders on your PC, devices and drives connected to your PC, and other PCs on your network.

4 ▸ If necessary, on the ribbon at the top of the window, on the View tab, in the Layout group, click Tiles. (You might have to expand your ribbon, as described in the table in Figure 1.13; also, you might have to scroll within the Layout group to view *Tiles*.) Compare your screen with Figure 1.12, and then take a moment to study the parts of the File Explorer window as shown in the table in Figure 1.13.

NOTE Does your ribbon show only the tab names? Does your Quick Access toolbar display below the ribbon?

By default, the ribbon is minimized and appears as a menu bar, displaying only the ribbon tabs. If your ribbon displays only tabs, click the Expand the Ribbon arrow ⌄ on the right side to display the full ribbon. If your Quick Access toolbar displays below the ribbon, point to it, right-click, and then click Show Quick Access Toolbar above the Ribbon.

The *File Explorer window* displays with the Quick access area selected by default. A File Explorer window displays the contents of the current location, and contains helpful parts so that you can *navigate*—explore within the file organizing structure of Windows. A *location* is any disk drive, folder, network, or cloud storage area in which you can store files and folders.

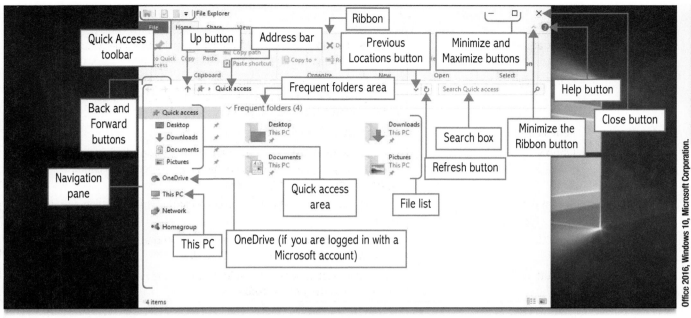

FIGURE 1.12

PARTS OF THE FILE EXPLORER WINDOW	
Address bar	Displays your current location in the folder structure as a series of links separated by arrows.
Back and Forward buttons	Provides the ability to navigate to other folders you have already opened without closing the current folder window. These buttons work with the address bar; that is, after you use the address bar to change folders, you can use the Back button to return to the previous folder.
Close button	Closes the window.
File list	Displays the contents of the current folder or location; if you type text into the Search box, only the folders and files that match your search will display here—including files in subfolders. This area is also referred to as the ***content pane***.
Frequent folders area	When Quick access is selected in the navigation pane, displays the folders you use frequently.
Help button	Opens a Bing search for Windows 10 help.
Maximize button	Increases the size of a window to fill the entire screen.
Minimize button	Removes the window from the screen without closing it; minimized windows can be reopened by clicking the associated button in the taskbar.
Minimize the Ribbon button	Collapses the ribbon so that only the tab names display.
Navigation pane	Displays—for the purpose of navigating to locations—the Quick access area, your OneDrive if you have one and are signed in, locations on the PC at which you are working, any connected storage devices, and network locations to which you might be connected.
OneDrive	Provides navigation to your free file storage and file sharing service provided by Microsoft that you get when you sign up for a Microsoft account; this is your personal cloud storage for files.
Previous Locations button	Displays the path to locations you have visited recently so that you can go back to a previously working directory quickly.

FIGURE 1.13 *(Continued)*

PARTS OF THE FILE EXPLORER WINDOW (continued)	
Quick access area	Displays commonly accessed locations—such as Documents and Desktop—that you want to access quickly.
Quick Access toolbar	Displays commonly used commands; you can customize this toolbar by adding and deleting commands and by showing the toolbar below the ribbon instead of above the ribbon.
Refresh button	Refreshes the current path.
Ribbon	Groups common tasks on related tabs at the top of the window; for example, copying and moving, creating new folders, emailing and zipping items, and changing views.
Search box	Locates files stored within the current location when you type a search term.
This PC	Provides navigation to your internal storage and attached storage devices including optical media such as a DVD drive.
Up button	Opens the location where the folder you are viewing is saved—also referred to as the *parent folder*.

Office 2016, Windows 10, Microsoft Corporation.

FIGURE 1.13

5 ▸ In the **navigation pane**, click **This PC**. On the right, under **Devices and drives**, locate **Windows (C:)**—or **OS (C:)**—point to the device name to display the ⬚ pointer, and then right-click to display a shortcut menu. Compare your screen with Figure 1.14.

A *shortcut menu* is a context-sensitive menu that displays commands and options relevant to the active object. The Windows logo on the C: drive indicates this is where the Windows 10 operating system is stored.

🔄 BY TOUCH   Press and hold briefly to display a shaded square and then release.

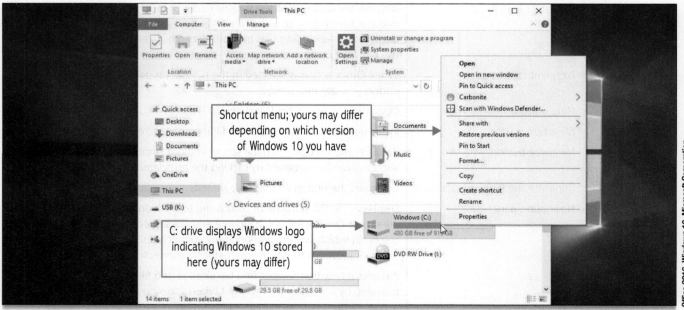

FIGURE 1.14

Office 2016, Windows 10, Microsoft Corporation.

6 On the shortcut menu, click **Open** to display the *file list* for this drive.

A file list displays the contents of the current location. This area is also referred to as the ***content pane***. If you enter a search term in the search box, your results will also display here. Here, in the C: drive, Windows 10 stores various files related to your operating system.

ANOTHER WAY   Point to the device name and double-click to display the file list for the device.

7 On the ribbon, notice that the **Drive Tools tab** displays above the **Manage tab**.

This is a ***contextual tab***, which is a tab added to the ribbon automatically when a specific object is selected and that contains commands relevant to the selected object.

8 To the left of the **address bar**, click **Up** ↑ to move up one level in the drive hierarchy and close the file list.

The ***address bar*** displays your current location in the folder structure as a series of links separated by arrows. Use the address bar to enter or select a location. You can tap or click a part of the path to go to that level, or tap or click at the end of the path to select the path for copying.

9 Under **Devices and drives**, click your **USB flash drive** to select it—or click the folder or location where you want to store your files for this Project—and notice that the drive or folder is highlighted in blue, indicating it is selected. At the top of the window, on the ribbon, click the **Computer tab**, and then in the **Location group**, click **Open**. Compare your screen with Figure 1.15.

The file list for the selected location displays. There may be no files or only a few files in the location you have selected. You can open a location by using the shortcut menu or by using this ribbon command.

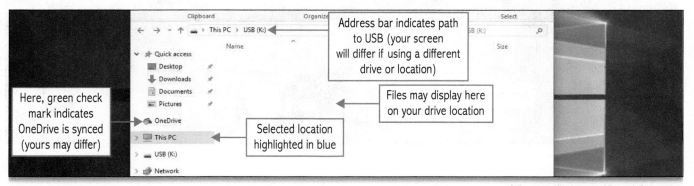

FIGURE 1.15

Office 2016, Windows 10, Microsoft Corporation.

10 On the ribbon, in the **New group**, click **New folder**.

11 With the text *New folder* highlighted in blue, type **Windows 10 Chapter 1** and press Enter to confirm the folder name and select—highlight in blue—the new folder. With the folder selected, press Enter again to open the File Explorer window for your **Windows 10 Chapter 1** folder. Compare your screen with Figure 1.16.

Windows creates a new folder in the location you selected. The address bar indicates the ***path*** from This PC to your folder. A path is a sequence of folders that leads to a specific file or folder.

To ***select*** means to specify, by highlighting, a block of data or text on the screen with the intent of performing some action on the selection.

**BY TOUCH**   You may have to tap the keyboard icon in the lower right corner of the taskbar to display the onscreen keyboard.

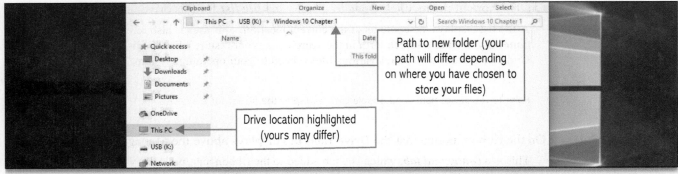

FIGURE 1.16

Office 2016, Windows 10, Microsoft Corporation.

Activity 1.08 | Creating and Saving a File

1 ▶ In the upper right corner of your **Windows 10 Chapter 1** folder window, click **Close** ☒.

2 ▶ In the lower left corner, click **Start** ⊞.

3 ▶ Point to the right edge of the **menu list** to display a **scroll bar**, and then drag the **scroll box** down to view apps listed under **G**. Compare your screen with Figure 1.17.

> To *drag* is to move something from one location on the screen to another while holding down the left mouse button; the action of dragging includes releasing the mouse button at the desired time or location.

FIGURE 1.17

Office 2016, Windows 10, Microsoft Corporation.

Jump to a Lettered Section of the Apps List Quickly

To move quickly to an alphabetic section of the apps list, click any alphabetic letter on the list to display an onscreen alphabet, and then click the letter of the alphabet to which you want to jump.

4 Click **Get Started**. If necessary, in the upper right, click **Maximize** ☐ so that the **Get Started** window fills your entire screen. On the left, click **Browse**, on the right, click **Start**, and then click **See what's on the menu**. Then, move your mouse pointer to the right edge of the screen to display the **scroll bar**. Compare your screen with Figure 1.18.

A vertical *scroll bar* displays on the right side of this window. A scroll bar displays when the contents of a window are not completely visible. A scroll bar can be vertical as shown or horizontal and displayed at the bottom of a window.

Within the scroll bar, you can move the *scroll box* to bring the contents of the window into view. The position of the scroll box within the scroll bar indicates your relative position within the window's contents. You can click the *scroll arrow* at either end of the scroll bar to move within the window in small increments.

In any window, the *Maximize* button will maximize the size of the window to fill the entire screen.

It is worth your time to explore this *Get Started* feature in Windows 10 to learn about all the things that Windows 10 can do for you.

FIGURE 1.18

5 On the taskbar, click **Snipping Tool** 🔖 to display the small **Snipping Tool** dialog box over the screen.

6 On the **menu bar** of the **Snipping Tool** dialog box, click the **arrow** to the right of *New*—referred to as the **New arrow**—and then compare your screen with Figure 1.19.

An arrow attached to a button will display a menu when clicked. Such a button is referred to as a *split button*—clicking the main part of the button performs a command and clicking the arrow opens a menu with choices. A *menu* is a list of commands within a category, and a group of menus at the top of a program window is referred to as the *menu bar*.

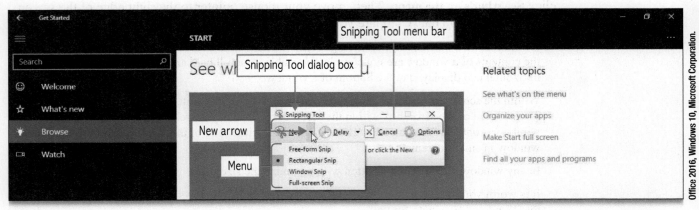

Office 2016, Windows 10, Microsoft Corporation.

FIGURE 1.19

7 On the menu, notice that there are four types of snips.

A *free-form snip* enables you to draw an irregular line such as a circle around an area of the screen. A *rectangular snip* enables you to draw a precise box by dragging the mouse pointer around an area of the screen to form a rectangle. A *window snip* captures the entire displayed window. A *full-screen snip* captures the entire screen.

8 On the menu, click **Rectangular Snip**, and move your mouse slightly. Notice that the screen dims and your pointer takes the shape of a plus sign ⊞.

9 Move the mouse pointer to the upper left corner of the white portion of the screen, hold down the left mouse button, and then drag down and to the right until you have captured the white portion of the screen as shown in Figure 1.20 and then release the mouse button. If you are not satisfied with your result, close the Snipping Tool window and begin again.

Your snip is copied to the Snipping Tool markup window. Here you can annotate—mark or make notes on—save, copy, or share the snip.

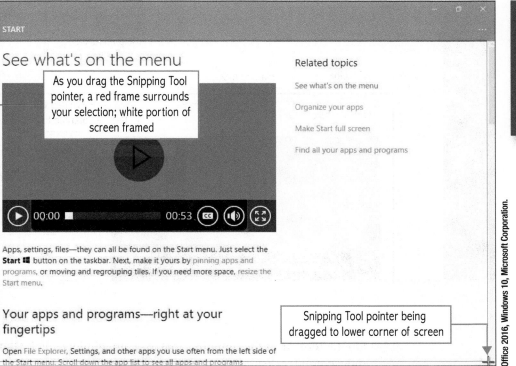

As you drag the Snipping Tool pointer, a red frame surrounds your selection; white portion of screen framed

Snipping Tool pointer being dragged to lower corner of screen

FIGURE 1.20

10 On the toolbar of the displayed **Snipping Tool** markup window, click the **Pen button arrow** ✏️, and then click **Red Pen**. Notice that your mouse pointer displays as a red dot.

11 At the top of the snip—remember that you are now looking at a picture of the portion of the screen you captured—point to the words *See what's on the menu* and use the red mouse pointer to draw a circle around the text—the circle need not be precise. If you are not satisfied with your circle, on the toolbar, click the Eraser button 🧽, point anywhere on the red circle, click to erase, and then begin again. Compare your screen with Figure 1.21.

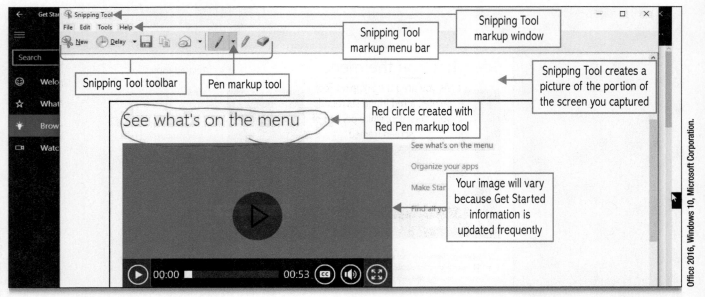

Snipping Tool markup window

Snipping Tool markup menu bar

Snipping Tool markup window

Snipping Tool creates a picture of the portion of the screen you captured

Snipping Tool toolbar

Pen markup tool

Red circle created with Red Pen markup tool

See what's on the menu

Your image will vary because Get Started information is updated frequently

FIGURE 1.21

12 On the toolbar of the **Snipping Tool** markup window, click **Highlighter**. Notice that your mouse pointer displays as a small yellow rectangle.

13 Point to the text *See what's on the menu*, hold down the left mouse button, and then drag over the text to highlight it in yellow. If you are not satisfied with your yellow highlight, on the toolbar, click the Eraser button, point anywhere on the yellow highlight, click to erase, and then begin again. Compare your screen with Figure 1.22.

BY TOUCH   Use your finger to draw the circle and to highlight text.

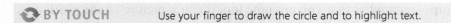

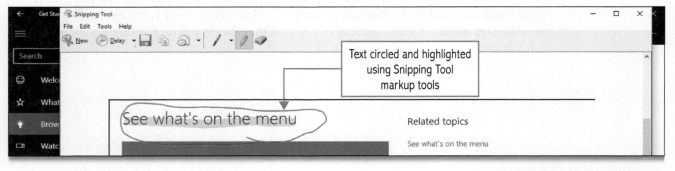

Text circled and highlighted using Snipping Tool markup tools

See what's on the menu

Related topics

See what's on the menu

FIGURE 1.22

14 On the **Snipping Tool** markup window's toolbar, click **Save Snip** to display the **Save As** dialog box.

15 In the **Save As** dialog box, in the **navigation pane**, drag the scroll box down as necessary to find and then click the location where you created your **Windows 10 Chapter 1** folder.

16 In the **file list**, scroll as necessary, locate and *double-click*—press the left mouse button two times in rapid succession while holding the mouse still—your **Windows 10 Chapter 1** folder. Compare your screen with Figure 1.23.

🔄 **ANOTHER WAY**   Right-click the folder name and click Open.

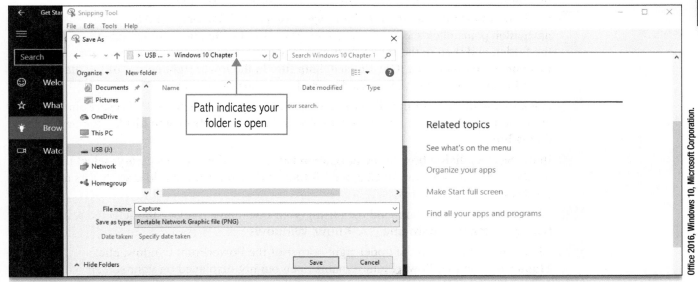

FIGURE 1.23

NOTE	Successful Double-Clicking Requires a Steady Hand

Double-clicking needs a steady hand. The speed of the two clicks is not as important as holding the mouse still between the two clicks. If you are not satisfied with your result, try again.

---

17 At the bottom of the **Save As** dialog box, locate **Save as type**, click anywhere in the box to display a list, and then on the displayed list click **JPEG file**.

JPEG, which is commonly pronounced *JAY-peg* and stands for Joint Photographic Experts Group, is a common file type used by digital cameras and computers to store digital pictures. JPEG is popular because it can store a high-quality picture in a relatively small file.

18 At the bottom of the **Save As** dialog box, click in the **File name** box to select the text *Capture*, and then using your own name, type **Lastname_Firstname_1A_Get_Started_Snip**

Within any Windows-based program, text highlighted in blue—selected—in this manner will be replaced by your typing.

NOTE	File Naming in This Textbook

Windows 10 recognizes file names with spaces. You can use spaces in file names, however, some programs, especially when transferring files over the Internet, may insert the extra characters *%20* in place of a space. In this instruction you will be instructed to save files using an underscore instead of a space. The underscore key is the shift of the ⊡ key—on most keyboards located two keys to the left of Backspace.

---

19 In the lower right corner of the dialog box, click **Save**.

20 **Close** ⊠ the **Snipping Tool** markup window, and then **Close** ⊠ the **Get Started** window.

You have successfully created a folder and saved a file within that folder.

1 If the Microsoft PowerPoint application is not pinned to your taskbar, use the same technique you used to search for and pin the Snipping Tool application to search for and pin the PowerPoint application to your taskbar.

2 From the taskbar, open **PowerPoint**. Click **Blank Presentation**, and then on the **Home tab**, in the **Slides group**, click **Layout**. In the displayed gallery, click **Blank**.

3 Click the **Insert tab**, and then in the **Images group**, click **Pictures**. In the **navigation pane**, click the location of your **Windows 10 Chapter 1** folder, open the folder, and then in the **Insert Picture** dialog box, click one time to select your **Lastname_Firstname_1A_Get_Started_Snip** file. In the lower right corner of the dialog box, click **Insert**. If necessary, close the Design Ideas pane on the right.

4 Click in a white area of the slide to deselect the image, and then on the PowerPoint ribbon, click the **File tab**. On the left, click **Save As**, and then click **Browse** to display the **Save As** dialog box.

5 In the **Save As** dialog box, in the **navigation pane**, scroll down as necessary, select the location of your **Windows 10 Chapter 1** folder, and then open the folder so that its name displays in the address bar.

6 Click in the **File name** box, and then using your own name, replace the selected text by typing **Lastname_Firstname_1A_Know_Windows**

7 Click **Save**, and then in the upper right corner of the PowerPoint window, click **Minimize** ▢ so that PowerPoint remains open but not displayed on your screen; you will need your PowerPoint presentation again as you progress through this Project.

Objective 3 | Identify the Functions of the Windows 10 Operating System

Traditionally, the three major tasks of an operating system are to:

- Manage your computer's hardware—the printers, scanners, disk drives, monitors, and other hardware attached to it.
- Manage the application software installed on your computer—programs like those in Microsoft Office and other programs you might install to manage your money, edit photos, or play games.
- Manage the *data* generated from your application software. Data refers to the documents, worksheets, pictures, songs, and so on that you create and store during the day-to-day use of your computer.

The Windows 10 operating system continues to perform these three tasks, and additionally is optimized for touchscreens; for example, tablets of all sizes and convertible laptop computers. Windows 10 works equally well with any input device, including a mouse, keyboard, touchscreen, and *pen*—a pen-shaped stylus that you tap on a computer screen.

In most instances, when you purchase a computer, the operating system software is already installed. The operating system consists of many smaller programs, stored as system files, which transfer data to and from the disk and transfer data in and out of your computer's memory. Other functions performed by the operating system include hardware-specific tasks such as checking to see if a key has been pressed on the keyboard and, if it has, displaying the appropriate letter or character on the screen.

When using a Windows 10 computer, you can write and create using traditional desktop apps, and you can also read and socialize and communicate by using the Windows Store apps.

With Windows 10, as compared to earlier versions of Windows, your PC has some of the characteristics of a smartphone or tablet—it is connected, it is mobile, and it is centered on people and activities. If, as Microsoft predicts, the laptop and tablet will ultimately merge into one device—like the Microsoft Surface—then you will be well prepared by learning to use Windows 10 and the Windows apps.

Activity 1.10 | Identifying Operating System Functions and Windows App Functions

Windows 10, in the same manner as other operating systems and earlier versions of the Windows operating system, has a desktop that uses a *graphical user interface*—abbreviated as *GUI* and pronounced *GOO-ee*. A graphical user interface uses graphics such as an image of a file folder or wastebasket that you click to activate the item represented. A GUI commonly incorporates the following:

- A *pointer*—any symbol that displays on your screen in response to moving your mouse and with which you can select objects and commands.
- A *pointing device*, such as a mouse or touchpad, to control the pointer.
- *Icons*—small images that represent commands, files, applications, or other windows. You can select an object icon and drag it to move it or double-click a program icon to start a program.
- A *desktop*—a simulation of a real desk that represents your work area; here you can arrange icons such as shortcuts to programs, files, folders, and various types of documents in the same manner you would arrange physical objects on top of a desk.

In Windows 10, you also have a Start menu with tiles on the right. The array of tiles serves as a connected dashboard to all of your important programs, sites, and services. On the Start menu, your view is tailored to your information and activities.

The physical parts of your computer such as the central processing unit (CPU), memory, and any attached devices such as a printer, are collectively known as *resources*. The operating system keeps track of the status of each resource and decides when a resource needs attention and for how long.

There will be times when you want and need to interact with the functions of the operating system; for example, when you want to install a new hardware device like a color printer. Windows 10 provides tools with which you can inform the operating system of new hardware that you attach to your computer.

Software application programs are the programs that enable you to do work on, and be entertained by, your computer—programs such as Word and Excel found in the Microsoft Office suite of products, Adobe Photoshop, and computer games. No application program, whether a larger desktop app or smaller Windows app, can run on its own—it must run under the direction of an operating system.

For the everyday use of your computer, the most important and most often used function of the operating system is managing your files and folders—referred to as *data management*. In the same manner that you strive to keep your paper documents and file folders organized so that you can find information when you need it, your goal when organizing your computer files and folders is to group your files so that you can find information easily. Managing your data files so that you can find your information when you need it is one of the most important computing skills you can learn.

FIGURE 1.24

Managing the data on all of your devices is an important computing skill; storing your data in the cloud—for example, on OneDrive—enables you to access your data from any device

hywards/Shutterstock

To check how well you can identify operating system functions, take a moment to think about the answers to the following questions:

Self-Check | Answer These Questions to Check Your Understanding

1 ▷ Of the three major functions of the operating system, the first is to manage your computer's _____ such as disk drives, monitors, and printers.

2 ▷ The second major function of the operating system is to manage the application _____ such as Microsoft Office, Adobe PhotoShop, and video games.

3 ▷ The third major function of the operating system is to manage the _____ generated from your applications—the files such as Word documents, Excel workbooks, pictures, and songs that you create and store during the day-to-day use of your computer.

4 ▷ The Start menu's array of tiles is your connected _____ to all of your important programs, sites, and services.

5 ▷ One of the most important computing skills you can learn is how to manage your _____ _____ so that you can find your information quickly.

Objective 4 | Discover Windows 10 Features

According to Microsoft, a billion people in the world use Windows and 93 percent of PCs in the world run some version of Windows. Increasingly people want to use Windows in a format that runs easily on mobile computing devices such as laptops, tablets, *2 in 1 PCs*, and smartphones; research shows this is where people now spend more time. A 2 in 1 PC is a laptop or notebook computer that can function as both a traditional laptop and as a tablet by either detaching the keyboard or by rotating the keyboard 360 degrees on hinges to look like a tablet.

With only desktop apps to choose from, Windows is centered around files—typing and creating things—and that will continue to be an important part of what you do on your computer, especially in the workplace.

Additionally, you are doing different kinds of things on your PC, and you probably expect your PC to be more like a smartphone—connected all the time, mobile, to have long battery life if it's a laptop, and be centered on the people and activities that are important to you. It is for those activities that the Windows apps will become useful to you.

Think of Windows 10 as a way to do work on your desktop or laptop computer, and then to read and be entertained on your laptop, tablet, or Xbox game console. Windows 10 is both serious for work and fun for entertainment and social networking.

Activity 1.11 | Using Windows Apps

On your own computer, an array of Windows apps displays on the Start menu immediately after you sign in to a Windows 10 computer. Keep in mind that a workplace computer may have a specific, locked-down arrangement of apps, or no apps at all.

On a new computer, the apps might be preselected by your computer manufacturer and by Microsoft. You can use these right away, and later you can add, delete, and rearrange the apps so that your Start menu tiles become your own personal dashboard. Recall that some apps are represented by live tiles that will update with information after you set them to do so. For example, the Mail app will show updates of incoming mail after you connect it to your email account.

Some of the built-in apps that will come with a new installation of Windows 10 on a consumer PC include:

- Mail, from which you can get email from all of your email accounts, all in one place!
- Weather, from which you can get hourly, daily, and 10-day forecasts.
- Voice Recorder, with which you can easily record a sound, and then trim, save, and replay it on your PC.
- News, which is a photo-rich app to keep up with what's happening in the world.

1 With your **desktop** displayed, to the right of Start ■, click in the Search box to display the insertion point, type **sports** and then at the top of the search pane, click **More**. Compare your screen with Figure 1.25.

The ***insertion point*** is a blinking vertical line that indicates where text will be inserted when you type.

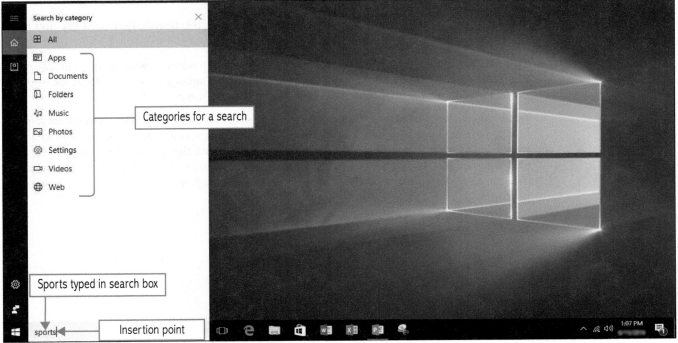

FIGURE 1.25

2▷ On the displayed list, click **Apps,** and then click to install, if necessary, the **MSN Sports** app. (If the app is already installed, the search result will indicate *Sports Windows Store Trusted app* and the Store will indicate *Install* instead of *Free*.) In the Windows Store, click **Free.** Wait a few moments for the app to install, and then click **Launch.**

3▷ Click **Start** ⊞ to display the **Start menu,** at the top of the list of apps, under **Recently added,** point to **Sports** and right-click. Click **Pin to Start,** and then compare your screen with Figure 1.26.

Up-to-date information may already begin to display.

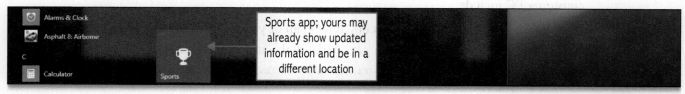

> Sports app; yours may already show updated information and be in a different location

Office 2016, Windows 10, Microsoft Corporation.

FIGURE 1.26

4▷ In the upper right corner of the **Sports** app, if necessary, click **Maximize** ☐ to have the app fill the entire window.

Here you can scroll down and click on many new sports stories. Across the top, you can click on *Scoreboard* to see up-to-date scores of games, or click *Slideshows* or *Videos* to see sports news stories portrayed in images or videos.

The features in the Sports app are representative of the features in many Windows apps.

5▷ At the top, click **Scoreboard,** in the upper left corner, click the **Hamburger** icon ▤, and then compare your screen with Figure 1.27.

This icon is commonly referred to as a ***hamburger menu*** or a ***menu icon*** or simply a ***hamburger.*** The name derives from the three lines that bring to mind a hamburger on a bun. This type of button is often used in mobile applications because it is compact to use on smaller screens.

When you click the hamburger icon, a menu displays that identifies the list of icons on the left so that you can navigate to more specific areas of the Microsoft Sports app. Sometimes this area is referred to as the ***app bar***. Regardless of the name, you can see that you can navigate directly to categories such as the NBA (National Basketball Association) or MLB (Major League Baseball). You can also create a list of favorite teams that you want to follow.

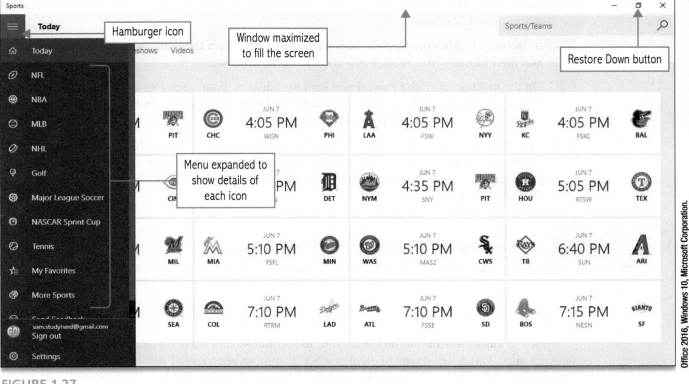

FIGURE 1.27

6 ▸ In the upper right corner, click **Restore Down** ▣ to return the window to its previous size.

Use the Maximize command ▢ to display a window in a full-screen view; use the ***Restore Down command*** ▣ to resize a window to its previous size.

7 ▸ **Close** ☒ the Sports app and the Store window.

8 ▸ With your **desktop** displayed, to the right of Start ⊞, click in the Search box to display the insertion point, type **money** and then at the top of the list of results, click **More**. On the list, click **Apps**, and then click to install the **MSN Money** app. Click **Free** (or Install), wait a moment for the app to download, and then click **Launch**. Skip any introductory messages. Click **Start** ⊞, at the top under **Recently added**, right-click **Money**, and then click **Pin to Start**.

9 ▸ **Maximize** ▢ the Money window, and then on the navigation bar at the top of the window, click **Watchlist**. On the list of stocks, click **MSFT**. If *MSFT* does not display, at the upper right, click +, type MSFT, and then on the list that displays, click MSFT to add it to the list.

Information about Microsoft's stock and a graph displays.

10 ▸ Below the graph, click **1 Year** to see a graph representing one year.

11 ▸ With your Microsoft graph displayed, in the lower left corner of your keyboard, press and hold down ⊞ and then press [PrintScrn]; release the two keys. Notice that your screen dims momentarily.

Use this technique to create a ***screenshot***. The screenshot file is automatically stored in the Pictures folder of your hard drive and also on the Clipboard.

A screenshot captured in this manner is saved as a ***.png*** file, which is commonly pronounced PING, and stands for Portable Network Graphic. This is an image file type that can be transferred over the Internet.

A ***keyboard shortcut*** is a combination of two or more keyboard keys and is useful to perform a task that would otherwise require a mouse.

12 ▸ Point to the right edge of the screen to display a scroll bar, and then scroll down to see news stories about Microsoft.

13 ▸ In the upper right corner, click **Restore Down** ☐ to return the window to its previous size, and then **Close** ☒ the Money app and the Store window.

14 ▸ On the taskbar, click the **PowerPoint icon** to redisplay your open PowerPoint presentation. On the **Home tab**, click the upper portion of the **New Slide** button, and then in the **Clipboard** group, click the upper portion of the **Paste** button.

15 ▸ Click in a white area of the slide to deselect the image. In the upper left corner of the screen, above the **File tab**, click **Save** ☐ to save the changes you have made to your PowerPoint presentation, and then in the upper right corner of the screen, click **Minimize** ☐ to leave PowerPoint open.

More Knowledge	**Where Did the Hamburger Icon Come From?**

For a brief history of the hamburger icon, visit http://blog.placeit.net/history-of-the-hamburger-icon

---

Activity 1.12 │ Using Task View, Snap Assist, and Virtual Desktops

Use the *Task View* button on the taskbar to see and switch between open apps—including desktop apps. Use *Snap Assist* to display a 50/50 split screen view of two apps. Begin by dragging the *title bar*—the bar across the top of the window that displays the program or app name—to the right or left until it snaps into place. Or, hold down ⊞ and press → or ← to snap the window right or left. As soon as you snap the first window, Task View displays all your other open windows, and you need to click only one to have it snap to the other half of the screen. You can also snap four apps by dragging their title bars into the corners of your screen.

1 ▸ Be sure all windows except the PowerPoint window are closed, and then on the taskbar, click **File Explorer** ☐. Navigate to the location for your **Windows 10 Chapter 1** folder, but do not open the folder. With your File Explorer window open, click **Start** ☐ and then open one of the displayed apps; for example, Weather. Then, from either the taskbar or the Start menu, open the **Windows Store**.

Including your PowerPoint presentation, four windows are now open with the Windows Store app window on top.

2 ▸ On the taskbar, click **Task View** ☐, point to one of the windows, and then compare your screen with Figure 1.28.

Task View displays a *thumbnail*—a reduced image of a graphic—of each open window. This command is convenient when you want to see all of your open windows.

When you point to an open window, a Close button displays in the upper right corner so that you can close the window from Task View.

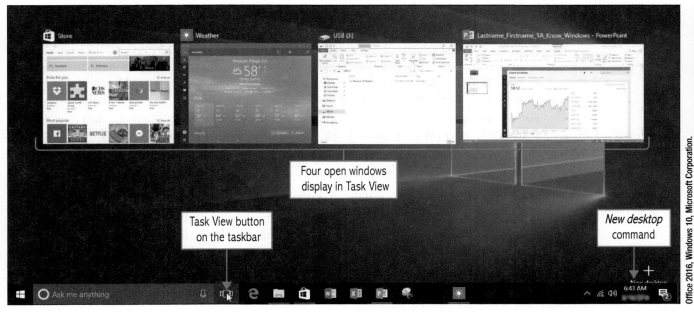

Office 2016, Windows 10, Microsoft Corporation.

Four open windows
display in Task View

Task View button
on the taskbar

New desktop
command

FIGURE 1.28

3 ▶ Click the **File Explorer** window, hold down ⊞, and then press →.

The File Explorer window snaps to the right side of the screen, and Snap Assist displays the other three open windows on the left.

4 ▶ On the left, click the Weather app, and then compare your screen with Figure 1.29.

The Weather window snaps to the left side of the screen.

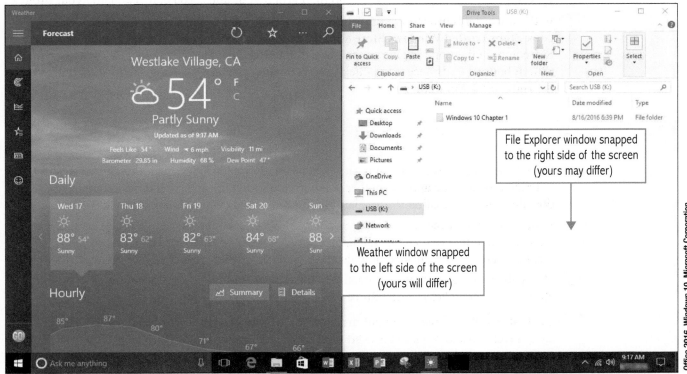

Office 2016, Windows 10, Microsoft Corporation.

File Explorer window snapped
to the right side of the screen
(yours may differ)

Weather window snapped
to the left side of the screen
(yours will differ)

FIGURE 1.29

5 On the taskbar, click **Task View** ▢ again, in the lower right corner, click **New desktop**, and notice that two thumbnail images display—**Desktop 1** with your two apps snapped and **Desktop 2**.

If you have a large number of apps open, you can create another *virtual desktop*—an additional desktop to organize and quickly access groups of windows—to work with just the apps you want by clicking + New desktop in the lower right corner of your screen. This can be a good way to organize and quickly access groups of windows.

For example, you could run your work email and Office apps on your desktop, and then open another virtual desktop for personal work. Then you can use Task View to switch between open desktops.

6 Click **Desktop 1** to bring that desktop back to full screen, and then on the taskbar, click **Task View** ▢.

7 From your desktop, drag the Windows Store window down to **Desktop 2**.

8 Click **Desktop 2** and maximize ▢ the window if necessary, and then click **Task View** ▢. With **Desktop 2** active—its icon is framed above the taskbar—drag the app on the screen back down to **Desktop 1**.

9 Point to **Desktop 2** and click **Close** ☒, and then in the upper right corner of each open window, except your PowerPoint window, click **Close** ☒. Click in an empty area of your desktop to minimize the PowerPoint program.

Create virtual desktops when you need to separate a group of windows while working on other things. Then you can close the virtual desktop when you no longer need it.

Activity 1.13 | Organizing Your Start Menu and Getting Apps from the Windows Store

On your own PC, you will want to organize your Start menu to become your personal dashboard. You will probably use your desktop apps like Microsoft Word and Microsoft Excel for work and school, but with the tiles on the Start menu, you can also use your PC like you use your smartphone—centered on the people and notifications that are important to you.

You can pin apps to the Start menu and then group your apps. You can also name your groups.

1 In the lower left corner, click in the **Search** box, type **store** and then at the top of the list, click **Store Trusted Windows Store app**. If necessary, Maximize ▢ the Store window. In the Store app, in the upper right corner, click in the **Search** box, type **travel** and then click the **Search** button ▢. If necessary, click in a white area to close the suggested list, and then on the right, click **Show all**.

ANOTHER WAY   On the taskbar, click the Store icon ▣; or, on the Start menu, click the Windows Store tile.

2 Click to select any free travel app, and then when the app displays, click **Free** (or click Install if your already own the app on another computer) to install the app; wait a few moments for the download and installation to complete and for *Launch* to display. Do not launch the app.

3 In the upper left corner of the **Store** window, click the **Back** button ◁. If necessary, click Show all again, and then find and install another travel app of your choice. When *Launch* displays, meaning the app has finished downloading, in the upper left corner, click the Back ◁ button.

4 Using the techniques you just practiced, install, but don't launch, a third travel app of your choice, and then **Close** ☒ the **Store** window.

5 Click **Start** ⊞ to display the Start menu. In the **Recently added** section on the left, right-click each travel app and pin it to the Start menu. Compare your screen with Figure 1.30.

The *Recently added* section of the Start menu displays apps that you have recently downloaded and installed.

FIGURE 1.30

6 ▶ Point to one of the three apps and right-click, and notice that you can Unpin an app from Start, or uninstall the app. Compare your screen with Figure 1.31.

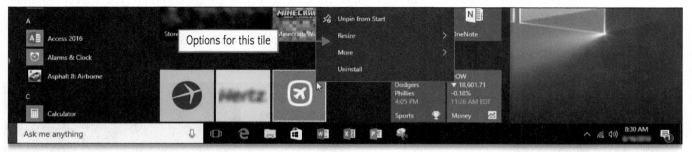

FIGURE 1.31

7 ▶ Click in a blank area of the Start menu to close the menu. Locate one of your travel apps you pinned to the Start menu. Drag the app tile into a blank space, and notice that a shaded bar displays indicating that you can create a new section on your Start menu, as shown in Figure 1.32.

> Your array of tiles and amount of space will differ from what is shown, because Windows 10 is *your* personal dashboard!

FIGURE 1.32

8 Drag the two remaining travel apps next to the first one, and then point to the area above the new group to display *Name group*, as shown in Figure 1.33.

Office 2016, Windows 10, Microsoft Corporation.

FIGURE 1.33

9 Click the double lines at the right or click the text *New group*, and then type **Travel** to name the group. Press Enter, and then compare your screen with Figure 1.34.

You can use the techniques you just practiced with the Windows Store, the apps menu, and the tiles on the Start menu to customize Windows 10 to be your personal dashboard.

Office 2016, Windows 10, Microsoft Corporation.

FIGURE 1.34

10 Point to one of the Travel app tiles, right-click, point to **Resize**, and then click **Small**. Point to another of the Travel app tiles, right-click, point to **Resize**, and then click **Wide**.

You might want to resize tiles on your Start menu to make them more or less visible—this is another way to personalize Windows 10 to make it work for you.

You probably want your PC to give you notifications—just like your smartphone does—and the Windows 10 Action Center does that. The *Action Center* is a vertical panel that displays on the right side of your screen when you click the icon in the notifications area of the taskbar. The upper portion displays notifications from apps you have installed and from which you have elected to receive notifications. The bottom portion displays Quick Actions—buttons that take you to frequently used system commands.

Both areas of the Action Center are customizable to suit your needs. When you have a new notification, the icon on the taskbar will light up white. There is even a Quiet Hours setting to turn off notifications when you don't want them.

1 At the right edge of your taskbar, click **Action Center** ▢ to display the **Action Center** pane on the right side of your screen. Compare your screen with Figure 1.35.

Although your arrangement and list will differ from what is shown in the figure, you can see that this is a convenient way to check mail and messages without leaving whatever you are working on.

Here you see email messages. If someone contacted you on Skype, you can reply here. You can set what notifications you want to see in the Action Center, and you will also see system messages here; for example, updates that were made to Windows.

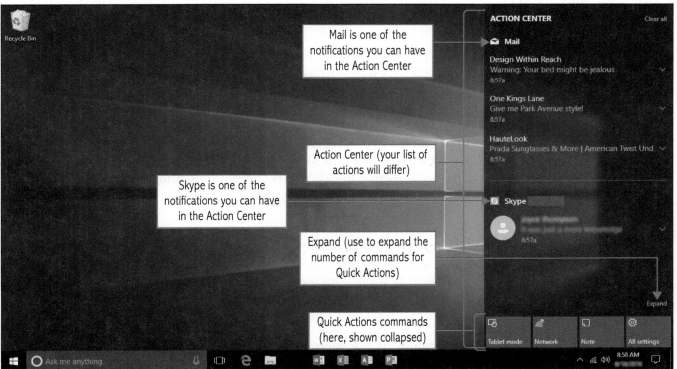

FIGURE 1.35

2 At the bottom of the **Action Center**, click **All settings**, and then in the **Settings** window, click **System**. On the left, click **Notifications & actions**, scroll down toward the bottom of the list on the right, and then compare your screen with Figure 1.36.

Here you can make decisions about what apps can send you notifications in the Action Center.

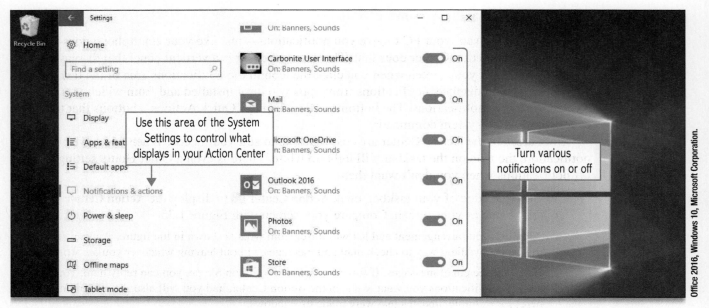

FIGURE 1.36

Office 2016, Windows 10, Microsoft Corporation.

3 Close ☒ the **Settings** window.

Activity 1.15 | Using Cortana and Searching for Help

Cortana, the name for the intelligent female character in the *Halo* video game series, is also the name for the personal digital assistant in Windows 10. With use, Cortana becomes more useful to you, and you can add features—such as reminders—that Cortana delivers to you.

On your own PC, starting with the Windows 10 Anniversary update released in August of 2016, Cortana is part of Windows 10 and cannot be entirely turned off. However, according to Microsoft, "you can use Cortana settings to control exactly what Cortana has access to and how personalized you'd like her assistance to be." You will benefit from using this powerful feature that can search the web, find things on your PC, and keep track of your calendar.

ALERT! **Are You Working in a College Lab?**

Some Education editions of Windows 10 do not include Cortana, so you may not have this feature in a college lab. You will know that Cortana is available if you see *Ask me anything* in the taskbar search box. If you do not have Cortana available, just read through the Activity, and then try Cortana on your own computer.

---

1 In the lower left corner of your desktop, locate the search box and notice the text *Ask me anything*, as shown in Figure 1.37.

If this area indicates *Search the web and Windows*, then Cortana is not active on your system.

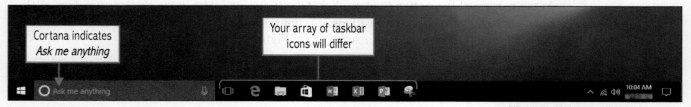

Cortana indicates
Ask me anything

Your array of taskbar
icons will differ

FIGURE 1.37

Office 2016, Windows 10, Microsoft Corporation.

2 Click in the Cortana search box, and then on the left, click **Settings** ⚙️. Compare your screen with Figure 1.38.

Here you can control how you use Cortana.

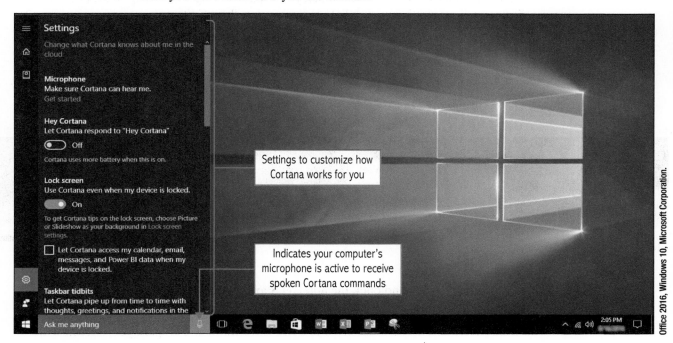

FIGURE 1.38

3 In the upper left corner, click the **menu** icon ▤ to display the menu commands. Click **Notebook**.

4 On the list, click **About Me**, and then compare your screen with Figure 1.39.

Here you can change the name that Cortana uses for you or change how Cortana pronounces your name. You can also edit your Favorites so that Cortana can gradually learn about you and offer you more useful information.

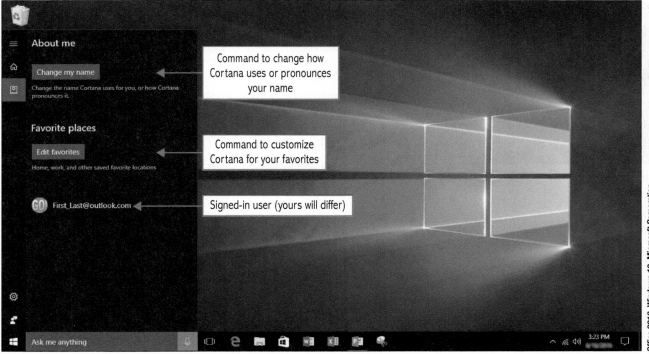

FIGURE 1.39

5 Click in the **Ask me anything** box, and then type **who is Cortana?** Then press Enter. If necessary, click *See more results on Bing.com*.

> Your **web browser**—software with which you display webpages and navigate the Internet— displays a Bing search with web links to information about Cortana.

6 **Close** ⊠ the browser window.

7 Click again in the **Ask me anything** box, and then in the upper left corner, click the **menu** icon ▤. Click **Notebook**, click **Reminders**, and then compare your screen with Figure 1.40.

> On this menu, you can have Cortana set reminders for you.

FIGURE 1.40

8 Click **Start** ⊞. Locate and click the app **Get Started**.

9 **Maximize** ⊡ the window, on the left, click **Browse**, and then click **Cortana**. Click **Make Cortana yours**, and take a moment to read this information. Compare your screen with Figure 1.41.

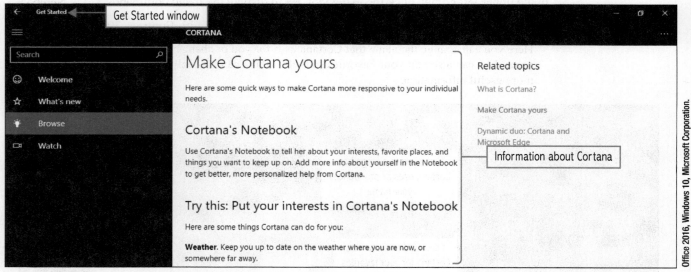

FIGURE 1.41

10 ▶ On your keyboard, hold down ⊞ and press (PrintScrn); notice that your screen dims momentarily while the image is copied to the Clipboard.

11 ▶ From the taskbar, open your PowerPoint presentation. On the **Home tab**, in the **Slides group**, click the upper portion of the **New Slide** button to insert a new slide in the **Blank** layout. Then in the **Clipboard group**, click the upper portion of the **Paste** button.

12 ▶ Click anywhere to deselect the image. In the upper left corner, click **Save** 🖫, and then in upper right corner, click **Minimize** ⊟.

13 ▶ **Close** ⊠ the **Get Started** window.

Activity 1.16 | Using the Microsoft Edge Browser

Microsoft Edge is the web browser program that comes with Windows 10. Among its many features are the ability to:

- Enter a search directly into the address bar
- Save sites and favorites and reading lists in the *Hub* feature
- Take notes and highlight directly on a webpage and then share that page with someone
- Pin a website to your Start menu

1 ▶ On the taskbar, click **Microsoft Edge** 🅴. If the icon is not on your taskbar, search for the app in the search box. **Maximize** ⊡ the window.

2 ▶ In the **Search or enter web address** box, or in the address bar, type the name of your college and then press (Enter).

It is not necessary to type a web address; Edge will search for you and present the results.

3 ▶ In the search results, locate and click the link for your college's official website. On your college website, search for or navigate to information about the college library.

4 ▶ With the webpage for your college library displayed, in the upper right corner, click **Make a Web Note** ✏, and then compare your screen with Figure 1.42.

The Web Note toolbar displays tools for marking a webpage. Tools include a Pen, a Highlighter, an Eraser, a Note maker, and a Clip for cutting out a portion of a webpage as a file. On the right of the toolbar, there are tools for saving and sharing a webpage on which you have made markups or notes.

FIGURE 1.42

5 > On the toolbar, point to the **Pen** ▽, click the **small white triangle** in the lower right corner, and then on the displayed gallery, click the **yellow square**. Click the **white triangle** again, and then click the largest size.

6 > With your mouse pointer, circle the name of—or some other information about—your college library. Compare your screen with Figure 1.43.

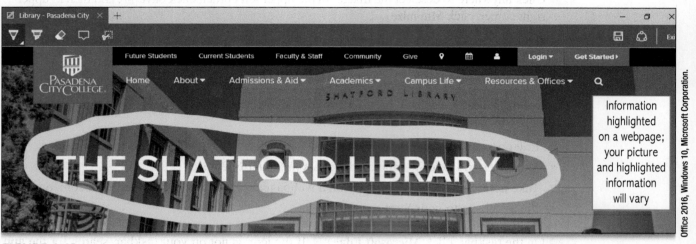

FIGURE 1.43

7 > On the toolbar, click **Share** 🔗 to display the **Share** pane on the right, and notice the various ways you can share this marked-up webpage with others.

8 > Using the techniques you have practiced, press [🪟] + [PrintScrn] to copy the image to the Clipboard, and then paste the image as the fourth slide in your PowerPoint presentation. **Save** 🖫 the presentation and **Minimize** [–] the window.

9 > Click in a blank area of the webpage to close the Share pane. In the upper right corner, on the toolbar, click **Exit**. If asked to save changes, click No.

10 > In the upper right corner, click **More** [⋯] and then on the list, click **Pin this page to Start** and if necessary, click Yes. **Close** [×] the browser window.

11 > Click **Start** ⊞, and then scroll as necessary to locate the pinned website on your Start menu. Compare your screen with Figure 1.44.

Use this technique to pin websites that you visit often to your Start menu.

FIGURE 1.44

Office 2016, Windows 10, Microsoft Corporation.

On your own computer, when you are done working, sign out from Windows 10, and then set your computer properly so that your data is saved, you save energy, and your computer remains secure.

When you turn off your computer by using the *Sleep* command, Windows 10 automatically saves your work, the screen goes dark, the computer's fan stops, and your computer goes to sleep. You need not close your programs or files because your work is saved. When you wake your computer by pressing a key, moving the mouse, or using whatever method is appropriate for your device, you need only to dismiss the lock screen and then enter your password or PIN; your screen will display exactly like it did when you initiated the Sleep command.

When you *shut down* your computer, all open programs and files close, network connections close, and the hard disk stops. No power is used. According to Microsoft, about half of all Windows users like to shut down so that they get a "fresh start" each time they turn on the computer. The other half use Sleep.

Activity 1.17 | Locking, Signing Out of, and Shutting Down Your Computer

In an organization, there might be a specific process for signing out from Windows 10 and turning off the computer. The following steps will work on your own PC.

1 Click **Start**, and then point to the icon that represents your user name. Compare your screen with Figure 1.45. Then click the icon.

Here you can sign out of or lock your computer, in addition to changing your account settings. If you click Sign out, the lock screen will display, and then on the lock screen, if you press [Enter], all the user accounts on the computer will display and you are able to sign in.

If you click Lock, the lock screen will display.

Office 2016, Windows 10, Microsoft Corporation.

FIGURE 1.45

2 Click **Lock**, and then with the lock screen displayed, press [Enter]. Sign in to your computer again as necessary.

If you want to shut down your computer, click **Start**, click Power, and then click Shut down.

Windows 10 supports multiple local account users on a single computer, and at least one user is the administrator—the initial administrator that was established when the system was purchased or when Windows 10 was installed.

As the administrator of your own computer, you can restrict access to your computer so that only people you authorize can use your computer or view its files. This access is managed through a local *user account*, which is a collection of information that tells Windows 10 what files and folders the account holder can access, what changes the account holder can make to the computer system, and what the account holder's personal preferences are.

Each person accesses his or her user account with a user name and password, and each user has his or her own desktop, files, and folders. Users with a local account should also establish a Microsoft account so that their Start menu arrangement—personal dashboard of tiles—displays when they sign in.

An *administrator account* allows complete access to the computer. Administrators can make changes that affect other users, change security settings, install software and hardware, access all files on the computer, and make changes to other user accounts.

1 Click **Start** ⊞. Above the Start button, click **Settings** ⚙, and then click **Accounts**. Compare your screen with Figure 1.46.

Here you can manage your Microsoft account, set various sign-in options, and change your account picture.

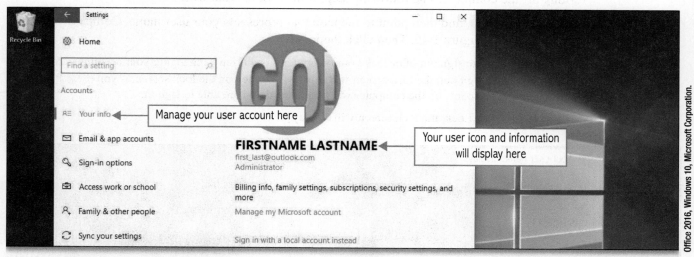

FIGURE 1.46

2 **Close** ⊠ the **Settings** window.

3 On the taskbar, click the **PowerPoint icon** to redisplay your **Lastname_Firstname_1A_Know_Windows** presentation. Press Ctrl + Home to display the first slide in your presentation; your presentation contains four slides.

4 **Close** ⊠ the PowerPoint window; if prompted, click **Save**. Submit your PowerPoint presentation as directed by your instructor. You do not need to submit your saved snip file.

On your own computer, you can change the default settings of some basic functions that will help you manage your Windows 10 system.

NOTE | **This Activity Is Optional**

Complete this Activity if you are able to do so; otherwise, simply read through the information. Some college labs may not enable these features. If you cannot practice in your college lab, practice this on another computer if possible.

Activity 1.19 | Managing Windows Updates, Notifications, and Backup

Windows 10 is a modern operating system, and just like the operating system on your smartphone or tablet, Windows 10 will receive regular updates. These updates will include improvements, new features, and new security updates to address new security issues that emerge. Apps in the Windows Store will also be continuously updated.

Because updates will be automatically installed, you will not have to be concerned about keeping your Windows 10 system up to date; however, you can still view updates and see when they will be installed.

In Windows 10, notifications keep you informed about your apps and messages. You can manage what notifications you get and see in the notifications area of the taskbar from the Settings window.

The backup and recovery tools available in Windows 10 include: *File History*, which can automatically back up your most important files to a separate location; *PC Reset*, which lets you return your PC to the condition it was on the day you bought it; and *system image backup*, which creates a full system image backup from which you can restore your entire PC.

1 On the taskbar, click **Action Center** [icon], and then at the bottom, in the **Quick Actions** area, click **All settings**. In the **Settings** window, *point to* **System**, and then notice that in this group of settings you can manage your display, your notifications, your apps, and the computer's power. Compare your screen with Figure 1.47.

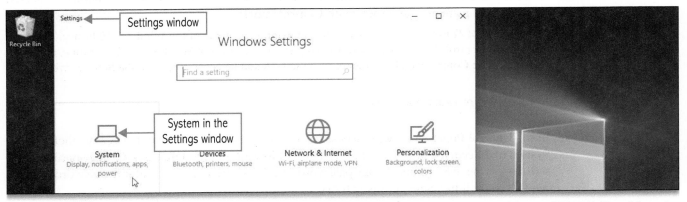

Office 2016, Windows 10, Microsoft Corporation.

FIGURE 1.47

2 Click **System**, and then on the left, click **Notifications & actions**.

Here you can manage your notifications.

3 Without making any changes, click **Back** $\boxed{\leftarrow}$ to redisplay the **Settings** window. Click **Update & security,** and then on the left, click **Backup.** On the right, click **Add a drive.** (This may vary depending on what drives are attached to your system.)

> A list of drives connected to your computer displays, and you can select a drive onto which you could make a backup.

4 **Close** $\boxed{\times}$ the **Settings** window without making a backup.

More Knowledge | **Consider a Commercial Backup Service Instead**

The backup system in Windows 10 is useful, but you might find it easier to use a commercial backup system like Carbonite or Mozy or IDrive. For a small annual fee, these systems back up your files automatically on their servers—in the cloud—and if your computer suffers a misfortune, you can get your files back easily by simply downloading them to your new or repaired system.

NOTE | **This Activity Is Optional**

Complete this Activity if you are able to do so; otherwise, simply read through the information. Some college labs may not enable these features. If you cannot practice in your college lab, practice this on another computer if possible.

Activity 1.20 | Managing Windows Defender and Windows Firewall

Windows Defender is protection built into Windows 10 that helps prevent viruses, spyware, and malicious or unwanted software from being installed on your PC without your knowledge. You can rely on Windows Defender without assistance from other software products that might come preinstalled on a PC you purchase; you can confidently uninstall and not pay for these products.

Windows Firewall is protection built into Windows 10 that can prevent hackers or malicious software from gaining access to your computer through a network or the Internet.

1 In the lower left corner of your screen, click in the search box, type **windows defender** and then press Enter to display **Windows Defender.** If a *What's new in Windows Defender* message displays, click Close.

> Here you can change settings related to real-time and cloud-based protection.

2 **Close** $\boxed{\times}$ the **Windows Defender** window.

3 In the lower left corner, point to **Start** ⊞, right-click to display a menu—sometimes referred to as the power menu—and then click **Control Panel.**

> The *Control Panel* is an area where you can manipulate some of the Windows 10 basic system settings. Control Panel is a carryover from previous versions of Windows, and over time, more and more of the Control Panel commands will move to and be accessible from the Settings window.

🔄 ANOTHER WAY | Type *control panel* in the search box.

---

4 In the **Control Panel** window, if necessary, on the right, set *View by* to *Category,* click **System and Security,** and then click **Windows Firewall.** On the left, click **Change notification settings**—if necessary, enter your password; or, if you are unable to enter a password, just read the remaining steps in this activity.

5 In the **Customize Settings** window, notice that you can receive notifications when Windows Firewall blocks a new app.

6 **Close** $\boxed{\times}$ the window.

7 If you have not already done so, as directed by your instructor, submit your **Lastname_Firstname_1A_Know_Windows** PowerPoint presentation.

END | You have completed Project 1A

Managing Files and Folders

In Activities 1.21 through 1.33, you will assist Barbara Hewitt and Steven Ramos, who work for the Information Technology Department at the Boston headquarters office of the Bell Orchid Hotels. Barbara and Steven have been asked to organize some of the files and folders that comprise the corporation's computer data. As you progress through the Project, you will insert screenshots of windows that you create into a PowerPoint presentation similar to Figure 1.48.

PROJECT FILES

For Project 1B, you will need the following student data files:

A new blank PowerPoint presentation

win10_01_Student_Data_Files

Student Data Files may be provided by your instructor, or you can download them from www.pearsonhighered.com/go which you will learn to do in the next Activity. If you already have the Student Data Files stored in a location that you can access, then begin with Activity 1.22.

You will save your results in a PowerPoint file as:

Lastname_Firstname_1B_Manage_Files

PROJECT RESULTS

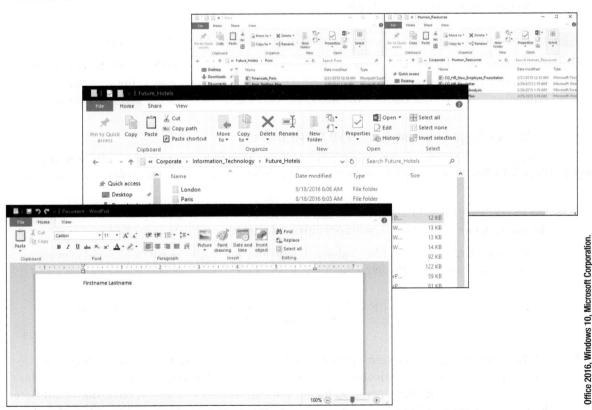

Office 2016, Windows 10, Microsoft Corporation.

FIGURE 1.48 Project 1B Managing Files and Folders

Objective 7 Download and Extract Files and Folders

Download refers to the action of transferring or copying a file from another location—such as a cloud storage location or from an Internet site—to your computer. Files that you download are frequently *compressed files*, which are files that have been reduced in size, take up less storage space, and can be transferred to other computers faster than uncompressed files.

A compressed folder might contain a group of files that were combined into one compressed folder, which makes it easier to share a group of files. To *extract* means to decompress, or pull out, files from a compressed form. The terms *zip* and *unzip* refer to the process of compressing (zipping) and extracting (unzipping). File Explorer includes *Compressed Folder Tools*, available on the ribbon, to assist you in extracting compressed files.

> **ALERT!** **Already Have the Student Data Files?**
>
> If your instructor has already provided you with the Student Data Files that accompany this chapter and you have stored them in a location that you can access, then skip to Activity 1.22. However, you can refer to these instructions when downloading files from other sites.

Activity 1.21 │ Downloading Files from a Website

To complete this Project and the Projects at the end of this chapter, you will need the Student Data Files that accompany this chapter. Follow the steps in this Activity to download the Student Data Files from the publisher's website; or, your instructor might provide the Student Data Files to you, for example, in your learning management system.

> **NOTE** **Using a Touchscreen**
>
> If you are using a touchscreen device to complete this Project, continue to use the tap and swipe gestures presented in Project 1A. The remainder of this instruction will assume that you are using a mouse and keyboard setup, but all the Projects can be completed using a touchscreen without a mouse or keyboard.

1 If necessary, sign in to your computer and display the Windows 10 desktop.

2 Determine the location where you want to store your downloaded Student Data Files; this example will assume you are using a USB flash drive. If you are working on your own computer, consider the Documents folder on This PC or your OneDrive cloud storage.

> **ALERT!** **In a College Lab, Use Your USB Flash Drive**
>
> If you are completing these Activities in a college lab, store your Student Data Files on a USB flash drive and use it to complete the steps, because in a college lab, any work you store on the computer at which you are working will likely be deleted as soon as you sign off the lab computer.

3 On the taskbar, click **Microsoft Edge** [e], click in the **Search or enter web address** box or in the address bar—type **www.pearsonhighered.com/go** and then press [Enter].

Microsoft Edge is Microsoft's Windows 10 *web browser*—software with which you display webpages and navigate the Internet.

> ↻ **ANOTHER WAY** You can use other browsers, such as Chrome or Firefox, to go to this website. Use the download techniques associated with that browser to download the files.

4 At the Pearson site, on the right, locate and then click the cover image for the book you are using, or narrow your selection by clicking a topic on the left and then locate the cover image. In the window that opens, on the left, under **Student Resources**, click **Download Data Files**. On the **Student Data Files** screen, click **Windows 10 Chapter 1: Getting Started with Windows 10**.

5 At the bottom of the screen, click **Save** to begin the download. When the file download completes, at the bottom of the screen, click **Open folder**.

Typically, files that you download from an Internet site are stored in the *Downloads folder* on your PC.

6 In the **file list** for the **Downloads** folder, with the **win10_01_Student_Data_Files** folder selected, on the **Home tab**, in the **Clipboard group**, click **Copy**, and then in the **navigation pane**, navigate to and open your **Windows 10 Chapter 1** folder. On the **Home tab**, in the **Clipboard group**, click **Paste**. With the zipped folder selected and the **Compressed Folder Tools** active, on the ribbon, click the **Extract tab**, and then click **Extract all**. In the displayed dialog box, click **Browse**.

7 In the **Select a destination** window, in the **navigation pane**, navigate to and open your **Windows 10 Chapter 1** folder, and then in the lower right corner, click **Select Folder**. In the lower right corner of the displayed window, click **Extract**.

After a few moments, the folder is extracted and placed in the location you selected.

8 Now that you have the extracted folder, you no longer need the zipped folder, so select the zipped folder and delete it. Also, if a folder for MAC files displays, you can delete that folder if you are not using a Mac computer. **Close** ⊠ all open windows to redisplay your desktop.

Objective 8   Use File Explorer to Display Locations, Folders, and Files

A file is the fundamental unit of storage that enables Windows 10 to distinguish one set of information from another. A folder is the basic organizing tool for files. In a folder, you can store files that are related to one another. You can also place a folder inside another folder, which is then referred to as a *subfolder*.

Windows 10 arranges folders in a structure that resembles a *hierarchy*—an arrangement where items are ranked and where each level is lower in rank than the item above it. The hierarchy of folders is referred to as the *folder structure*. A sequence of folders in the folder structure that leads to a specific file or folder is a *path*.

Activity 1.22 │ Navigating with File Explorer

Recall that File Explorer is the program that displays the contents of locations, folders, and files on your computer and also in your OneDrive and other cloud storage locations. File Explorer also enables you to perform tasks related to your files and folders such as copying, moving, and renaming. When you open a folder or location, a window displays to show its contents. The design of the window helps you navigate—explore within the file structure for the purpose of finding files and folders—so that you can save and find your files and folders efficiently.

In this Activity, you will open a folder and examine the parts of its window.

1 Close all open windows. With your desktop displayed, on the taskbar, *point to* but do not click **File Explorer** ▣, and notice the ScreenTip *File Explorer*.

A *ScreenTip* displays useful information when you perform various mouse actions, such as pointing to screen elements.

2 Click **File Explorer** ▣ to display the **File Explorer** window.

File Explorer is at work anytime you are viewing the contents of a location or the contents of a folder stored in a specific location. By default, the File Explorer button on the taskbar opens with the *Quick access* location selected, which is a list of files you have been working on and folders you use often.

The default list will likely display the Desktop, Downloads, Documents, and Pictures folders, and then folders you worked on recently or work on frequently will be added automatically, although you can change this behavior.

The benefit of the Quick access list is that you can customize a list of folders that you go to often. To add a folder to the list quickly, you can right-click a folder in the file list and click Pin to Quick Access.

For example, if you are working on a project, you can pin it—or simply drag it—to the Quick access list. When you are done with the project and not using the folder so often, you can remove it from the list. Removing it from the list does not delete the folder, it simply removes it from the Quick access list.

> **NOTE** | **You Can Change the Behavior of the Quick Access List in File Explorer**
>
> If you prefer to have File Explorer default to the This PC view—which was the default in Windows 8—on the View tab, click Options to display the Folder Options dialog box. On the General tab, click the Open File Explorer to arrow, and then click This PC. If you want to prevent recently and frequently used items from displaying on the Quick access list, on the same tab, at the bottom under Privacy, clear the check boxes and then clear the File Explorer history. Click Apply and click OK.

3 On the left, in the **navigation pane**, scroll down if necessary, and then click **This PC** to display folders, devices, and drives in the **file list** on the right. Compare your screen with Figure 1.49.

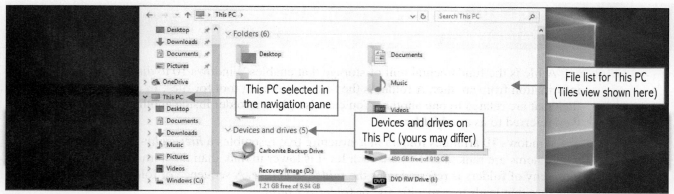

FIGURE 1.49

Office 2016, Windows 10, Microsoft Corporation.

4 If necessary, in the upper right corner, click Expand the Ribbon ⌄. In the **file list**, under **Folders**, click **Documents** one time to select it, and then on the ribbon, on the **Computer tab**, in the **Location group**, click **Open**. On the ribbon, click the **View tab**, and then in the **Layout group**, if necessary, click **Details**.

The window for the Documents folder displays. You may or may not have files and folders already stored here. Because this window typically displays the file list for a folder, it is also referred to as the *folder window*.

> **ANOTHER WAY** | Point to Documents, right-click to display a shortcut menu, and then click Open; or, point to Documents and double-click.

5 Compare your screen with Figure 1.50, and then take a moment to study the parts of the window as described in the table in Figure 1.51.

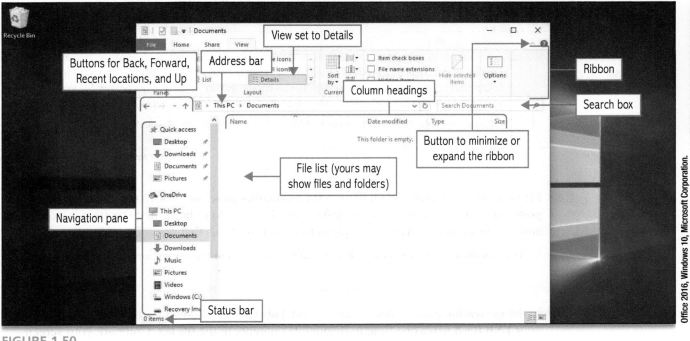

FIGURE 1.50

PARTS OF THE FILE EXPLORER WINDOW	
WINDOW PART	**FUNCTION**
Address bar	Displays your current location in the file structure as a series of links separated by arrows. Tap or click a part of the path to go to that level or tap or click at the end to select the path for copying.
Back, Forward, Recent locations, and Up buttons	Enable you to navigate to other folders you have already opened without closing the current window. These buttons work with the address bar; that is, after you use the address bar to change folders, you can use the Back button to return to the previous folder. Use the Up button to open the location where the folder you are viewing is saved—also referred to as the *parent folder*.
Column headings	Identify the columns in Details view. By clicking the column heading name, you can change how the files in the file list are organized; by clicking the arrow on the right, you can select various sort arrangements in the file list. By right-clicking a column heading, you can select other columns to add to the file list.
File list	Displays the contents of the current folder or location. If you type text into the Search box, a search is conducted on the folder or location only, and only the folders and files that match your search will display here—including files in subfolders.
Minimize the Ribbon or Expand the Ribbon button	Changes the display of the ribbon. When minimized, the ribbon shows only the tab names and not the full ribbon.
Navigation pane	Displays locations to which you can navigate; for example, your OneDrive, folders on This PC, devices and drives connected to your PC, folders listed under Quick access, and possibly other PCs on your network. Use Quick access to open your most commonly used folders and searches. If you have a folder that you use frequently, you can drag it to the Quick access area so that it is always available.
Ribbon	Groups common tasks such as copying and moving, creating new folders, emailing and zipping items, and changing views of the items in the file list.

FIGURE 1.51 *(continued)*

PARTS OF THE FILE EXPLORER WINDOW (*continued*)	
WINDOW PART	**FUNCTION**
Search box	Enables you to type a word or phrase and then searches for a file or subfolder stored in the current folder that contains matching text. The search begins as soon as you begin typing; for example, if you type *G*, all the file and folder names that start with the letter *G* display in the file list.
Status bar	Displays the total number of items in a location, or the number of selected items and their total size.

FIGURE 1.51

Office 2016, Windows 10, Microsoft Corporation.

6 ▶ Move your ⬚ pointer anywhere into the **navigation pane**, and notice that a downward pointing arrow ⬇ displays to the left of *Quick access* to indicate that this item is expanded, and a right-pointing arrow ⬆ displays to the left of items that are collapsed.

You can click these arrows to collapse and expand areas in the navigation pane.

Activity 1.23 │ Using File Explorer to Display Locations, Folders, and Files

1 ▶ In the **navigation pane**, if necessary expand **This PC**, scroll down if necessary, and then click your **USB flash drive** one time to display its contents in the **file list**. Compare your screen with Figure 1.52.

In the navigation pane, *This PC* displays all of the drive letter locations attached to your computer, including the internal hard drives, CD or DVD drives, and any connected devices such as a USB flash drive.

Your extracted student data files display if this is your storage location.

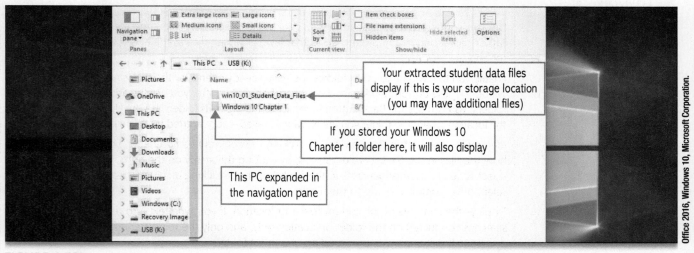

FIGURE 1.52

2 In the **file list**, double-click the uncompressed **win10_01_Student_Data_Files** folder to display the subfolders and files. Then double-click the folder for this Project, which is the folder **win01_1B_Bell_Orchid**.

Recall that the corporate office of the Bell Orchid Hotels is in Boston. The corporate office maintains subfolders labeled for each of its large hotels in Honolulu, Orlando, San Diego, and Santa Barbara.

⟳ ANOTHER WAY   Right-click the folder, and then click Open; or, select the folder and then on the ribbon, on the Home tab, in the Open group, click Open.

3 In the **file list**, double-click **Orlando** to display the subfolders, and then look at the **address bar** to view the path. Compare your screen with Figure 1.53.

Within each city's subfolder, there is a structure of subfolders for the Accounting, Engineering, Food and Beverage, Human Resources, Operations, and Sales and Marketing departments.

Because folders can be placed inside other folders, such an arrangement is common when organizing files on a computer.

In the address bar, the path from the flash drive to the win01_1B_Bell_Orchid folder to the Orlando folder displays as a series of links.

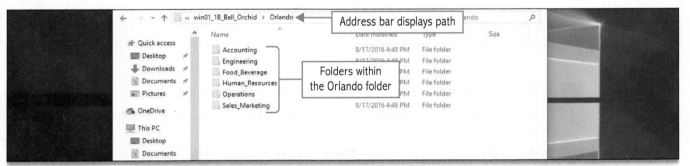

Office 2016, Windows 10, Microsoft Corporation.

FIGURE 1.53

4 In the **address bar**, to the right of **win01_1B_Bell_Orchid**, click the ⟩ arrow to display a list of the subfolders in the **win01_1B_Bell_Orchid** folder. On the list that displays, notice that **Orlando** displays in bold, indicating it is open in the file list. Then, on the list, click **Honolulu**.

The subfolders within the Honolulu folder display.

5 In the **address bar**, to the right of **win01_1B_Bell_Orchid**, click the ⟩ arrow again to display the subfolders in that folder. Then, on the **address bar**—not on the list—point to **Honolulu** and notice that the list of subfolders in the **Honolulu** folder displays.

After you display one set of subfolders in the address bar, all of the links are active and you need only point to them to display the list of subfolders.

Clicking an arrow to the right of a folder name in the address bar displays a list of the subfolders in that folder. You can click a subfolder name to display its contents. In this manner, the address bar is not only a path, but it is also an active control with which you can step from the current folder directly to any other folder above it in the folder structure just by clicking a folder name.

6 On the list of subfolders for **Honolulu**, click **Sales_Marketing** to display its contents in the **file list**. On the **View tab**, in the **Layout group**, if necessary, click **Details**. Compare your screen with Figure 1.54.

ANOTHER WAY   In the file list, double-click the Sales_Marketing folder.

The files in the Sales_Marketing folder for Honolulu display in the Details layout. To the left of each file name, an icon indicates the program that created each file. Here, there is one PowerPoint file, one Excel file, one Word file, and four JPEG images.

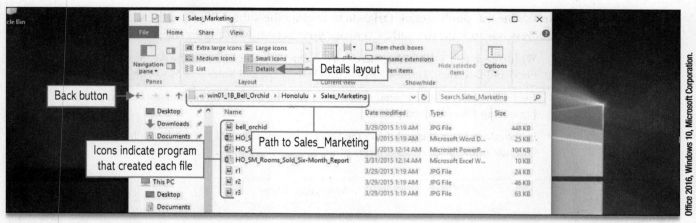

FIGURE 1.54

7 In the upper left portion of the window, click **Back** ← one time.

The Back button retraces each of your clicks in the same manner as clicking the Back button when you are browsing the Internet.

8 In the **file list**, point to the **Human_Resources** folder, and then double-click to open the folder.

9 In the **file list**, click one time to select the PowerPoint file **HO_HR_New_Employee_Presentation**, and then on the ribbon, click the **View tab**. In the **Panes group**, click **Details pane**, and then compare your screen with Figure 1.55.

The *Details pane* displays the most common *file properties* associated with the selected file. File properties refer to information about a file, such as the author, the date the file was last changed, and any descriptive *tags*—properties that you create to help you find and organize your files.

Additionally, a thumbnail image of the first slide in the presentation displays, and the status bar displays the number of items in the folder.

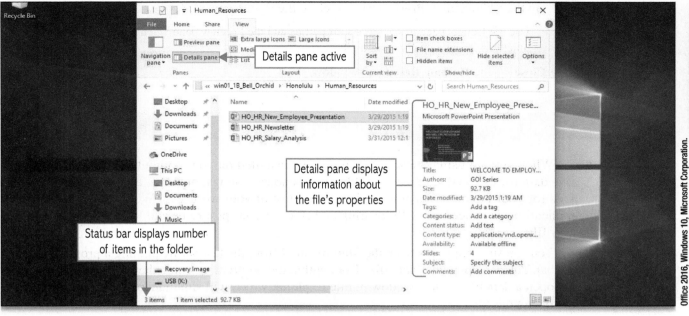

FIGURE 1.55

10 On the right, in the **Details pane**, click **Add a tag**, type **New Employee meeting** and then at the bottom of the pane click **Save**.

Because you can search for tags, adding tags to files makes them easier to find.

🔄 ANOTHER WAY   With the file selected, on the Home tab, in the Open group, click Properties to display the Properties dialog box for the file, and then click the Details tab.

11 On the ribbon, on the **View tab**, in the **Panes group**, click **Preview pane** to replace the **Details pane** with the **Preview pane**. Compare your screen with Figure 1.56.

In the Preview pane that displays on the right, you can use the scroll bar to scroll through the slides in the presentation; or, you can click the up or down scroll arrow to view the slides as a miniature presentation.

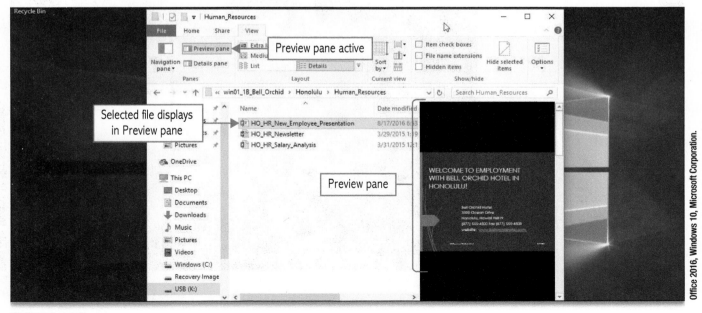

FIGURE 1.56

12 On the ribbon, click **Preview pane** to close the right pane.

Use the Details pane to see a file's properties and the Preview pane when you want to look at a file quickly without actually opening it.

13 **Close** ☒ the **Human_Resources** window.

Objective 9 Start Programs and Open Data Files

When you are using the software programs installed on your computer, you create and save data files—the documents, workbooks, databases, songs, pictures, and so on that you need for your job or personal use. Therefore, most of your work with Windows 10 desktop applications is concerned with locating and starting your programs and locating and opening your files.

You can start programs from the Start menu or from the taskbar by pinning a program to the taskbar. You can open your data files from within the program in which they were created, or you can open a data file from a window in File Explorer, which will simultaneously start the program and open your file.

Activity 1.24 │ Starting Programs

1 Close any open windows. Click **Start** ⊞ to place the insertion point in the search box, and then type **paint** At the top of the search results, click **More**, and then click **Apps**. Compare your screen with Figure 1.57.

The Windows 10 search feature will immediately begin searching your PC and the web when you type in the search box. To refine your search, select a category; for example, Apps.

Paint is a Windows desktop application that comes with Windows 10 with which you can create and edit drawings and display and edit stored photos.

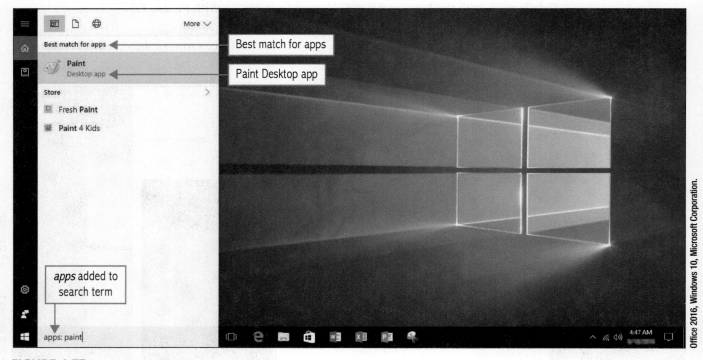

FIGURE 1.57

2 With the **Paint Desktop app** selected—also referred to as *in focus*—as the result of your search, press Enter to open this Windows desktop application.

3 On the ribbon of the Paint program, with the **Home tab** active, in the **Tools group**, click the **Pencil** icon. Move your mouse pointer into the white drawing area, hold down the left mouse button, and then with your mouse, try drawing the letters of your first name in the white area of the window.

BY TOUCH   Use your finger to draw on the screen.

4 In the upper left corner, to the left of the **Home tab,** click the **File tab** to display a menu of commands for things you can do with your image.

5 At the bottom of the menu, click **Exit.** In the displayed message, click **Don't Save.**

Messages like this display in most programs to prevent you from forgetting to save your work. A file saved in the Paint program creates a graphic file in the JPEG format.

6 Click **Start** ⊞ to place the insertion point in the search box, type **wordpad** at the top click **More,** click **Apps,** and then open the **WordPad Desktop app.** Notice that this program window has characteristics similar to the Paint program window; for example, it has a ribbon of commands.

7 With the insertion point blinking in the document window, type your first and last name.

8 If the Microsoft PowerPoint application is not pinned to your taskbar, use the same technique you used to search for and pin the Snipping Tool application to search for and pin the PowerPoint application to your taskbar.

9 From the taskbar, open **PowerPoint.** Click **Blank Presentation,** and then on the **Home tab,** in the **Slides group,** click **Layout.** In the displayed gallery, click **Blank.** If necessary, Maximize ▢ the PowerPoint window.

10 On the **Insert tab,** in the **Images group,** click **Screenshot,** and then under **Available Windows,** click the image of the WordPad program with your name typed to insert the image in the PowerPoint presentation. Click in a blank area of the slide to deselect the image; if necessary, close the Design Ideas pane on the right.

11 Click the **File tab,** on the left click **Save As,** click **Browse,** and then in the **Save As** dialog box, navigate to and open your **Windows 10 Chapter 1 folder;** open the folder so that its name displays in the address bar.

12 Click in the **File name** box, and then using your own name, replace the selected text by typing **Lastname_Firstname_1B_Manage_Files**

13 Click **Save,** and then in the upper right corner of the PowerPoint window, click **Minimize** ▬ so that PowerPoint remains open but not displayed on your screen; you will need your PowerPoint presentation again as you progress through this Project.

14 **Close** ⊠ **WordPad,** and then click **Don't Save.**

15 Search for the **steps recorder** desktop app and open it. Search for the **alarms & clock** Windows Store app and open it. Search for the **calculator** Windows Store app and open it. Search for **network and sharing center** in the **Control Panel** and open it. Compare your screen with Figure 1.58.

Steps Recorder captures the steps you perform on your computer, including a text description of where you clicked and a picture of the screen during each click. The *Network and Sharing Center* is a Windows 10 feature in the Control Panel where you can view your basic network information.

You can open multiple programs and apps, and each one displays in its own window. Each open program displays an icon on the taskbar.

You can see that for both desktop apps that come with Windows 10 and Windows Store apps, the easiest way to find a program is to simply search for it, and then open it from the list of results.

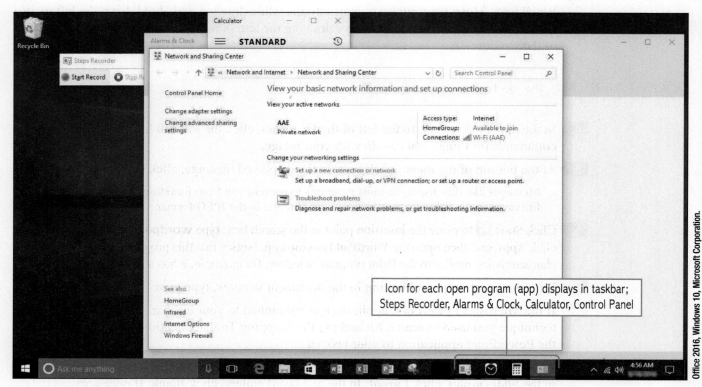

Icon for each open program (app) displays in taskbar; Steps Recorder, Alarms & Clock, Calculator, Control Panel

FIGURE 1.58

16 Click **Start** , and then above the apps that begin with A, click the letter **A** to display an onscreen alphabet. Then click **W** to quickly jump to the W section of the list. Click **Windows Accessories**. Compare your screen with Figure 1.59.

These are programs that come with Windows 10. You can open them from this list or search for them as you just practiced. Additionally, use the technique you just practiced to quickly jump to a section of the apps list without scrolling.

Programs (apps) included
with Windows Accessories

FIGURE 1.59

17 On the taskbar, click the **Steps Recorder** icon ▣, and then on the taskbar, click the **Alarms & Clocks** icon ◉.

Use the taskbar to quickly move among open apps.

18 **Close** ✕ all open windows and redisplay the desktop.

Activity 1.25 │ **Opening Data Files**

NOTE	You Need Microsoft Word 2016 or Word 2013
For this Project you need Microsoft Word 2016 or Word 2013 on your computer; you can use a trial version if necessary.	

1 Open **Word** from your taskbar, or click **Start** ▦, type **word 2016** (or type *word 2013* if that is the version of Word on your computer) and then open the **Word** desktop app. Maximize ▢ the window if necessary. Compare your screen with Figure 1.60.

The Word program window has features that are common to other programs you have opened; for example, commands are arranged on tabs. When you create and save data in Word, you create a Word document file.

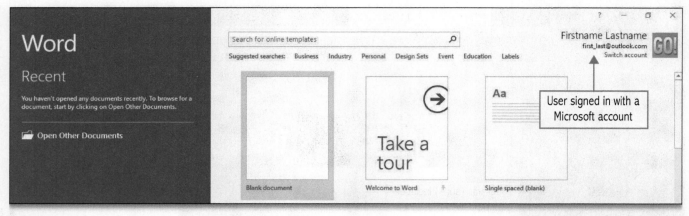

FIGURE 1.60

Word 2016, Windows 10, Microsoft Corporation.

2 On the left, click **Open Other Documents**. Notice the list of places from which you can open a document, including your OneDrive if you are logged in. Click **Browse** to display the **Open** dialog box. Compare your screen with Figure 1.61, and then take a moment to study the table in Figure 1.62.

Recall that a dialog box is a window containing options for completing a task; its layout is similar to that of a File Explorer window. When you are working in a desktop application, use the Open dialog box to locate and open existing files that were created in the desktop application.

When you click Browse, typically the Documents folder on This PC displays. You can use the skills you have practiced to navigate to other locations on your computer, such as your removable USB flash drive.

FIGURE 1.61

Office 2016, Windows 10, Microsoft Corporation.

DIALOG BOX ELEMENT	FUNCTION
Address bar	Displays the path in the folder structure.
File list	Displays the list of files and folders that are available in the folder indicated in the address bar.
File name box	Enables you to type the name of a specific file to locate it—if you know it.
File type arrow	Enables you to restrict the type of files displayed in the file list; for example, the default *All Word Documents* restricts (filters) the type of files displayed to only Word documents. You can click the arrow and adjust the restrictions (filters) to a narrower or wider group of files.
Navigation pane	Navigate to files and folders and get access to Quick access, OneDrive, and This PC.
Search box	Search for files in the current folder. Filters the file list based on text that you type; the search is based on text in the file name (and for files on the hard drive or OneDrive, in the file itself), and on other properties that you can specify. The search takes place in the current folder, as displayed in the address bar, and in any subfolders within that folder.
Toolbar	Displays relevant tasks; for example, creating a new folder.

FIGURE 1.62

Office 2016, Windows 10, Microsoft Corporation.

3 In the **navigation pane**, scroll down as necessary, and then under **This PC**, click your **USB flash drive** or whatever location where you have stored your student data files. In the **file list**, double-click your **win10_01_Student_Data_Files** folder to open it and display its contents. Then double-click the **win01_1B_Bell_Orchid** folder to open it and display its contents.

4 In the upper right portion of the **Open** dialog box, click the **More options arrow** [⌄], and then set the view to **Large icons**. Compare your screen with Figure 1.63.

The Live Preview feature indicates that each folder contains additional subfolders.

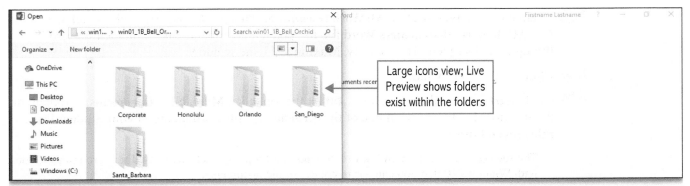

FIGURE 1.63

Office 2016, Windows 10, Microsoft Corporation.

5 In the **file list**, double-click the **Corporate** folder, and then double-click the **Accounting** folder.

The view returns to the Details view.

6 In the **file list**, notice that only one document—a Word document—displays. In the lower right corner, locate the **File type** button, and notice that *All Word Documents* displays as the file type. Click the **File type arrow**, and then on the displayed list, click **All Files**. Compare your screen with Figure 1.64.

When you change the file type to *All Files*, you can see that the Word file is not the only file in this folder. By default, the Open dialog box displays only the files created in the *active program*; however, you can display variations of file types in this manner.

Microsoft Office file types are identified by small icons, which is a convenient way to differentiate one type of file from another. Although you can view all the files in the folder, you can open only the files that were created in the active program, which in this instance is Microsoft Word.

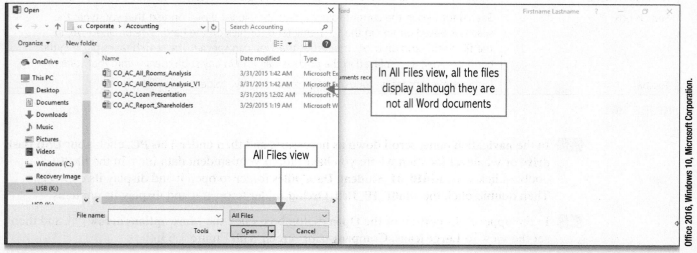

FIGURE 1.64

7 Change the file type back to **All Word Documents**. Then in the **file list**, double-click the **CO_AC_Report_Shareholders** Word file to open the document. Take a moment to scroll through the document. If necessary, Maximize ▢ the window.

8 **Close** ✕ the Word window.

9 Click **Start** ⊞, and then search for **.txt** At the top, click **More**, click **Documents**, and then, on the list, double-click to open one of the **Structure.txt** files, which are in your Student Data Files several times.

The file opens using the Windows 10 *Notepad* desktop app—a basic text-editing program included with Windows 10 that you can use to create simple documents.

In the search box, you can search for files on your computer, and you can search for a file by its *file name extension*—a set of characters at the end of a file name that helps Windows understand what kind of information is in a file and what program should open it. A *.txt file* is a simple file consisting of lines of text with no formatting and that almost any computer can open and display.

10 **Close** ✕ all open windows.

More Knowledge | **Do Not Clutter Your Desktop by Creating Desktop Shortcuts**

On your desktop, you can add or remove *desktop shortcuts*, which are desktop icons that can link to items accessible on your computer such as a program, file, folder, disk drive, printer, or another computer. In previous versions of Windows, many computer users commonly did this.

Now the Start menu is your personal dashboard for all your programs and online activities, and increasingly you will access programs and your own files in the cloud. So do not clutter your desktop with shortcuts—doing so is more confusing than useful. Placing desktop shortcuts for frequently used programs or folders directly on your desktop may seem convenient, but as you add more icons, your desktop becomes cluttered and the shortcuts are not easy to find. A better organizing method is to use the taskbar for shortcuts to programs. For folders and files, the best organizing structure is to create a logical structure of folders within your Documents folder.

You can also drag frequently-used folders to the Quick access area in the navigation pane so that they are available any time you open File Explorer. As you progress in your use of Windows 10, you will discover techniques for using the taskbar and the Quick access area of the navigation pane to streamline your work, instead of cluttering your desktop.

Activity 1.26 | Searching, Pinning, Sorting, and Filtering in File Explorer

1 From the taskbar, open **File Explorer** ▢. On the right, at the bottom, you may notice that under **Recent files**, you can see files that you have recently opened.

2 In the **navigation pane**, click your **USB flash drive**—or click the location where you have stored your student data files for this Project. In the upper right, click in the **Search** box, and then type **pool** Compare your screen with Figure 1.65.

Files that contain the word *pool* in the title display. If you are searching a folder on your hard drive or OneDrive, files that contain the word *pool* within the document will also display. Additionally, Search Tools display on the ribbon.

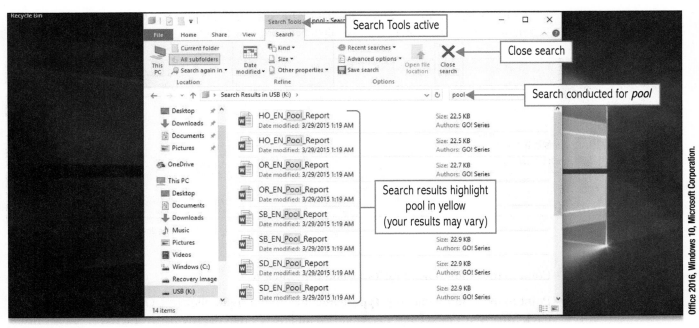

FIGURE 1.65

3 In the search box, clear the search by clicking ☒, and then in the search box type **dogs.jpg** Notice that you can also search by using a file extension as part of the search term.

4 **Clear** ☒ the search. In the **file list**, double-click your **win10_01_Student_Data_Files** folder to open it in the file list, and then click one time on your **win01_1B_Bell_Orchid** folder to select it.

5 On the **Home tab**, in the **Clipboard group**, click **Pin to Quick access**. Compare your screen with Figure 1.66.

You can pin frequently used folders to the Quick access area, and then unpin them when you no longer need frequent access. Folders that you access frequently will also display in the Quick access area without the pin image. Delete them by right-clicking the name and clicking Remove from Quick access.

FIGURE 1.66

Office 2016, Windows 10, Microsoft Corporation.

🔄 ANOTHER WAY   In the file list, right-click a folder name, and then click Pin to Quick access; or, drag the folder to the Quick access area in the navigation pain and release the mouse button when the ScreenTip displays Pin to Quick access.

6 In the **file list**—or from the Quick access area—double-click your **win01_1B_Bell_Orchid** folder to display its contents in the file list. Double-click the **Corporate** folder and then double-click the **Engineering** folder.

7 On the **View tab**, in the **Current view group**, click **Sort by**, and then click **Type**. Compare your screen with Figure 1.67.

Use this technique to sort files in the file list by type. Here, the JPG files display first, and then the Microsoft Excel files, and so on—in alphabetic order by file type.

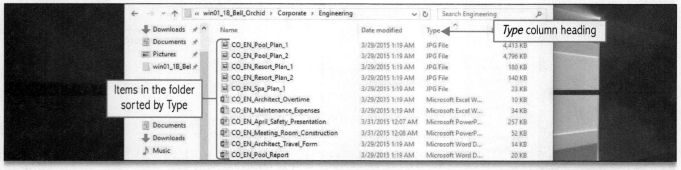

FIGURE 1.67

Office 2016, Windows 10, Microsoft Corporation.

8 Point to the column heading **Type**, and then click ∧.

9 Point to the column heading **Type** again, and on the right, click ☑. On the displayed list, click **Microsoft PowerPoint Presentation**, and notice that the file list is filtered to show only PowerPoint files.

A *filtered list* is a display of files that is limited based on specified criteria.

10 Click the check box to clear the Microsoft PowerPoint filter and redisplay all of the files.

11 **Close** ☒ all open windows.

Objective 10   Create, Rename, and Copy Files and Folders

File management includes organizing, copying, naming, renaming, moving, and deleting the files and folders you have stored in various locations—both locally and in the cloud.

Activity 1.27 | Copying Files from a Removable Storage Device to the Documents Folder on the Hard Disk Drive

Barbara and Steven have the assignment to transfer and then organize some of the corporation's files to a computer that will be connected to the corporate network. Data on such a computer can be accessed by employees at any of the hotel locations through the use of sharing technologies. For example, ***SharePoint*** is a Microsoft technology that enables employees in an organization to access information across organizational and geographic boundaries.

1 Close any open windows. If necessary, insert the USB flash drive that contains the Student Data Files that accompany this chapter that you downloaded from the Pearson website or obtained from your instructor.

2 From the taskbar, open **File Explorer** 📁. In the **navigation pane**, if necessary expand **This PC**, and then click your USB flash drive or the location where you have stored your student data files to display its contents in the file list.

Recall that in the navigation pane, under This PC, you have access to all the storage areas inside your computer, such as your hard disk drives, and to any devices with removable storage, such as CDs, DVDs, or USB flash drives.

3 In the **file list**, double-click **win10_01_Student_Data_Files** (not the zipped folder if you still have it) to open it, and then click one time on **win01_1B_Bell_Orchid** to select the folder. Compare your screen with Figure 1.68.

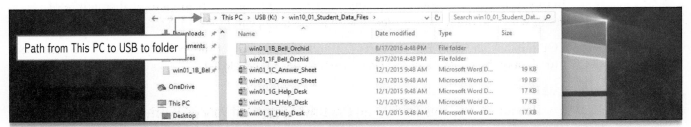

Office 2016, Windows 10, Microsoft Corporation.

FIGURE 1.68

4 With the **win01_1B_Bell_Orchid** folder on your USB drive selected, on the ribbon, on the **Home tab**, in the **Clipboard group**, click **Copy**.

The Copy command places a copy of your selected file or folder on the *Clipboard* where it will be stored until you use the Paste command to insert the copy somewhere else. The Clipboard is a temporary storage area for information that you have copied or moved from one place and plan to use somewhere else.

In Windows 10, the Clipboard can hold only one piece of information at a time. Whenever something is copied to the Clipboard, it replaces whatever was there before. In Windows 10, you cannot view the contents of the Clipboard nor place multiple items there in the manner that you can in Microsoft Word.

ANOTHER WAY   With the item selected in the file list, press Ctrl + C to copy the item to the Clipboard.

5 To the left of the address bar, click **Up** ↑ two times. In the **file list**, double-click your **Documents** folder to open it, and then on the **Home tab**, in the **Clipboard group**, click **Paste**.

A *progress bar* displays in a dialog box, and also displays on the File Explorer taskbar button with green shading. A progress bar indicates visually the progress of a task such as a copy process, a download, or a file transfer.

The Documents folder is one of several folders within your *personal folder* stored on the hard disk drive. For each user account—even if there is only one user on the computer—Windows 10 creates a personal folder labeled with the account holder's name.

ANOTHER WAY   With the destination location selected, press Ctrl + V to paste the item from the clipboard to the selected location. Or, on the Home tab, in the Organize group, click Copy to, find and then click the location to which you want to copy. If the desired location is not on the list, use the Choose location command at the bottom.

6 Close ✕ the **Documents** window.

Activity 1.28 | Creating Folders, Renaming Folders, and Renaming Files

Barbara and Steven can see that various managers have been placing files related to the new European hotels in the *Future_Hotels* folder. They can also see that the files have not been organized into a logical structure. For example, files that are related to each other are not in separate folders; instead they are mixed in with other files that are not related to the topic.

In this Activity, you will create, name, and rename folders to begin a logical structure of folders in which to organize the files related to the European hotels project.

1 On the taskbar, click **File Explorer** 🗂, and then use any of the techniques you have practiced to display the contents of the **Documents** folder in the **file list**.

NOTE   **Use the Documents Folder and OneDrive Instead of Your USB Drive**

In this modern computing era, you should limit your use of USB drives to those times when you want to quickly take some files to another computer without going online. Instead of using a USB drive, use your computer's hard drive, or better yet, your free OneDrive cloud storage that comes with your Microsoft account.

There are two excellent reasons to stop using USB flash drives. First, searching is limited on a USB drive—search does not look at the content inside a file. However, when you search files on your hard drive or OneDrive, the search extends to words and phrases actually *inside* the files. Second, if you delete a file or folder from a USB drive, it is gone and cannot be retrieved. Files you delete from your hard drive or OneDrive go to the Recycle Bin where you can retrieve them later.

---

2 In the **file list**, double-click the **win01_1B_Bell_Orchid** folder, double-click the **Corporate** folder, double-click the **Information_Technology** folder, and then double-click the **Future_Hotels** folder to display its contents in the file list; sometimes this navigation is written as *Documents > win01_1B_Bell_Orchid > Corporate > Information_Technology > Future_Hotels*.

Some computer users prefer to navigate a folder structure by double-clicking in this manner. Others prefer using the address bar as described in the following Another Way box. Use whatever method you prefer—double-clicking in the file list, clicking in the address bar, or expanding files in the navigation pane.

ANOTHER WAY In the navigation pane, click Documents, and expand each folder in the navigation pane. Or, In the address bar, to the right of Documents, click >, and then on the list, click win01_1B_Bell_Orchid. To the right of win01_1B_Bell_Orchid, click > and then click Corporate. To the right of Corporate, click > and then click Information_Technology. To the right of Information_Technology, click >, and then click Future_Hotels.

3 In the **file list**, be sure the items are in alphabetical order by **Name**. If the items are not in alphabetical order, recall that by clicking the small arrow in the column heading name, you can change how the files in the file list are ordered.

4 On the ribbon, click the **View tab**, and then in the **Layout group**, be sure **Details** is selected.

The ***Details view*** displays a list of files or folders and their most common properties.

ANOTHER WAY Right-click in a blank area of the file list, point to View, and then click Details.

5 On the ribbon, click the **Home tab**, and then in the **New group**, click **New folder**. With the text *New folder* selected, type **Paris** and press Enter. Click **New folder** again, and then type **Venice** and press Enter. Create a third **New folder** named **London**

In a Windows 10 file list, folders are listed first, in alphabetic order, followed by individual files in alphabetic order.

6 Click the **Venice** folder one time to select it, and then on the ribbon, in the **Organize group**, click **Rename**. Notice that the text *Venice* is selected. Type **Rome** and press Enter.

ANOTHER WAY Point to a folder or file name, right-click, and then on the shortcut menu, click Rename.

7 In the **file list**, click one time to select the Word file **Architects**. With the file name selected, click the file name again to select all the text. Click the file name again to place the insertion point within the file name, edit the file name to **Architects_Local** and press Enter. Compare your screen with Figure 1.69.

You can use any of the techniques you just practiced to change the name of a file or folder.

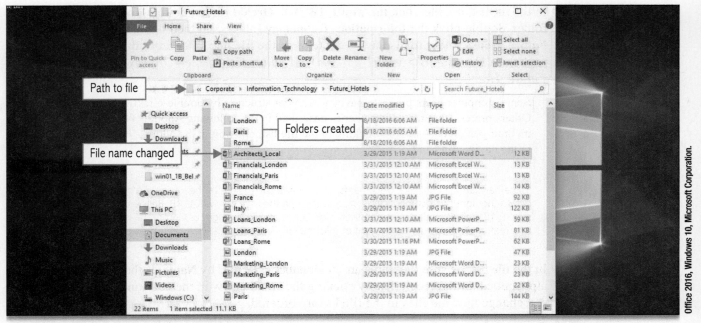

FIGURE 1.69

8 ▸ On the taskbar, click the **PowerPoint** icon to redisplay your **Lastname_Firstname_1B_Manage_Files** presentation, and then on the **Home tab**, click the upper portion of the **New Slide** button to insert a new slide with the **Blank** layout.

9 ▸ On the **Insert tab**, in the **Images group**, click **Screenshot**, and then under **Available Windows**, click the image of the **Future_Hotels** window to insert the image in the PowerPoint presentation. Click in a blank area of the slide to deselect the image; if necessary, close the Design Ideas pane on the right.

10 ▸ Above the **File tab**, on the Quick Access toolbar, click **Save** 🖫 and then in the upper right corner, click **Minimize** ⊟ so that PowerPoint remains open but not displayed on your screen.

11 ▸ **Close** ☒ all open windows.

Activity 1.29 | Copying Files

Copying, moving, renaming, and deleting files and folders comprise the most heavily used features within File Explorer. Probably half or more of the steps you complete in File Explorer relate to these tasks, so mastering these techniques will increase your efficiency.

When you *copy* a file or a folder, you make a duplicate of the original item and then store the duplicate in another location. In this Activity, you will assist Barbara and Steven in making copies of the Staffing_Plan file and then placing the copies in each of the three folders you created—London, Paris, and Rome.

1 ▸ From the taskbar, open **File Explorer** 🗔, and then by double-clicking in the file list or following the links in the address bar, navigate to **This PC > Documents > win01_1B_Bell_Orchid > Corporate > Information_Technology > Future_Hotels**.

2 ▸ **Maximize** ▢ the window. On the **View tab**, if necessary set the **Layout** to **Details**, and then in the **Current view group**, click **Size all columns to fit** 🎛.

3 ▸ In the **file list**, click the file **Staffing_Plan** one time to select it, and then on the **Home tab**, in the **Clipboard group**, click **Copy**.

4 At the top of the **file list**, double-click the **London folder** to open it, and then in the **Clipboard group**, click **Paste**. Notice that the copy of the **Staffing_Plan** file displays. Compare your screen with Figure 1.70.

FIGURE 1.70

Office 2016, Windows 10, Microsoft Corporation.

ANOTHER WAY Right-click the file you want to copy, and on the menu click Copy. Then right-click the folder into which you want to place the copy, and on the menu click Paste. Or, select the file you want to copy, press Ctrl + C to activate the Copy command, open the folder into which you want to paste the file, and then press Ctrl + V to activate the Paste command.

5 With the **London** window open, by using any of the techniques you have practiced, rename this copy of the **Staffing_Plan** file to **London_Staffing_Plan**

6 To the left of the **address bar**, click **Up** ↑ to move up one level in the folder structure and redisplay the file list for the **Future_Hotels** folder.

ANOTHER WAY In the address bar, click Future_Hotels to redisplay this window and move up one level in the folder structure.

7 Click the **Staffing_Plan** file one time to select it, hold down Ctrl, and then drag the file upward over the **Paris** folder until the ScreenTip + *Copy to Paris* displays, and then release the mouse button and release Ctrl.

When dragging a file into a folder, holding down Ctrl engages the Copy command and places a *copy* of the file at the location where you release the mouse button. This is another way to copy a file or copy a folder.

8 Open the **Paris** folder, and then rename the **Staffing_Plan** file to **Paris_Staffing_Plan** Then, move up one level in the folder structure to display the **Future_Hotels** window.

9 Double-click the **Rome** folder to open it. With your mouse pointer anywhere in the **file list**, right-click, and then from the shortcut menu click **Paste**.

A copy of the Staffing_Plan file is copied to the folder. Because a copy of the Staffing_Plan file is still on the Clipboard, you can continue to paste the item until you copy another item on the Clipboard to replace it.

10 Rename the file **Rome_Staffing_Plan**

11 On the **address bar**, click **Future_Hotels** to move up one level and open the **Future_Hotels** window—or click Up ↑ to move up one level. Leave this folder open for the next Activity.

Activity 1.30 | Moving Files

When you move a file or folder, you remove it from the original location and store it in a new location. In this Activity, you will move items from the Future_Hotels folder into their appropriate folders.

1 With the **Future_Hotels** folder open, in the **file list**, click the Excel file **Financials_London** one time to select it. On the **Home tab**, in the **Clipboard group**, click **Cut**.

The file's Excel icon dims. This action places the item on the Clipboard.

> **ANOTHER WAY** Right-click the file or folder, and on the shortcut menu, click Cut; or, select the file or folder, and then press Ctrl + X.

2 Double-click the **London** folder to open it, and then on the **Home tab**, in the **Clipboard group**, click **Paste**.

> **ANOTHER WAY** Right-click the folder, and on the shortcut menu, click Paste; or, select the folder, and then press Ctrl + V.

3 Click **Up** ↑ to move up one level and redisplay the **Future_Hotels** folder window. In the **file list**, point to **Financials_Paris**, hold down the left mouse button, and then drag the file upward over the **Paris** folder until the ScreenTip ➔*Move to Paris* displays, and then release the mouse button.

4 Open the **Paris** folder, and notice that the file was moved to this folder. Click **Up** ↑—or on the address bar, click Future_Hotels to return to that folder.

5 In the **file list**, click **Loans_London**, hold down Ctrl, and then click **London** and **Marketing_London** to select the three files. Release the Ctrl key. Compare your screen with Figure 1.71.

Use this technique to select a group of noncontiguous items in a list.

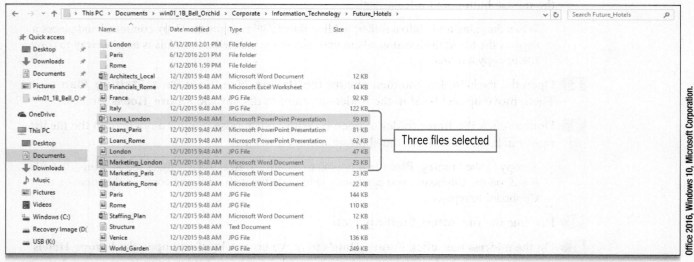

FIGURE 1.71

6 Point to any of the selected files, hold down the left mouse button, and then drag upward over the **London** folder until the ScreenTip ➔*Move to London* displays and *3* displays over the files being moved, and then release the mouse button.

> You can see that by keeping related files together—for example, all the files that relate to the London hotel—in folders that have an appropriately descriptive name, it will be easier to locate information later.

7 By dragging, move the **Architects_Local** file into the **London** folder.

8 In an empty area of the file list, right-click, and then click **Undo Move**. Leave the **Future_Hotels** window open for the next Activity.

> Any action that you make in a file list can be undone in this manner.

🔄 ANOTHER WAY   Press Ctrl + Z to undo an action in the file list.

More Knowledge **Using Shift + Click to Select Files**

If files to be selected are contiguous (next to each other in the file list), click the first file to be selected, hold down Shift and then click the left mouse button on the last file to select all of the files between the top and bottom file selections.

Activity 1.31 │ Copying and Moving Files by Snapping Two Windows

Sometimes you will want to open, in a second window, another instance of a program that you are using; that is, two copies of the program will be running simultaneously. This capability is especially useful in the File Explorer program, because you are frequently moving or copying files from one location to another.

In this Activity, you will open two instances of File Explorer, and then use the *Snap* feature to display both instances on your screen.

To copy or move files or folders into a different level of a folder structure, or to a different drive location, the most efficient method is to display two windows side by side and then use drag and drop or copy (or cut) and paste commands.

In this Activity, you will assist Barbara and Steven in making copies of the Staffing_Plan files for the corporate office.

1 In the upper right corner, click **Restore Down** ⯗ to restore the **Future_Hotels** window to its previous size and not maximized on the screen.

2 Hold down ⊞ and press ← to snap the window so that it occupies the left half of the screen.

3 On the taskbar, right-click **File Explorer** 🗎, and then on the list, click **File Explorer** to open another instance of the program. With the new window active, hold down ⊞ and press → to snap the window so that it occupies the right half of the screen.

🔄 ANOTHER WAY   Drag the title bar of a window to the left or right side of the screen and when your mouse pointer reaches the edge, it will snap it into place.

4 In the window on the right, click in a blank area to make the window active. Then navigate to **Documents > win01_1B_Bell_Orchid > Corporate > Human_Resources**. Compare your screen with Figure 1.72.

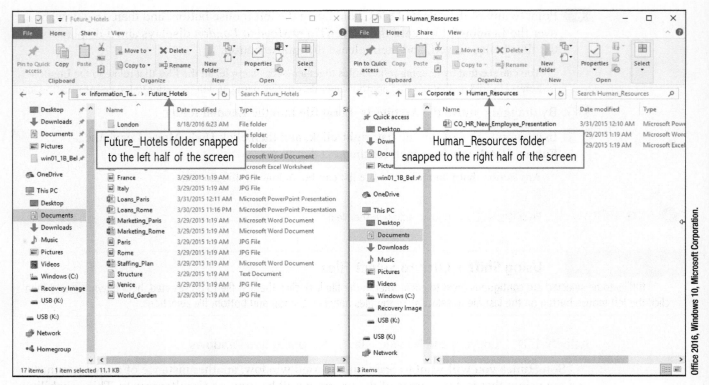

FIGURE 1.72

5 In the left window, double-click to open the **Rome** folder, and then click one time to select the file **Rome_Staffing_Plan**.

6 Hold down Ctrl, and then drag the file into the right window, into an empty area of the **Human_Resources file list**, until the ScreenTip + *Copy to Human_Resources* displays and then release the mouse button and Ctrl.

7 In the left window, on the **address bar**, click **Future_Hotels** to redisplay that folder. Open the **Paris** folder, point to **Paris_Staffing_Plan** and right-click, and then click **Copy**.

You can access the Copy command in various ways; for example, from the shortcut menu, on the ribbon, or by using the keyboard shortcut Ctrl + C.

8 In the right window, point anywhere in the **file list**, right-click, and then click **Paste**.

9 On the taskbar, click the PowerPoint icon to redisplay your **Lastname_Firstname_1B_Manage_Files** presentation, and then on the **Home tab**, click the upper portion of the **New Slide** button to insert a new slide with the **Blank** layout.

10 On the **Insert tab**, in the **Images group**, click **Screenshot**, and then click **Screen Clipping**. When the dimmed screen displays, move the + pointer to the upper left corner of the screen, hold down the left mouse button, and then drag to the lower right corner but do not include the taskbar, and then release the mouse button.

Because you have two windows displayed, each window displays under Available Windows. To capture an entire screen that contains more than one window, use the **Screen Clipping** tool with which you can capture a snapshot of your screen.

11 Click in a blank area of the slide to deselect the image; if necessary, close the Design Ideas pane on the right.

12 Press Ctrl + Home to to display the first slide in your presentation; your presentation contains three slides.

13 In the upper right, **Close** × the PowerPoint window, and when prompted, click **Save**. Submit this file to your instructor as directed.

14 **Close** ⌧ the two File Explorer windows to redisplay your desktop.

15 To properly eject your USB flash drive, if you are using one, on the right end of your taskbar, click **Show hidden icons** ⌃, and then click **Safely Remove Hardware and Eject Media** 🔌. When the Eject USB message displays, click the drive for your USB; a check mark will display indicating, or a message will indicate, that it is safe to remove your USB drive.

Activity 1.32 | Deleting Files and Using the Recycle Bin

It is good practice to delete files and folders that you no longer need from your hard disk drive and removable storage devices. Doing so makes it easier to keep your data organized and also frees up storage space.

When you delete a file or folder from any area of your computer's hard disk drive or from OneDrive, the file or folder is not immediately deleted. Instead, the deleted item is stored in the *Recycle Bin* and remains there until the Recycle Bin is emptied. Therefore, you can recover an item deleted from your computer's hard disk drive or OneDrive so long as the Recycle Bin has not been emptied. Items deleted from removable storage devices like a USB flash drive and from some network drives are immediately deleted and cannot be recovered from the Recycle Bin.

To permanently delete a file without first moving it to the Recycle Bin, click the item, hold down ⒮ⒽⒾⒻⓉ, and then press ⒟ⒺⓁ. A message will display indicating *Are you sure you want to permanently delete this file?* Use caution when using ⒮ⒽⒾⒻⓉ + ⒟ⒺⓁ to permanently delete a file because this action is not reversible.

You can restore items by dragging them from the file list of the Recycle Bin window to the file list of the folder window in which you want to restore them. Or, you can restore them to the location from which they were deleted by right-clicking the items in the file list of the Recycle Bin window and selecting Restore.

To check how well you understand the Recycle Bin, take a moment to think about the answers to the following questions:

Self-Check | Answer These Questions to Check Your Understanding

1 When you delete a file or folder from any area of your computer's hard disk drive or from OneDrive, the file or folder is not deleted; it is automatically stored in the _____ _____.

2 Files deleted from the computer's hard drive or OneDrive can be recovered from the Recycle Bin until the Recycle Bin is _____.

3 Items deleted from removable storage devices such as a USB flash drive are immediately deleted and cannot be _____ from the Recycle Bin.

4 You can permanently delete a file from the hard drive or OneDrive without first moving it to the Recycle Bin, but a warning message will indicate *Are you sure you want to _____ delete this file?*

5 To restore items from the Recycle Bin to the location from which they were deleted, right-click the items and then click _____.

Objective 11 Use OneDrive as Cloud Storage

OneDrive is Microsoft's *cloud storage* product. Cloud storage means that your data is stored on a remote server that is maintained by a company so that you can access your files from anywhere and from any device so long as you can access the Internet and then sign into Windows with your Microsoft account. The idea of having all of your data on a single device—your desktop or laptop PC—has become old fashioned. Because cloud storage from large companies like Microsoft is secure, many computer users now store their information on cloud services like OneDrive. Anyone with a Microsoft account has a large amount of free storage on OneDrive, and if you have an

Office 365 account—free to many college students if your college offers such a program—you have 1 terabyte or more of OneDrive storage that you can use across all Microsoft products. That amount of storage is probably all you will ever need—even if you store lots of photos on your OneDrive.

OneDrive is no longer just an app, as it was in Windows 8. Rather, OneDrive is integrated into the Windows 10 operating system. Similarly, Google's cloud storage called *Google Drive* is integrated into its Chrome operating system, and Apple's cloud storage called *iCloud* is integrated into both the Mac and iOS operating systems.

> **ALERT!** **To complete this final Activity, you must have a Microsoft account, be signed in to Windows 10 with that account, and be able to access your OneDrive from File Explorer**
>
> To complete this Activity, you must be able to access your OneDrive account from File Explorer. To do so, you must sign into Windows with your Microsoft account. If you cannot do this in your college lab, read through the steps, and if you can, practice on another computer on which you can sign in with your Microsoft account.

Activity 1.33 | Using OneDrive as Cloud Storage

When you install Windows 10 or use it for the first time, you will be prompted to set up your OneDrive. The setup process involves determining which folders—if not all—that you want to *sync* to OneDrive. Syncing—also called synchronizing—is the process of updating OneDrive data to match any updates you make on your device, and vice versa. This setup is optional, and you can always come back to it later. Your OneDrive storage, however, will be available from the navigation pane in File Explorer. Additionally, you will always have instant access to your OneDrive from any web browser.

1 **Close** ☒ any open windows. From the taskbar, start **File Explorer** 🗂 and then navigate to **Documents > win01_1B_Bell_Orchid > Santa_Barbara > Sales_Marketing > Media**.

2 Hold down Ctrl, click **Scenic1** and **Scenic2**, and then release Ctrl. With the two files selected, press Ctrl + C, which is the keyboard shortcut for the Copy command.

Although you see no screen action, the two files are copied to the Clipboard.

3 In the **navigation pane**, click **OneDrive**. If a dialog box regarding Customizing your OneDrive settings displays, in the lower right corner, click Cancel.

If you have decided on syncing options, you can do so in this dialog box; or, postpone these decisions by clicking Cancel.

Your OneDrive folders display in the file list.

4 On the ribbon, on the **Home tab**, in the **New group**, click **New folder**. Name the new folder **Marketing Photos** and then press Enter. Double-click the new folder to open it.

5 Press Ctrl + V, which is the keyboard shortcut for the Paste command, to paste the two photos into the folder. On the **View tab**, set the **Layout** to **Details**. Compare your screen with Figure 1.73.

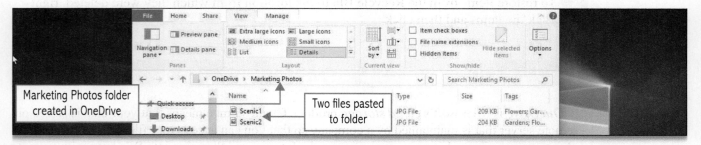

FIGURE 1.73

Office 2016, Windows 10, Microsoft Corporation.

6 **Close** ☒ all open windows.

> **END | You have completed Project 1B**

END OF CHAPTER

SUMMARY

Windows 10 is optimized for touchscreens and also works with a mouse and keyboard. You will probably use touch when you are reading or communicating on the web and a keyboard when creating files.

The Windows 10 Start menu is your connected dashboard—this is your one-screen view of information that updates continuously with new information and personal communications that are important to you.

The Windows Store apps you use from the Start menu display in separate Windows, similar to your other files, so you can move them on the desktop or display them side by side. These apps typically have a single purpose.

File Explorer is at work anytime you are viewing the contents of a location, a folder, or a file. Use File Explorer to navigate your Windows 10 structure that stores and organizes the files you create.

GO! LEARN IT ONLINE

Review the concepts and key terms in this chapter by completing these online challenges, which you can find in **MyITLab**:

Matching and Multiple Choice: Answer matching and multiple choice questions to test what you learned in this chapter.

GO! FOR JOB SUCCESS

Discussion: Managing Your Computer Files

Your instructor may assign this discussion to your class, and then ask you to think about, or discuss with your classmates, these questions:

FotolEdhar/Fotolia

Question 1: Why do you think it is important to follow specific guidelines when naming and organizing your files?

Question 2: Why is it impractical to store files and programs on your desktop?

Question 3: How are you making the transition from storing all of your files on physical media, such as flash drives or the hard drive of your computer, to storing your files in the cloud where you can access them from any computer with an Internet connection?

	Review and Assessment Guide for Windows 10 Chapter 1		
Project	**Apply Skills from These Chapter Objectives**	**Project Type**	**Project Location**
1A	Objectives 1-6 from Project 1A	**1A Instructional Project (Scorecard Grading)** Guided instruction to learn the skills in Project 1A.	In text
1B	Objectives 7-11 from Project 1B	**1B Instructional Project (Scorecard Grading)** Guided instruction to learn the skills in Project 1B.	In text
1C	Objectives 1-6 from Project 1A	**1C Chapter Review (Scorecard Grading)** A guided review of the skills from Project 1A.	In text
1D	Objectives 7-11 from Project 1B	**1D Chapter Review (Scorecard Grading)** A guided review of the skills from Project 1B.	In text
1E	Objectives 1-6 from Project 1A	**1E Mastery (Scorecard Grading) Mastery and Transfer of Learning** A demonstration of your mastery of the skills in Project 1A with decision-making.	In text
1F	Objectives 7-11 from Project 1B	**1F Mastery (Scorecard Grading) Mastery and Transfer of Learning** A demonstration of your mastery of the skills in Project 1B with decision-making.	In text
1G	Combination of Objectives from Projects 1A and 1B	**1G GO! Think (Rubric Grading) Critical Thinking** A demonstration of your understanding of the chapter concepts applied in a manner that you would outside of college. An analytic rubric helps you and your instructor grade the quality of your work by comparing it to the work an expert in the discipline would create.	In text
1H	Combination of Objectives from Projects 1A and 1B	**1H GO! Think (Rubric Grading) Critical Thinking** A demonstration of your understanding of the chapter concepts applied in a manner that you would outside of college. An analytic rubric helps you and your instructor grade the quality of your work by comparing it to the work an expert in the discipline would create.	In text
1I	Combination of Objectives from Projects 1A and 1B	**1I GO! Think (Rubric Grading) Critical Thinking** A demonstration of your understanding of the chapter concepts applied in a manner that you would outside of college. An analytic rubric helps you and your instructor grade the quality of your work by comparing it to the work an expert in the discipline would create.	In text

GLOSSARY

GLOSSARY OF CHAPTER KEY TERMS

.png An image file format, commonly pronounced *PING*, that stands for Portable Network Graphic; this is an image file type that can be transferred over the Internet.

.txt file A simple file consisting of lines of text with no formatting that almost any computer can open and display.

2 in 1 PC A laptop or notebook computer that can function as both a traditional laptop and as a tablet by either detaching the keyboard or by rotating the keyboard 360 degrees on hinges to look like a tablet.

Access work or school A Windows 10 feature with which you can connect to your work or school system based on established policies.

Action Center A vertical panel that displays on the right side of your screen when you click the icon in the notifications area of the taskbar; the upper portion displays notifications you have elected to receive such as mail and social network updates and the lower portion displays buttons for frequently used system commands.

Address bar (File Explorer) The area at the top of a File Explorer window that displays your current location in the folder structure as a series of links separated by arrows.

Administrator account A user account that lets you make changes that will affect other users of the computer; the most powerful of the two account types, because it permits the most control over the computer.

App The shortened version of the term *application*, and which typically refers to a smaller application designed for a single purpose.

App bar A term used to describe a horizontal or vertical array of command icons in a Windows app.

Application A set of instructions that a computer uses to accomplish a task; also called a program.

Application developer An individual who writes computer applications.

Badge An icon that displays on the Lock screen for lock screen apps that you have selected.

Bing Microsoft's search engine, which powers Cortana.

Booting the computer The process of turning on a computer when the computer has been completely shut down.

Click The action of pressing the left mouse button.

Clipboard A temporary storage area for information that you have copied or moved from one place and plan to use somewhere else.

Cloud storage Storage space on an Internet site that may also display as a drive on your computer.

Compressed file A file that has been reduced in size and that takes up less storage space and can be transferred to other computers faster than uncompressed files.

Compressed Folder Tools File Explorer tools, available on the ribbon, to assist you in extracting compressed files.

Content pane Another term for *file list*.

Contextual tab A tab that is added to the ribbon automatically when a specific object, such as a zipped file, is selected and that contains commands relevant to the selected object.

Control Panel An area of Windows 10 where you can manipulate some of the Windows 10 basic system settings—a carryover from previous versions of Windows.

Cortana Microsoft's intelligent personal assistant that is part of the Windows 10 operating system.

Dashboard A descriptive term for the Windows 10 Start menu because it provides a one-screen view of links to information and programs that matter most to the signed-in user.

Data All the files—documents, spreadsheets, pictures, songs, and so on—that you create and store during the day-to-day use of your computer.

Data management The process of managing your files and folders in an organized manner so that you can find information when you need it.

Desktop The main Windows 10 screen that serves as a starting point and surface for your work, like the top of an actual desk.

Desktop app A computer program that is installed on the hard drive of a personal computer and that requires a computer operating system like Microsoft Windows or macOS to run.

Desktop background Displays the colors and graphics of your desktop; you can change the desktop background to look the way you want.

Desktop shortcuts Desktop icons that link to any item accessible on your computer or on a network, such as a program, file, folder, disk drive, printer, or another computer.

Details pane Displays the most common properties associated with the selected file in File Explorer.

Details view A view in File Explorer that displays a list of files or folders and their most common properties.

Dialog box A small window that displays options for completing a task.

Double-click The action of pressing the left mouse button twice in rapid succession while holding the mouse still.

Download The action of transferring or copying a file from another location—such as a cloud storage location or from an Internet site—to your computer.

Downloads folder A folder that holds items that you have downloaded from the Internet.

Drag The action of moving something from one location on the screen to another while holding down the left mouse button; the action of dragging includes releasing the mouse button at the desired time or location.

Drive An area of storage that is formatted with a file system compatible with your operating system and is identified by a drive letter.

Extract The action of decompressing— pulling out—files from a compressed form.

File A collection of information that is stored on a computer under a single name, for example, a text document, a picture, or a program.

File Explorer window A window that displays the contents of the current location and contains helpful parts so that you can navigate within the file organizing structure of Windows.

File History A backup and recovery tool that automatically backs up your files to a separate location.

File list Displays the contents of the current folder or location; if you type text into the Search box, only the folders and files that match your search will display here—including files in subfolders; also referred to as the *content pane*.

File name extension A set of characters at the end of a file name that helps Windows 10 understand what kind of information is in a file and what program should open it.

File properties Information about a file such as its author, the date the file was last changed, and any descriptive tags.

Filtered list A display of files that is limited based on specified criteria.

Folder A container in which you store files.

Folder window Another name for the window that displays the contents of the current folder or location.

Folder structure The hierarchy of folders in Windows 10.

Free-form snip When using Snipping Tool, the type of snip that lets you draw an irregular line, such as a circle, around an area of the screen.

Full-screen snip When using Snipping Tool, the type of snip that captures the entire screen.

Get Started A feature in Windows 10 to learn about all the things that Windows 10 can do for you.

Google Drive Google's cloud storage.

Graphical user interface The system by which you interact with your computer and that uses graphics such as an image of a file folder or wastebasket that you click to activate the item represented.

GUI The acronym for a graphical user interface, pronounced *GOO-ee*.

Hamburger Another name for the hamburger menu.

Hamburger menu An icon made up of three lines that evoke a hamburger on a bun.

Hard disk drive The primary storage device located inside your computer and where most of your files and programs are typically stored; usually labeled as drive C.

Hierarchy An arrangement where items are ranked and where each level is lower in rank than the item above it.

HoloLens A see-through holographic computer developed by Microsoft.

Hub A feature in Microsoft Edge where you can save favorite websites and create reading lists.

iCloud Apple's cloud storage that is integrated into its Mac and iOS operating systems.

Icons Small images that represent commands, files, or other windows.

Insertion point A blinking vertical line that indicates where text or graphics will be inserted.

Internet of Things A growing network of physical objects that will have sensors connected to the Internet.

IoT The common acronym for the Internet of Things.

JPEG An acronym for Joint Photographic Experts Group, and which is a common file type used by digital cameras and computers to store digital pictures; JPEG is popular because it can store a high-quality picture in a relatively small file.

Jump list A list that displays when you right-click a button on the taskbar, and that displays locations (in the upper portion) and tasks (in the lower portion) from a program's taskbar button.

Keyboard shortcut A combination of two or more keyboard keys, used to perform a task that would otherwise require a mouse.

Live tiles Tiles on the Windows 10 Start menu that are constantly updated with fresh information relevant to the signed-in user; for example, the number of new email messages, new sports scores of interest, or new updates to social networks such as Facebook or Twitter.

Location Any disk drive, folder, or other place in which you can store files and folders.

Lock screen The first screen that displays after turning on a Windows 10 device and that displays the time, day, and date, and one or more icons representing the status of the device's Internet connection, battery status on a tablet or laptop, and any lock screen apps that are installed such as email notifications.

Lock screen apps Apps that display on a Windows 10 lock screen and that show quick status and notifications, even if the screen is locked.

Maximize The command to display a window in full-screen view.

Menu A list of commands within a category.

Menu bar A group of menus.

Menu icon Another name for the hamburger menu.

Microsoft account A single login account for Microsoft systems and services.

Microsoft Edge The web browser program included with Windows 10.

Mobile device platform The hardware and software environment for smaller-screen devices such as tablets and smartphones.

Mouse pointer Any symbol that displays on your screen in response to moving your mouse.

Navigate Explore within the file organizing structure of Windows 10.

Navigation pane The area on the left side of a folder window in File Explorer that displays the Quick access area and an expandable list of drives and folders.

Network and Sharing Center A Windows 10 feature in the Control Panel where you can view your basic network information.

Notepad A basic text-editing program included with Windows 10 that you can use to create simple documents.

OneDrive A free file storage and file sharing service provided by Microsoft when you sign up for a free Microsoft account.

Operating system A specific type of computer program that manages the other programs on a computer—including computer devices such as desktop computers, laptop computers, smartphones, tablet computers, and game consoles.

Parent folder In the file organizing structure of File Explorer, the location where the folder you are viewing is saved—one level up in the hierarchy.

Path A sequence of folders (directories) that leads to a specific file or folder.

PC Reset A backup and recovery tool that returns your PC to the condition it was in the day you purchased it.

Pen A pen-shaped stylus that you tap on a computer screen.

Personal folder A folder created for each user account on a Windows 10 computer, labeled with the account holder's name, and that contains the subfolders *Documents, Pictures, Music,* and *Videos.*

PIN Acronym for personal identification number; in Windows 10 Settings, you can create a PIN to use in place of a password.

Platform An underlying computer system on which application programs can run.

Point to The action of moving the mouse pointer over a specific area.

Pointer Any symbol that displays on your screen in response to moving your mouse and with which you can select objects and commands.

Pointing device A mouse, touchpad, or other device that controls the pointer position on the screen.

Program A set of instructions that a computer uses to accomplish a task; also called an application.

Progress bar In a dialog box or taskbar button, a bar that indicates visually the progress of a task such as a download or file transfer.

Quick access The navigation pane area in File Explorer where you can pin folders you use frequently and that also adds folders you are accessing frequently.

Quick Access toolbar (File Explorer) The small row of buttons in the upper left corner of a File Explorer window from which you can perform frequently used commands.

Recently added On the Start menu, a section that displays apps that you have recently downloaded and installed.

Rectangular snip When using Snipping Tool, the type of snip that lets you draw a precise box by dragging the mouse pointer around an area of the screen to form a rectangle.

Recycle Bin A folder that stores anything that you delete from your computer, and from which anything stored there can be retrieved until the contents are permanently deleted by activating the Empty Recycle Bin command.

Removable storage device A portable device on which you can store files, such as a USB flash drive, a flash memory card, or an external hard drive, commonly used to transfer information from one computer to another.

Resources A term used to refer collectively to the parts of your computer such as the central processing unit (CPU), memory, and any attached devices such as a printer.

Restore Down A command to restore a window to its previous size before it was maximized.

Ribbon The area at the top of a folder window in File Explorer that groups common tasks such as copying and moving, creating new folders, emailing and zipping items, and changing views on related tabs.

Right-click The action of clicking the right mouse button.

Screen Clipping A snapshot of all or part of your screen that you can add to a document.

Screenshot Another name for a screen capture.

ScreenTip Useful information that displays in a small box on the screen when you perform various mouse actions, such as pointing to screen elements.

Scroll arrow An arrow at the top, bottom, left, or right, of a scroll bar that when clicked, moves the window in small increments.

Scroll bar A bar that displays on the bottom or right side of a window when the contents of a window are not completely visible; used to move the window up, down, left, or right to bring the contents into view.

Scroll box The box in a vertical or horizontal scroll bar that you drag to reposition the document on the screen.

Select To specify, by highlighting, a block of data or text on the screen with the intent of performing some action on the selection.

SharePoint A Microsoft technology that enables employees in an organization to access information across organizational and geographic boundaries.

Shortcut menu A context-sensitive menu that displays commands and options relevant to the active object.

Shut down Turning off your computer in a manner that closes all open programs and files, closes your network connections, stops the hard disk, and discontinues the use of electrical power.

Sleep Turning off your computer in a manner that automatically saves your work, stops the fan, and uses a small amount of electrical power to maintain your work in memory.

Snap Assist The ability to drag windows to the edges or corners of your screen, and then having Task View display thumbnails of other open windows so that you can select what other windows you want to snap into place.

Snip The image captured using Snipping Tool.

Snipping Tool A program included with Windows 10 with which you can capture an image of all or part of a computer screen, and then annotate, save, copy, or share the image via email.

Split button A button that has two parts—a button and an arrow; clicking the main part of the button performs a command and clicking the arrow opens a menu with choices.

Start menu The menu that displays when you click the Start button, which consists of a list of installed programs on the left and a customizable group of app tiles on the right.

Steps Recorder A tool that captures the steps you perform on your computer, including a text description of where you clicked and a picture of the screen during each click.

Subfolder A folder within another folder.

System image backup A backup and recovery tool that creates a full system image backup from which you can restore your entire PC.

System tray Another name for the notification area on the taskbar.

Tags Properties that you create and add to a file to help you find and organize your files.

Task View A button on the taskbar that displays thumbnail images of all open apps enabling you to switch quickly between open apps.

Taskbar The area of the desktop that contains program buttons, and buttons for all open programs; by default, it is located at the bottom of the desktop, but you can move it.

This PC An area on the navigation pane that provides navigation to your internal storage and attached storage devices including optical media such as a DVD drive.

Thumbnail A reduced image of a graphic.

Tiles Square and rectangular boxes on the Windows 10 Start menu from which you can access apps, websites, programs, and tools for using the computer by simply clicking or tapping them.

Title bar The bar across the top of the window that displays the program name.

Universal apps Windows apps that use a common code base to deliver the app to any Windows device.

Unzip Extract files.

User account A collection of information that tells Windows 10 what files and folders the account holder can access, what changes the account holder can make to the computer system, and what the account holder's personal preferences are.

Virtual desktop An additional desktop display to organize and quickly access groups of windows.

Wallpaper Another term for the desktop background.

Web browser Software with which you display webpages and navigate the Internet.

Window snip When using Snipping Tool, the type of snip that captures the entire displayed window.

Windows 10 An operating system developed by Microsoft Corporation designed to work with mobile computing devices of all types and also with traditional PCs.

Windows apps Apps that run not only on a Windows phone and a Windows tablet, but also on your Windows desktop PC or laptop PC.

Windows Defender Protection built into Windows 10 that helps prevent viruses, spyware, and malicious or unwanted software from being installed on your PC without your knowledge.

Windows Firewall Protection built into Windows 10 that can prevent hackers or malicious software from gaining access to your computer through a network or the Internet.

Windows Store The program where you can find and download Windows apps.

Zip Compress files.

Apply 1A skills from these Objectives:

1 Explore the Windows 10 Environment

2 Use File Explorer and Desktop Apps to Create a New Folder and Save a File

3 Identify the Functions of the Windows 10 Operating System

4 Discover Windows 10 Features

5 Sign Out of Windows 10, Turn Off Your Computer, and Manage User Accounts

6 Manage Your Windows 10 System

Skills Review   Project 1C Exploring Windows 10

 PROJECT FILES

For Project 1C, you will need the following files:

Your USB flash drive—or other location—containing the student data files
win01_1C_Answer_Sheet (Word document)

You will save your file as:

Lastname_Firstname_1C_Answer_Sheet

1 Close all open windows. On the taskbar, click **File Explorer**, navigate to the location where you are storing your student data files for this chapter, and then open the file **win01_1C_Answer_Sheet**. If necessary, at the top click Enable Editing; be sure the window is maximized.

In the upper left corner, click **File**, click **Save As**, click **Browse**, and then navigate to your **Windows 10 Chapter 1** folder. Using your own name, save the document as **Lastname_Firstname_1C_Answer_Sheet**

With the Word document displayed, on the taskbar, click the **Word** button to minimize the window and leave your Word document accessible from the taskbar. **Close** the **File Explorer** window. As you complete each step in this project, write the letter of your answer on a piece of paper; you will fill in your Answer Sheet after you complete all the steps in this project.

Click **Start**, and then with the insertion point blinking in the search box, type **lock screen** Which of the following is true?

A. Search terms that include the text *lock screen* display in the search results.

B. The System settings window opens on the desktop.

C. From this screen, you can remove or change your lock screen picture from your computer.

2 At the top of the search results, click **Lock screen settings**. What is your result?

A. Your lock screen picture fills the screen.

B. The Settings window displays with *Background* selected on the left.

C. The Settings window displays with *Lock screen* selected on the left.

3 **Close** the **Settings** window. Click **Start**, scroll to the **G** section of installed apps, click **Get Started**, on the left, click **Browse**, and then click **Windows Hello**. According to this information, which of the following is true?

A. You cannot activate Windows Hello by using a fingerprint.

B. Windows Hello enables you to sign in to your computer without typing a password.

C. To set up Windows Hello, you must open a Windows Store app.

4 **Close** the **Get Started** window. On the taskbar, click **File Explorer**. What is your result?

A. The window for your USB flash drive displays.

B. The File Explorer window displays.

C. The Documents window displays.

(Project 1C Exploring Windows 10 continues on the next page)

5 On **This PC**, locate and open **Documents**. What is your result?

A. The first document in the folder opens in its application.

B. The contents of the Documents folder display in the file list.

C. The contents of the Documents folder display in the address bar.

6 In the **navigation pane**, click **This PC**. What is your result?

A. The storage devices attached to your computer display in the file list.

B. All of the files on the hard drive display in the file list.

C. Your computer restarts.

7 **Close** the **This PC** window. Click **Start**, and then in the search box, type **paint** Open the **Paint desktop app**, and then pin the program to the taskbar. **Close** the **Paint** window. Which of the following is true?

A. On the taskbar, the Paint program icon on the taskbar displays with a line under it.

B. The Paint program tile displays on the right side of the Start menu.

C. The Paint program icon displays on the taskbar with no line under it.

8 On the taskbar, point to the **Paint** button, right-click, and then click **Unpin from taskbar**. Click **Start**, type **store** and then with the **Store app** at the top of the search results, press [Enter]. What is your result?

A. All the storage devices attached to your computer display on the Start menu.

B. The Store app displays.

C. A list of games that you can download displays.

9 **Close** the **Store** app. Click **Start**, type **maps** and then with the **Maps Trusted Windows Store** app selected, press [Enter]; if necessary, follow any prompts until a map displays. Click **Start**, type **weather** and then with **Weather Trusted Windows Store app** selected, press [Enter]. On the taskbar, click **Task View**. What is your result?

A. The Start menu displays.

B. The Weather app opens and fills the screen.

C. All the open apps display as smaller images.

10 Point to the **Weather** app, and then click its **Close** button. In the same manner, close the **Maps** app. What is your result?

A. Your Word document displays as a small image on the desktop.

B. The search results for *Weather* redisplay.

C. The Start menu displays.

To complete this project: On the taskbar, click the Word icon to redisplay your Word document. Type your answers into the correct boxes. Save and close your Word document, and submit as directed by your instructor. **Close** all open windows.

END | You have completed Project 1C

Apply 1B skills from these Objectives:

7 Download and Extract Files and Folders

8 Use File Explorer to Display Locations, Folders, and Files

9 Start Programs and Open Data Files

10 Create, Rename, and Copy Files and Folders

11 Use OneDrive as Cloud Storage

Skills Review | Project 1D Working with Windows, Programs, and Files

 PROJECT FILES

For Project 1D, you will need the following files:

Your USB flash drive—or other location—containing the student data files

win01_1D_Answer_Sheet (Word document)

You will save your file as:

Lastname_Firstname_1D_Answer_Sheet

1▶ Close all open windows. On the taskbar, click **File Explorer**, navigate to the location where you are storing your student data files for this chapter, and then open the file **win01_1D_Answer_Sheet**. If necessary, at the top click Enable Editing; be sure the window is maximized.

In the upper left corner, click **File**, click **Save As**, click **Browse**, and then navigate to your **Windows 10 Chapter 1** folder. Using your own name, save the document as **Lastname_Firstname_1D_Answer_Sheet**

With the Word document displayed, on the taskbar, click the **Word** button to minimize the window and leave your Word document accessible from the taskbar. **Close** the **File Explorer** window. As you complete each step in this project, write the letter of your answer on a piece of paper; you will fill in your Answer Sheet after you complete all the steps in this project.

Open **File Explorer**, navigate to your student data files, and then open your **win01_1D_Bell_Orchid** folder. If necessary, on the **View tab**, set the **Layout** to **Details**.

In the **file list**, how many *folders* display?

A. Four

B. Five

C. Six

2▶ Navigate to **Corporate ＞ Food_Beverage**. If necessary, change the view to **Details**. How many *folders* are in the **Food_Beverage** folder?

A. Three

B. Two

C. One

3▶ Open the **Restaurants** folder, and then click one time to select the file **Breakfast_Continental**. On the ribbon, click the **Home tab**. In which group of commands can you change the name of this file?

A. New

B. Select

C. Organize

(Project 1D Working with Windows, Programs, and Files continues on the next page)

4 With the **Breakfast_Continental** file still selected, point to the file name and right-click. Which of the following is *not* true?

A. From this menu, you can rename the file.

B. From this menu, you can print the file.

C. From this menu, you can move the folder to another folder within Corporate.

5 Click on the desktop to close the shortcut menu, and then click the **Up** button to move up one level in the hierarchy and display the file list for the **Food_Beverage** folder. On the ribbon, click the **View tab**. In the **Layout group**, click **Large icons**. What is your result?

A. The window fills the entire screen.

B. Files that are pictures are visible as pictures.

C. Only picture files display in the file list.

6 On the **View tab**, return the **Layout** to **Details**. In the **file list**, click one time to select the file **CO_FB_Menu_Presentation**. In the **Panes group**, click the **Details pane** button. (*Hint*: You can point to a button to see its ScreenTip.) By looking at the displayed details about this file on the right, which of the following is an information item you can determine about this file?

A. The number of words on each slide

B. The number of slides in the presentation

C. The slide layout used in the title slide

7 In the **Panes group**, click **Preview pane**. In the **Preview pane**, drag the scroll box to the bottom of the scroll bar. Which of the following is *not* true?

A. The slide title displays as you drag the scroll box.

B. The PowerPoint program opens as you drag the scroll box.

C. The slide number displays as you drag the scroll box.

8 On the **View tab**, in the **Current view group**, click the **Sort by arrow**, and then click **Type**. In the Type column, if necessary, click the arrow so that the column is sorted in ascending order. Which of the following is true?

A. The Restaurants folder displays at the bottom of the list.

B. The files are in alphabetic order by name.

C. The files are in alphabetic order by Type.

9 In the **Corporate > Food_Beverage** folder, create a new folder named **Dining_Rooms** Select the three JPG files, and then move them into the new folder. Which of the following is true?

A. The status bar indicates that there are five items in the current folder.

B. The three JPG files display in the file list for Food_Beverage.

C. The Dining_Rooms folder is selected.

(Project 1D Working with Windows, Programs, and Files continues on the next page)

10 Open the **Restaurants** folder, and then in the upper right portion of the window, in the **search** box, type **sales** How many files display with the word *Sales* in the document name?

  A. Three

  B. Four

  C. Five

To complete this project: Close the File Explorer window. On the taskbar, click the Word icon to redisplay your Word document. Type your answers into the correct boxes. Save and close your Word document, and submit as directed by your instructor. **Close** any open windows.

> **END | You have completed Project 1D**

Mastering Windows 10 — Project 1E Create a File and Use Windows Apps

Apply 1A skills from these Objectives:

1 Explore the Windows 10 Environment
2 Use File Explorer and Desktop Apps to Create a New Folder and Save a File
3 Identify the Functions of the Windows 10 Operating System
4 Discover Windows 10 Features
5 Sign Out of Windows 10, Turn Off Your Computer, and Manage User Accounts
6 Manage Your Windows 10 System

PROJECT ACTIVITIES

In the following Mastering Windows 10 project, you will capture two screens and save them in a PowerPoint presentation that will look similar to Figure 1.74.

 PROJECT FILES

For Project 1E, you will need the following file:

A new PowerPoint presentation

You will save your PowerPoint file as:

Lastname_Firstname_1E_Cortana_and_Snap

PROJECT RESULTS

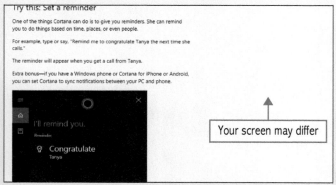

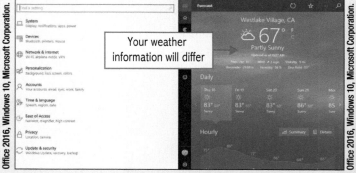

FIGURE 1.74

(Project 1E Create a File and Use Windows Apps continues on the next page)

Mastering Windows 10 | **Project 1E Create a File and Use Windows Apps** (continued)

1 Click **Start**, click any letter above the alphabetized list of apps to display an onscreen alphabet, click **G** to jump to the G section, and then click **Get Started**.

2 On the left, click **Browse**, click **Cortana**, and then click **What is Cortana?** Scroll down to view the information about setting a reminder.

3 Open PowerPoint, if necessary maximize the PowerPoint window, and then click **Blank Presentation**. In the **Slides group**, click **Layout**, and then click **Blank**.

4 On the **Insert tab**, in the **Images group**, click **Screenshot**, and then click **Screen Clipping**. Position the + pointer in the upper left corner of the white portion of the screen, hold down the left mouse button, and then drag to the lower right corner of the screen; do not include the taskbar. Release the mouse button to insert the screen clipping into the first slide.

5 Click anywhere in the white area of the slide to deselect the image. Click the **File tab**, on the left click **Save As**, click **Browse**, and then in the **Save As** dialog box, navigate to and open your **Windows 10 Chapter 1 folder**. Using your own name, save the file as **Lastname_Firstname_1E_Cortana_and_Snap**

6 **Minimize** the PowerPoint presentation. **Close** the **Get Started** window.

7 Click **Start**, click any letter to display an onscreen alphabet, click **S** to jump to the S section, and then click **Settings**. Display the **apps** list again, jump to the **W** section, and then click **Weather**.

8 Press ⊞ + → to snap the Weather app to the right side of the screen. Click the **Settings** window to snap it to the left side of the screen.

9 From the taskbar, redisplay your PowerPoint presentation. On the **Home tab**, click the upper portion of the **New Slide** button. On the **Insert tab**, in the **Images group**, click **Screenshot**, and then click **Screen Clipping**. Using the technique you have practiced, drag the + pointer from the upper left to the lower right, but do not include the taskbar, and then release the left mouse button to insert the screen clipping into the second slide.

10 Click in a white area of the slide to deselect the image, press Ctrl + Home, close the PowerPoint window, and then click **Save**.

11 Close all open windows, and then submit your PowerPoint file to your instructor as directed.

END | You have completed Project 1E

Mastering Windows 10 | **Project 1F Working with Windows, Programs, and Files**

PROJECT ACTIVITIES

In the following Mastering Windows 10 project, you will capture two screens and save them in a PowerPoint presentation that will look similar to Figure 1.75.

 PROJECT FILES

For Project 1F, you will need the following file:

A new PowerPoint presentation

You will save your PowerPoint file as:

Lastname_Firstname_1F_San_Diego_and_Filter

PROJECT RESULTS

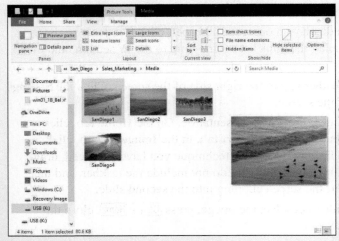
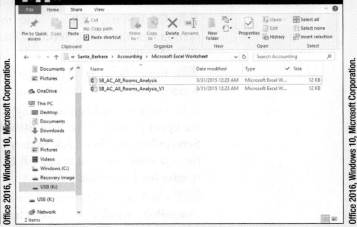

FIGURE 1.75

(Project 1F Working with Windows, Programs, and Files continues on the next page)

Mastering Windows 10 | **Project 1F Working with Windows, Programs, and Files** (continued)

1 Close all open windows, and then on the taskbar, click **File Explorer**. Display the window for your **USB flash drive**—or the location of your student data files—and then navigate to **win01_1F_Bell_Orchid > San_Diego > Sales_Marketing > Media**.

2 From the **View tab**, change the **Layout** to **Large icons**, and then in the **file list**, click one time to select the file **SanDiego1**.

3 Display the **Preview pane** for this file.

4 Open PowerPoint, if necessary maximize the PowerPoint window, and then click **Blank Presentation**. In the **Slides group**, click **Layout**, and then click **Blank**.

5 On the **Insert tab**, in the **Images group**, click **Screenshot**, and then under **Available Windows**, click the image of your File Explorer window.

6 Click anywhere in the white area of the slide to deselect the image. Click the **File tab**, on the left click **Save As**, click **Browse**, and then in the **Save As** dialog box, navigate to and open your **Windows 10 Chapter 1** folder. Using your own name, save the file as **Lastname_Firstname_1F_San_Diego_and_Filter**

7 **Minimize** the PowerPoint window. Turn off the display of the **Preview pane**. **Close** the window.

8 Open **File Explorer**, and then from your student data files, navigate to **win01_1F_Bell_Orchid > Santa_Barbara > Accounting**.

9 From the **Type** column heading, filter the list to display only **Microsoft Excel Worksheet**.

10 From the taskbar, redisplay your PowerPoint presentation. On the **Home tab**, click the upper portion of the **New Slide** button. On the **Insert tab**, in the **Images group**, click **Screenshot**, and then under **Available Windows**, click the image of your File Explorer window.

11 Click in a white area of the slide to deselect the image, press [Ctrl] + [Home], close the PowerPoint window, and then click **Save**.

12 **Close** the **File Explorer** window. Submit your PowerPoint file as directed by your instructor.

END | You have completed Project 1F

OUTCOMES-BASED ASSESSMENTS

RUBRIC

The following outcomes-based assessments are *open-ended assessments*. That is, there is no specific correct result; your result will depend on your approach to the information provided. Make *Professional Quality* your goal. Use the following scoring rubric to guide you in *how* to approach the problem, and then to evaluate *how well* your approach solves the problem.

The *criteria*—Software Mastery, Content, Format and Layout, and Process—represent the knowledge and skills you have gained that you can apply to solving the problem. The *levels of performance*—Professional Quality, Approaching Professional Quality, or Needs Quality Improvements—help you and your instructor evaluate your result.

	Your completed project is of Professional Quality if you:	Your completed project is Approaching Professional Quality if you:	Your completed project Needs Quality Improvements if you:
1-Software Mastery	Choose and apply the most appropriate skills, tools, and features and identify efficient methods to solve the problem.	Choose and apply some appropriate skills, tools, and features, but not in the most efficient manner.	Choose inappropriate skills, tools, or features, or are inefficient in solving the problem.
2-Content	Construct a solution that is clear and well organized, contains content that is accurate, appropriate to the audience and purpose, and is complete. Provide a solution that contains no errors of spelling, grammar, or style.	Construct a solution in which some components are unclear, poorly organized, inconsistent, or incomplete. Misjudge the needs of the audience. Have some errors in spelling, grammar, or style, but the errors do not detract from comprehension.	Construct a solution that is unclear, incomplete, or poorly organized, contains some inaccurate or inappropriate content, and contains many errors of spelling, grammar, or style. Do not solve the problem.
3-Format and Layout	Format and arrange all elements to communicate information and ideas, clarify function, illustrate relationships, and indicate relative importance.	Apply appropriate format and layout features to some elements, but not others. Overuse features, causing minor distraction.	Apply format and layout that does not communicate information or ideas clearly. Do not use format and layout features to clarify function, illustrate relationships, or indicate relative importance. Use available features excessively, causing distraction.
4-Process	Use an organized approach that integrates planning, development, self-assessment, revision, and reflection.	Demonstrate an organized approach in some areas, but not others; or, use an insufficient process of organization throughout.	Do not use an organized approach to solve the problem.

GO! Think   Project 1G Help Desk

In this Project, you will construct a solution by applying any combination of the skills you practiced from the Objectives in Projects 1A and 1B.

 PROJECT FILES

For Project 1G, you will need the following file:

win01_1G_Help_Desk (Word file)

You will save your document as:

Lastname_Firstname_1G_Help_Desk

From the student files that accompany this chapter, open the Word document **win01_1G_Help_Desk**. Save the document in your chapter folder as **Lastname_Firstname_1G_Help_Desk**

The following email question arrived at the Help Desk from an employee at the Bell Orchid Hotel's corporate office. In the Word document, construct a response based on your knowledge of Windows 10. Although an email response is not as formal as a letter, you should still use good grammar, good sentence structure, professional language, and a polite tone. Save your document and submit the response as directed by your instructor.

To: Help Desk

We have a new employee in our department, and as her user picture, she wants to use a picture of her dog. I know that Corporate Policy says it is OK to use an acceptable personal picture on a user account. Can she change the picture herself within her standard user account, or does she need an administrator account to do that?

END | You have completed Project 1G

GO! Think   Project 1H Help Desk

In this Project, you will construct a solution by applying any combination of the skills you practiced from the Objectives in Projects 1A and 1B.

 PROJECT FILES

For Project 1H, you will need the following file:

win01_1H_Help_Desk (Word file)

You will save your document as:

Lastname_Firstname_1H_Help_Desk

From the student files that accompany this chapter, open the Word document **win01_1H_Help_Desk**. Save the document in your chapter folder as **Lastname_Firstname_1H_Help_Desk**

The following email question arrived at the Help Desk from an employee at the Bell Orchid Hotel's corporate office. In the Word document, construct a response based on your knowledge of Windows 10. Although an email response is not as formal as a letter, you should still use good grammar, good sentence structure, professional language, and a polite tone. Save your document and submit the response as directed by your instructor.

To: Help Desk

When I'm done using my computer at the end of the day, should I use the Sleep option or the Shut down option, and what's the difference between the two?

END | You have completed Project 1H

GO Think! Project 1I Help Desk

In this Project, you will construct a solution by applying any combination of the skills you practiced from the Objectives in Projects 1A and 1B.

 PROJECT FILES

For Project 1I, you will need the following file:

win01_1I_Help_Desk (Word file)

You will save your document as:

Lastname_Firstname_1I_Help_Desk

From the student files that accompany this chapter, open the Word document **win01_1I_Help_Desk**. Save the document in your chapter folder as **Lastname_Firstname_1I_Help_Desk**

The following email question has arrived at the Help Desk from an employee at the Bell Orchid Hotel's corporate office. In the Word document, construct a response based on your knowledge of Windows 10. Although an email response is not as formal as a letter, you should still use good grammar, good sentence structure, professional language, and a polite tone. Save your document and submit the response as directed by your instructor.

To: Help Desk

I am not sure about the differences between copying and moving files and folders. When is it best to copy a file or a folder and when is it best to move a file or folder? Can you also describe some techniques that I can use for copying or moving files and folders? Which do you think is the easiest way to copy or move files and folders?

END | You have completed Project 1I

Use Backup and Recovery Tools and Discover Windows Apps

Dragonstock/Fotolia

In This Chapter

Always protect against any loss of data by making a backup copy of all of your data. Additionally, there is always a chance that your computer could be damaged physically resulting in a catastrophic hardware failure. In this chapter, you will learn how to use the backup and recovery tools built into Windows 10 to ensure that you never suffer a loss of your data and that you can restore your computer in the event of a hard drive failure.

Windows 10 comes with many pre-installed apps, which you will find to be helpful and easy to use—after you know about them! With so many small but useful apps within Windows, and also available from the Windows store, it can be hard to find those that work the best and will be of the most benefit to you. In this

chapter, you will discover many of the apps that you will want to use for entertainment, information gathering, and productivity.

The projects in this chapter relate to the **Bell Orchid Hotels**, headquartered in Boston, and which own and operate resorts and business-oriented hotels. Resort properties are located in popular destinations, including Honolulu, Orlando, San Diego, and Santa Barbara. The resorts offer deluxe accommodations and a wide array of dining options. Other Bell Orchid hotels are located in major business centers and offer the latest technology in their meeting facilities. The company plans to open new properties and update existing properties over the next ten years.

PROJECT 2A Using Backup and Recovery Tools

PROJECT ACTIVITIES

In Activities 2.01 through 2.07, you will train with Steven Ramos and Barbara Hewitt, employees in the Information Technology Department at the Bell Orchid Hotels, so that you will be able to back up and restore your computer system, safeguard your files, and restore previous versions of your files. As you progress through this Project, you will insert screenshots of windows that you create into a PowerPoint presentation similar to Figure 2.1.

PROJECT FILES

For Project 2A, you will need the following file:

A new blank PowerPoint presentation

You will save your PowerPoint presentation as:

Lastname_Firstname_2A_Backup_Recovery

PROJECT RESULTS

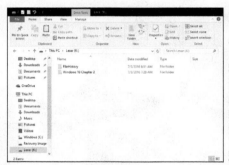

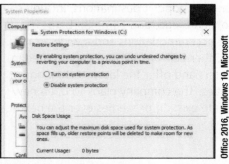

FIGURE 2.1 Project 2A Using Backup and Recovery Tools

Objective 1 Use File History

Backing up is the process of creating a copy of your files somewhere other than on your computer. For example, you can create copies of your files on cloud storage such as your Microsoft OneDrive, Google Drive, iCloud, or Dropbox. Or you can create backups on an *external hard drive*, also known as a *portable hard drive*, which is a disk drive that plugs into an external port on your computer, typically into a USB port. Or you can use an *online backup service*—also referred to as a *remote backup service* or a *managed backup service*—which is a service that provides a system for backing up your computer files over the Internet on a scheduled basis and then storing the data securely on their computers. Three popular companies that provide this type of service are Carbonite, IDrive, and Mozy.

Back up your files so that you can restore them in the event of a virus attack on your computer, a hard disk drive failure, theft of your laptop computer, or a disaster such as a fire or flood. In the event of a fire, flood, or some other disaster in which you also lose your physical backups, you will be glad that you backed up your files to cloud storage or invested in an online backup service.

If you work in an organization, there is likely an automatic backup system in place, although it is always a good idea to confirm this with someone in your organization's Information Technology department. On your own computer, you will want to back up regularly to preserve your documents, photos, music, and all of the important information you have.

Activity 2.01 | Using File History

File History is a Windows 10 tool that enables you to back up your files to another drive and restore those files if the originals are lost, damaged, or deleted. First, you must select where your backups will be saved. You can select an externally connected drive—an external hard drive—or you can save to a drive on a network. On your own computer, a good choice is an external hard drive connected to a USB port on your computer.

You can purchase an external hard drive from most retail stores that sell computers or from online retailers such as Amazon and Newegg. You should select an external drive with at least 1 terabyte (1 TB) of storage, and you can find these at prices under $60. Seagate and Western Digital are brand names to consider, but there are many others.

File History will back up copies of files that you have stored in your Documents, Music, Pictures, Videos, and Desktop folders. It will also back up OneDrive files available offline on your PC. After you have set up File History properly and connected an external drive to your computer, you can be assured that Windows 10 is automatically backing up your files.

1 ▶ Insert a USB flash drive into your computer.

> For purposes of this Activity, you need only a small USB flash drive. On your own computer, you will want to connect a larger external storage device with at least 1 terabyte of storage space.

2 ▶ From the taskbar, or by searching, open **PowerPoint**, and then click **Blank Presentation**. On the **Home tab**, in the **Slides group**, click **Layout**, and then as shown in Figure 2.2, click **Blank**.

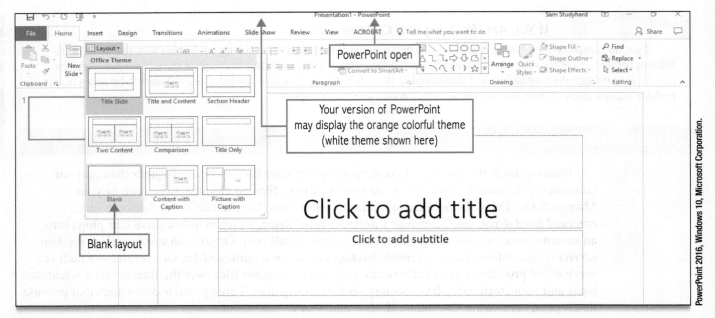

FIGURE 2.2

3 ▸ Click the **File tab**, on the left click **Save As**, click **Browse**, and then in the **Save As** dialog box, navigate to the storage location where you will store your files for this chapter. Click **New folder**, as the folder name type **Windows 10 Chapter 2** and then press Enter. Click **Open** to open the new folder in the **Save As** dialog box.

4 ▸ In the **File name** box, using your own name, type **Lastname_Firstname_2A_Backup_Recovery**

5 ▸ In the **Save As** dialog box, click **Save**. In the upper right corner, click **Minimize** ⎯ to display the desktop and leave the presentation open.

6 ▸ On the right end of the taskbar, click **Action Center** ⬛, click **All settings**, and then click **Update & security**. Compare your screen with Figure 2.3.

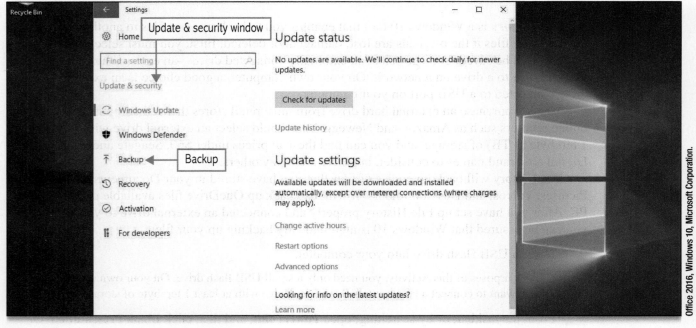

FIGURE 2.3

7 On the left, click **Backup**, and then on the right, click **Add a drive**. Compare your screen with Figure 2.4.

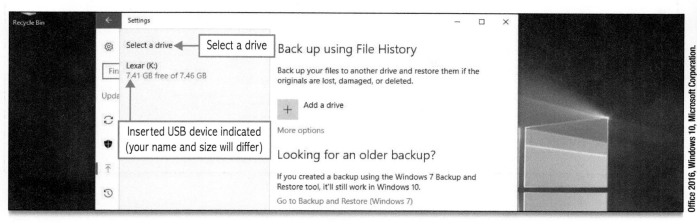

FIGURE 2.4

8 On the left, click the drive letter of the USB flash drive that you inserted. **Close** ✕ the **Settings** window.

9 Click **Start** ⊞, and then click **Settings** ⚙; notice that this is another method to open the **Settings** window.

10 Click **Update & security**, and then on the left click **Backup**. Notice that the button for *Automatically back up my files* is set to **On**. Compare your screen with Figure 2.5.

After you have selected a drive on which to back up files, File History is automatically on.

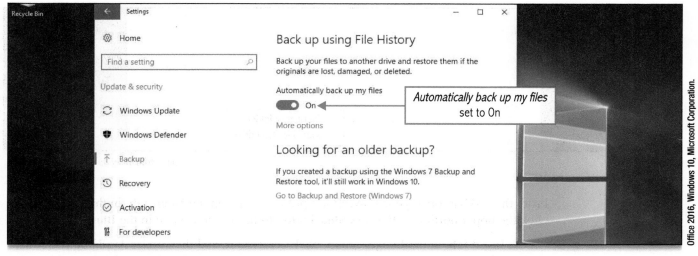

FIGURE 2.5

11 From the taskbar, open your PowerPoint presentation. On the **Insert tab**, in the **Images group**, click **Screenshot**, and then click **Screen Clipping**. Position the + pointer in the upper left corner of the **Settings** window, hold down the left mouse button, drag down and to the lower right corner of the window, and then release the mouse button to insert the clipping into your PowerPoint presentation. Click outside of the image to deselect it. If necessary, close the Design Ideas pane on the right. Compare your screen with Figure 2.6.

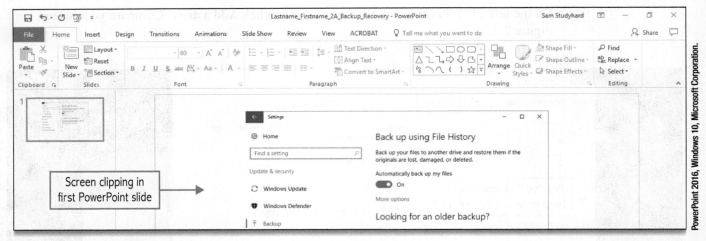

Screen clipping in first PowerPoint slide

FIGURE 2.6

PowerPoint 2016, Windows 10, Microsoft Corporation.

12 In the upper left corner, click **Save** 🖫, and then in the upper right corner, click **Minimize** ⊟.

13 **Close** ⊠ the **Settings** window.

14 On your taskbar, check to see if the **File Explorer icon** 📁 displays. If it does not, in the taskbar search box, type **file explorer** and then under **Best Match**, point to *File Explorer Desktop app*, right-click, and then click **Pin to taskbar**. From the taskbar, open **File Explorer** 📁, and then navigate to and open your USB flash drive. Compare your screen with Figure 2.7.

Because this is the drive you selected to store your File History, Windows 10 creates the FileHistory folder to begin storing your files. From this folder, you can recover lost files if you experience a hard drive failure. You can see that it is worth your money and time to purchase an external hard drive and set up File History. If your hard drive fails, all your files are available on the external drive.

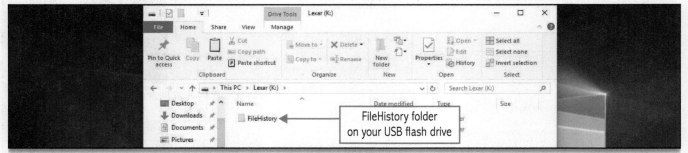

FileHistory folder on your USB flash drive

FIGURE 2.7

Office 2016, Windows 10, Microsoft Corporation.

15 From the taskbar, open your PowerPoint presentation. On the **Home tab**, in the **Slides group**, click the upper portion of the **New Slide** button to insert a new slide in the **Blank** layout.

16 On the **Insert tab**, in the **Images group**, click **Screenshot**, and then under **Available Windows**, click the image of your **File Explorer** window to insert it into the slide. Click in a white area to deselect the image; in your image, the ribbon may display in black. In the upper left corner, click **Save** 🖫, and then in the upper right corner, click **Minimize** ⊟.

Windows 10 Is an Evolving Operating System

Like all modern operating systems, Windows 10 is constantly evolving with new features, updates, and security enhancements. Therefore, you may encounter occasional differences in techniques and screens as you progress through the Projects. You can often look at the screens in Windows 10 to determine how to complete steps, or you can search for information about new features.

Activity 2.02 | Restoring Previous Versions from File History

Another convenient task you can perform with File History is to recover a previous (older) version of a file.

1 If necessary, from the taskbar, open **File Explorer** ▣, open your **Documents** folder, point to any file in any folder, and then right-click.

2 On the shortcut menu, click **Restore previous versions**. Compare your screen with Figure 2.8.

The Properties dialog box for the file you selected displays with the Previous Versions tab active. Because you may have not started saving your File History yet, no files display. However, after your File History is saved for a few days, you will be able to recover previous versions of files from this dialog box.

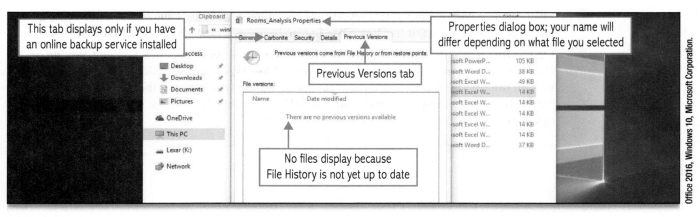

FIGURE 2.8

3 **Close** ☒ the dialog box and **Close** ☒ the File Explorer window.

Activity 2.03 | Adding or Excluding Folders to Back Up

You can view which folders are being backed up with File History, and then add to or exclude folders from the list.

1 Using either of the methods you have practiced, display the **Settings** window, click **Update & security**, and then on the left, click **Backup**.

2 On the right, click **More options**, and then scroll down about half way in the window. Compare your screen with Figure 2.9.

Here you can see exactly which folders are being backed up, and you can add folders to or exclude folders from your backup.

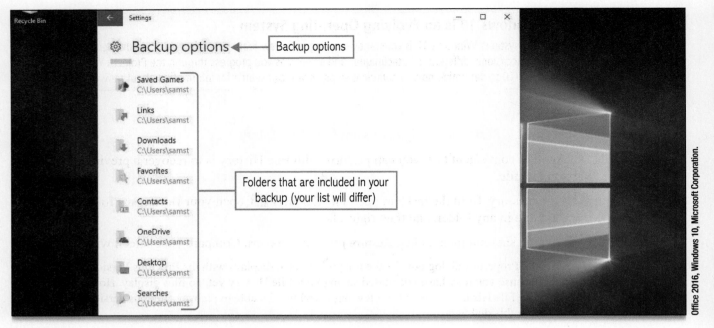

FIGURE 2.9

3 From the taskbar, display your PowerPoint presentation. On the **Home tab**, in the **Slides group**, click the upper portion of the **New Slide** button to insert a new slide in the **Blank** layout.

4 On the **Insert tab**, in the **Images group**, click **Screenshot**, and then click **Screen Clipping**. Position the **+** pointer in the upper left corner of **Settings** window, hold down the left mouse button, drag down and to the lower right corner of the window, and then release the mouse button to insert the clipping into your PowerPoint presentation. Click outside of the image to deselect it. Compare your screen with Figure 2.10.

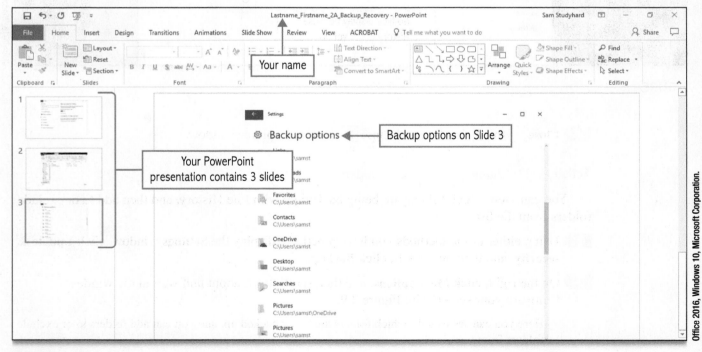

FIGURE 2.10

5 In the upper left corner, click **Save** 🖫, and then in the upper right corner, click **Minimize** −.

6 **Close** ✕ the **Settings** window.

Keep in mind that hard drives fail. It's not really a matter of if, it's a matter of when. Many PC users replace their PCs frequently enough that they never experience a hard drive failure—typically referred to as a *crash*. But even the hard drive on a brand new PC can fail.

In a hard drive failure, you not only lose your files—all those documents, songs, pictures, and videos that you have been accumulating during the life of your PC—but you also lose your operating system, and that includes all of your installed programs and the updates and patches to those programs that have occurred over time. If you have set File History to back up your files to an external hard drive, they are easily recovered. But getting your PC's operating system and all your programs and their updates back can take a long time.

The ***System Image*** backup is an exact copy—sometimes referred to as an image—of your hard drive, and you can use this image to completely restore your computer in the event of a hard drive failure. The backup created using this tool includes the complete operating system, settings, desktop programs, apps from the Windows store, and all of your files.

You may not need to make a system image if you are using other tools discussed in this chapter. However, it's good to know where it is if you decide you would like to make this type of backup.

ALERT! | **You Will Need Admin Access to Complete Some of the Remaining Activities in This Project**

If you do not have admin access, read through the steps.

Activity 2.04 | Creating a System Image

It is good practice to make a new system image every few months. Doing so will create an image that includes any updates you have made to programs or settings, as well as creating a new backup of your files separate from File History.

1 Point to the **Start** button ⊞ and right-click. On the displayed menu, click **Control Panel**. If necessary, in the upper right, click the View by arrow, and then click Category. Compare your screen with Figure 2.11.

The Control Panel, which is gradually being replaced by the Settings window, still exists in Windows 10, and some tools are easily available here.

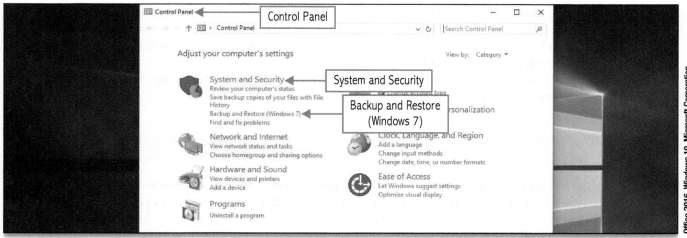

FIGURE 2.11

2 In the **Control Panel**, under **System and Security**, click **Backup and Restore (Windows 7)**.

3 On the left, click **Create a system image**, if necessary, type the password for your admin account. Then in the **Create a system image** dialog box, click the first **arrow**, as shown in Figure 2.12.

Although Windows may suggest creating the image on a portion of your hard drive, the best idea is to connect an external hard drive and store the image there. In the event of hard drive failure, you will have your image on another separate drive.

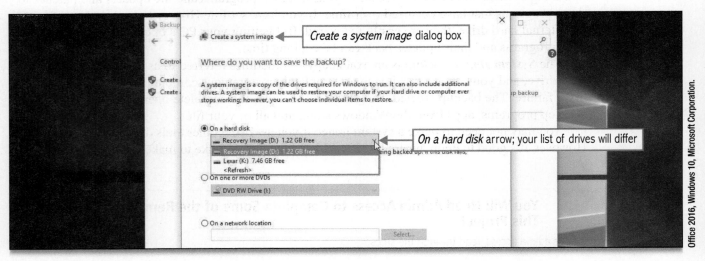

FIGURE 2.12

4 From the taskbar, display your PowerPoint presentation. On the **Home tab**, in the **Slides group**, click the upper portion of the **New Slide** button to insert a new slide in the **Blank** layout.

5 On the **Insert tab**, in the **Images group**, click **Screenshot**, and then click **Screen Clipping**. Position the + pointer in the upper left corner of the **Control Panel** window, hold down the left mouse button, drag down and to the lower right corner of the window—capturing both the window and the dialog box as you drag—and then release the mouse button to insert the clipping into your PowerPoint presentation. Click outside of the image to deselect it.

6 In the upper left corner, click **Save** 🔲, and then in the upper right corner, click **Minimize** ⊟.

7 **Close** ☒ the dialog box and the open window.

If you experience a hard drive failure, you can restore your entire system from your System Image. Because the backup of your files from a system image is not as up to date as your File History, which is on all the time, you will probably want to restore your files from File History after restoring your system image.

This process will reformat your hard drive and will delete all of your data and files. Your restored image will overwrite the entire drive.

Objective 3 | Use System Restore and Create a Recovery Drive

System Restore enables you to take your computer back to a previous point in time—when it was working exactly the way you wanted it to. When enabled, Windows creates a *restore point*—a snapshot of your computer's settings—which it takes at regular intervals and also when you install a new program or device driver or when Windows itself updates. This is a useful tool if a change made to your computer suddenly results in unstable behavior.

For example, in rare instances the installation of a program or a *driver* can cause an unexpected change to your computer or cause Windows 10 to behave in an unpredictable manner. A driver is software that enables hardware or devices such as a printer, mouse, or keyboard to work with your computer. Every device needs a driver for it to work. Usually you can uninstall the program or driver to correct the problem, but if uninstalling fails to solve the problem, you can restore your computer's system to an earlier date when everything worked correctly.

System Restore differs from a backup in that reverting to a restore point will not affect any of your files or settings.

By default, System Restore is not enabled, but you can easily enable it, and you can also create a restore point manually; for example, right before you install a large program or make a major change to your computer.

Activity 2.05 | Using System Restore

1 On the taskbar, click in the search box, type **create a restore point** and then at the top of the search results, click **Create a restore point Control panel** as shown in Figure 2.13. If necessary, type your admin password.

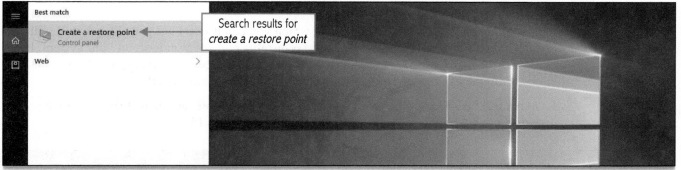

FIGURE 2.13

Office 2016, Windows 10, Microsoft Corporation.

2 In the **System Properties** dialog box, on the **System Protection tab**, under **Protection Settings**, notice that **Protection** is set to **Off** for the available hard drives. Compare your screen with Figure 2.14.

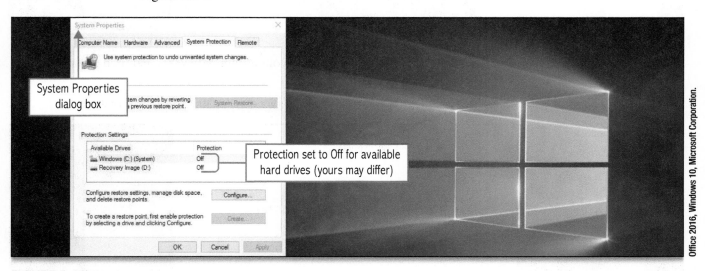

FIGURE 2.14

Office 2016, Windows 10, Microsoft Corporation.

3 Click **Configure**.

On your own computer, you can select Turn on system protection. In a college lab, you might not be able to change or view this setting.

4 From the taskbar, display your PowerPoint presentation. On the **Home tab**, in the **Slides group**, click the upper portion of the **New Slide** button to insert a new slide in the **Blank** layout.

5 On the **Insert tab**, in the **Images group**, click **Screenshot**, and then click **Screen Clipping**. Position the + pointer in the upper left corner of the two dialog boxes, hold down the left mouse button, drag down and to the lower right corner capturing both dialog boxes as you drag—and then release the mouse button to insert the clipping into your PowerPoint presentation. Click outside of the image to deselect it.

6 In the upper left corner, click **Save** 🖫, and then in the upper right corner, click **Minimize** ⊟.

7 **Close** ✕ the two open dialog boxes.

More Knowledge | **Performing a System Restore**

To perform a system restore, assuming that the protection has been turned on, redisplay the System Properties dialog box with the System Protection tab active. Click System Restore, and then select a restore point.

Activity 2.06 | Creating a USB Recovery Drive

You should create a USB recovery drive, which you can use to boot your PC when it will not start. You can also set the recovery drive to reinstall a copy of Windows on your system. If you must use the recovery drive to restart your system, the process will delete all of your files, programs, settings, and drivers and install a clean version of Windows 10.

1 On the taskbar, click in the search box, type **recovery drive** and then at the top of the search results, click **Create a recovery drive** as shown in Figure 2.15.

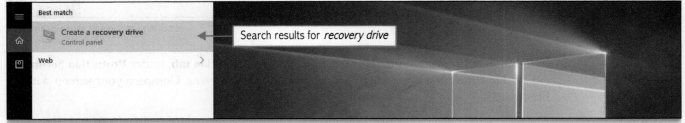

Office 2016, Windows 10, Microsoft Corporation.

FIGURE 2.15

2 If a User Account Control box displays, type your admin password, and then compare your screen with Figure 2.16.

On your own computer, you can follow the steps for creating this USB recovery drive.

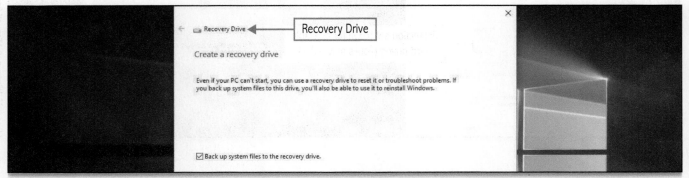

Office 2016, Windows 10, Microsoft Corporation.

FIGURE 2.16

3 **Close** ✕ the dialog box.

PC Reset is a set of tools that you can use to bring your PC back to its original factory settings. You have the option to either remove your files or remove files and clean the drive. PC Reset is useful if you are planning to sell or give your computer to someone else. You can delete all of your information and present the new owner with a computer that behaves and looks like it did the day you bought it.

Activity 2.07 | Using PC Reset

1 Using any of the techniques you have practiced, display the **Settings** window, and then click **Update & security**.

2 On the left click **Recovery**, and then compare your screen with Figure 2.17; you must be signed in as an administrator to display the Reset this PC command.

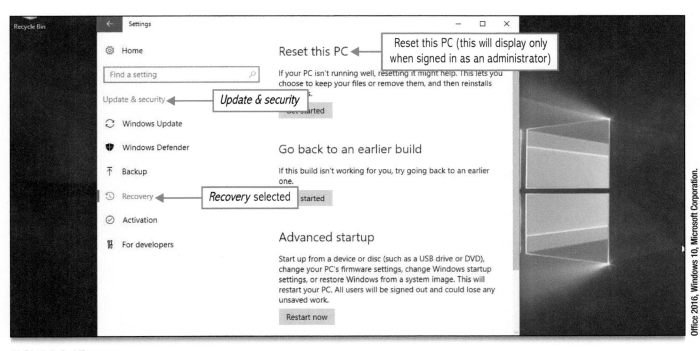

FIGURE 2.17

3 Under **Reset this PC**, click **Get started**, and then compare your screen with Figure 2.18.

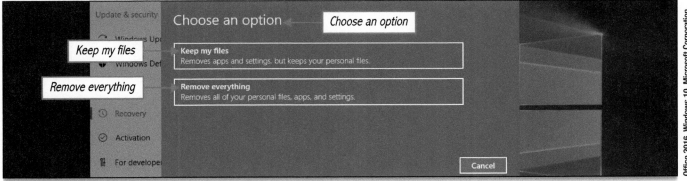

FIGURE 2.18

4 In the lower right corner, click **Cancel**.

Be sure to use this option if you plan to sell or donate your PC to someone else.

5 **Close** ☒ the **Settings** window.

6 From the taskbar, redisplay your PowerPoint presentation. In the upper left corner, click **Save** 🖫, and then in the upper right corner, click **Close** ☒. Submit your completed PowerPoint presentation as directed by your instructor.

END | You have completed Project 2A

Discover Windows Apps

PROJECT ACTIVITIES

In Activities 2.08 through 2.20, you will participate in training along with Barbara Hewitt and Steven Ramos, both of whom work for the Information Technology Department at the headquarters office of the Bell Orchid Hotels, to discover the Windows apps that can be most useful to employees and individuals. As you progress through this Project, you will insert screenshots of windows that you create into a PowerPoint presentation similar to Figure 2.19.

PROJECT FILES

For Project 2B, you will need the following file:

A new blank PowerPoint presentation

You will save your PowerPoint presentation as:

Lastname_Firstname_2B_Windows_Apps

PROJECT RESULTS

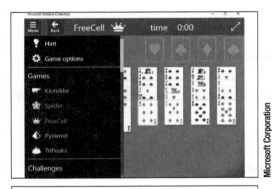

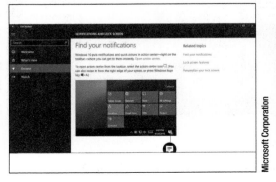

FIGURE 2.19 Project 2B Discover Windows Apps

Objective 5 Discover Windows Entertainment Apps

Gone are the days when you used your PC only for dreary work or school tasks; for example, working on spreadsheets or college reports. Now you probably expect your PC to offer you entertainment so that you can play games, listen to music, watch movies and TV shows, and look at your photos—all from your desktop or laptop PC. Windows 10 comes with entertainment apps that you can use to enjoy all of these types of activities, and all of these apps are free and either pre-installed on Windows 10 systems or are easily downloaded from the Windows Store.

> **NOTE** **User Rights and App Availability May Vary in College Labs**
>
> The setup of user rights and the availability of Windows apps varies among colleges; you may not have access to as many Windows 10 features in a college lab as you would have on your own computer.

Activity 2.08 | Using the Microsoft Solitaire Collection

In Windows 8, Microsoft removed the popular Solitaire game, but it's back in Windows 10 with five different versions.

1 In the lower left corner of your screen, click **Start** ⊞, and then above the group of apps that begin with the letter *A*, click the letter **A** to display a layout of the alphabet. Compare your screen with Figure 2.20.

> Use this shortcut to display the alphabet, from which you can click any letter and then move to installed apps that begin with that letter. This saves you from unnecessary scrolling on the list of apps that are installed on your computer.

FIGURE 2.20

2 On the displayed alphabet, click **M**, and then compare your screen with Figure 2.21.

> Apps installed on your computer that begin with the letter *M* display.

FIGURE 2.21

Office 2016, Windows 10, Microsoft Corporation.

3 On the list, click **Microsoft Solitaire Collection**; if necessary wait a few moments for the app to load. If a message box offers you an **Xbox profile**, click **Not now**, and then if necessary, click **Play as a guest**.

4 Click **FreeCell**, if necessary, in the **How to play** message, click **Close**, and then in the upper left corner, click the **Menu** button. Compare your screen with Figure 2.22.

The menu offers you hints and game options, and also provides links to the other games.

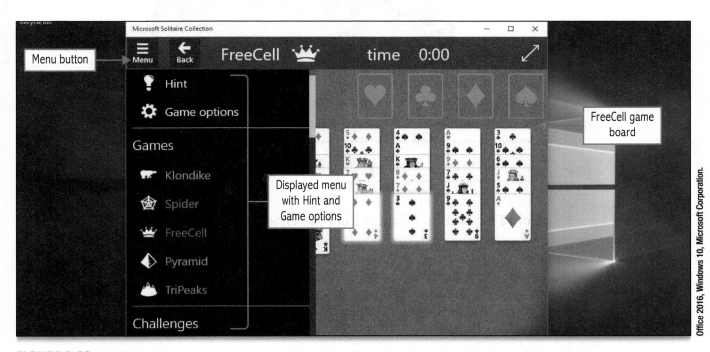

FIGURE 2.22

Office 2016, Windows 10, Microsoft Corporation.

5 From the taskbar, or by searching, open **PowerPoint**, and then click **Blank Presentation**. On the **Home tab**, in the **Slides group**, click **Layout**, and then click **Blank**.

6 Click the **File tab**, on the left click **Save As**, click **Browse**, and then in the **Save As** dialog box, navigate to the location of your **Windows 10 Chapter 2** folder and open the folder.

7 In the **File name** box, using your own name, type **Lastname_Firstname_2B_Windows_Apps** and then press **Enter** to save and redisplay your PowerPoint presentation.

8 On the **Insert tab**, in the **Images group**, click **Screenshot**, and then click **Screen Clipping**. Position the **+** pointer in the upper left corner of the **Microsoft Solitaire Collection** window, hold down the left mouse button, drag down and to the lower right corner of the window, and then release the mouse button to insert the clipping into your PowerPoint presentation. Click outside of the image to deselect it, and then compare your screen with Figure 2.23.

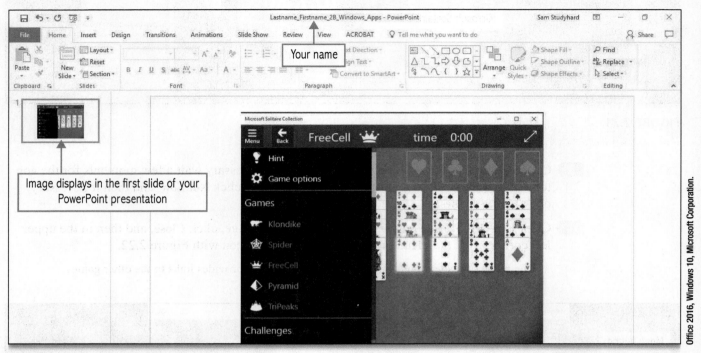

FIGURE 2.23

9 In the upper left corner, click **Save** 🖫, and then in the upper right corner, click **Minimize** ▭ to display the desktop and leave the presentation open.

10 **Close** ✕ the **Microsoft Solitaire Collection** window.

More **Knowledge** | **More Free and Paid Games from the Windows Store**

There are hundreds of free and paid games available from the Windows store. Highly rated and fun ones include Sonic Dash, Fairway Solitaire, and for kids—Madagascar Math Ops.

Activity 2.09 | Using Groove Music

Of course you want to listen to music on your PC. In Windows 10, the ***Groove Music*** app enables you to play the music from a collection that exists on your PC. Additionally, this app is where you can play music from Microsoft's Groove music service, which is Microsoft's version of services like Spotify or Apple Music—and is similarly priced. Groove Music was formerly known as Xbox Music.

1 In the lower left corner of your screen, click **Start** 🖽, and then above the group of apps that begin with the letter *A*, click the letter **A** to display a layout of the alphabet. Click the letter **G**, and then click **Groove Music**. Compare your screen with Figure 2.24.

Commands display on the left.

Office 2016, Windows 10, Microsoft Corporation.

FIGURE 2.24

2 On the left, click the Menu icon ☰ at the top, click **Albums** and then compare your screen with Figure 2.25.

Here you see the easy-to-use interface that you can use if you want to use Groove Music to organize and play your music collection.

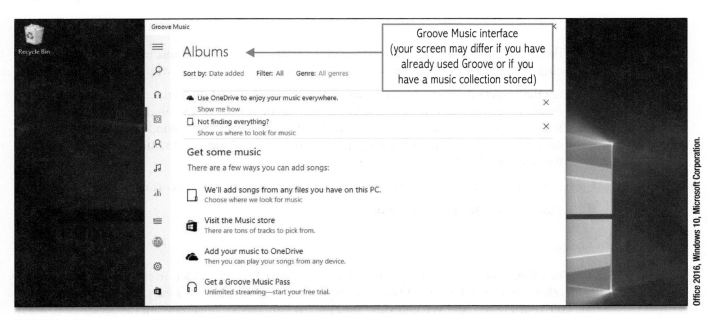

Office 2016, Windows 10, Microsoft Corporation.

FIGURE 2.25

3 **Close** ⊠ the **Groove Music** window.

Activity 2.10 | Using Movies & TV

The *Movies & TV* app is where you can either buy or rent movies and episodes of TV shows. The app acts as a video player, so you can play videos from your own files too, including ripped DVD movies and movies or TV shows that you have purchased from Microsoft's online store. You can link to the store directly from the app.

1 Using the techniques you have practiced, locate and open the **Movies & TV** app.

2 On the left, click **Videos** 📹, and then compare your screen with Figure 2.26.

> Here you can play videos that you have stored on your PC.

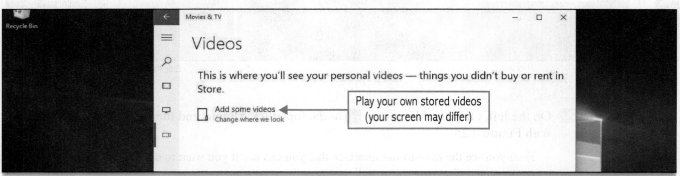

FIGURE 2.26

Office 2016, Windows 10, Microsoft Corporation.

3 From the taskbar, display your PowerPoint presentation. On the **Home tab**, in the **Slides group**, click the upper portion of the **New Slide** button to insert a new slide with the **Blank** layout.

4 On the **Insert tab**, in the **Images group**, click **Screenshot**, and then click **Screen Clipping**. Position the + pointer in the upper left corner of the **Movies & TV** window, hold down the left mouse button, drag down and to the lower right corner of the window, and then release the mouse button to insert the clipping into your PowerPoint presentation. Click outside of the image to deselect it.

5 In the upper left corner, click **Save** 🖫, and then in the upper right corner, click **Minimize** −.

6 **Close** × the **Movies & TV** window.

Activity 2.11 | Using Photos

The *Photos* app will display photo albums from your Pictures folder, from your OneDrive, and from other connected devices and then display them all in one place. It's easy to navigate, organize, and edit your Photos, and you can view your photos either as a Collection or as an Album.

1 Using the techniques you have practiced, locate and open the **Photos** app. Compare your screen with Figure 2.27.

> If you have any photos stored in your Pictures folder or OneDrive, you can immediately view them by scrolling on the right.

Office 2016, Windows 10, Microsoft Corporation.

FIGURE 2.27

2 In Figure 2.28, notice that if you select a picture, editing tools display at the top.

The editing tools provided with the Photos app are quite sophisticated. You can quickly perform photo editing tasks without the need for other programs. For example, you can rotate, crop, adjust brightness and contrast and color, and add special effects like blur.

Office 2016, Windows 10, Microsoft Corporation.

FIGURE 2.28

3 As shown in Figure 2.29, if you click Edit, a wide variety of editing tools display on the left and the right.

Editing tools for Basic fixes

Editing tools for Enhancement

Office 2016, Windows 10, Microsoft Corporation.

FIGURE 2.29

4 **Close** ✕ the **Photos** window.

Objective 6   Discover Windows Information Apps

Microsoft has developed informative and beautifully displayed apps from which you can get information about the latest news, sports, and weather. Additionally, you can view maps for both information and directions.

Activity 2.12 │ Using Maps

The *Maps* app is powered by Bing. Just type in an address and see it plotted on a map! The Maps app also includes spoken driving directions and alerts about traffic jams.

1 Using the techniques you have practiced, locate and open the **Maps** app, if necessary, click Let's go and click Yes to let Windows Maps access your location. Compare your screen with Figure 2.30.

If you are connected to the Internet, Maps will likely display a map of your current location, unless the Location settings are turned off for Maps in your Privacy settings.

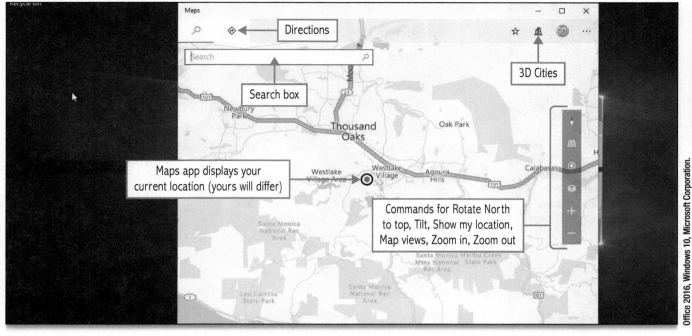

FIGURE 2.30

2 At the top of the Maps window, click in the **Search** box, and then type the address of your college; notice that as you type, suggested addresses will display, as shown in Figure 2.31.

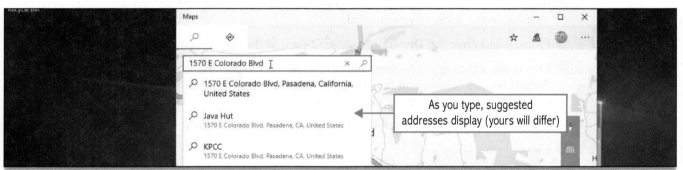

Office 2016, Windows 10, Microsoft Corporation.

FIGURE 2.31

3 When you see the complete address of your college, click it, and then click **Streetside**, if it is available.

4 If a Streetside photo displays, point to it, hold down the left mouse button, and then move your mouse left and right to get a panoramic view, similar to Figure 2.32.

Streetside view of typed address

FIGURE 2.32

5 In the upper right corner, click **Exit Streetside** ⊗.

6 In the upper left corner, click **Directions** ◇, and notice that you can get directions from your location to the address you entered.

7 Press Esc to clear the **Directions** box, and then in the upper right, click **3D Cities** 🏛.

8 Locate the 3D map for **Boston**, and then click on the picture. Point to the picture, hold down the left mouse button, and then drag left and right and up and down, and notice that as you drag, the names of landmarks display on the map.

> When you can take time to further explore the Maps app; you will find it very useful.

9 **Close** ✕ the **Maps** window.

Activity 2.13 | Using News

Two apps that present news, *News* and *Money*, are photo rich and interesting. The News app is a daily publication that acquires articles from large news sites such as The New York Times, CNN, and The Huffington Post. These apps are both customizable to your own interests, and you can add topics or news sources. The Money app provides financial news and current stock information. The Sports app provides sports news in many formats and can be organized by type of sport. Both the Money and Sports apps must be installed from the Windows store.

1 Using the techniques you have practiced, locate and open the **News** app. Compare your screen with Figure 2.33.

> If you have not used the app before, you may be invited to personalize the app.

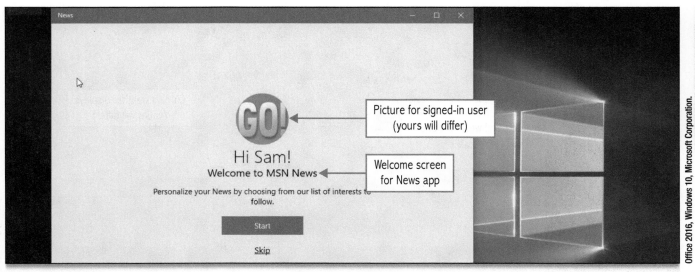

Picture for signed-in user
(yours will differ)

Welcome screen
for News app

Office 2016, Windows 10, Microsoft Corporation.

FIGURE 2.33

2 If necessary, click **Skip**. If the Breaking News Alerts dialog box displays, click Yes or Turn Off. At the top, notice the various categories of news, and then click **Technology**. In the upper left corner, click **Expand** ☰, and then compare your screen with Figure 2.34.

Many of the Windows apps share this menu interface.

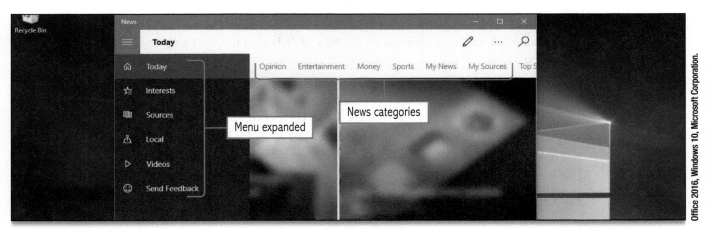

Menu expanded

News categories

Office 2016, Windows 10, Microsoft Corporation.

FIGURE 2.34

3 **Close** ☒ the **News** window.

Activity 2.14 | Using Weather

Everyone likes to check the weather, and the **Weather** app provides a visually appealing and informative view of your weather or of the weather in a location that you designate. The app also offers meteorological data.

1 Using the techniques you have practiced, locate and open the **Weather** app, and then **Maximize** ☐ the window. If necessary, fill out information to personalize your weather content and start the app. In the upper left corner, click **Expand** ☰. Compare your screen with Figure 2.35.

Your location will display. Here you can click to view weather maps, historical weather (did it rain on this date 5 years ago?), or go to favorite locations.

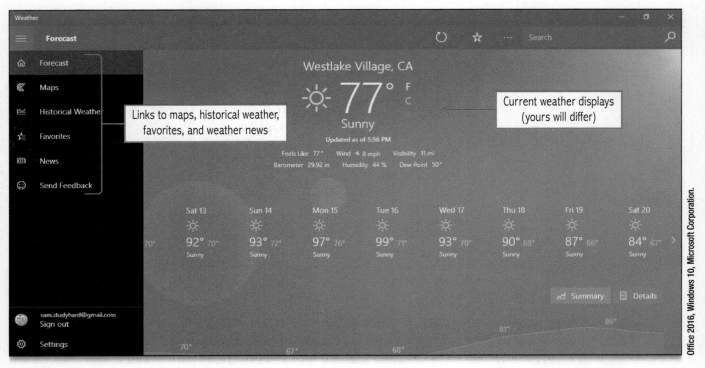

FIGURE 2.35

2 From the taskbar, display your PowerPoint presentation. On the **Home tab**, in the **Slides group**, click the upper portion of the **New Slide** button to insert a new slide with the **Blank** layout.

3 On the **Insert tab**, in the **Images group**, click **Screenshot**, and then click **Screen Clipping**. Position the **+** pointer in the upper left corner of the **Weather** window, hold down the left mouse button, drag down and to the lower right corner of the window but not including the taskbar, and then release the mouse button to insert the clipping into your PowerPoint presentation. Click outside of the image to deselect it.

4 In the upper left corner, click **Save** 🔲, and then in the upper right corner, click **Minimize** ⊟.

5 **Close** ✕ the **Weather** window.

Objective 7   Discover Windows Productivity Apps

Some Windows apps, while not exhibiting beautiful pictures and interesting content, are nonetheless valuable for the assistance they can offer as you work on your PC each day. In the Activities in this Objective, you will discover useful apps for helping your productivity.

Activity 2.15 | Using Contact Support

You may not have noticed this, but there is no built-in Help system for Windows 10—unlike previous versions of Windows. The Internet is exceptionally good at finding answers, so Microsoft expects that you will use the powerful Internet search capabilities built into Windows to find answers to your questions. However, there is an app that can link you to many useful help sites; this is the *Contact Support* app.

1 Using the techniques you have practiced, locate and open the **Contact Support** app, and then compare your screen with Figure 2.36.

Here you can get help with Accounts & billing or with Windows, Office, Services & Apps. For example, if you have an Office 365 subscription for which you pay, you can get billing help here.

FIGURE 2.36

2 Click **Get started**. Compare your screen with Figure 2.37.

Whether or not you can get *free* support usually depends on when and where you got your copy of Windows. However, do not expect any support system—Microsoft's or any others—to hold your hand through a problem that you yourself cannot properly explain. Be ready to explain your problem clearly. Typically the Microsoft support is of high quality, especially if you can explain your problem succinctly.

FIGURE 2.37

3 From the taskbar, display your PowerPoint presentation. On the **Home tab**, in the **Slides group**, click the upper portion of the **New Slide** button to insert a new slide with the **Blank** layout.

4 On the **Insert tab**, in the **Images group**, click **Screenshot**, and then click **Screen Clipping**. Position the **+** pointer in the upper left corner of the **Contact Support** window, hold down the left mouse button, drag down and to the lower right corner of the window, and then release the mouse button to insert the clipping into your PowerPoint presentation. Click outside of the image to deselect it.

5 In the upper left corner, click **Save** 🖫, and then in the upper right corner, click **Minimize** ⊟.

6 **Close** ☒ the **Contact Support** window.

Activity 2.16 | Using Get Started

Although there is no built-in Help system for Windows 10, you will find very useful information in the **Get Started** app, which contains lots of videos that explain how to do things; for example, how to use Cortana. This app especially is good at giving you an overview about something that you are not sure about.

1 ▶ Using the techniques you have practiced, locate and open the **Get Started** app. If necessary, **Maximize** ☐ the window. On the left, click **Browse**, and then compare your screen with Figure 2.38.

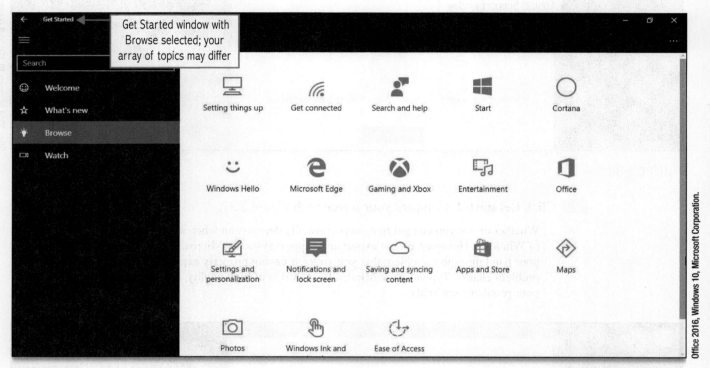

FIGURE 2.38

2 ▶ Click **Notifications and lock screen**, click **Find your notifications**, and then take a moment to read through the information.

3 ▶ From the taskbar, display your PowerPoint presentation. On the **Home tab**, in the **Slides group**, click the upper portion of the **New Slide** button to insert a new slide with the **Blank** layout.

4 ▶ On the **Insert tab**, in the **Images group**, click **Screenshot**, and then click **Screen Clipping**. Position the + pointer in the upper left corner of the **Get Started** window, hold down the left mouse button, drag down and to the lower right corner of the window but not including the taskbar, and then release the mouse button to insert the clipping into your PowerPoint presentation. Click outside of the image to deselect it.

5 ▶ In the upper left corner, click **Save** 🖫, and then in the upper right corner, click **Minimize** ☐.

6 ▶ **Close** ☒ the **Get Started** window.

Activity 2.17 | Using Mail for Windows 10

Although text messaging and chat platforms on mobile devices are an increasingly popular way to communicate, email will continue to be a primary way to communicate with others. This is especially true in a work setting. Most organizations expect that their employees will use email as a primary means of communication.

You may have struggled to manage your personal email, because you probably have multiple personal email addresses, plus an email address from your college and perhaps an email address provided by an employer.

Understanding who provides your email and where it is stored can be confusing. And navigating the interface for each email provider can also be challenging. For example, if you have a Yahoo account and a Gmail account, each one has a different display of email messages. And if you have an email address from your college or work, it also has a display of messages that varies from system to system.

Microsoft Outlook, which is part of the Microsoft Office suite of programs, is a popular *email client*—a program that enables you to view and manage your email from multiple email providers. However, the Outlook program—not to be confused with *Outlook.com*, which is a free web-based email system like Gmail and Yahoo mail—can be more than you need to manage your personal email accounts. Even for a small business, Microsoft Outlook, which has hundreds of features and commands, may be overly complicated for everyday communication.

Mail for Windows 10 is an app that comes with Windows 10, and with it you can efficiently read and respond to messages from multiple email accounts from a single user interface. You can also send files, pictures, and set up an automatic reply when you are away. Additionally, you can access the Mail app on any Windows 10 computer or device when you are signed in to Windows 10 with your Microsoft account.

Mail for Windows 10 may be the ideal app to manage all of the email in your life without having to navigate many different interfaces and without mastering the intricacies of Microsoft Outlook.

1 ▶ On the taskbar, click **Start** ⊞, and then click the **Mail** app as shown in Figure 2.39. If you cannot see the app tile, search for the app by typing in the search box on the left end of the taskbar.

Office 2016, Windows 10, Microsoft Corporation.

FIGURE 2.39

2 ▶ A **Welcome** screen similar to Figure 2.40 displays if you have not previously used the app.

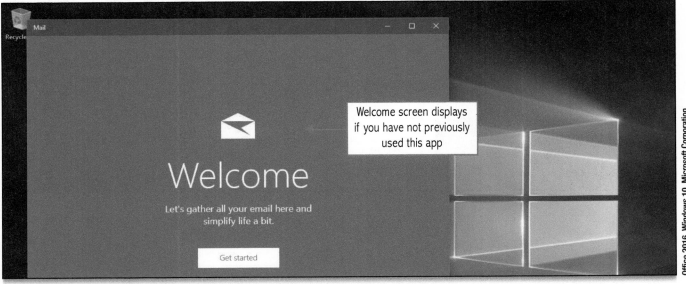

FIGURE 2.40

3 On the **Welcome** screen, click **Get started**, and then compare your screen with Figure 2.41.

The account with which you are signed in to Windows 10 displays.

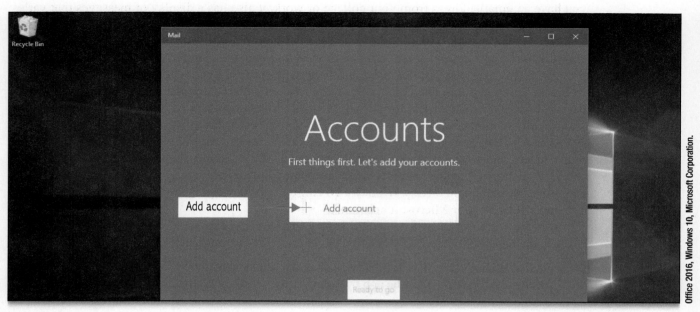

FIGURE 2.41

4 Click **Add account**, and then compare your screen with Figure 2.42.

The advantage to using the Windows 10 Mail app is that you can configure multiple accounts from various email providers.

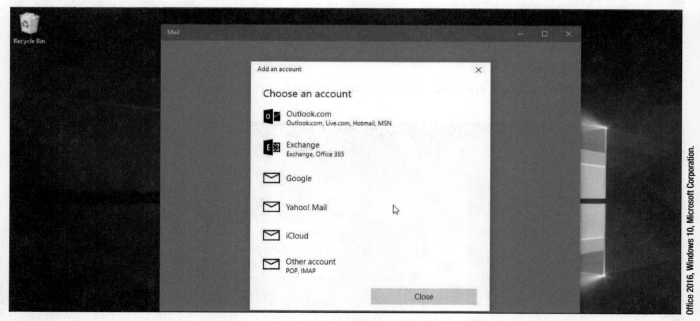

FIGURE 2.42

5 If you want to do so, select an account from the list, fill in the appropriate information, and then compare your screen with Figure 2.43.

If this is a new account, some introductory emails from Microsoft will display. If this is an email address that you already use, your current messages may display.

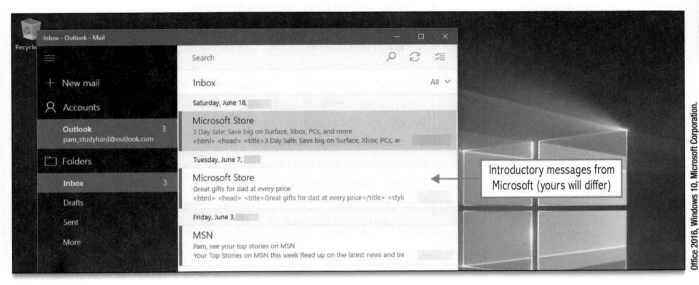

FIGURE 2.43

6 In the upper right corner of the screen, click **Maximize** ☐, compare your screen with Figure 2.44, and then take a moment to study the table in Figure 2.45 that describes the parts of the Mail for Windows 10 window.

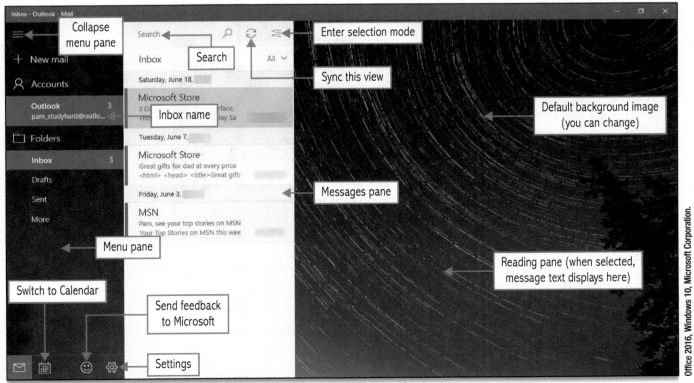

FIGURE 2.44

MAIL FOR WINDOWS 10	
SCREEN PART	**DESCRIPTION**
Background image	Displays if no message is selected (can be customized).
Calendar	Switches the view to the Windows 10 calendar.
Collapse	Collapses the pane on the left to increase viewing area.
Enter selection mode	Displays selection boxes to the left of messages, similar to Item check boxes in File Explorer.
Feedback	Enables you to give feedback to Microsoft about this app.
Inbox name	Indicates the provider of the current inbox, in this instance, Outlook.com.
Menu pane	Displays the Windows 10 for Mail menu.
Messages pane	Displays the messages for the selected folder, in this instance the Inbox folder.
Reading pane	Displays the contents of a message when it is selected (none selected here).
Search	Provides a place to type a search of your email account.
Settings	Displays various settings that you can configure.
Sync this view	Syncs all of your configured accounts to display in Mail for Windows 10.

Office 2016, Windows 10, Microsoft Corporation.

FIGURE 2.45

7 Examine Figure 2.46; it is not necessary to click anything.

Here you can click *Accounts* to display the Manage Accounts pane, or you can click Add account to add another email account.

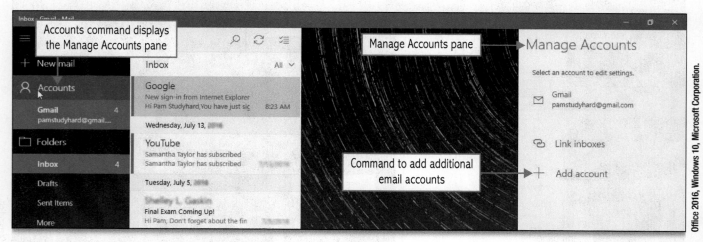

FIGURE 2.46

8 Examine Figure 2.47; it is not necessary to click anything.

Here you can add any email account that you have so that you can have multiple accounts displayed in one place.

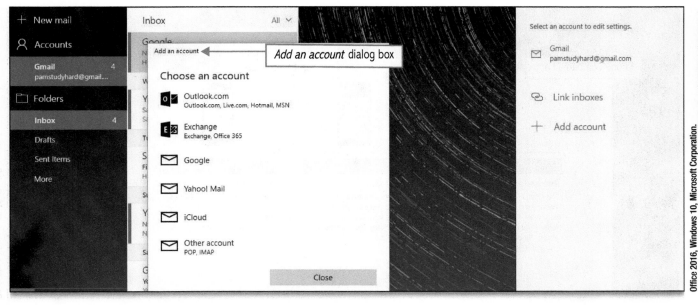

FIGURE 2.47

Office 2016, Windows 10, Microsoft Corporation.

9 ▶ Examine Figure 2.48; it is not necessary to click anything.

If you add an email address, a message similar to this will display to confirm that you can view email from the account in the Mail for Windows 10 app.

Office 2016, Windows 10, Microsoft Corporation.

FIGURE 2.48

10 ▶ **Close** ☒ the **Mail** window.

More **Knowledge**	**Expect Enhancements to Windows 10 Mail App**

Microsoft is expected to continue adding features and enhancements to the Windows 10 Mail app, so that you will find the app to be increasingly useful in managing multiple email accounts.

Activity 2.18 | Using Phone Companion

Do you have an iPhone or an Android phone? If you do, you can get your music, photos, Word documents, Cortana reminders, and more, on your phone by using *Phone Companion*.

1 ▶ Click in the taskbar search box, type **phone companion** and then at the top of the search pane, click **Find results in apps** ⊞. Click to install the **Microsoft Phone Companion** app from the Windows Store. Click **Free**, wait a moment for the app to download, close the **Store** window, and then click **Start** ⊞. At the top of the **Start menu**, on the left, under **Recently added**, click **Phone Companion**. Compare your screen with Figure 2.49.

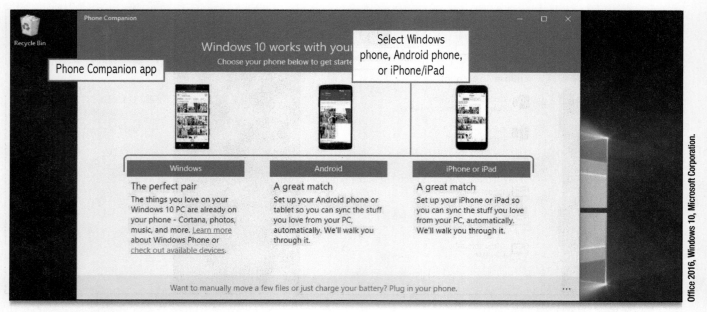

Phone Companion app

Select Windows phone, Android phone, or iPhone/iPad

FIGURE 2.49

> **2** Click **Android**, and then compare your screen with Figure 2.50.

> Here you can see which Microsoft applications you can connect to your phone. In the Apple app store, and in the Google Play store on an Android phone, you can also download most of these apps on your phone, but here you can get them all at one time.

> For each option, if you click Get started, a step-by-step wizard will walk you through what you need to do to connect the app to your phone.

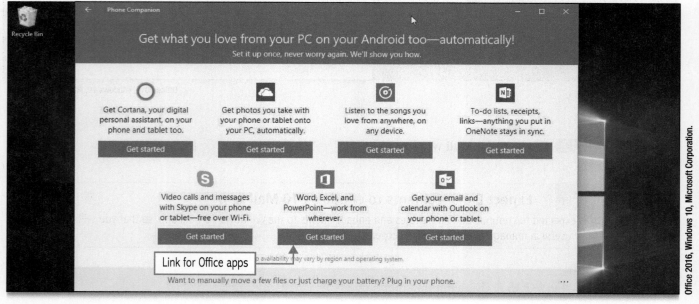

Link for Office apps

FIGURE 2.50

> **3** Under the **Office** logo (*Word, Excel and PowerPoint*), click **Get started**, and then click **Yes, this is me**.

> The first step in the step-by-step wizard displays. You can use these steps to connect the apps that you want.

> **4** Close ⊠ the **Phone Companion** window.

Activity 2.19 | Using Snipping Tool

Snipping Tool is a program within Windows 10 that captures an image of all or part of your computer's screen. A ***snip***, as the captured image is called, can be annotated, saved, copied, or shared via email.

1 Using the techniques you have practiced, open the **Weather** app and be sure the screen is maximized.

2 With the Weather app displayed, in the lower left corner of your screen, click **Start** ▦, and then above the group of apps that begin with the letter *A*, click the letter **A** to display a layout of the alphabet. Within the group of letters, click **W**, and then click **Windows Accessories**. Compare your screen with Figure 2.51.

Snipping Tool is one of the programs included in the group of system tools called ***Windows Accessories***. Also included here are some of the programs you have used such as Paint and WordPad. You could also locate Snipping Tool by searching for it in the search box.

FIGURE 2.51

3 On the list of **Windows Accessories**, click **Snipping Tool** to display the small **Snipping Tool** window on your screen. Click the **New arrow**.

An arrow attached to a button will display a menu when clicked. Such a button is referred to as a ***split button***—clicking the main part of the button performs a command and clicking the arrow opens a menu with choices. A ***menu*** is a list of commands within a category, and a group of menus at the top of a program window is referred to as the ***menu bar***.

A ***free-form snip*** lets you draw an irregular line such as a circle around an area of the screen. A ***rectangular snip*** lets you draw a precise box by dragging the mouse pointer around an area of the screen to form a rectangle. A ***window snip*** captures the entire displayed window. A ***full-screen snip*** captures the entire screen.

4 Click **Rectangular Snip**, and then with the + pointer, hold down the left mouse button and capture the displayed city and state and current conditions, release the left mouse button, and then compare your screen with Figure 2.52.

Your snip displays in the Snipping Tool mark-up window. Here you can annotate—mark or make notes on—save, copy, or share the snip.

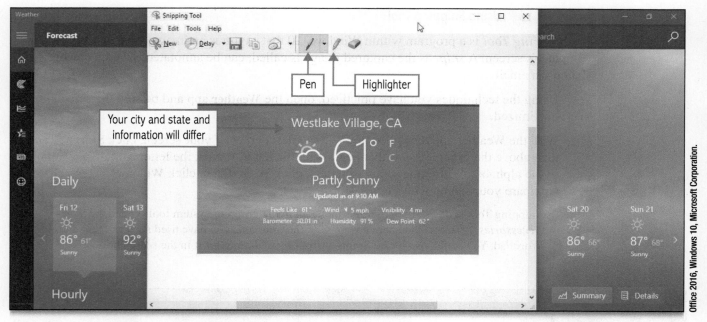

FIGURE 2.52

5 On the toolbar of the displayed **Snipping Tool** mark-up window, click the **Pen button arrow** 🖊, and then click **Red Pen**. Notice that your mouse pointer displays as a red dot. With the pen, circle the current temperature.

6 On the toolbar of the **Snipping Tool** mark-up window, click **Highlighter** 🖊. Notice that your mouse pointer displays as a small yellow rectangle. Drag the mouse pointer to highlight the city and state. Compare your screen with Figure 2.53.

FIGURE 2.53

7 On the toolbar of the **Snipping Tool** mark-up window, click **Copy** 📋. This will copy your snip to the Clipboard.

8 From the taskbar, display your PowerPoint presentation. On the **Home tab**, in the **Slides group**, click the upper portion of the **New Slide** button to insert a new slide with the **Blank** layout.

9 On the **Home tab**, in the **Clipboard group**, click the upper portion of the **Paste** button.

Your copied snip is pasted into the blank slide.

10 In the upper left corner, click **Save** 💾, and then in the upper right corner, click **Minimize** ▬.

11 Close ⊠ the **Snipping Tool** window, and then click **No**. **Close** ⊠ the **Weather** window.

> You can save a snip as an image if you need to do so. Use this convenient tool anytime you want to capture all or part of a screen; for example, to send in an email message.

Activity 2.20 | Using Snip From Microsoft Garage

Microsoft Garage, as described by Microsoft, is an "outlet for experimental projects." For the most part, the projects consist of small apps that you can download and use.

One such app is *Snip*, with which you can capture a screenshot, photo, or whiteboard drawing, annotate it with voice and ink, and share it. Being able to add your voice to a snip is a great advantage compared to the Snipping Tool that you just practiced. You can capture a snip, add your voice to it, and then include it in an email!

ALERT!	**Microsoft Garage Projects Are Subject to Change**

Projects created in Microsoft Garage are, by nature, experimental and subject to change.

---

1 Open **Microsoft Edge** , navigate to **www.mix.office.com/Snip** and then compare your screen with Figure 2.54.

> Here you can get information about how Snip works, view some sample snips, and download the app if you want to do so.

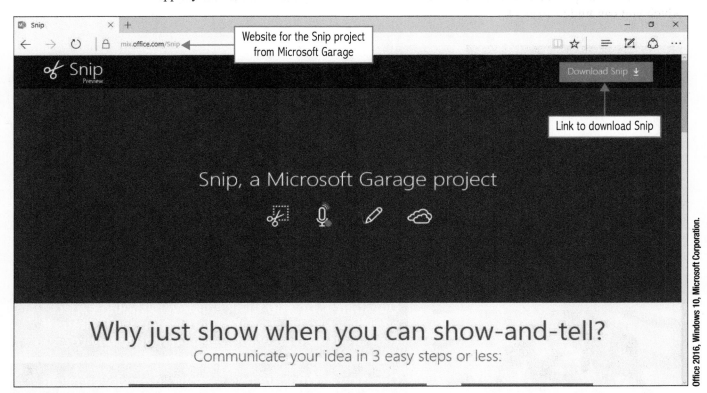

Office 2016, Windows 10, Microsoft Corporation.

FIGURE 2.54

2 Close ⊠ your browser window.

3 From the taskbar, redisplay your PowerPoint presentation. In the upper left corner, click **Save** , and then in the upper right corner, click **Close** ⊠. Submit your completed PowerPoint presentation, which contains six slides, as directed by your instructor.

> **END | You have completed Project 2B**

END OF CHAPTER

SUMMARY

Back up your files so that you can restore them in the event of a virus attack on your computer, a hard disk drive failure, theft of your laptop computer, or a disaster such as a fire or flood.

File History will back up copies of files that you have stored in your Documents, Music, Pictures, Videos, and Desktop folders. It will also back up OneDrive files available offline on your PC.

You expect your PC to offer you entertainment so that you can play games, listen to music, watch movies and TV shows, and look at your photos—all from your PC. Use Windows 10 apps for entertainment.

Microsoft has developed beautifully displayed apps from which you can get information about the latest news, sports, and weather. You can also view maps for both information and directions.

GO! LEARN IT ONLINE

Review the concepts and key terms in this chapter by completing these online challenges, which you can find in **MyITLab**:

Matching and Multiple Choice: Answer matching and multiple choice questions to test what you learned in this chapter.

Lessons on the GO!: Learn how to use all the new apps and features as they are introduced by Microsoft.

GO! FOR JOB SUCCESS

Discussion: Mobile Devices

Mobile devices that can do more at low cost are popular for employers and employees. Employers who provide a smartphone or tablet to employees benefit by having employees available to handle customer or production issues quickly from any location. Employees like not being tied to a desk and a phone. A downside, however, is that many employees feel they have to be available 24 hours a day and are constantly tempted to check their work emails even when they are on personal time.

FotoEdhar/Fotolia

Question 1: Do you think employers should expect employees to be available during non-work hours if they are issued an employer-paid mobile device?

Question 2: What are two reasons an employee might prefer having mobile access to work rather than being at a desk in the office?

Question 3: What are two strategies an employee can implement to avoid looking at work emails during non-work hours?

	Review and Assessment Guide for Windows 10 Chapter 2		
Project	**Apply Skills from These Chapter Objectives**	**Project Type**	**Project Location**
2A	Objectives 1-4 from Project 2A	**2A Instructional Project (Scorecard Grading)** Guided instruction to learn the skills in Project 2A.	In text
2B	Objectives 5-7 from Project 2B	**2B Instructional Project (Scorecard Grading)** Guided instruction to learn the skills in Project 2B.	In text
2C	Objectives 1-4 from Project 2A	**2C Skills Review (Scorecard Grading)** A guided review of the skills from Project 2A.	In text
2D	Objectives 5-7 from Project 2B	**2D Skills Review (Scorecard Grading)** A guided review of the skills from Project 2B.	In text
2E	Objectives 1-4 from Project 2A	**2E Mastery (Scorecard Grading) Mastery and Transfer of Learning** A demonstration of your mastery of the skills in Project 2A with decision-making.	In text
2F	Objectives 5-7 from Project 2B	**2F Mastery (Scorecard Grading) Mastery and Transfer of Learning** A demonstration of your mastery of the skills in Project 2B with decision-making.	In text
2G	Combination of Objectives from Projects 2A and 2B	**2G GO! Think (Rubric Grading) Critical Thinking** A demonstration of your understanding of the Chapter concepts applied in a manner that you would outside of college. An analytic rubric helps you and your instructor grade the quality of your work by comparing it to the work an expert in the discipline would create.	In text
2H	Combination of Objectives from Projects 2A and 2B	**2H GO! Think (Rubric Grading) Critical Thinking** A demonstration of your understanding of the Chapter concepts applied in a manner that you would outside of college. An analytic rubric helps you and your instructor grade the quality of your work by comparing it to the work an expert in the discipline would create.	In text
2I	Combination of Objectives from Projects 2A and 2B	**2I GO! Think (Rubric Grading) Critical Thinking** A demonstration of your understanding of the Chapter concepts applied in a manner that you would outside of college. An analytic rubric helps you and your instructor grade the quality of your work by comparing it to the work an expert in the discipline would create.	In text

GLOSSARY

GLOSSARY OF CHAPTER KEY TERMS

Backing up The process of creating a copy of your files somewhere other than on your computer.

Contact Support A Windows 10 app that can link you to many useful help sites.

Driver Software that enables hardware or devices such as a printer, mouse, or keyboard to work with your computer.

Email client A program that enables you to view and manage your email from multiple email providers; for example, Microsoft Outlook or Mail for Windows 10.

Enter selection mode In Mail for Windows 10, a command that displays selection boxes to the left of messages, similar to Item check boxes in File Explorer.

External hard drive A disk drive that plugs into an external port on your computer, typically into a USB port; also referred to as a portable hard drive.

File History A Windows 10 tool that enables you to back up your files to another drive and restore those files if the originals are lost, damaged, or deleted.

Free-form snip When using Snipping Tool, the type of snip that lets you draw an irregular line, such as a circle, around an area of the screen.

Full-screen snip When using Snipping Tool, the type of snip that captures the entire screen.

Get Started A Windows 10 app that contains information and videos to explain how to do things; for example, how to use Cortana.

Groove Music A Windows 10 app that enables you to play the music from a collection that exists on your PC.

Mail for Windows 10 A Windows 10 app with which you can efficiently read and respond to messages from multiple email accounts from a single user interface.

Managed backup service A service that provides a system for backing up your computer files over the Internet on a scheduled basis and then storing the data securely on their computers; also referred to as remote backup or online backup service.

Maps A Windows 10 app that provides maps and directions.

Menu A list of commands within a category.

Menu bar A group of menus at the top of a program window.

Messages pane In Mail for Windows 10, an area that displays the messages for the selected folder, such as the Inbox folder.

Microsoft Garage A group at Microsoft that develops experimental projects.

Microsoft Outlook A program in the Microsoft Office suite of programs that enables you to view and manage your email from multiple email providers.

Money A Windows 10 app that provides financial news and information such as stock market quotes.

Movies & TV A Windows 10 app where you can either buy or rent movies and episodes of TV shows and that also acts as a video player so you can play videos from your own files.

News A Windows 10 app that provides world and national news and that you can customize to your interests.

Online backup services A service that provides a system for backing up your computer files over the Internet on a scheduled basis and then storing the data securely on their computers; also referred to as remote backup or managed backup service.

Outlook.com A free web-based email system from Microsoft similar to Gmail and Yahoo mail.

PC Reset A set of Windows 10 tools that you can use to bring your PC back to its original factory settings.

Phone Companion A Windows 10 app from the Store that assists you in adding Microsoft services to an iPhone, iPad, or Android phone.

Photos A Windows 10 app that will display photo albums from your Pictures folder, from your OneDrive, and from other connected devices and then display them all in one place.

Portable hard drive A disk drive that plugs into an external port on your computer, typically into a USB port; also referred to as an external hard drive.

Reading pane In Mail for Windows 10, an area that displays the contents of a message when it is selected.

Rectangular snip When using Snipping Tool, the type of snip that lets you draw a precise box by dragging the mouse pointer around an area of the screen to form a rectangle.

Remote backup service A service that provides a system for backing up your computer files over the Internet on a scheduled basis and then storing the data securely on their computers; also referred to as online backup or managed backup service.

Restore point A snapshot of your computer's settings created by the System Restore tool.

Snip (from Microsoft Garage) A Microsoft Garage project that enables you to capture a screenshot, photo, or whiteboard drawing, annotate it with voice and ink, and share it.

Snip (Snipping Tool) The name for an image captured with Snipping Tool.

Snipping Tool A program within Windows 10 that captures an image of all or part of your computer's screen.

Split button A button that has two parts—a button and an arrow; clicking the main part of the button performs a command and clicking the arrow opens a menu with choices.

Sports A Windows 10 app that provides sports news and that can be viewed by individual sport type.

Sync this view In Mail for Windows 10, a command that syncs all of your configured accounts to display.

System Image A Windows 10 tool that makes an exact copy of your hard drive and that you can use to completely restore your computer in the event of a hard drive failure.

System Restore A Windows 10 tool that enables you to take your computer back to a previous point in time.

Weather A Windows 10 app that provides a visually appealing and informative view of your weather or of the weather in a location that you designate.

Window snip When using Snipping Tool, the type of snip that captures the entire displayed window.

Windows Accessories A group of system tools in Windows 10 that includes programs like Snipping Tool, WordPad, and Paint.

Apply 2A skills from these Objectives:

1 Use File History
2 Use System Image
3 Use System Restore and Create a Recovery Drive
4 Use PC Reset

Skills Review Project 2C Using Backup and Recovery Tools

 PROJECT FILES

For Project 2C, you will need the following file:

win02_2C_Answer_Sheet (Word document) from the student data files that accompany this textbook

You will save your results as:

Lastname_Firstname_2C_Answer_Sheet

1 From your **win10_02_student_data_files** that accompany this chapter, open the Word document **win02_2C_Answer_Sheet**. Using your own name, save it in your **Windows Chapter 2** folder as **Lastname_Firstname_2C_Answer_Sheet** and then minimize the document to leave it open.

Close all File Explorer windows and display your desktop. As you complete each step in this Project, write the letter of your answer on a piece of paper; you will fill in your Answer Sheet after you complete all the steps in this Project.

On the right end of the taskbar, click **Action Center**, click **All settings**, and then click **Update & security**. On the left, click **Backup**. What is your result?

A. The File History dialog box displays.

B. Information and commands regarding File History display on the right.

C. A list of files backed up with File History displays.

2 On the right, click **More options**. What is your result?

A. The Backup options screen displays.

B. Options for viewing previous versions of files display.

C. The Data backup screen displays.

3 **Close** the **Settings** window. Point to the **Start** button and right-click. Which of the following is true?

A. The Settings window redisplays.

B. A menu displays.

C. File Explorer opens.

4 Click **Control Panel**. In the **Search Control Panel** box, type **Backup and Restore** Which of the following is true?

A. Here you can activate File History.

B. Here you can click a link for Backup and Restore (Windows 7).

C. Here you can initiate a PC Reset.

(Project 2C Using Backup and Recovery Tools continues on the next page)

Project 2C Using Backup and Recovery Tools (continued)

5 **Close** the **Control Panel** window. On the keyboard, press ⊞ to place the insertion point in the search box. Type **backup and restore** Under **Best match**, click **Backup and Restore (Windows 7)**. What is your result?

A. The Control Panel window for Backup and Restore (Windows 7) displays.

B. A message displays regarding which drive you would like to back up.

C. Neither A or B.

6 Point to **Start** ⊞, right-click, click **Control Panel**, click in the Control Panel search box, and then, type **restore point** What is your result?

A. Detailed instructions for creating a restore point display.

B. The System Properties dialog box displays.

C. Here you can initiate the command to create a restore point.

7 **Close** all **Control Panel** windows, display the **Settings** window, click **Update & security**, and then click **Recovery**. Which of the following is true?

A. Here you can learn how to start fresh with a clean installation of Windows.

B. Here you can designate what folders to recover.

C. Here you can create a USB recovery drive.

8 Close any open windows. Based on the information in the chapter, which of the following is true?

A. An external hard drive is a good option for storing File History.

B. Multiple DVDs are a good option for storing File History.

C. iCloud is a good option for storing File History.

9 Based on the information in the chapter, which of the following is true?

A. If your hard drive fails, only your files are lost.

B. If your hard drive fails, only your programs are lost.

C. If your hard drive fails you lose your files, your operating system, and your programs.

10 Based on the information in the chapter, how often should you make a new system image?

A. Every few months

B. Every week

C. Every day

To complete this Project: Close any open windows to display the **desktop**, on the taskbar click the **Word** button, type your answers into the correct boxes. Save and close your Word document, and submit as directed by your instructor. **Close** ⊠ any open windows.

END | You have completed Project 2C

Apply 2B skills from these Objectives:

5 Discover Windows Entertainment Apps

6 Discover Windows Information Apps

7 Discover Windows Productivity Apps

Skills Review | **Project 2D Discover Windows Apps**

 PROJECT FILES

For Project 2D, you will need the following file:

win02_2D_Answer_Sheet (Word document) from the student data files that accompany this textbook

You will save your results as:

Lastname_Firstname_2D_Answer_Sheet

1 From your **win10_02_student_data_files** that accompany this chapter, open the Word document **win02_2D_Answer_Sheet**. Using your own name, save it in your **Windows Chapter 2** folder as **Lastname_Firstname_2D_Answer_Sheet** and then minimize the document to leave it open.

Close all File Explorer windows and display your desktop. As you complete each step in this Project, write the letter of your answer on a piece of paper; you will fill in your Answer Sheet after you complete all the steps in this Project.

By using the techniques you have practiced, locate and open the **Microsoft Solitaire Collection**, and then open the **Spider** game. What is the goal of this game?

A. To clear as many boards as possible by tapping face-up cards.

B. To remove all the cards from the table by creating "runs" of cards.

C. To clear as many boards as possible by tapping any two cards that add up to 13.

2 **Close** the **Microsoft Solitaire Collection** window. Locate and open the **Groove Music** app. Display the **Albums** menu. Under *Use OneDrive to enjoy your music everywhere*, click **Show me how**. Scroll down to view the Frequently asked questions. Which of the following is true?

A. You must have a Groove Music Pass subscription to play your own music from OneDrive.

B. The MP3 file format is not supported.

C. You can play OneDrive music on an Xbox One console.

3 **Close** all open windows, and then display the **Movies & TV** app. In the lower left corner, click the **Settings** button. Which of the following is true?

A. Here you can select the download quality.

B. Here you purchase movies.

C. Here you can read movie reviews.

4 **Close** all open windows, and then display the **Photos** app. In the lower left corner, click the **Settings** button. Which of the following is *not* true?

A. Here you can add a folder as a source of photos.

B. Here you can choose what photo or photos to show on the Photos tile.

C. Here you can change the picture on your user account.

(Project 2D Discover Windows Apps continues on the next page)

5 **Close** all open windows, and then display the **Weather** app. In the Search box, type **Chicago** and then click **Chicago Illinois, United States**. On the left, click the icon for **Historical Weather**. What is your result?

    A. A map of Chicago displays.

    B. A photo of Chicago displays.

    C. A graph displays.

6 On the left, click the **Maps** icon. On what lake is Chicago located?

    A. Lake Ontario

    B. Lake Michigan

    C. Lake Erie

7 **Close** all open windows, and then display the **Get Started** app. On the left click **Browse**, click **Office**, and then click **Get started with Office 365**. Which of the following is true?

    A. Office 365 is a subscription service.

    B. You can install an Office 365 subscription on only one device.

    C. Office 365 includes only PowerPoint and Outlook.

8 On the left, click **Browse**, click **Get connected**, and then click **Connect to Bluetooth devices**. Which of the following is true?

    A. Bluetooth is for wired devices.

    B. The first step in connecting a Bluetooth device is to start pairing.

    C. You turn on Bluetooth on your PC from the File Explorer window.

9 On the left, click **Browse**, click **Settings and personalization**, and then click **Change desktop background and colors**. Which of the following is true?

    A. As your desktop background, you can choose only from among the images provided by Microsoft.

    B. If you select an accent color, you cannot show it on the Action Center.

    C. As your desktop background, you can create a slideshow of pictures.

10 **Close** all open windows. In the taskbar **Search** box, search for **fetch garage project** Based on the information you see, what does this app do?

    A. Finds and launches apps on an Android device.

    B. Recognizes dogs and classifies them by breed.

    C. Helps small business owners manage contact information.

To complete this Project: Close any open windows to display the **desktop**, on the taskbar click the **Word** button, type your answers into the correct boxes. Save and close your Word document, and submit as directed by your instructor. **Close** ☒ any open windows.

END | You have completed Project 2D

Apply 2A skills from these Objectives:

1 Use File History

2 Use System Image

3 Use System Restore and Create a Recovery Drive

4 Use PC Reset

Mastering Windows 10 | **Project 2E Using Backup and Recovery Tools**

In the following Mastering Windows 10 Project, you will find information about backing up your computer. As you progress through the Project, you will insert a screenshot that you create into a PowerPoint presentation similar to Figure 2.55.

📁 PROJECT FILES

For Project 2E, you will need the following file:

A new PowerPoint presentation

You will save your results in a PowerPoint presentation as:

Lastname_Firstname_2E_Backup

Office 2016, Windows 10, Microsoft Corporation.

FIGURE 2.55

Mastering Windows 10 | **Project 2E Using Backup and Recovery Tools** (continued)

1 Display the **Settings** window, click **Update & security**, and then on the left, click **Backup**. Click **Go to Backup and Restore (Windows 7)**. In the lower left corner, click **Security and Maintenance**.

2 Click **Maintenance**, and then **Maximize** the window.

3 Open a new blank PowerPoint presentation, and then using your own name, save it in your **Windows Chapter 2** folder as **Lastname_Firstname_2E_Backup**

4 In PowerPoint, set the **Layout** to **Blank**, insert the **Screenshot** of your **Security and Maintenance** window, and then click to deselect the image.

5 **Close** the PowerPoint window; when prompted, click **Save**.

6 In the upper right corner of the **Control Panel** window, click **Restore Down**. **Close** all open windows, and then submit your PowerPoint file as directed by your instructor.

END | You have completed Project 2E

Apply 2B skills from these Objectives:

5 Discover Windows Entertainment Apps

6 Discover Windows Information Apps

7 Discover Windows Productivity Apps

Mastering Windows 10 | **Project 2F Discover Windows Apps**

In the following Mastering Windows 10 Project, you will use the Get Started app and the Snipping Tool app. As you progress through this Project, you will insert a screenshot that you create into a PowerPoint presentation similar to Figure 2.56.

 PROJECT FILES

For Project 2F, you will need the following file:

A new PowerPoint presentation

You will save your results in a PowerPoint presentation as:

Lastname_Firstname_2F_Snip

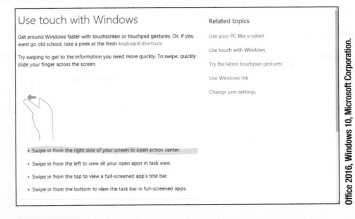

FIGURE 2.56

(Project 2F Discover Windows Apps continues on the next page)

Mastering Windows 10 | **Project 2F Discover Windows Apps** (continued)

1 Display the **Get Started** app. On the left, click **Browse**, click **Windows Ink and touch**, and then click **Use touch with Windows**.

2 Open the **Snipping Tool** app, and then use the **Rectangular Snip** to capture the white portion of the window.

3 Use the highlighter to highlight the text *Swipe in from the right side of your screen to open action center*.

4 On the **Snipping Tool** markup toolbar, click **Copy**.

5 Open a new PowerPoint presentation, and then using your own name, save it in your **Windows Chapter 2** folder as **Lastname_Firstname_2F_Snip**

6 In PowerPoint, set the **Layout** to **Blank**, and then on the **Home tab**, in the **Clipboard group**, use the **Paste** command to paste your snip into the PowerPoint slide.

7 **Close** the PowerPoint window; when prompted, click **Save**.

8 **Close** all open windows; you need not save your snip. Submit your PowerPoint file as directed by your instructor.

> **END | You have completed Project 2F**

OUTCOMES-BASED ASSESSMENTS

RUBRIC

The following outcomes-based assessments are *open-ended assessments*. That is, there is no specific correct result; your result will depend on your approach to the information provided. Make *Professional Quality* your goal. Use the following scoring rubric to guide you in *how* to approach the problem, and then to evaluate *how well* your approach solves the problem.

The *criteria*—Software Mastery, Content, Format and Layout, and Process—represent the knowledge and skills you have gained that you can apply to solving the problem. The *levels of performance*—Professional Quality, Approaching Professional Quality, or Needs Quality Improvements—help you and your instructor evaluate your result.

	Your completed project is of Professional Quality if you:	Your completed project is Approaching Professional Quality if you:	Your completed project Needs Quality Improvements if you:
1-Software Mastery	Choose and apply the most appropriate skills, tools, and features and identify efficient methods to solve the problem.	Choose and apply some appropriate skills, tools, and features, but not in the most efficient manner.	Choose inappropriate skills, tools, or features, or are inefficient in solving the problem.
2-Content	Construct a solution that is clear and well organized, contains content that is accurate, appropriate to the audience and purpose, and is complete. Provide a solution that contains no errors of spelling, grammar, or style.	Construct a solution in which some components are unclear, poorly organized, inconsistent, or incomplete. Misjudge the needs of the audience. Have some errors in spelling, grammar, or style, but the errors do not detract from comprehension.	Construct a solution that is unclear, incomplete, or poorly organized, containing some inaccurate or inappropriate content, and contains many errors of spelling, grammar, or style. Do not solve the problem.
3-Format and Layout	Format and arrange all elements to communicate information and ideas, clarify function, illustrate relationships, and indicate relative importance.	Apply appropriate format and layout features to some elements, but not others. Overuse features, causing minor distraction.	Apply format and layout that does not communicate information or ideas clearly. Do not use format and layout features to clarify function, illustrate relationships, or indicate relative importance. Use available features excessively, causing distraction.
4-Process	Use an organized approach that integrates planning, development, self-assessment, revision, and reflection.	Demonstrate an organized approach in some areas, but not others; or, use an insufficient process of organization throughout.	Do not use an organized approach to solve the problem.

Problem Solving　Project 2G Help Desk

In this Project, you will construct a solution by applying any combination of the skills you practiced from the Objectives in Projects 2A and 2B.

For Project 2G, you will need the following file:

win02_2G_Help_Desk

You will save your document as:

Lastname_Firstname_2G_Help_Desk

From the student files that accompany this textbook, locate and open the Word document **win02_2G_Help_Desk**. Save the document in your chapter folder as **Lastname_Firstname_2G_Help_Desk**

The following e-mail question has arrived at the Help Desk from an employee at the Bell Orchid Hotel's corporate office. In the Word form, construct a response based on your knowledge of Windows 10. Although an email response is not as formal as a letter, you should still use good grammar, good sentence structure, professional language, and a polite tone. Save your document and submit the response as directed by your instructor.

To: Help Desk

What's a simple way to assure that my files are backed up in the event my hard drive crashes, without purchasing online services?

End | You have completed Project 2G

Problem Solving | Project 2H Help Desk

In this Project, you will construct a solution by applying any combination of the skills you practiced from the Objectives in Projects 2A and 2B.

For Project 2H, you will need the following file:

win02_2H_Help_Desk

You will save your document as:

Lastname_Firstname_2H_Help_Desk

From the student files that accompany this textbook, locate and open the Word document **win02_2H_Help_Desk**. Save the document in your chapter folder as **Lastname_Firstname_2H_Help_Desk**

The following e-mail question has arrived at the Help Desk from an employee at the Bell Orchid Hotel's corporate office. In the Word form, construct a response based on your knowledge of Windows 10. Although an email response is not as formal as a letter, you should still use good grammar, good sentence structure, professional language, and a polite tone. Save your document and submit the response as directed by your instructor.

To: Help Desk

Is there a simple way to view email from multiple accounts in one place without using Microsoft Outlook? If so, how would I set up such a system?

END | You have completed Project 2H

Problem Solving   Project 2I Help Desk

In this Project, you will construct a solution by applying any combination of the skills you practiced from the Objectives in Projects 2A and 2B.

For Project 2I, you will need the following file:

win02_2I_Help_Desk

You will save your document as:

Lastname_Firstname_2I_Help_Desk

From the student files that accompany this textbook, locate and open the Word document **win02_2I_Help_Desk**. Save the document in your chapter folder as **Lastname_Firstname_2I_Help_Desk**

The following e-mail question has arrived at the Help Desk from an employee at the Bell Orchid Hotel's corporate office. In the Word document, construct a response based on your knowledge of Windows 10. Although an email response is not as formal as a letter, you should still use good grammar, good sentence structure, professional language, and a polite tone. Save your document and submit the response as directed by your instructor.

To: Help Desk

I am the Corporate Director of Food and Beverage. I have hundreds of photos from various banquets and wedding receptions that I would like to share with potential customers who would like to see how we set up and display for these events. Is there a simple way—without investing in a paid photo-sharing service—that I could share photos when customers request to see examples of our work—without the cost of printing brochures? I would also like to organize them into some kind of groups; for example, Spring Weddings and Sports Banquets. Is there a Windows 10 app that I could use for this purpose?

End | You have completed Project 2I

Advanced File Management and Advanced Searching

PROJECT 3A

OUTCOMES
Navigate and display your files and folders for maximum ease of use and efficiency in completing tasks.

PROJECT 3B

OUTCOMES
Conduct a search of your computer that includes multiple criteria and administer the search engine and index.

OBJECTIVES

1. Navigate by Using the Address Bar and Quick Access List
2. Manage Folder Options and Views
3. Recognize File Types and Associate Files with Programs

OBJECTIVES

4. Use Search Tools in File Explorer
5. Use the Taskbar Search Box and Search with Cortana

Loftflow/Shutterstock

In This Chapter

In this chapter, you will learn that although most of the work with your data occurs inside the program in which the file was created, there are still many times when you are outside of the program and using File Explorer to find or organize your files and folders. You will use the address bar to navigate within File Explorer and use the Quick access area to increase your efficiency. The search features in Windows 10 are powerful; searching properly can reduce frustration when you are trying to find your files. In this chapter, you will practice additional search techniques so that you will always be able to find your files quickly.

The projects in this chapter relate to the **Bell Orchid Hotels**, headquartered in Boston, and which own and operate resorts and business-oriented hotels. Resort properties are located in popular destinations, including Honolulu, Orlando, San Diego, and Santa Barbara. The resorts offer deluxe accommodations and a wide array of dining options. Other Bell Orchid Hotels are located in major business centers and offer the latest technology in their meeting facilities. Bell Orchid offers extensive educational opportunities for employees. The company plans to open new properties and update existing properties over the next decade.

Using Advanced File Management Techniques

PROJECT 3A

PROJECT ACTIVITIES

In Activities 3.01 through 3.09, you will work with Barbara Hewitt and Steven Ramos, employees in the Information Technology department at the headquarters office of Bell Orchid Hotels, as they explore how to navigate and display the files and folders on a computer for maximum efficiency and ease of use. As you progress through the Project, you will insert screenshots of windows that you create into a PowerPoint presentation similar to Figure 3.1.

PROJECT FILES

For Project 3A, you will need the following files:

win03_3A_Bell_Orchid folder from the student data files that accompany this textbook

A new blank PowerPoint presentation

You will save your results in a PowerPoint file as:

Lastname_Firstname_3A_File_Management

PROJECT RESULTS

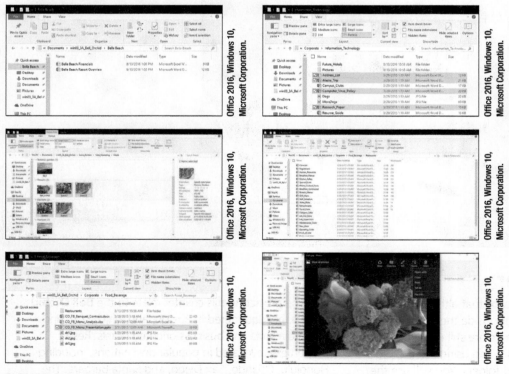

FIGURE 3.1 Project 3A Using Advanced File Management Techniques

Recall that in File Explorer, the address bar displays your current location as a series of links separated by arrows. The term *location* is used, rather than the term *folder*, because you can navigate to both folders and to other resources.

Every element of the address bar—the folder names and each arrow—is an active control. That is, you can move from the currently displayed folder directly to any folder above it in the path just by clicking on a folder name. Additionally, you can click the Forward and Back buttons to the left of the address bar to navigate through folders you have already visited, just as if you were surfing the Internet. You can go directly to the Internet by typing a Web address into the address bar, which causes your browser to open in a new window.

ALERT!   **You Will Need a USB Flash Drive**

Be sure you have a USB flash drive ready to insert when instructed to do so.

Activity 3.01 | Navigating by Using the Address Bar

A primary function of your operating system is to store and keep track of your files. A file folder on a disk in which you store files is referred to as a ***directory***. The location of any file can be described by its ***path***. A path is a sequence of folders—*directories*—that leads to a specific file or folder.

> **1** Sign in to your computer to display the **desktop**. From the taskbar, open **File Explorer** 📁. (If necessary, search for and pin File Explorer to the taskbar.) If necessary, in the upper right corner of the File Explorer window, click Expand the Ribbon ⌄ so that you can view all of the ribbon commands.

> **2** From the student data files for Chapter 3—**win10_03_Student_Data_Files**—that you downloaded from www.pearsonhighered.com/go or obtained from your instructor, copy the folder **win03_3A_Bell_Orchid** and paste it to your **Documents** folder.

> **3** Navigate to **This PC > Documents > win03_3A_Bell_Orchid > Corporate**. On the ribbon, click the **View tab**, and then if necessary, set the **Layout** to **Details**.

> **4** In the **address bar**, locate the **location icon**, as shown in Figure 3.2.

> The *location icon* depicts the location—disk drive, folder, and so on—you are currently accessing. Here, a buff-colored folder displays.

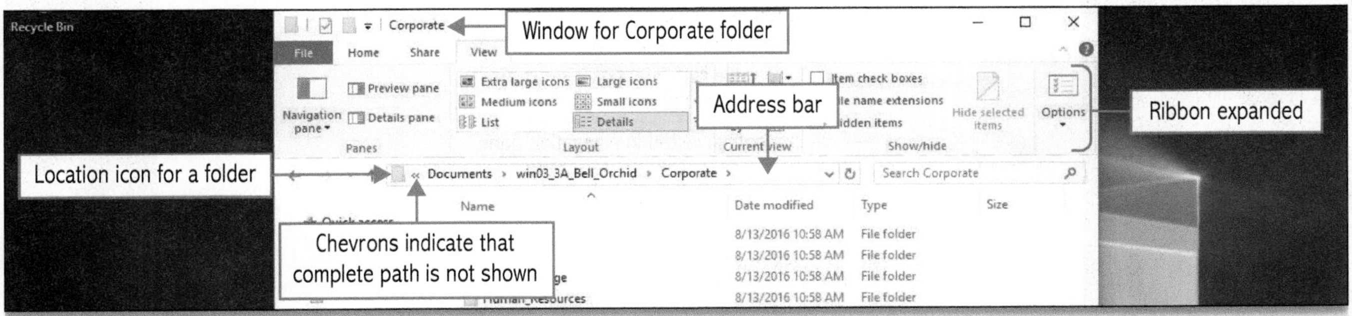

Office 2016, Windows 10, Microsoft Corporation.

FIGURE 3.2

> **5** In the **address bar**, click the **location icon** one time, and then compare your screen with Figure 3.3.

> The path that describes the folder's location displays and is highlighted. The path begins with the disk, which is indicated by *C:*—the main hard disk drive of your computer.

> Following the disk is the sequence of subfolders, each separated by a backslash (\). On the *C:* hard disk drive, the folder *Users* contains your personal folder with an abbreviation of your name. Your personal folder contains your *Documents* folder, which contains the *win03_3A_Bell_Orchid* folder that you copied there. The *win03_3A_Bell_Orchid* folder contains the *Corporate* folder.

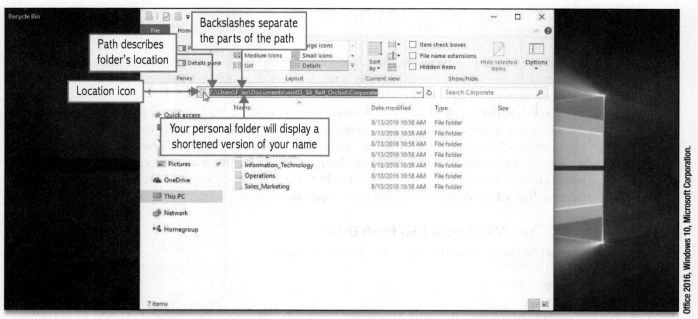

Path describes folder's location

Backslashes separate the parts of the path

Location icon

C:\Users\F las\Documents\win03_3A_Bell_Orchid\Corporate

Your personal folder will display a shortened version of your name

Information_Technology   8/13/2016 10:58 AM   File folder
Operations   8/13/2016 10:58 AM   File folder
Sales_Marketing   8/13/2016 10:58 AM   File folder

FIGURE 3.3

> 6   Click in a blank area of the **file list** to cancel the display of the path.

ANOTHER WAY   Press Esc to cancel the path display.

> 7   On the left, in the **navigation pane**, if necessary expand > **This PC**, click **Documents**, and then compare your screen with Figure 3.4.

The location icon changes to depict the location being accessed—Documents.

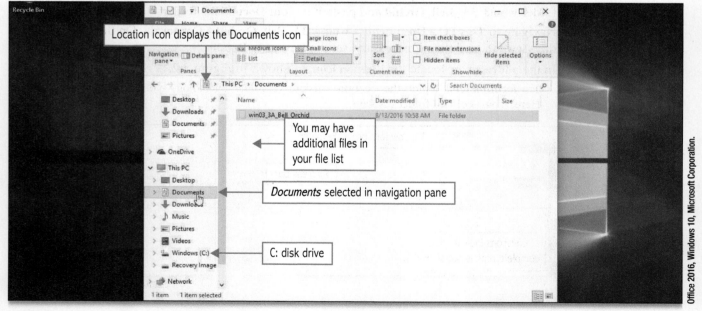

Location icon displays the Documents icon

This PC ▸ Documents ▸

win03_3A_Bell_Orchid   8/13/2016 10:58 AM   File folder

You may have additional files in your file list

Documents selected in navigation pane

C: disk drive

FIGURE 3.4

> 8   In the **navigation pane**, under **This PC**, click your **C: disk drive**. In the **address bar**, notice the disk drive icon that displays as the **location icon**—a small Windows logo may display there.

> 9   Insert your USB flash drive. In the **navigation pane**, click your **USB flash drive**, and notice the **location icon**.

> 10   Under **This PC**, click **Music**. Compare your screen with Figure 3.5.

The location icon is a music note.

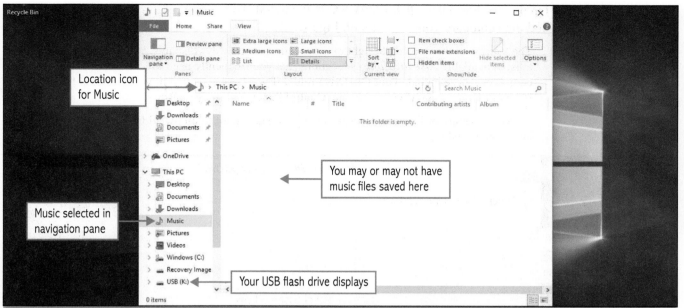

Office 2016, Windows 10, Microsoft Corporation.

FIGURE 3.5

11 ▶ To the left of the **address bar**, click **Back** ← as many times as necessary to redisplay the **Corporate** window.

Recall that the Forward and Back buttons enable you to navigate to locations you have already visited. In a manner similar to browsing the Web, the locations you have visited are stored in a location history, and you can browse that location history by clicking the Back and Forward buttons.

Activity 3.02 | Navigating by Using Recent Locations, Base Locations, and Links on the Address Bar

1 ▶ To the immediate right of the **Forward** button →, point to the **Recent locations** button ⌄, and then click one time. Compare your screen with Figure 3.6.

The *Recent locations* button displays a list of recently accessed locations, and the current location is indicated by a check mark. By clicking an item on this list, you can move to a recently accessed location quickly. The list is limited to the current session, so only locations you have accessed since starting File Explorer display on the list.

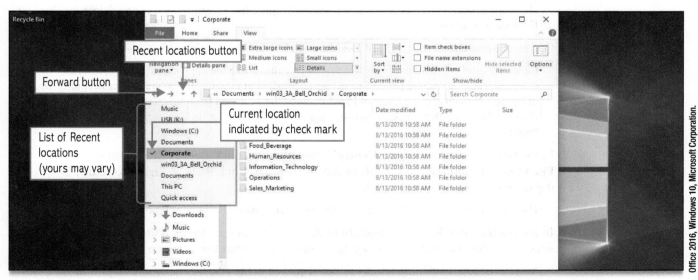

Office 2016, Windows 10, Microsoft Corporation.

FIGURE 3.6

2 On the displayed list, click **win03_3A_Bell_Orchid**. To the right of the **location icon**, click >
and then compare your screen with Figure 3.7.

The > arrow to the immediate right of the location icon always displays, *below* the separator line,
a list of available *base locations*—locations that you frequently need to access to manage your
computer. These include your OneDrive folder if you have activated it, your personal folder, This
PC, your Homegroup if you have one, Control Panel, and Recycle Bin.

Above the separator line, any folders in the path that cannot fit on the address bar will display,
along with Desktop.

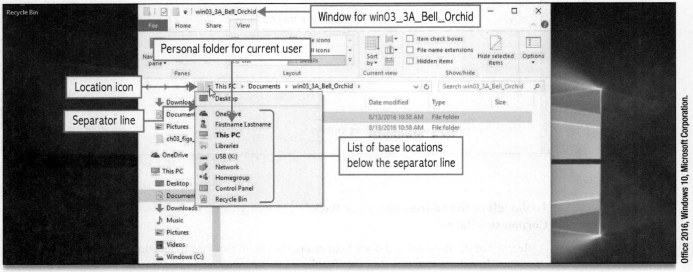

FIGURE 3.7

3 On the displayed list, notice the **separator line** below **Desktop**.

Locations above the separator line are part of the current path. Recall that your desktop is
considered the top of your hierarchy; it is created for each user account name on the computer and
contains your personal folder.

4 On the displayed list, click **Desktop**.

Here you can view and work with any shortcuts, files, or folders that you have stored on the
desktop. In the file list, you can open items in the same manner you do in any other file list.

This is a convenient view to help you clean up any clutter on your desktop or to *find* items on a
cluttered desktop. For example, here you could right-click a shortcut name and delete the shortcut
from your desktop.

5 On the **address bar**, to the right of **Desktop**, click >. On the displayed list, click **Control Panel**.

Control Panel is a window from which you can customize the appearance and functionality of your
computer, add or remove programs, set up network connections, and manage user accounts. Most
of the functionality of the Control Panel can now be accessed from the Windows 10 Start menu by
clicking Start and then clicking Settings ⚙, or by clicking Action Center ⬛ on the taskbar, and
then clicking All settings.

6 In the upper left corner of the **Control Panel** window, click **Back** ⬅ to return to
File Explorer, and then to the left of the **address bar**, click **Back** ⬅ again to return to
the **win03_3A_Bell_Orchid** window.

Use the features of the address bar in this manner to navigate your computer efficiently.

7 In the **file list**, double-click **Honolulu** to display its window. In the **address bar**, to the right of
win03_3A_Bell_Orchid, click > and then on the displayed list, click **Orlando**.

You can access a subfolder of any folder displayed in the address bar by clicking the arrow to the
right of the folder and displaying its list of subfolders.

8 In the **address bar**, to the right of **win03_3A_Bell_Orchid_Orlando**, click **>**, and then on the displayed list, click **Corporate**. In the **file list**, double-click **Information_Technology** to display its window.

9 To the right of the location icon, notice the **double chevrons <<**. Compare your screen with Figure 3.8.

Double chevrons indicate that the current path is too long to fit in the address bar. If your window is larger than the one shown in Figure 3.8, you might not see the double chevrons.

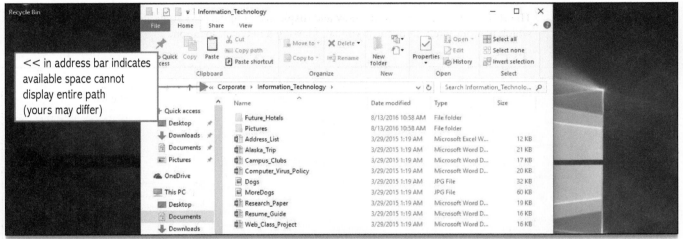

Office 2016, Windows 10, Microsoft Corporation.

FIGURE 3.8

10 If the double chevrons **<<** display in your folder window, click them, and then compare your screen with Figure 3.9. If they do not display, just examine Figure 3.9.

The part of the path that cannot display is shown above the separator line. Below the separator line, the base locations display.

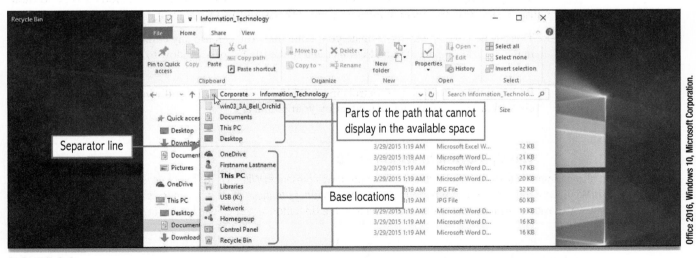

FIGURE 3.9

11 Press **Esc** to close the list, and then in the upper right corner, click **Maximize** ☐ to maximize the window. Notice that the entire path displays, and double chevrons no longer display.

Even with the folder window maximized, a path that contains numerous subfolders will be forced to display double chevrons. When you see double chevrons in this manner, you will know that the entire path is not visible.

12 ▸ Be sure your computer is connected to the Internet. In the **address bar**, click in the empty area at the end of the current path. With the path selected—highlighted in blue—type **www.bls.gov** and press Enter.

The website for the U.S. Department of Labor's Bureau of Labor Statistics displays. In this manner, you can type a Web address directly in the address bar without opening your Web browser.

13 ▸ **Close** ☒ the webpage to redisplay the **Information_Technology** window. Compare your screen with Figure 3.10, and notice the two buttons at the end of the address bar.

The Previous Locations button provides a drop-down list of locations you have accessed.

The Refresh button updates the view and displays any updates to contents in the selected location, which is more likely to occur if you are viewing a network location.

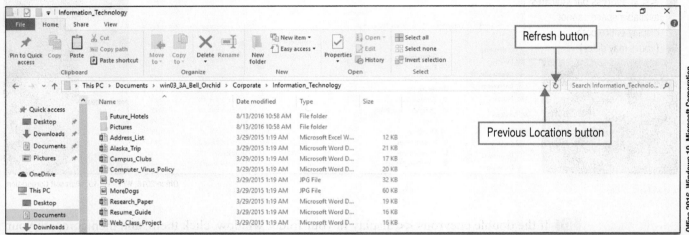

FIGURE 3.10

14 ▸ In the upper right, click **Restore Down** ⧉ to return the window to its previous size, and then **Close** ☒ the **File Explorer** window. If any other windows remain open, close them.

There is no *correct* way to navigate your computer. You can use any combination of techniques in the navigation pane, the address bar, and in the file list of a window to display the location you want.

By using the various active controls in the address bar, you can significantly reduce the number of clicks that you perform when navigating your computer.

More **Knowledge** | **The Up Button in Windows 10**

You can also navigate by using the Up button ↑. This button was present in Windows XP, but removed in Windows Vista and Windows 7. In Windows 8, Microsoft brought back this button and continues to incorporate it in Windows 10. It provides you with another easy way to navigate the hierarchy of the folder structure. The Up button moves up one level in the hierarchy with each click.

Activity 3.03 | Managing the Quick Access List

Think of the navigation pane in File Explorer as a map of your computer that lists the places and things you most often need to access. Each item that displays in the navigation pane is sometimes referred to as a *node*—a central point of connection or a place where things come together. The first node in the navigation pane is the *Quick access list*, which contains links to folders and files that Windows determines that you access frequently or that you pin there yourself for easy access.

The Quick access list, which is new in Windows 10, has two categories of links to folders and files: items that you use frequently as determined by Windows and items that you pin there yourself because you need to access them frequently.

Because the Quick access list is so useful, by default it is the location that opens when you open File Explorer. You can change this default behavior, but that is not recommended because you will find this list to be very useful, especially if you take the time to pin your frequently used files and folders here.

However, you may decide to modify the behavior of the Quick access list to suit your needs. For example, you can turn off the option of having Windows automatically display recently used files and organize the Quick access list with only the items *you* want to see there. Also, you can remove any of the default locations.

If you have a folder or file for a project that you are working on, you can pin it to the Quick access list, and then unpin it from the Quick access list when you no longer need to access it frequently.

1 If necessary, search for and then pin the Word, Excel, and PowerPoint desktop apps to the taskbar—or they may already be pinned there from your work in a previous chapter.

2 From the taskbar, open **File Explorer** ▣. In the **navigation pane**, if necessary, expand **> Quick access**.

3 On the left, in the **navigation pane**, if necessary expand **This PC**, and then under **This PC**, click **Documents**. In the **file list**, point to your **win03_3A_Bell_Orchid** folder, and then right-click. Compare your screen with Figure 3.11.

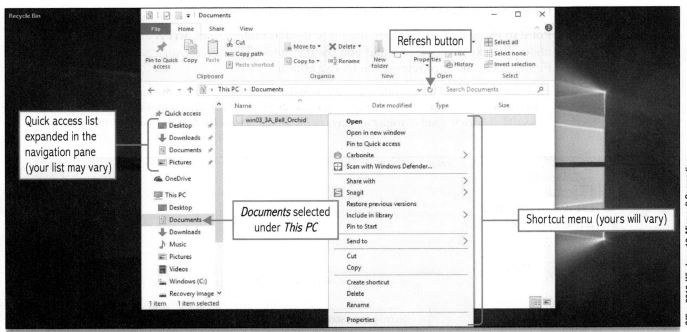

FIGURE 3.11

4 On the shortcut menu, click **Pin to Quick access**, and then compare your screen with Figure 3.12.

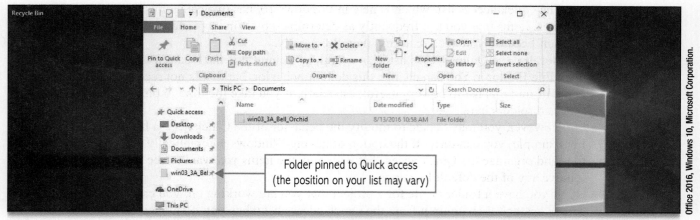

FIGURE 3.12

ALERT!   **Documents and Pictures Under Quick Access May Link to OneDrive**

If you are signed in to your computer with a Microsoft account, rather than a local account, the links to the Documents folder and the Pictures folder under Quick Access may link to your OneDrive and not to these folders on This PC. Always check the path in the address bar so that you know where your files are being stored or what location you are accessing.

> **5** In the **file list**, double-click **win03_3A_Bell_Orchid**, and then on the ribbon, on the **Home tab**, in the **New group**, click **New folder**. Type **Bella Beach** and then press [Enter] to name the new folder. Notice that the list of folders re-alphabetizes.

> **6** Point to the **Bella Beach** folder, drag it to the left under **Quick access** until a line displays under the text *Quick access* and you see the ScreenTip *Pin to Quick access* as shown in Figure 3.13, and then release the mouse button.

> A link to the *Bella Beach* folder is created in the Quick access list in the navigation pane. The position is determined by where the black line displays as you drag into the Quick access area. Your win03_3A_Bell_Orchid folder displays in the Quick access list because you recently accessed it.

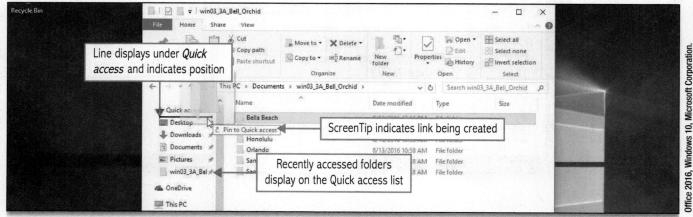

FIGURE 3.13

> **7** In the upper right corner, **Close** [×] the **win03_3A_Bell_Orchid** window, and then on the taskbar, click the **Word** program button to launch the Word desktop app.

> **8** Click **Blank document**, and then type **Information regarding this new resort near Bella Beach will be added to this document at a later date.**

9 ▸ Click the **File tab**, on the left click **Save As**, and then click **Browse** to display the **Save As** dialog box. In the **navigation pane**, scroll up as necessary, and then under **Quick access**, click one time on the link to the **Bella Beach** folder to display its path in the **address bar**. Click in the **File name** box to select the default text, type **Bella Beach Resort Overview** as the file name, and then compare your screen with Figure 3.14.

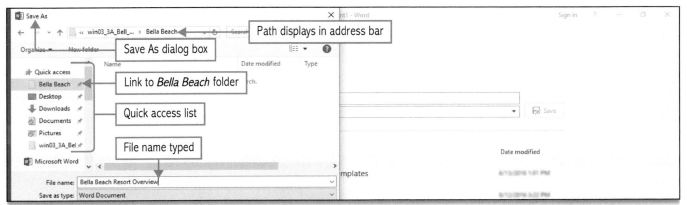

FIGURE 3.14

Office 2016, Windows 10, Microsoft Corporation.

10 ▸ In the lower right corner, click **Save**, and then **Close** ☒ Word. Start **Excel**. Click **Blank workbook**, and then in cell **A1** type **Financial information for the new resort in Bella Beach will be added to this file at a later date.** Press ⏎.

11 ▸ Click the **File tab**, click **Save As**, and then click **Browse** to display the **Save As** dialog box. In the **navigation pane**, scroll up as necessary, and then under **Quick access**, click **Bella Beach** to display its path in the **address bar**.

12 ▸ Click in the **File name** box to select the default text, and then type **Bella Beach Financials** Click **Save**, and then **Close** ☒ Excel.

13 ▸ From the taskbar, open **File Explorer** ▣, and then in the **navigation pane**, in the **Quick access list**, click one time on the **Bella Beach** link. Compare your screen with Figure 3.15.

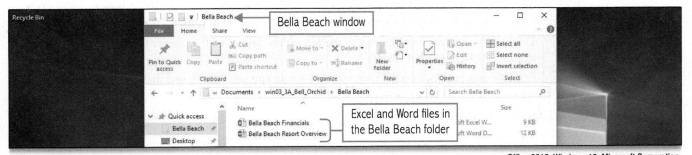

FIGURE 3.15

Office 2016, Windows 10, Microsoft Corporation.

14 ▸ With the **Bella Beach** window still displayed in File Explorer, from the taskbar, open **PowerPoint**. Click **Blank Presentation**, and then on the **Home tab**, in the **Slides group**, click **Layout**. In the displayed gallery, click **Blank**.

15 ▸ Click the **Insert tab**, in the **Images group** click **Screenshot**, and then under **Available Windows**, click the image of your File Explorer window. Click in a white area to deselect the image; the title bar in the image may display as black. If necessary, close the Design Ideas pane on the right, and then compare your screen with Figure 3.16.

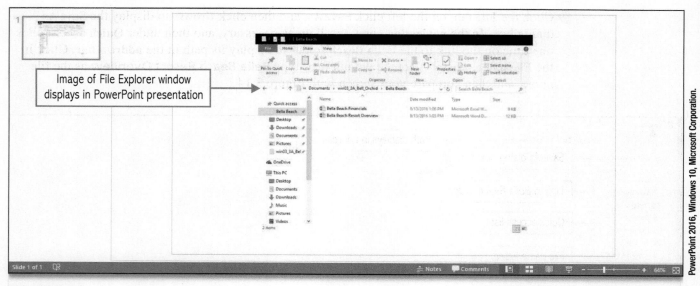

Image of File Explorer window displays in PowerPoint presentation

PowerPoint 2016, Windows 10, Microsoft Corporation.

FIGURE 3.16

16 ▶ In PowerPoint, click the **File tab**, on the left click **Save As**, and then click **Browse** to display the **Save As** dialog box.

17 ▶ In the **Save As** dialog box, in the **navigation pane**, scroll down as necessary, and then click your **USB flash drive**, or navigate to the location where you are storing your files for this chapter, so that it displays in the **address bar**. On the toolbar, click **New folder**, type **Windows 10 Chapter 3** and press ⏎.

18 ▶ In the **file list**, double-click your **Windows 10 Chapter 3** folder to open it. Click in the **File name** box, and then using your own name, replace the selected text by typing **Lastname_Firstname_3A_File_Management** Click **Save**, and then in the upper right corner of the PowerPoint window, click **Minimize** ☐ so that PowerPoint remains open but not displayed on your screen.

You will need your PowerPoint presentation again as you progress through this Project.

19 ▶ In the **navigation pane**, if necessary expand **›** **Quick access**, point to **Bella Beach**, right-click, and then on the displayed shortcut menu, click **Unpin from Quick access**.

This action removes only the *link* to the folder; the folder itself is still contained in your win03_3A_Bell_Orchid folder.

Place folders and files on the Quick access list as you need them, and then remove them when you are no longer accessing them frequently.

20 ▶ **Close** ☒ the **Bella Beach** window.

Objective 2 Manage Folder Options and Views

A Microsoft blog once noted that building Windows is like ordering pizza for a billion people—there are so many options that various users need! Although you will not need many of the numerous options for setting the behavior of files and folders on your own PC, it's helpful to understand what the options are and where to locate them should you ever have the need.

Recall that Windows 10 is a multi-user operating system. That means that your computer can have multiple user accounts; for example, one for you and one for each member of your family. As you use your computer—download files, change the desktop color, create files and folders—these changes are made only to *your* account. If you create a user account for another person on your computer, when he or she signs in, the Windows 10 defaults will be in place until they are changed by the new user.

When a new user account is created on your PC, Windows 10 creates a new user account folder in the Users folder, which is located in the path This PC > Windows (C:) > Users. Each user account folder—also referred to as a ***personal folder***—contains subfolders and information for one specific user—for example, the Documents and Pictures folders for a specific user can be accessed only when that user is signed in. This is how Windows keeps each user's information and settings separate—by storing the information in the personal folder created for each user account.

In this Activity, you will locate and identify the subfolders in your personal folder.

ALERT!   **The Steps in This Activity May Not Work on a Campus Computer**

On a lab computer at your college, you may not be able to access the C: drive to view the Users folder. If you are unable to complete the steps, just read the information, and then try this on your own computer when you are able to do so.

---

1 ▸ On the taskbar, click **File Explorer** ▦, and then in the **navigation pane**, under **This PC**, click your **Windows C: drive**—or whatever name is assigned to your drive C. In the **file list**, locate and then double-click the **Users** folder.

Each user of this PC for which a user account has been created has a folder in the Users folder with his or her name.

2 ▸ Locate the folder with your user name—this might be the first five letters of your sign-on name—and then double-click to open the folder. Compare your screen with Figure 3.17.

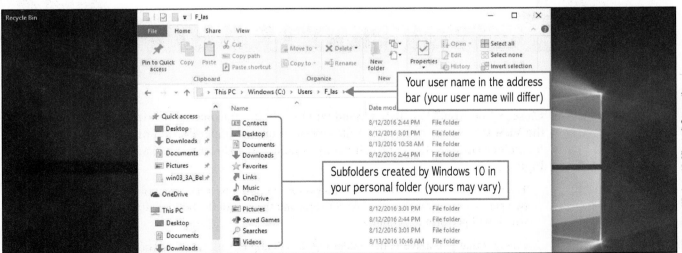

FIGURE 3.17

3 ▸ **Close** ☒ the window for your personal folder.

You can personalize the way your folders look and behave to suit your needs. For example, if you have difficulty performing a double-click, you can set all your files and folders to open with a single click. Many computer users make this change to their computers.

1 From the taskbar, open **File Explorer** 📁, and notice in the lower portion of the window, you may see your two Bella Beach files under Recent files. In the **navigation pane**, under **This PC**, click to open your **Documents** folder.

2 In the **file list**, point to your **win03_3A_Bell_Orchid** folder, right-click, and then on the displayed shortcut menu, click **Open in new window**. Compare your screen with Figure 3.18.

> The win03_3A_Bell_Orchid folder opens in a new window. Open a folder in a new window if you want to keep open all the folders you are working with on the screen at the same time; for example, you could snap one window to the right and the other to the left to drag files from one location to another.

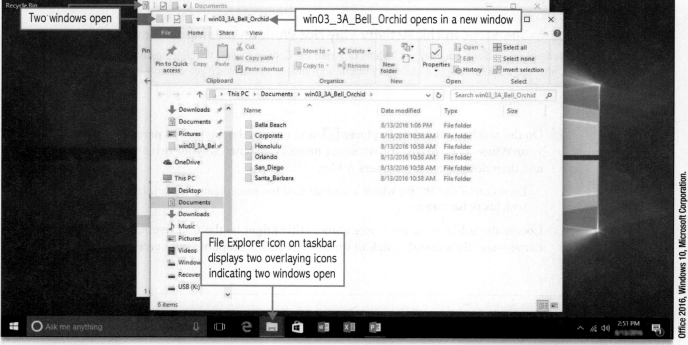

FIGURE 3.18

3 **Close** ✕ the **win03_3A_Bell_Orchid** window. In the **Documents** window, on the ribbon, click the **View tab**. At the right end of the ribbon, click the upper portion of the **Options** button. In the **Folder Options** dialog box, if necessary, click the **General tab**. Compare your screen with Figure 3.19.

> The Options button is an example of a *split button*; that is, when you point to the button there are two parts—the arrow that displays a menu, and the part of the button with the command name, which will perform the command.

> Changes that you make in the Folder Options dialog box affect *all* of your File Explorer windows, regardless of what disk drive or folder's content displays. On the General tab, there are three significant changes you can make to the behavior of *all* of your File Explorer windows.

> Under *Browse folders*, you can choose to open *each* folder in its own window, in the manner that you did in Step 1 of this Activity. Recall that this keeps *all* the folder windows you are working with on the screen at the same time. If you change this default setting, keep in mind that this behavior

will apply to *all* folder windows *all* the time. Because you can easily do this on a folder-by-folder basis, as you did in Step 2, you will probably want to leave the default option selected.

Under *Click items as follows*, you can change the behavior of clicking items to open them. Changing the default setting by choosing the first option will change the behavior of your mouse as follows: to select an item, you need only point to it and it will be selected; to open an item, you need only single-click. This is similar to the manner in which you select and open links in a webpage. Many individuals like this option and make this change.

Under *Privacy*, you can choose to show recently used files in Quick access and show frequently used folders in Quick access. Deselect these two options if you want to prevent Windows from placing files or folders on your Quick access list based on your usage—you may prefer to limit the Quick access list only to items *you* pin there. This is a personal preference.

If you select some of these changes and then decide you want to restore all of the original behaviors, you can click the Restore Defaults button in this dialog box.

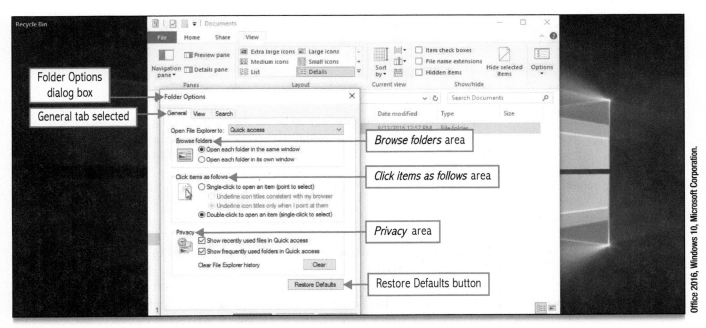

Folder Options dialog box

General tab selected

Browse folders area

Click items as follows area

Privacy area

Restore Defaults button

FIGURE 3.19

4 In the **Folder Options** dialog box, click the **View tab**, and then notice the two buttons under **Folder views**.

Here you can select one of the Windows 10 views—for example, the *Details* view or the *Icons* view—to apply to every folder window you open. To accomplish this, open any folder's window and change it to the view you want for all folder windows. Then display this dialog box and click the Apply to Folders button.

Recall that Windows 10 selects a view that is appropriate for the type of data; for example, the Icon view for pictures and the Details view for documents. Because you can change the view easily on a folder-by-folder basis, you will probably not want to adjust this setting. If you make the adjustment and do not like it, display the dialog box and click the Reset Folders button.

5 Locate the **Advanced settings** portion of the dialog box, as shown in Figure 3.20. Take a moment to scroll down the list under **Advanced settings** and study the table in Figure 3.21.

Becoming familiar with these settings will enable you to further personalize the manner in which your folders display to suit your own comfort and ease of use.

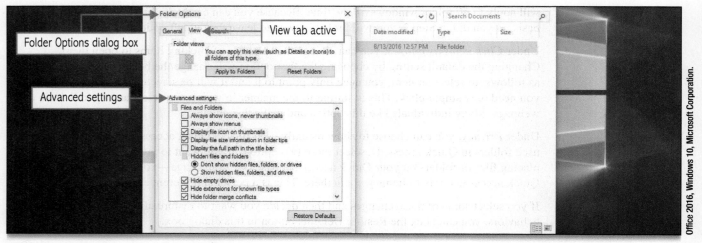

FIGURE 3.20

ADVANCED SETTINGS IN THE VIEW TAB OF THE FOLDER OPTIONS DIALOG BOX	
SETTING	**DESCRIPTION AND DEFAULT SETTING**
Always show icons, never thumbnails	Replaces Live Icons with a standard image. Off by default.
Always show menus	Displays a menu bar below the address bar on the Control Panel. Off by default.
Display file icon on thumbnails	Displays a small version of the application icon, for example the green Excel icon, on the file name, which makes it easier to determine visually which application opens the file. On by default.
Display file size information in folder tips	Displays the size of the file in a ScreenTip when you point to the file. On by default.
Display the full path in the title bar	Displays the full path of the file in the title bar of the folder window. Off by default.
Hidden files and folders	Displays hidden files and displays them as a paler ghost image. Off by default. By not showing hidden files, it is less likely that you will delete an important system file.
Hide empty drives	Hides the display of drive letters in which there is no device attached. On by default.
Hide extensions for known file types	Hides the display of the file extensions for files, for example *.docx* for a Word file. On by default (by default, extensions are hidden from view).
Hide folder merge conflicts	If you copy a *file* into a folder that contains a file with the same name, Windows will warn you by displaying the Replace or Skip Files dialog box. However, if you copy a *folder* into a location with the same folder name, you will get no warning if this check box is selected. By default, this check box is selected.
Hide protected operating system files (Recommended)	Hides files with the *System* attribute from file listings. On by default. It is recommended to hide protected operating system files to prevent accidental deletion or movement of critical Windows files.
Launch folder windows in a separate process	Launches each folder window in a separate memory space, increasing stability but decreasing performance. Rarely necessary; off by default.
Restore previous folder windows at logon	Redisplays, upon restart, any windows that you had open when Windows 10 was shut down. Off by default, but can be a useful feature to enable.
Show drive letters	Displays both the drive letter and the friendly name for a drive. If you clear this setting, only the friendly name will display. On by default.
Show encrypted or compressed NTFS files in color	Changes the text color for any files that use NTFS (New Technology File System) compression or NTFS encryption. Off by default.
Show pop-up description for folder and desktop items	Displays a ScreenTip when you point to an item. On by default.

FIGURE 3.21 *(Continued)*

ADVANCED SETTINGS IN THE VIEW TAB OF THE FOLDER OPTIONS DIALOG BOX (*continued*)	
SETTING	**DESCRIPTION AND DEFAULT SETTING**
Show preview handlers in preview pane	Displays the contents of a file in the Preview pane when the Preview pane is enabled. On by default.
Show status bar	Displays the status bar at the bottom of the window. On by default.
Show sync provider notifications	Enables notifications from providers you select.
Use check boxes to select items	Displays a selection check box when you point to an item; off by default. This is a useful feature that you might want to enable and can also be enabled on the View tab on the ribbon.
Use Sharing Wizard (Recommended)	Limits the capability to assign complex permissions to files, which simplifies the process. On by default.
When typing into list view	Lets you choose between typing the value into the Search Box automatically or displaying the results in the view. By default, set to *Select the typed item in the view*.
Expand to open folder	In the navigation pane, the path to the open folder is expanded. Off by default.
Show all folders	In the navigation pane, all folders are displayed. Off by default. Traversing the navigation pane becomes increasingly more difficult as folders are added.
Show libraries	In the navigation pane, the libraries on your computer are displayed in a separate Libraries area. Off by default.

Office 2016, Windows 10, Microsoft Corporation.

FIGURE 3.21

6 At the bottom of the **Folder Options** dialog box, click **Cancel** to close the dialog box without changing any settings. In the **file list**, double-click your **win03_3A_Bell_Orchid** folder to open it. Then navigate to **Corporate > Information_Technology**.

7 On the **View tab**, in the **Show/hide group**, if it is not already selected, click to select the **Item check boxes** check box, and notice that a small check box displays in the file list to the left of *Name*.

Three settings from the Folder Options dialog box are commonly used—*Item check boxes*, *File name extensions*, and *Hidden items*—so they also appear on the ribbon.

ALERT! **Is *Item check boxes* Already Selected on Your Computer?**

On a computer with a touchscreen, the *Item check boxes* option is selected by default.

---

8 In the **file list**, *point* to the **Future_Hotels** folder, and notice the check box that displays to the left. Click one time to select the file **Computer_Virus_Policy**, and then compare your screen with Figure 3.22.

A check box displays to the left of the file you selected with a checkmark. By enabling the ***check box feature***, when you point to a file or folder, a check box displays. Selecting the file or folder places a checkmark in the check box.

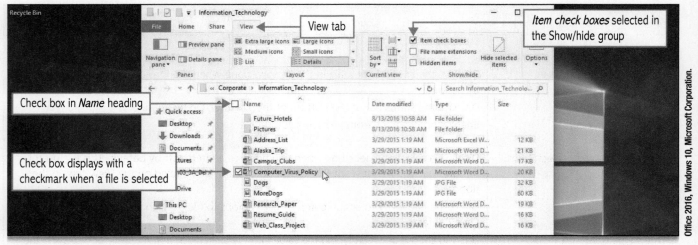

FIGURE 3.22

9 ▶ Point to the file **Alaska_Trip**, and then click its **check box**. Notice that two files remain selected.

10 ▶ Point to and then click the **check box** for the **Address_List** file, the **Research_Paper** file, and the **Web_Class_Project** file. Compare your screen with Figure 3.23.

The files you select by clicking directly in the check box remain selected. Thus, you need not remember to hold down ⌈Ctrl⌋ to select a noncontiguous group of files. This setting also makes it easier to see which files are selected and which files are not selected.

Many individuals enable this feature to make selecting multiple files easier and visually distinctive. If you like this feature, consider enabling it on your own system.

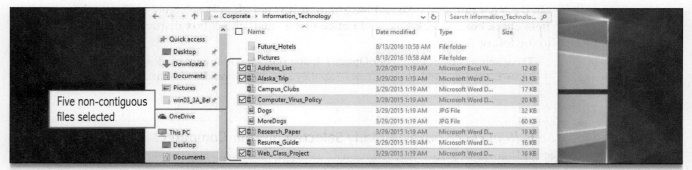

FIGURE 3.23

Office 2016, Windows 10, Microsoft Corporation.

11 ▶ On the taskbar, click the **PowerPoint icon** to redisplay your **3A_File_Management** presentation. On the **Home tab**, in the **Slides group**, click the upper portion of the **New Slide** button to insert a new slide with the Blank layout.

12 ▶ Click the **Insert tab**, in the **Images group**, click **Screenshot**, and then under **Available Windows**, click the image of your File Explorer window. If necessary, close the Design Ideas pane on the right, and then click in a white area to deselect the image. Compare your screen with Figure 3.24.

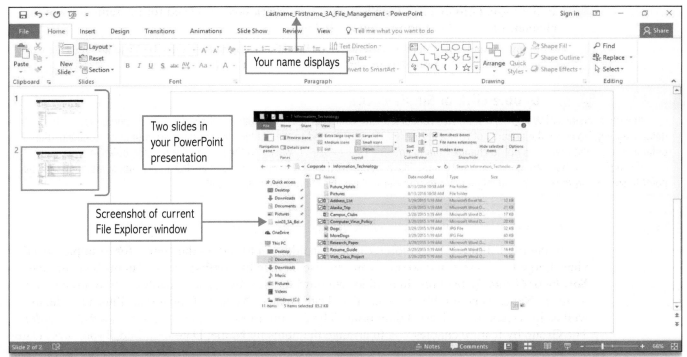

Your name displays

Two slides in your PowerPoint presentation

Screenshot of current File Explorer window

FIGURE 3.24

PowerPoint 2016, Windows 10, Microsoft Corporation.

13 In the upper right corner of the PowerPoint window, click **Minimize** $\boxed{-}$ to minimize the PowerPoint window.

14 Click the check box that displays to the left of the *Name* column heading to select all the items in the file list. Then click the same check box to deselect all files.

15 Open the **Future_Hotels** folder, set the view to **Large icons**, and then point to various files in this folder. Notice that the check box feature continues to display by placing a small check box in the upper left corner of files you point to, and that on the ribbon, on the View tab, the Item check boxes check box is selected. Compare your screen with Figure 3.25.

Recall that any setting you change in the Folder Options dialog box will be applied to *all* files and folders on your computer.

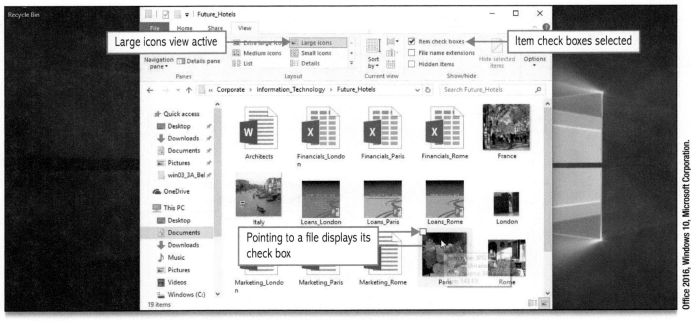

Large icons view active

Item check boxes selected

Pointing to a file displays its check box

Office 2016, Windows 10, Microsoft Corporation.

FIGURE 3.25

16 In the **Layout group**, click **Details**. Leave **Item check boxes** selected for the remainder of this chapter. **Close** ⊠ the **Future_Hotels** window.

Many computer users opt to leave the Item check boxes option selected, because it makes it easier to view which files or folders in a list are selected.

More Knowledge | **Double-click or Single-click?**

In earlier versions of Windows, testing was conducted with computer users on making the *single-click to open behavior* the default setting. However, the majority of computer users were accustomed to the double-click method, so double-click remains the default. Many computer users opt to change from the *double-click to open behavior* to the *single-click to open behavior*.

If you prefer to have Windows 10 behave more like a webpage, that is, you perform a single-click to activate something and you point to something to select it, you might want to consider making this change on your computer.

Activity 3.06 | Personalizing Views and Using the Sort By and Group By Features

In the file list of a File Explorer window, in addition to setting the *view*—for example Details view, Large icons view, and so on—you can also change the *arrangement* of items by using the ***Sort by*** or ***Group by*** features. In a folder window, the Sort by feature enables you to arrange the items by Name, Date modified, Type, Size, Date created, Authors, Categories, Tags, or Title, as well as in Ascending or Descending order. The default arrangement is Name in Ascending order. The Group by feature enables you to arrange the items by Name, Date modified, Type, Size, Date created, Authors, Categories, Tags, or Title, as well as in Ascending or Descending order.

1 On the taskbar, click **File Explorer** 🗖, and then in the upper right corner, **Maximize** ▢ the window.

2 Navigate to **Documents › win03_3A_Bell_Orchid › Corporate › Food_Beverage**. If necessary, on the **View tab**, set the layout to **Details**, and then click one time to select the Word file **CO_FB_Banquet_Contract**.

3 On the **View tab**, in the **Panes group**, click **Details pane** to display the **Details pane** on the right, and then compare your screen with Figure 3.26.

When a folder or file in the file list is selected, the Details pane—if open on the right side of the window—displays information about the selected item.

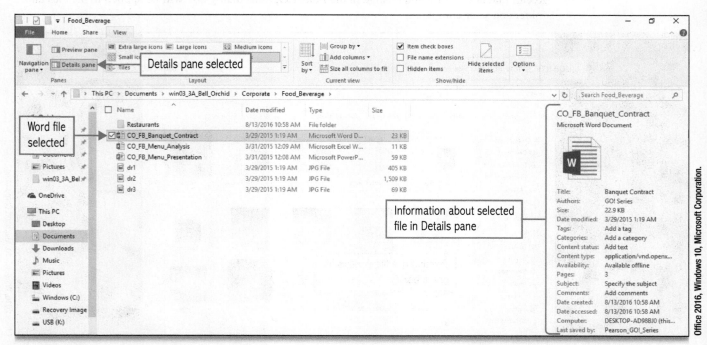

FIGURE 3.26

4 In the **Layout group**, click **Tiles**.

The Tiles view displays medium-sized icons with the following file properties: Name, Type, and Size.

5 In the **Layout group**, *point* to—but do not click—**Large icons**, and notice that you can see a preview of the view before you actually select it. Click **Large icons**.

The Large icons view makes it easy to see the content of files that use the Live Icon preview. For example, here you can see the actual picture files and the first slide of the PowerPoint presentation.

6 In the **Layout group**, click **List**.

The List view displays only the file icon and the file name. The advantage of the List view is that you can see the full file name without widening the Name column.

7 In the **Layout group**, click **Content**.

The Content view combines icons with some of the file properties.

8 In the **Layout group**, click **Details**.

The Details view enables you to view the most common properties of the files, including the Name, Date modified, Type, and Size.

9 In the lower left corner of the screen, notice that this **Food_Beverage** folder contains 7 items, including the **Restaurants** folder. On the **View tab**, in the **Current view group**, click **Sort by**, and notice that *Name* is the current sort arrangement and the order is Ascending.

The default order displays all *folders* first in alphabetical order, and then all *files* in alphabetical order.

10 On the **Sort by** list, click **Type**, and notice that in the **Type column**, the items in the file list are alphabetically arranged by Type.

11 Click **Sort by** again, and then return the sort arrangement to **Name**. Notice that the **Food_Beverage** folder contains only one PowerPoint file and one Excel file.

12 On the **View tab**, in the **Current view group**, click **Group by**, and then click **Type**. Notice that the **JPG File** section displays **3** files.

13 Set **Group by** to **(None)** and **Sort by** back to **Name**, which are the defaults. Navigate to **win03_3A_Bell_Orchid** > **Santa_Barbara** > **Sales_Marketing** > **Media**, and then set **Group by** to **Tags**. Notice that Windows 10 sorts the group of files into groups by tag.

14 If necessary, set the **Layout** to **Large icons**. Scroll down as necessary, and then click the Group name *Gardens*. Compare your screen with Figure 3.27.

The **Details pane** displays the number of files with the *Gardens* tag.

FIGURE 3.27

15 On the taskbar, click the **PowerPoint icon** to redisplay your **3A_File_Management** presentation. On the **Home tab**, in the **Slides group**, click the upper portion of the **New Slide** button to insert a new slide with the Blank layout.

16 Click the **Insert tab**, in the **Images group**, click **Screenshot**, and then under **Available Windows**, click the image of your File Explorer window. If necessary, close the Design Ideas pane on the right, and then click in a white area to deselect the image.

17 In the upper left corner of the PowerPoint window, on the Quick Access toolbar, click **Save** 🖫 to save the changes you have made to your PowerPoint presentation.

18 In the upper right corner of the PowerPoint window, click **Minimize** ⊟ to minimize the PowerPoint window.

19 On the **View tab**, in the **Current view group**, click **Group by**, and then click (**None**). In the **Panes group**, click **Details pane** to turn off the **Details pane**. In the **Layout group**, click **Details**.

20 In the upper right corner, click **Restore Down** 🗗, and then **Close** ⊠ the **Media** window.

Activity 3.07 | Sorting Files by Properties

You can select any property that a file supports, and use it to sort files.

1 From the taskbar, open **File Explorer** 🗀, and then navigate to **This PC > Documents > win03_3A_Bell_Orchid > Corporate > Food_Beverage > Restaurants**. In the upper right corner, **Maximize** 🗖 the window.

2 In the **file list**, point to any of the column headings, right-click, and then at the bottom of the displayed menu, click **More**.

The Choose Details dialog box displays. From this dialog box, you can select any property that the file supports and use that property to sort files.

3 In the **Choose Details** dialog box, scroll down to the end of the list or type **w** to display the details that begin with *w*, and then select the **Word count** check box. Click **OK**.

4 Point to the *Word count* **column heading**, and then click two times so that a small arrow at the upper edge of the column heading points downward. Compare your screen with Figure 3.28.

A Word count column is added to the folder window, and the files that support Word count—Microsoft Word files—are sorted in descending order. Microsoft Excel files do not contain a word count.

Properties such as those you can see in the Choose Details dialog box offer many ways to sort and find files.

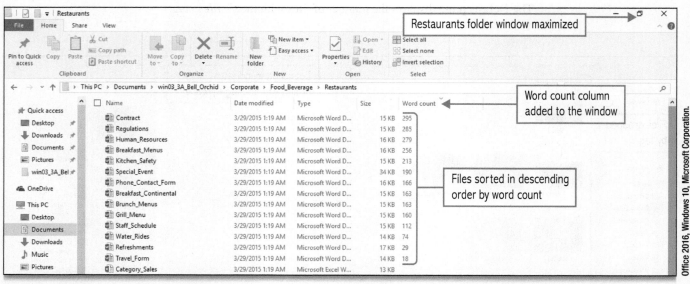

FIGURE 3.28

5 On the taskbar, click the **PowerPoint icon** to redisplay your **3A_File_Management** presentation. On the **Home tab**, in the **Slides group**, click the upper portion of the **New Slide** button to insert a new slide with the Blank layout.

6 Click the **Insert tab**, in the **Images group**, click **Screenshot**, and then under **Available Windows**, click the image of your File Explorer window. If necessary, close the Design Ideas pane on the right, and then click in a white area to deselect the image.

7 In the upper left corner of the PowerPoint window, on the Quick Access toolbar, click **Save** to save the changes you have made to your PowerPoint presentation.

Four slides display in your PowerPoint presentation.

8 In the upper right corner of the PowerPoint window, click **Minimize** − to minimize the PowerPoint window.

9 Point to any of the column headings, right-click, click **More**, and then notice that **Word count** moved to the upper portion of the list in the group of Details that currently display in this window. Click to *clear* the **Word count** check box, and then click **OK**.

The Word count column no longer displays in the window.

10 In the upper right corner, click **Restore Down** . Click *Name* in the **Name** column so that the small arrow at the upper edge of the column heading points upward to re-sort the items alphabetically.

11 **Close** × all windows.

More Knowledge | **Reverse the Current Selection of Files**

In a list of files, if you need to select all but a few of the files, select only the ones that you do *not* want, and then on the Home tab, in the Select group, click the Invert selection command. This command reverses the current selection, so all the files *except* the ones you clicked will be selected.

Objective 3 | Recognize File Types and Associate Files with Programs

A ***file name extension*** is a set of characters that indicates to Windows 10 what kind of information is in a file and what program should open it. A file name extension displays at the end of the file name, following a period. In the file name *Address_List.xlsx*, the extension *.xlsx* indicates to Windows 10 that this is an Excel file.

Activity 3.08 | Recognizing File Types

1 From the taskbar, open **File Explorer** , and then navigate to **This PC** > **Documents** > **win03_3A_Bell_Orchid** > **Corporate** > **Food_Beverage**.

2 In the **file list**, click to select the Word file **CO_FB_Banquet_Contract**, and then on the **Home tab**, in the **Open group**, notice the **Word icon** . Compare your screen with Figure 3.29.

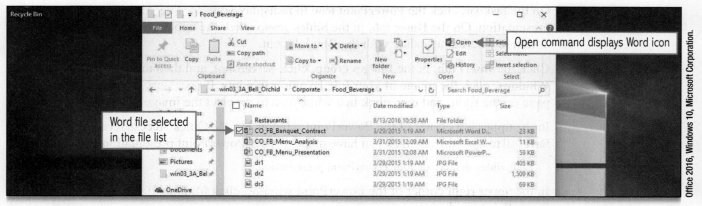

Open command displays Word icon

Word file selected in the file list

FIGURE 3.29

3 Maximize ▢ the **Food_Beverage** folder window. On the **Home tab**, in the **Open group**, click the **Open button arrow**.

When you open a file from the file list, Windows 10 uses the file extension of the file to determine which program to use to open the file. For most files, such as a Word document, Windows 10 not only determines which program to use to open the file, but also displays the icon representing the program on the Open button.

On the Open button, you can see by the icon which program will be used to open the file. If you are unfamiliar with an icon, click the Open button *arrow* to display the name of the program associated with the icon that will open the file.

4 On the list, view the program names, click **Choose another app**, and then if necessary, click **More apps**. Compare your screen with Figure 3.30.

The *How do you want to open this file?* dialog box displays. Here you can view the file extension for a file. For a file created in Microsoft Word, the file extension is *.docx*. For most files, you will probably open the file in the program in which it was created. Two programs on this computer that can open a file with a .docx extension are Word and *WordPad*—a simple word processing program that comes with Windows 10.

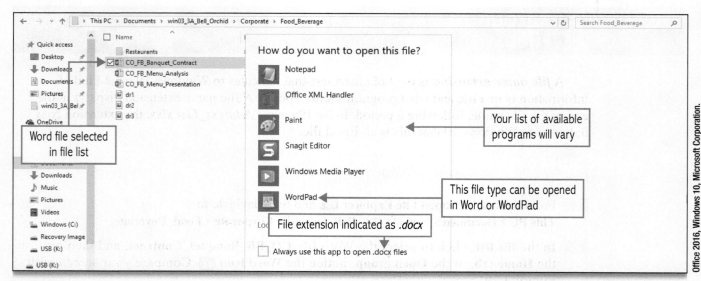

Word file selected in file list

How do you want to open this file?

Your list of available programs will vary

This file type can be opened in Word or WordPad

File extension indicated as *.docx*

FIGURE 3.30

5 Press Esc to cancel the dialog box. In the **file list**, select the file **CO_FB_Menu_Presentation**. On the ribbon, in the **Open group**, notice the **Microsoft PowerPoint icon** displays on the **Open** button. Click the **Open button arrow**, and then click **Choose another app**.

By viewing the information next to *Always use this app to open...*, you can see that the file extension for a file created with Microsoft PowerPoint is *.pptx*.

6 Press Esc to cancel the dialog box. Click the **View tab**, and then in the **Show/hide** group, select the **File name extensions** check box. In the upper right corner, click **Restore Down** ⧉ to restore the window down to its previous size.

⟳ **ANOTHER WAY** To display file extensions, on the View tab, click Options to display the Folder Options dialog box. On the View tab, under Advanced settings, click to clear the Hide extensions for known file types check box, and then click OK.

7 In the **Food_Beverage** window, in the **file list**, point to the *Name* column heading, right-click, and then click **Size Column to Fit**. Compare your screen with Figure 3.31.

By default, Windows 10 hides file name extensions to make file names easier to read. If for any reason you need to do so, you can choose to make extensions visible by changing this default setting on the ribbon or in the Folder Options dialog box.

On your screen, you can see that displaying the file extensions results in a list of file names that are more difficult to read.

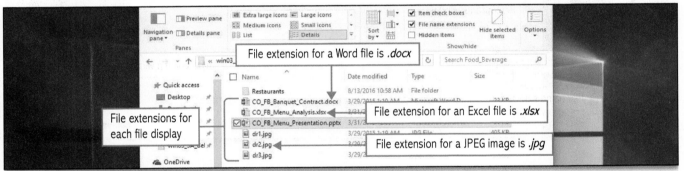

FIGURE 3.31

Office 2016, Windows 10, Microsoft Corporation.

8 On the taskbar, click the **PowerPoint icon** to redisplay your **3A_File_Management** presentation. On the **Home tab**, in the **Slides group**, click the upper portion of the **New Slide** button to insert a new slide with the Blank layout.

9 Click the **Insert tab**, in the **Images group**, click **Screenshot**, and then under **Available Windows,** click the image of your File Explorer window. Click in a white area to deselect the image.

10 In the upper left corner of the PowerPoint window, on the Quick Access toolbar, click **Save** 🖫 to save the changes you have made to your PowerPoint presentation.

Five slides display in your PowerPoint presentation.

11 In the upper right corner of the PowerPoint window, click **Minimize** ⊟ to minimize the PowerPoint window.

12 Leave your **Food_Beverage** window displayed for the next Activity.

1 ▶ Double-click **Restaurants** to open its window. On the **View tab**, be sure the **Layout** is **Details**. If necessary, click the column heading *Name* so that the column is sorted alphabetically.

2 ▶ Right-click the *Name* column heading, and then click **Size Column to Fit**. Right-click the *Type* column heading, and then click **Size Column to Fit**.

Because the Type column displays in a window in Details view, and because file names commonly display an identifying icon, for most individuals, there is probably no need to display the file extensions.

3 ▶ Click to select the Word file **Brunch_Menus.docx**, and then click the file again to select the file name. Notice that only the file name, and not the file extension, is selected. Compare your screen with Figure 3.32.

Usually, file extensions should *not* be changed, because you might not be able to open or edit the file after doing so. Because Windows 10 keeps track of which file is associated with which program—referred to as the ***file association***—you do not have to be concerned about typing a file extension when you name a new file.

Here you can see that even if you choose to display file extensions, Windows 10 will help you avoid changing the file extension by only highlighting the portion of the name that you would normally rename.

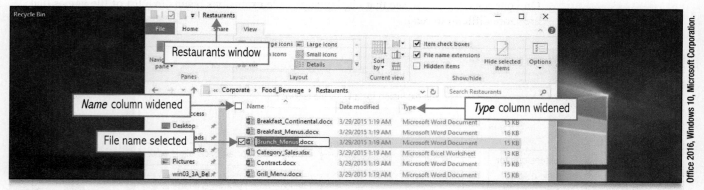

FIGURE 3.32

> **NOTE** Sometimes It Is Useful to Change a File Extension
>
> There are times when it is useful to change a file extension; for example, when you want to change a text file (.txt) to an HTML file (.htm) so that you can view it in a Web browser. Delete the file extension and type the new one. Windows 10 will warn you that changing the file name extension might cause the file to become unusable. Click Yes if you are certain that the extension you typed is appropriate for your file.

4 ▶ On the **View tab**, in the **Show/hide group**, click to deselect the **File name extensions** check box.

In the file list of the Restaurants folder window, the file extensions no longer display; they are hidden.

5 ▶ Maximize ☐ the folder window. In the **address bar**, to the right of **Corporate**, click ›, and then on the displayed list, click **Information_Technology**. Display the **Future_Hotels** window. If necessary, set the **Layout** to **Details**.

6 ▶ Select the JPG file **Italy**. On the **Home tab**, in the **Open group**, click the **Open button arrow**, and then click **Choose another app**. Notice the icon for each program, and then compare your screen with Figure 3.33.

Images differ somewhat from other files in that there may be two or more programs on your computer that can display them. If a program has already been selected on the computer you are using, you might see a message *Keep using...* with the program name.

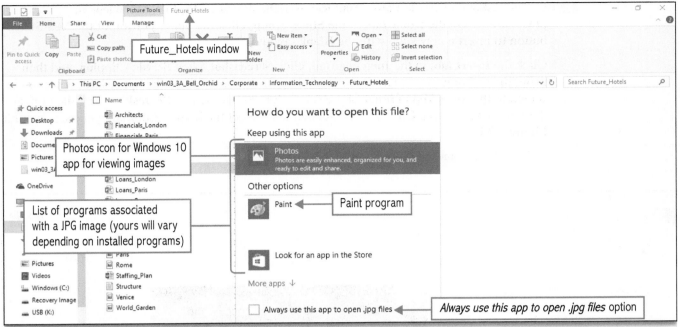

FIGURE 3.33

Office 2016, Windows 10, Microsoft Corporation.

ANOTHER WAY   In the file list, point to the file Italy, right-click, point to Open with, and then click Choose another app.

7 On the list, click **Paint**, and then click **OK** to display the photo in the Paint app. Then, in the upper right corner of the displayed photo of Venice, click **Close** ⊠.

8 In the **file list**, click the JPG file **Paris**. Click the **Open button arrow**, and then on the list, click **Photos**. In the upper right corner of the displayed photo, click **See more** ▦. Compare your screen with Figure 3.34.

The photo of flowers in Paris opens in the Windows 10 Photos app, which is the Windows 10 default app for opening pictures from File Explorer. Commands in the upper right corner enable you to Share the photo, display the photo in Slideshow mode, edit the photo, and rotate the photo. By clicking the See more button, you have additional commands that you can use with this image file.

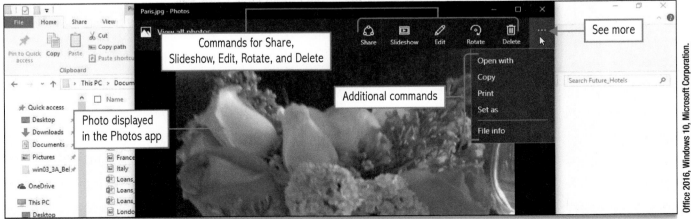

FIGURE 3.34

Office 2016, Windows 10, Microsoft Corporation.

9 On the taskbar, click the **PowerPoint icon** to redisplay your **3A_File_Management** presentation. On the **Home tab**, in the **Slides group**, click the upper portion of the **New Slide** button to insert a new slide with the Blank layout.

10 Click the **Insert tab**, in the **Images group**, click **Screenshot**, click **Screen Clipping**, and then using the techniques you have practiced, drag the + pointer from the upper left corner of the screen to the lower right corner of the screen but do not include the taskbar, and then release the left mouse button. Click in a white area to deselect the image. Compare your screen with Figure 3.35.

> Your PowerPoint presentation contains six slides.

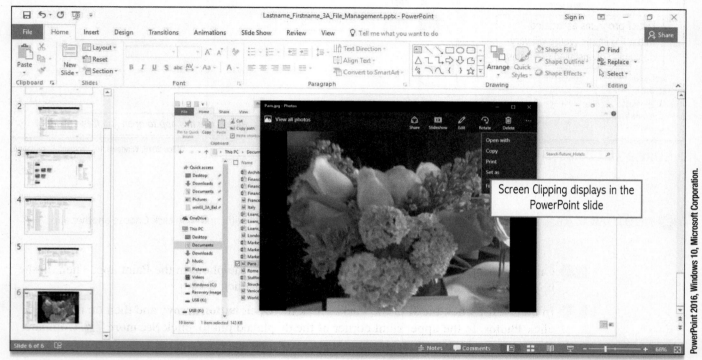

Screen Clipping displays in the PowerPoint slide

PowerPoint 2016, Windows 10, Microsoft Corporation.

FIGURE 3.35

11 Close ⊠ the PowerPoint window; when prompted, click **Save**.

12 In the upper right corner of the displayed photo, click **Close** ⊠.

> On the ribbon, the Photos icon displays on the Open button. In this manner, you can use different programs to open image files.

13 In the upper right corner of the window, click **Restore Down** ⬚, and then **Close** ✕ the **Future_Hotels** window.

14 On the right end of the taskbar, click the **Action Center** button ▨, at the bottom click **All settings**, click **System**, and then on the left, click **Default apps**. On the right, scroll as necessary to view the lower portion of the dialog box, and then click **Choose default apps by file type**. Compare your screen with Figure 3.36.

Here you can choose default apps by file type.

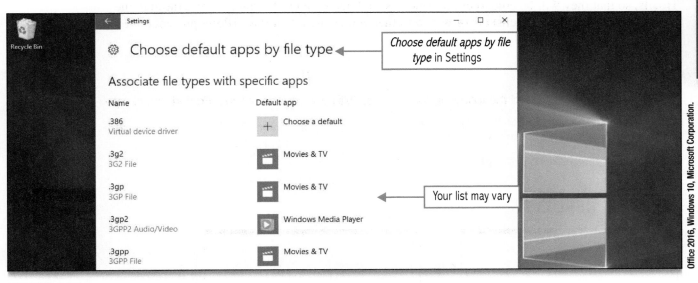

FIGURE 3.36

15 **Close** ✕ the **Settings** window; if necessary, close any other open windows.

16 As directed by your instructor, submit your PowerPoint presentation as evidence of your work on this Project.

More **Knowledge** **Wrong Program? What if the wrong program loads a file or if no program will open a file?**

In most instances, when you open a file from File Explorer, Windows 10 automatically knows which program should open the file because of the file extension. If a program other than the one you intended opens your file, close the program, display the folder window, right-click the file, click Open with, and then in the displayed dialog box, use the techniques you have practiced to set a default program for this type of file.

End | You have completed Project 3A

Using Advanced Search Techniques

In Activities 3.10 through 3.20 you will train with Steven Ramos and Barbara Hewitt, employees in the Information Technology Department at the headquarters office of Bell Orchid Hotels, so that they will be able to use advanced search techniques. As you progress through the Project, you will insert screenshots of windows that you create into a PowerPoint presentation similar to Figure 3.37.

PROJECT FILES

For Project 3B, you will need the following files:

win03_3B_Bell_Orchid folder from the student data files that accompany this textbook

A new blank PowerPoint presentation

You will save your results in a PowerPoint file as:

Lastname_Firstname_3B_Advanced_Search

PROJECT RESULTS

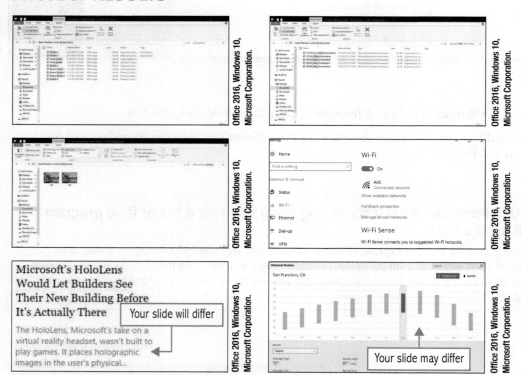

FIGURE 3.37 Project 3B Using Advanced Search Techniques

Your documents, music, videos, photos, and email messages are created, stored, and accessed in electronic form on your computer, resulting in an ever-increasing number of files. Large hard drives and the ability to store files in the cloud make it increasingly challenging to keep track of your computer files, regardless of how careful you are when organizing your files in a structure of folders.

Rely on Windows 10 search features to help you find what you are looking for. If you can remember any detail about a file or a saved email message that you need to access—for example, when it was created or some of its content—Windows 10 can find it for you quickly. Additionally, Windows 10 can help you visualize your files by arranging them in various ways; for example, by date or by author name.

Recall that every File Explorer window contains a search box in which you can enter part of a word, a complete word, or a phrase. The search feature immediately searches file names, *file properties*—also called *metadata*—and text within each file, and then returns results instantly. File properties display information about your files, such as the name of the author and the date that the file was last modified. Metadata is the data that describes other data. For example, the collective group of a file's properties, such as its title, subject, author, and file size, comprise that file's metadata.

Three features define the search capabilities in Windows 10:

- *Search is everywhere.* You are never more than a few keystrokes away from what you are looking for, because a search box displays in every window and you can also search from the search box on the taskbar and with Cortana.

- *Search is fast.* Recall that Windows 10 produces search results almost instantly because it employs an *index*, which is a collection of detailed information about the files on your computer. When you start a search for a file, Windows 10 searches this summary information in the index rather than searching file by file on your hard disk drive or OneDrive.

- *Any search can be saved.* You can save any search that you conduct in File Explorer and then rerun that search. The results will include any new files that meet the search criteria since the last time the search was conducted. In this manner, the search that you rerun is said to be *live*. By default, a saved search is saved in the Searches folder, which is one of your personal folders. This folder is not shown by default on the navigation pane, but you can pin it there if you need to save numerous searches.

Activity 3.10 | Adding Tags to Files

Recall that a *tag* is a property that you create and add to a file. Tags help you to find and organize your files, because you can include a tag in a search of your files.

1 Sign in to your computer and display the **desktop**. From the taskbar, open **File Explorer** 📁. (If necessary, search for, and then pin, File Explorer to the taskbar.)

2 From the student data files for Chapter 3—**win10_03_Student_Data_Files**—that you downloaded from www.pearsonhighered.com/go or obtained from your instructor, copy the folder **win03_3B_Bell_Orchid** to the **Documents** folder on your hard drive. If necessary, on the View tab, in the Show/hide group, select Item check boxes so that a checkmark displays and the feature is active.

3 Navigate to **Documents > win03_3B_Bell_Orchid > Montecito > Activities**, and then **Maximize** ☐ the folder window. On the **View tab**, in the **Panes group**, click **Details pane**, and if necessary set the **Layout** to **Details**. Click one time to select the Word file **Fishing**, and then compare your screen with Figure 3.38.

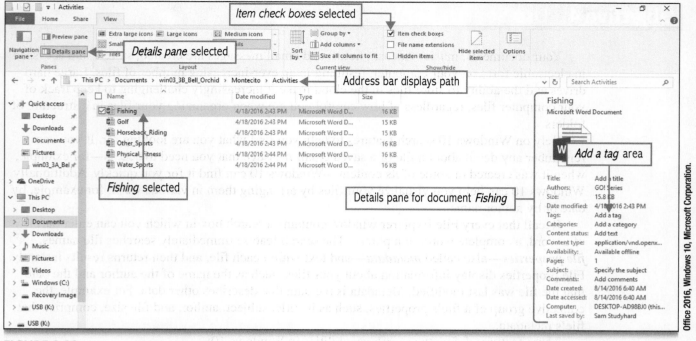

FIGURE 3.38

> **4** In the **Details pane**, to the right of *Tags*, click **Add a tag**, type **Fishing** and then at the bottom of the pane, click **Save** or press [Enter].

🔄 **ANOTHER WAY**   To add a tag, right-click the file name, click Properties, click the Details tab, under Description, click Tags, type the new tag, press [Enter], and then click OK.

> **5** In the **file list**, click the Word file **Golf**, and then use the technique you just practiced to add the tag **Golf** to this file.

> **6** Select the file **Other_Sports**, and then add the tag **Volleyball** Select the file **Water_Sports**, add then add the tag **Water Sports**

NOTE   Adding Tags to Multiple Word Files

You can select a group of Word files in the file list and the Details pane will indicate that all the files in the group are selected. Then you can add the same tag to the selected group.

> **7** On the **address bar**, to the right of **Montecito**, click **>**, and then on the list click **Photos** to display this folder window. Be sure the **Layout** is set to **Large icons**. Select the file **Fly Fishing 1**, and then in the **Details pane**, to the right of *Tags*, click **Add a tag**. Begin by typing **F** and when the list of possible tags displays, click the **Fishing** check box. At the bottom of the **Details pane**, click the **Save** button or press [Enter].

> After a tag is created, you can select it from a list in this manner.

ALERT!   Tags Can Vary Depending on Recent Use of Your Computer

The list of possible tags that displays on the computer you are using can vary depending on previous usage. Pictures on the computer that have been downloaded from other sources might have tags that will display on the list.

8 Select the file **Golf 1**, hold down Ctrl and select the file **Golf 2**. Release Ctrl. With both files selected, in the **Details pane**, add the tag **Golf** to the two selected items, and then at the bottom click **Save** or press Enter. Notice that as soon as you begin typing you will be able to select the tag from a list.

9 Scroll up as necessary, select the file **Beach Sports 3**, hold down Ctrl, and then select **Beach Sports 4**. In the **Details pane**, notice that *2 items* are selected. Click in the **Tags** box, type **V** and then from the displayed list of existing tags, click **Volleyball** to add this tag to both files. Press Enter, or at the bottom of the pane, click **Save**.

10 Select the file **Beach Sports 1**, hold down Ctrl and select the file **Beach Sports 2**. While holding down Ctrl, scroll down by using the scroll bar so the two files remain selected, and then select **Surfing 1**, and **Surfing 2**. In the **Details pane**, notice that *4 items selected* displays. Release Ctrl, click in the **Tags** box, add the tag **Water Sports** and press Enter or at the bottom of the pane click **Save**. Compare your screen with Figure 3.39.

Use the Ctrl key to select a group of files and then add the same tag to each.

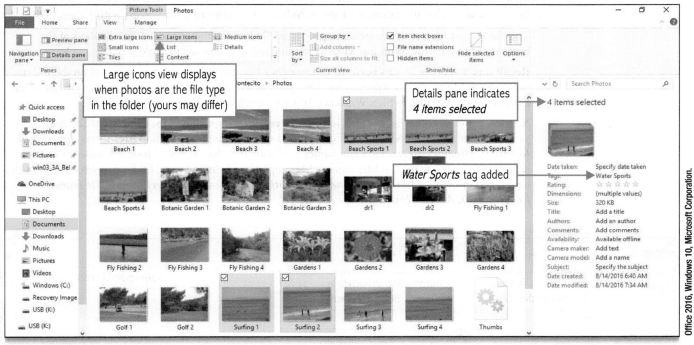

FIGURE 3.39

11 Select the files **Tours 1** and **Tours 2**. Add the tag **Tours** to these two files, then press Enter or click **Save**.

12 By using the techniques you have just practiced, add the tag **Santa Barbara** to the following four files: **Beach 1**, **Beach 4**, **Gardens 1** and **Gardens 3**.

13 Navigate to **Montecito ▸ Tours**. To the Word file **Tours**, add the tag **Tours** and press Enter.

Recall that the list of possible tags that displays will vary depending on previous usage of your computer.

14 On the **View tab**, in the **Panes group**, click **Details pane** to close the pane. In the upper right corner, click **Restore Down** ☐ and then **Close** ☒ all open windows.

Activity 3.11 | Clearing Search History and Refining a Search by Using the Tags Property

Windows 10 will search all of the files in the current folder window for whatever you type in the search box. In the indexed locations, it will search by looking in the file name, file contents, and file properties—including tags. For example, if you type *April*, Windows 10 will find any file that contains *April* in the file name, in the file contents, in the tag, or authored by someone named *April*.

If you want to search more selectively, you can refine your search in the search box by specifying which file property to search. To refine by a file property, separate the name of the property and the search term with a colon.

1 ▶ Open **File Explorer** 📁, and then navigate to **Documents ▸ win03_3B_Bell_Orchid**.

2 ▶ **Maximize** ☐ the window. In the upper right corner, click in the **search** box to activate the **Search Tools** on the ribbon. In the **Options group**, click **Recent searches** if it is not dimmed, and then at the bottom of the list, click **Clear search history**.

> This action will clear any recent searches conducted at the computer you are using.

3 ▶ In the search box, type **water** and then on the **View tab**, if necessary, change the **Layout** to **Content**. In the displayed **water – Search Results in win03_3B_Bell_Orchid** window, at the bottom of the window, notice the number of items indicated. Compare your screen with Figure 3.40.

> The number of files with one or more properties that match the criteria *water* displays at the bottom of the window. With the window maximized, you can see the folder path.

> Recall that Windows 10 can perform fast searches because the search is conducted on the *index*, not on each file on the hard disk drive. The index is a collection of detailed information about the files on your computer, which Windows 10 keeps track of and stores.

> Your Documents folder is included in the **Indexed locations**, which includes *all* of the folders in your personal folder (Documents, Pictures, and so on), email, and offline files if any. *In indexed locations, Windows 10 searches file names and contents*; that is, it will look for matches to your search term in file names, folder names, file properties including tags, folder properties, and in the actual text content of files. *In non-indexed locations, Windows 10 searches only file names and folder names. A USB flash drive is not indexed.*

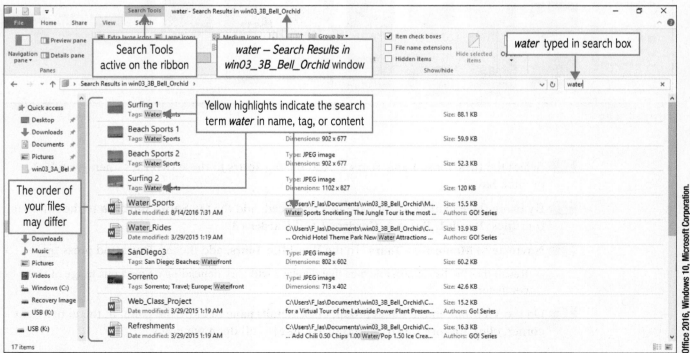

FIGURE 3.40

4 In the **search** box, click ✕ to clear the search.

5 On the **Search tab**, in the **Refine group**, click **Other properties**, click **Tags**, and then notice that the **search** box displays *tags:*.

6 With the insertion point blinking to the right of *tags:*, type **water** Click the **View tab**, and then in the **Layout group**, click **Details**. Right-click any column name and then if necessary, click **Tags**. Right-click the *Tags* column heading and click **Size Column to Fit**. Right-click the *Name* column and click **Size Column to Fit**.

> The Tags column displays in the file list, and in this view, the Folder path column is added. You can refine a search by searching only on the tags attached to files. Within all the subfolders in the Bell_Orchid folder, seven items have *water* as part of their tag, and in the Tags column, *water* is highlighted.

🔄 **ANOTHER WAY**   In the search box, type tags:water and then arrange the display in the file list the way you want it.

7 In the list of files that matched the search criteria, look at the tag for the files **SanDiego3** and **Sorrento**. Notice that *Waterfront* is among the tags attached to these two files, and thus these files are considered a match. Compare your screen with Figure 3.41.

> By default, Windows 10 uses ***partial matching***—matching to part of a word or phrase rather than to whole words. Thus, *waterfront* is a match for the criteria *water*. If you prefer to search by whole words only, use quote marks around the whole word.

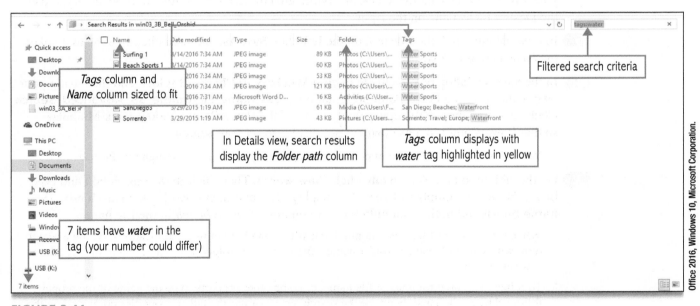

FIGURE 3.41

8 In the **search** box, click ✕ to clear the search. On the **Search tab**, in the **Refine group**, click **Other properties**, and then click **Tags**. In the search box, with the insertion point blinking after *tags:*, type **water sports**

> Five items display in the Search Results folder window. The files that match the criteria are those in the win03_3B_Bell_Orchid folder that have the exact tag *water sports*. Additionally, the word *Sports* is highlighted in yellow in the file names where it occurs.

9 Clear ☒ the **search** box, click **Other properties**, click **Tags**, and then type **golf**

Three files display.

10 On the ribbon, on the **Search tab**, click **Close search**.

Activity 3.12 | Refining a Search by Using the Name and Camera Properties

Recall that to refine a search by a file property, in the search box separate the name of the property and the search term with a colon. In this Activity, you will search by using the Name property and the Camera property. You can use this technique to refine a search by any property.

1 In the upper right corner, click in the **search** box to activate the **Search Tools** on the ribbon. In the **Refine group**, click **Other properties**, click **Name**, and then type **surfing**

Four files that contain *surfing* in the file name display. *Name* is a property that you can use as criteria to refine a search. The search is conducted only on file names.

2 Clear ☒ the **search** box, click **Other properties**, click **Name**, and then type **garden** Set the **View** to **Details**. Size the *Name* column to fit.

Nine items contain *garden* somewhere in the file name.

3 From the taskbar, open a new blank PowerPoint presentation, set the **Layout** to **Blank**, and then click the **Insert tab**.

4 In the **Images group**, click **Screenshot**, and then under **Available Windows**, click the image of your File Explorer window. Click in a white area to deselect the image. If necessary, close the Design Ideas pane on the right.

5 In PowerPoint, click the **File tab**, on the left click **Save As**, and then click **Browse** to display the **Save As** dialog box.

6 In the **Save As** dialog box, navigate to your **Windows 10 Chapter 3** folder, and then using your own name, save the PowerPoint presentation as **Lastname_Firstname_3B_Advanced_Search** Click **Save**, and then in the upper right corner of the PowerPoint window, click **Minimize** ☐ so that PowerPoint remains open but not displayed on your screen.

You will need your PowerPoint presentation again as you progress through this Project.

7 On the ribbon, on the **Search tab**, click **Close search**. Then click in the **search** box and type **beach** Notice the number of files that display (27), and then **Clear** ☒ the **search** box. Type **name:beach** and notice that only *9 items* contain the word *beach* in the file name.

When searching for files, keep in mind that when searching in indexed locations, typing a search term will search file names, folder names, file properties, folder properties, and in the actual text content of files.

To refine the search for a tag, a file name, or some other property, type the name of the property followed by a colon and then type the search term—or use the Other properties command on the ribbon to insert the property without typing it.

8 Clear ☒ the **search** box, and then type **camera:canon** In the list of files that match the search criteria, right-click the file **Gardens 3**, and then on the shortcut menu, click **Properties**. In the displayed dialog box, click the **Details tab**, drag the scroll box down about half way, and then compare your screen with Figure 3.42.

There are numerous properties for picture files, many of which are applied to the file by the camera's software.

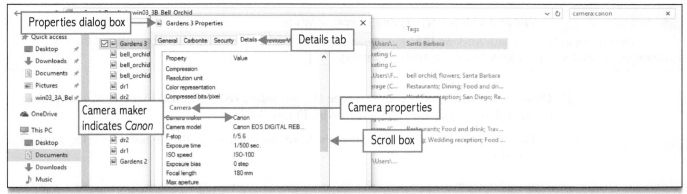

FIGURE 3.42

9 At the bottom of the **Gardens 3 Properties** dialog box, click **Cancel**. On the **View tab**, if necessary, set the **Layout** to **Details**.

10 In the **file list**, point to the column heading *Name*, and then right-click. At the bottom of the shortcut menu, click **More**. Take a moment to scroll down the list and examine the properties that might be assigned to a file by one or more software programs.

> CDs and DVDs usually have various tags so that you can search by Artist or Genre—for example Jazz or Classical. Software programs such as those from a digital camera or a video camera commonly attach numerous properties to a file to make it easy to find the files based on specific technical details such as *F-stop*.

> Likewise, properties such as *Cell phone* and *Business phone* are assigned by contact management programs such as Microsoft Outlook.

11 **Close** ☒ the **Choose Details** dialog box, and then on the ribbon, on the **Search tab**, click **Close search**.

More Knowledge | **What's the Difference Between a Tag and a Property?**

A tag is simply another type of property, but one that *you* create and add to a file. Whereas most file properties are added by either Windows 10 or the software that creates the file, a tag is probably the most useful property, because you can add tags that contain words or phrases that are meaningful to you.

An increasing number of software programs enable you to add tags at the time you create and save your file, which will enable you to rely more on tag searches to find what you are looking for. For example, in the Microsoft Office programs, you can add tags directly in the Save As dialog box at the time you save the file. Or, you can add tags in Backstage view.

Activity 3.13 | **Refining a Search by Using Boolean Operators and Quotes**

In addition to refining by various properties, you can also refine a search by using the *Boolean operators* AND, OR, and NOT. The term Boolean is taken from the name George Boole, who was a 19th century mathematician. Boole developed the mathematics of logic that govern the logical functions—true and false. A statement using Boolean operators expresses a condition that is either true or false. You can also use quotes to search for an exact phrase in a file.

1 With your File Explorer window still maximized, if necessary navigate to **Documents > win03_3B_Bell_Orchid**. Click in the **search** box and type **shareholders AND orlando**

> Boolean filters such as AND must be typed in all uppercase letters. The *AND filter* finds files that contain both the word *shareholders* and the word *orlando*—even if those words are not next to each other.

> As you type *shareholders*, Windows 10 begins refining the search based on the search term found in file names, folder names, file properties, folder properties, and in the actual text content of files. After you refine the search by typing *AND orlando*, the search is narrowed down to one file.

> You can see that if you know something about the contents or name of the file you are looking for, it might be easier to search for the file than to navigate your folder structure.

Windows 10 Search Ignores Capitalization

You need not capitalize to have Windows 10 find your search term. For example, you can type *orlando* instead of *Orlando*. However, you must use uppercase letters for the Boolean operators.

2 Clear ⊠ the **search** box, and then type **shareholders NOT orlando** Size the *Name* column to fit, and then compare your screen with Figure 3.43.

The *NOT filter* finds files that contain the word *shareholders* but that do not contain the word *orlando*.

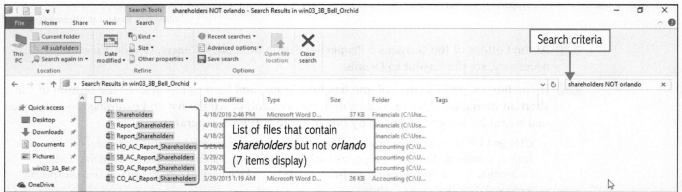

FIGURE 3.43

3 Clear ⊠ the **search** box, and then type **shareholders OR orlando**

A total of 49 items display. The *OR filter* finds files that contain either the word *shareholders* or the word *orlando*. Because either of the conditions can be present, OR typically produces a large number of results, but the OR filter will assist you in refining your search nonetheless.

4 Clear ⊠ the **search** box, and then including the quote marks, type **"teenage restaurant workers"**

One file—*Kitchen_Safety*—displays. The exact phrase *teenage restaurant workers* is contained within the text of this document.

The *quotes filter* finds files that contain the exact phrase placed within the quotes. You can see that if you know just a little about what you are looking for, refined searches can help you find files quickly without navigating a folder structure.

Files on a USB Drive Are Not Indexed

You can search for files and folders on a USB drive, but these drives are not indexed. So the search will *not* be conducted on the *contents* of the files.

5 Clear ⊠ the **search** box. On the **Search tab**, in the **Refine group**, click **Other properties**, and then click **Type**. In the search box type **pptx** and notice that only PowerPoint files display.

File *type* is one of the properties on which you can search. You can use the file extension associated with a program as the search criteria, or you can type the program name, for example *PowerPoint*.

6 Press Spacebar one time, and then continue typing so that the **search** box criteria indicates **type:pptx AND name:safety** Size the *Name* column to fit, size the *Type* column to fit, be sure the Name column is sorted in ascending order, and then compare your screen with Figure 3.44.

In this manner, you can combine different properties with Boolean operators to locate a file. Five items meet this criteria; that is, each file is a PowerPoint file and contains the word *safety* in the file name.

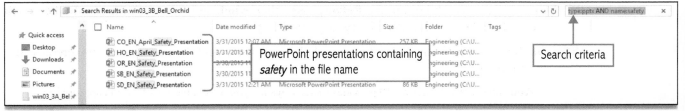

PowerPoint presentations containing
safety in the file name

Search criteria

FIGURE 3.44

PowerPoint 2016, Windows 10, Microsoft Corporation.

7 From the taskbar, open your PowerPoint presentation, add a new slide using the Blank layout, and then insert a screenshot of this File Explorer window. On the Quick Access toolbar, click **Save** 🖫. **Minimize** – your PowerPoint window.

8 **Clear** ✕ the **search** box, and then type **type:.jpg** and notice your results include 88 JPEG files. **Clear** ✕ the **search** box, and then type **type:.tif** and notice that your results include three TIFF files.

9 **Clear** ✕ the **search** box, type **type:.jpg OR type:.tif** and then click on the *Type* column heading to sort the files alphabetically by Type. Notice your results include 88 JPEG files and 3 TIFF files, for a total of 91 items.

10 On the **Search tab**, click **Close search**.

Activity 3.14 | Refining a Search by Kind

1 Click in the **search** box to activate **Search Tools**. In the **Refine group**, click **Kind**.

Refine your search by Kind when you want to locate a specific kind of file; for example, an e-mail message, a music file, or a contact.

2 On the list, click **Document**.

Microsoft Office files—Word, Excel, and PowerPoint—display because they are considered a kind of document. Additionally, one Text document displays.

3 With the insertion point blinking in the **search** box, type **:cheese** Be sure the Name column is sorted in alphabetical order, and then compare your screen with Figure 3.45.

Within Documents, seven files contain the word *cheese* somewhere in the text of the document.

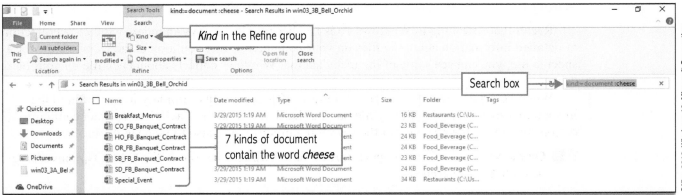

Kind in the Refine group

Search box

7 kinds of document
contain the word *cheese*

FIGURE 3.45

Office 2016, Windows 10, Microsoft Corporation.

4 Clear ✕ the **search** box. In the **Refine group**, click **Kind**, and then click **Picture**. In the **search** box, refine the search further by typing **:wedding**

5 On the **View tab**, in the **Layout group**, click **Large icons**, and then compare your screen with Figure 3.46.

You can see that Windows 10 provides many ways for you to find the files that you are looking for.

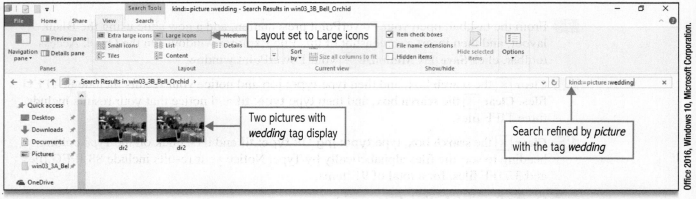

FIGURE 3.46

6 From the taskbar, open your PowerPoint presentation, add a new slide using the Blank layout, and then insert a screenshot of this File Explorer window. On the Quick Access toolbar, click **Save** 🖫. **Minimize** ▭ your PowerPoint window.

7 On the **View tab**, in the **Layout group**, click **Details**. Click the **Search tab**, and then click **Close search**.

More Knowledge | **Saving a Search**

After you have built a search, you can save it. When you save a search, you are saving its criteria, not its current results. After the search is saved, it becomes a **virtual folder**—a folder that does not represent a physical location—in the Searches folder in your personal folder. To save a search, conduct your search, and then on the Search tab, in the Options group, click Save search. In the displayed Save As dialog box, click Save to accept the default name.

Activity 3.15 | Managing Search Behavior and Managing the Index

Recall that searching in Windows 10 is fast because it employs an index, which is a collection of detailed information about the files on your computer. When you look at the Details pane for a specific file, you can see some of the metadata that Windows collects about each file on your hard drive.

When you start a search for a file, Windows 10 searches this summary information in the index rather than searching file by file on your hard disk drive or OneDrive. You can configure options to control the behavior of the search feature itself and also to manage the index.

1 On the **View tab**, click the upper portion of the **Options** button. In the **Folder Options** dialog box, click the **Search tab**.

Here you can manage how the Search feature behaves. You can make changes to how the search is conducted and include additional files and directories when searching non-indexed locations. You will probably want to maintain the default settings.

2 At the bottom of the **Folder Options** dialog box, click **Cancel**.

3 In the upper right corner, click **Restore Down** 🗗, and then **Close** ✕ the window.

4 On the right end of the taskbar, click **Action Center** 🖵, at the bottom click **All settings**, and then click **System**.

5 In the **Find a setting** box, type **index** and then click **Indexing Options**. Notice that if you use Outlook as your email client, your emails will also be indexed. Compare your screen with Figure 3.47.

At the top of this dialog box, you can see if your index is up to date. For example, if you just added a number of new folders and files—perhaps by copying them into your Documents folder from another source—you might have to wait a short time for the index to be complete.

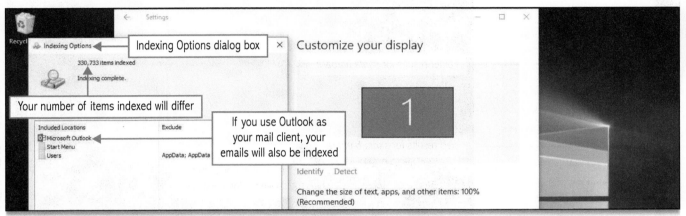

Office 2016, Windows 10, Microsoft Corporation.

FIGURE 3.47

6 Close ⨯ the **Indexing Options** dialog box and the **Settings** window.

Objective 5   Use the Taskbar Search Box and Search with Cortana

Search boxes in Windows are in two different places—File Explorer windows and the main search box on the taskbar.

As you have practiced in the previous Activities, searching in File Explorer is limited to files—it does not conduct a search for apps or for websites or for settings. And File Explorer search is conducted only on the files and folders contained in the window in which you are searching. So, for example, if you have the Bell Orchid Corporate folder window displayed, Windows will search only the files, folders, and subfolders within that location.

The search box located at the left end of the taskbar searches both your computer and the Web simultaneously (unless you disable that feature).

Activity 3.16 | Searching for Files by Using the Taskbar Search Box

The taskbar search box is labeled either *Search the web and Windows* or *Ask me anything*—depending on whether or not you have enabled Cortana on your computer. The Bing search engine provides the fast power for Windows 10 to locate items on your computer, in connected storage locations, and on the Web.

To position your insertion point in the search box, either click in the search box or press ⊞ to simultaneously display the Start menu and position the insertion point in the search box.

> **NOTE**
>
> For this Activity, Cortana is enabled. If you do not have Cortana enabled, your search results may differ slightly.

1 ▶ Close any open windows or apps. Press ⊞ to display the Start menu and place the insertion point in the search box. Type **santa barbara** and then compare your screen with Figure 3.48.

> Windows displays *likely* results—there is not enough space to show all results—from both your system and on the Web.

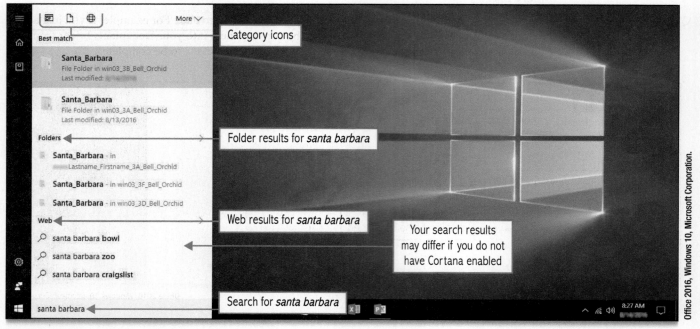

FIGURE 3.48

2 ▶ In the search results, click **Folders**, point to the first folder on the list, and then compare your screen with Figure 3.49.

> Folders that contain the text *santa barbara* in the title display. The search is conducted on your entire Personal folder, not just on the Bell Orchid folder. If you point to a folder name, details about the folder's location display.

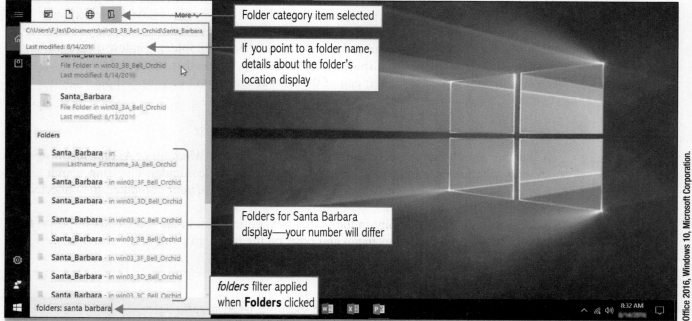

FIGURE 3.49

3 At the top of the search results pane, in the row of category icons, click **More**, on the displayed list click Photos ▨, and then compare your screen with Figure 3.50.

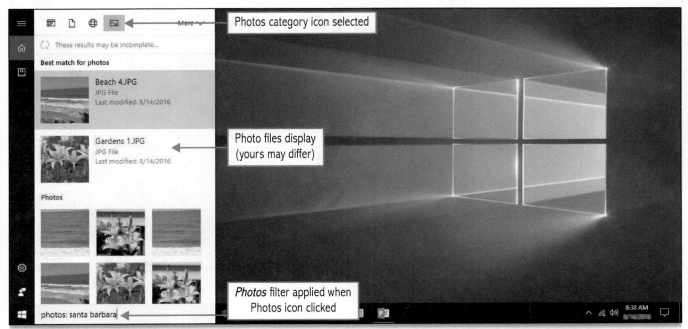

Photos category icon selected

Photo files display (yours may differ)

Photos filter applied when Photos icon clicked

FIGURE 3.50

Office 2016, Windows 10, Microsoft Corporation.

4 Point to one of the photos to view a ScreenTip; you may have duplicate photos because there are similar photos for each project.

5 Point to any photo, right-click, and then click **Open file location** to display the File Explorer window containing the photo you selected.

You may decide this is an easier way to search for files and folders rather than using the search techniques in File Explorer.

6 **Close** ⊠ the File Explorer window.

7 Press 🪟 to position the insertion point in the search box, type **spa** and then at the top of the search pane, click **More** to view the list of category icons as shown in Figure 3.51.

You can click any of the category icons to narrow your search for the type of file you are looking for.

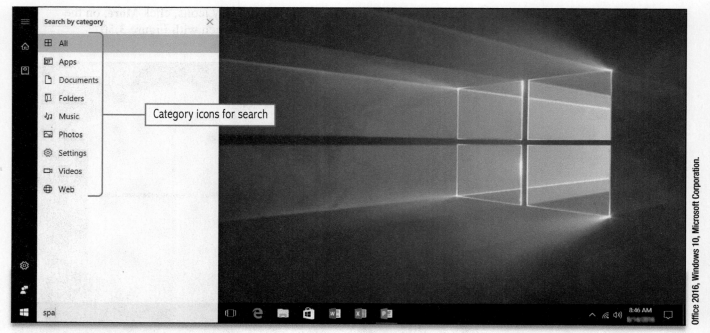

Category icons for search

FIGURE 3.51

8 Click the **Documents** category and then point to one of the PowerPoint presentations; notice that you can see details about the file before you open it. Then click one of the PowerPoint presentations.

You can see how easy it is to find files quickly using the taskbar search box.

9 In the PowerPoint window, click the **File tab**, and then on the left click **Close**. Your PowerPoint presentation for this Project remains open on the taskbar.

Activity 3.17 | Searching for Settings by Using the Taskbar Search Box

> **NOTE**
>
> For this Activity, Cortana is enabled. If you do not have Cortana enabled, your search results may differ slightly.

> **ALERT!** **Windows 10 Is an Evolving Operating System**
>
> Like all modern operating systems, Windows 10 is constantly evolving with new features, updates, and security enhancements. Therefore, you may encounter occasional differences in techniques and screens as you progress through the Projects. You can often look at the screens in Windows 10 to determine how to complete steps, or you can search for information about new features.

1 Click in the taskbar search box—if you have Cortana enabled you might see some action by Cortana above the search box. Type **wi-fi settings** and then at the top of the search results pane, click **More**. On the list of category icons, click **Settings** . Compare your screen with Figure 3.52.

You can filter results by selecting one of the Category icons. Here, you can go directly to the setting on your computer to change or view the wi-fi settings.

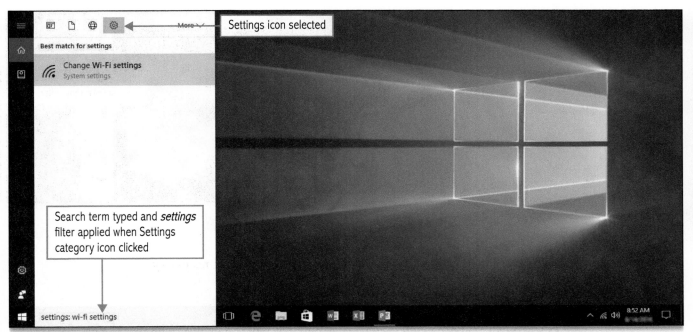

FIGURE 3.52

Office 2016, Windows 10, Microsoft Corporation.

2 ▶ Under **Best match for settings,** click **Change Wi-Fi Settings System settings**.

3 ▶ From the taskbar, open your PowerPoint presentation, add a new slide, and then on the **Insert tab,** click **Screenshot.** Click **Screen Clipping,** move the mouse to display the + pointer, position the + pointer in the upper left corner of the **Settings** window, and then drag down and to the right to capture only the white **Settings** window. Release the mouse button to place the clipping in your PowerPoint slide. On the Quick Access toolbar, click **Save** [□]. **Minimize** [–] your PowerPoint window.

4 ▶ **Close** [×] **Settings**.

Activity 3.18 | Searching in the Windows Store

The Windows Store is where you find and download both free and paid apps. Because your Windows 10 settings move with you from device to device, any app you install will always be available to you—on any device—so long as you sign in with your Microsoft account. The app will automatically scale to fit the device screen you are using, from tablets to desktops.

Some Windows Store apps display as live tiles—that is, the information in the app is updated on the tile, for example for sports scores, weather updates, or new Twitter messages. Some Windows Store apps are provided by Microsoft, but most are provided by other companies or independent *app developers*—individuals who make money by developing and selling apps on the Windows Store, or more generically, who create apps for any mobile computing platform.

1 ▶ On the taskbar, click **Store** [■]. If necessary search for the Store app.

2 ▶ With the **Store** displayed, click in the search box, type **microsoft sway** and press [Enter].

3 ▶ Locate and click the free app **Sway,** and then click **Free** or **Get** to install the app. Wait a few moments for the app to download and install, and then click **Launch.** Compare your screen with Figure 3.53.

> Sway is a digital storytelling app that you can use for personal use, for work, or for school. You can add pictures or import documents; it's quick and easy to create and share.

FIGURE 3.53

4 **Close** ☒ the Sway app and the Windows Store window, if necessary.

Activity 3.19 | Searching Within Installed Apps

A Universal Windows App (UWP) is an app that will run on any Windows device; for example, on a Windows phone, a Windows tablet, and a Windows PC. Microsoft is encouraging developers to write Universal Apps, and some apps that are already built come with Windows 10. These apps include Mail, Photos, News, and Weather, among others. Within an installed app, you can conduct searches.

> **NOTE**
>
> For this Activity, Cortana is enabled. If you do not have Cortana enabled, your search results may differ slightly.

1 Click in the taskbar search box, type **news** at the top of the Search pane click **More**, then click the **Apps** ▦ category. Compare your screen with Figure 3.54.

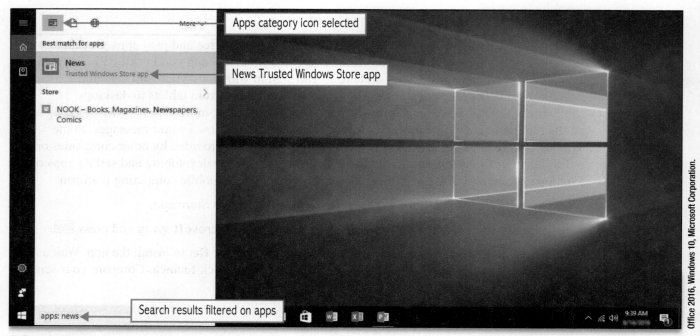

FIGURE 3.54

2 At the top of the search pane, under **Best match for apps**, click **News Trusted Windows Store app**. If a message displays regarding personalizing news or news alerts, click Skip or Turn Off—you can turn these on again later if you want to do so.

3 In the upper right, **Maximize** ☐ the window, click in the search box, type **microsoft hololens** and press Enter.

> News about and related to Microsoft's HoloLens technology displays.

4 From the taskbar, open your PowerPoint presentation, and add a new slide. On the **Insert tab**, in the **Images group**, click **Screenshot**, and then click **Screen Clipping**— recall that some windows are only available as a screen clipping and not a window.

5 Drag the + pointer around any HoloLens article and then release the mouse button—your clip need not be precise.

> Your clip displays in the PowerPoint slide. If you are not satisfied with your result, delete the image and try again.

6 On the Quick Access toolbar, click **Save** ☐. **Minimize** ☐ your PowerPoint window.

7 Close ☒ the **News** app.

8 Using the skills you just practiced, locate and open the Windows Trusted Store app for **Weather**.

9 If necessary, enable Weather to detect your location, and click Start. **Maximize** ☐ the window. In the upper right corner, in the **Search** box, type **san francisco** and press Enter. In the upper left corner, click the hamburger icon ☰, and then click **Historical Weather**.

10 From the taskbar, open your PowerPoint presentation, and add a new slide. On the **Insert tab**, in the **Images group**, click **Screenshot**, and then click **Screen Clipping**.

11 Drag the + pointer around the Historical Weather graph but not the taskbar, and then release the mouse button—your clip need not be precise.

> Your clip displays in the PowerPoint slide. If you are not satisfied with your result, delete the image and try again.

12 On the Quick Access toolbar, click **Save** ☐.

13 Click in a white area to deselect the image. Press Ctrl + Home to display the first slide. **Close** ☒ PowerPoint, and submit your PowerPoint file to your instructor as evidence of your work in this Project.

14 **Close** ☒ the **Weather** app.

ALERT!   **The Following Final Activity is Optional**

This Activity uses Cortana, which might not be installed on a lab computer at your college. If you have Cortana on the computer you are using, you might want to complete this Activity now. If you are unable to complete the steps, just read the information, and then try this on your own computer when you are able to do so.

Cortana is Microsoft's digital assistant, and is named after a female character in the video game Halo. You can speak to Cortana in a natural voice using natural language. Similar voice-activated digital assistants have been available for several years. Siri for the iPhone was introduced by Apple in 2011, and Google introduced Google Now for Android phones in 2012. In 2014, Amazon released the Amazon Echo, a stationary device for your home or office that can answer questions, play music, and maintain shopping lists—all by speaking.

What differentiates Cortana from Siri and Google Now is that Cortana runs on a PC—not just on a phone. Additionally, you can also type commands instead of speaking—for example in your computer classroom. Finally, Cortana most often speaks with the recorded voice of a real person.

When you install Windows 10, or get a new computer with Windows 10, you will need to follow the prompts to activate Cortana. Then, click the microphone button in the search box, say "hey Cortana," and then ask your question.

1 In the taskbar search box, be sure that *Ask me anything* displays, indicating that Cortana is active.

2 In the search box, click the microphone button. Cortana may ask for help in learning to recognize your voice; you can click Maybe Later and Got it (or similar prompts). Compare your screen with Figure 3.55.

Cortana indicates that she is listening.

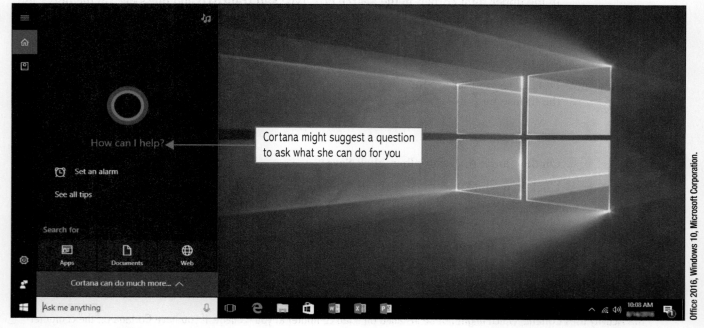

FIGURE 3.55

3 Speak the words *weather in boston*

Cortana displays weather information for Boston.

4 Press (Esc) to close the search pane. If you have not already done so, submit your **Lastname_Firstname_3B_Advanced_Search** PowerPoint presentation to your instructor as evidence of your work in this chapter.

END | You have completed Project 3B

END OF CHAPTER

SUMMARY

Every element of the address bar—the folder names and each arrow—is an active control, so you can move from the current folder directly to any folder above it in the path by clicking on a folder name.

When you open a file from the file list, Windows 10 uses the file extension of the file to determine which program to use to open the file and displays the program's icon on the Open button on the ribbon.

If you can remember any detail about a file or a saved email message that you need to access—for example, when the file was created or some of its content or its tag—Windows 10 can find it for you quickly.

Cortana is Microsoft's digital assistant, which you can use on a mobile phone and also on a PC. Cortana is named for a female character in the video game Halo. You can speak or type commands to Cortana.

GO! LEARN IT ONLINE

Review the concepts and key terms in this chapter by completing these online challenges, which you can find in **MyITLab**:

Matching and Multiple Choice: Answer matching and multiple choice questions to test what you learned in this chapter.

Lessons on the GO!: Learn how to use all the new apps and features as they are introduced by Microsoft.

GO! FOR JOB SUCCESS

Discussion: 3D-Printing

Your instructor may assign this discussion to your class, and then ask you to think about, or discuss with your classmates, these questions:

3D printing is a manufacturing process where three-dimensional objects are created from a digital file. You're familiar with laser printers that read digital files, like a Word document, and place ink on paper. 3D "printers" are machines that lay down layers of materials based on instructions from a digital file. The result is an object, like a part for an automobile, instead of a document.

FotoEdhar/Fotolia

Question 1: What are some industries that could benefit from trying out completely new products without having to build new manufacturing plants?

Question 2: What are some medical devices that could be improved by being made specifically for you or a friend or family member?

Question 3: If a 3D printer could be sent into space and receive instructions from earth, what are some objects it could create that would help scientists understand space objects?

Project	Apply Skills from These Chapter Objectives	Project Type	Project Location
		Review and Assessment Guide for Windows 10 Chapter 3	
3A	Objectives 1-3 from Project 3A	**3A Instructional Project (Scorecard Grading)** Guided instruction to learn the skills in Project 3A.	In text
3B	Objectives 4-5 from Project 3B	**3B Instructional Project (Scorecard Grading)** Guided instruction to learn the skills in Project 3B.	In text
3C	Objectives 1-3 from Project 3A	**3C Skills Review (Scorecard Grading)** A guided review of the skills from Project 3A.	In text
3D	Objectives 4-5 from Project 3B	**3D Skills Review (Scorecard Grading)** A guided review of the skills from Project 3B.	In text
3E	Objectives 1-3 from Project 3A	**3E Mastery (Scorecard Grading) Mastery and Transfer of Learning** A demonstration of your mastery of the skills in Project 3A with decision-making.	In text
3F	Objectives 4-5 from Project 3B	**3F Mastery (Scorecard Grading) Mastery and Transfer of Learning** A demonstration of your mastery of the skills in Project 3B with decision-making.	In text
3G	Combination of Objectives from Projects 3A and 3B	**3G GO! Think (Rubric Grading) Critical Thinking** A demonstration of your understanding of the Chapter concepts applied in a manner that you would outside of college. An analytic rubric helps you and your instructor grade the quality of your work by comparing it to the work an expert in the discipline would create.	In text
3H	Combination of Objectives from Projects 3A and 3B	**3H GO! Think (Rubric Grading) Critical Thinking** A demonstration of your understanding of the Chapter concepts applied in a manner that you would outside of college. An analytic rubric helps you and your instructor grade the quality of your work by comparing it to the work an expert in the discipline would create.	In text
3I	Combination of Objectives from Projects 3A and 3B	**3I GO! Think (Rubric Grading) Critical Thinking** A demonstration of your understanding of the Chapter concepts applied in a manner that you would outside of college. An analytic rubric helps you and your instructor grade the quality of your work by comparing it to the work an expert in the discipline would create.	In text

GLOSSARY

GLOSSARY OF CHAPTER KEY TERMS

AND filter When used in a search, finds files that contain both search terms even if those terms are not next to each other.

App developer An individual who makes money by developing and selling apps on the Windows Store, or more generically that develops apps for any computing platform, especially for mobile computing platforms.

Base locations Locations that you frequently need to access to manage your computer; includes your OneDrive folder, your personal folder, This PC, your Homegroup if you have one, Control Panel, and Recycle Bin.

Boolean operators The terms AND, OR, and NOT that govern the logical functions and express a condition that is either true or false.

Check box feature A folder option which, when applied, displays a check box to the left of folders and files.

Control Panel A window from which you can customize the appearance and functionality of your computer, add or remove programs, set up network connections, and manage user accounts.

Directory A file folder on a disk in which you store files; also called a *path*.

File association The association between a file and the program that created the file.

File name extension A set of characters at the end of a file name that helps Windows 10 understand what kind of information is in a file and what program should open it.

File properties Information about your files, such as the name of the author and the date that the file was last modified.

Group by In a folder window, a feature that enables you to group the items by Name, Date modified, Type, Size, Date created, Authors, Tags, and Title, in Ascending or Descending order.

Index A collection of detailed information about the files on your computer that Windows 10 maintains for the purpose of conducting fast searches; when you begin a search, Windows 10 searches this summary information rather than searching file by file on your hard disk drive.

Indexed locations All of the folders in your personal folder (Documents, Pictures, and so on) and offline files, if any, that Windows 10 includes in a search.

Location icon An icon on the address bar that depicts the location—disk drive, folder, and so on—you are accessing.

Metadata The data that describes other data; for example, the collective group of a file's properties, such as its title, subject, author, and file size.

Node The locations on the Quick access list that indicate a central point of connection or a place where things come together.

NOT filter When used in a search, finds files that contain the first word but that do not contain the second word.

OR filter When used in a search, finds files that contain either search term.

Partial matching A technique employed by the Windows 10 search feature that matches your search criteria to part of a word or phrase rather than to whole words.

Path A sequence of folders that leads to a specific file or folder.

Personal folder The folder created for a user account in Windows 10 that contains subfolders and information for one specific user.

Quick access list The first node in the navigation pane, which contains links to folders and files that Windows determines you access frequently and links that you add yourself.

Quotes filter When used in a search, finds files that contain the exact phrase placed within the quotes.

Recent locations A button on the address bar that displays a list of recently accessed locations; the current location is indicated by a check mark.

Sort by In a folder window, a feature that enables you to sort the items by Name, Date modified, Type, Size, Date created, Authors, Tags, and Title, in Ascending or Descending order.

Split button A button, that when pointed to, displays in two parts—an arrow that displays a list and a button that starts the command.

Tag A property that you create and add to a file.

Virtual folder A folder that does not represent a physical location.

WordPad A simple word processing program that comes with Windows 10.

Skills Review **Project 3C Using Advanced File Management Techniques**

 PROJECT FILES

For Project 3C, you will need the following files:

win03_3C_Bell_Orchid folder from the student data files that accompany this textbook

win03_3C_Answer_Sheet (Word document) from the student data files that accompany this textbook

You will save your results as:

Lastname_Firstname_3C_Answer_Sheet

1 Close any open apps and windows and display your desktop. On the taskbar, click **File Explorer**. From your **win10_03_Student_Data_Files**, copy the folder **win03_3C_Bell_Orchid** to your **Documents** folder on your hard drive.

From your **win10_03_Student_Data_Files**, open the Word document **win03_3C_Answer_Sheet**. Using your own name, save this Word document in your **Windows 10 Chapter 3** folder as **Lastname_Firstname_3C_Answer_Sheet** and then minimize the document to leave it open.

Close all File Explorer windows and display your desktop. As you complete each step in this Project, write the letter of your answer on a piece of paper; you will fill in your Answer Sheet after you complete all the steps in this Project.

Display your **Documents** folder, and then navigate to **win03_3C_Bell_Orchid** > **Corporate** > **Information_Technology** > **Future _Hotels**. At the left end of the **address bar**, click the **location icon**. What is your result?

A. All of the files in the Future_Hotels folder are selected.

B. In the address bar, the path that describes the folder's location displays separated by backslashes and is highlighted.

C. The Documents folder window displays.

2 Press Esc, and then **Maximize** ☐ the **Future_Hotels** window. In the **address bar** click **Corporate** to display this folder window. In the **address bar**, to the immediate right of the **location icon**, click >. What is your result?

A. A list of available base locations displays below the separator line.

B. A list of the subfolders within the Corporate folder displays.

C. The path that describes the folder's location displays and is highlighted.

(Project 3C Using Advanced File Management Techniques continues on the next page)

Skills Review | **Project 3C Using Advanced File Management Techniques** (continued)

3 Display the **win03_3C_Bell_Orchid** folder window. On the **Home tab**, in the **New group**, click **New folder**, and then create a new folder named **Florida_Keys** Drag the **Florida_Keys** folder to the **navigation pane** to become the first item under **Quick access**. Which of the following is true?

A. The Florida_Keys folder no longer displays in the file list.

B. The Florida_Keys folder window opens.

C. The Florida_Keys folder displays in the Quick access list with a buff-colored folder icon.

4 On the **View tab**, click the upper portion of the **Options** button, and then in the **Folder Options** dialog box, click the **General tab**. Which of the following is *not* true?

A. On this tab, you can change folder behavior so that every folder opens in its own window.

B. On this tab, you can set items to open with a single click.

C. On this tab, you can change folder behavior so that no folders display in the navigation pane.

5 In the **Folder Options** dialog box, click the **View tab**. From the **Advanced settings** area, which of the following settings can be adjusted on your computer?

A. Hiding or showing file extensions.

B. Changing the desktop color.

C. Both A and B.

6 **Close** the **Folder Options** dialog box. Navigate to **Corporate > Information_Technology > Future_Hotels**. Be sure the layout is set to **Details**, and then from the **View tab**, sort the file list by **Type**. How many different file types display?

A. Four

B. Five

C. Six

7 How many **PowerPoint** files are in the file list?

A. Three

B. Four

C. Five

8 Navigate to the **Corporate > Food_Beverage** folder, and then group by **Tags**. How many files are in the **Wedding reception** group?

A. One

B. Two

C. Three

9 Set **Group by** back to **(None)**. Navigate to **Corporate > Food_Beverage > Restaurants**. In the **file list**, click **Grill_Menu**, and then on the **Home tab**, in the **Select group**, click **Invert selection**. What is your result?

A. Only files containing the word *menu* are selected.

B. All the files *except* Grill_Menu are selected.

C. No files in the list are selected.

(Project 3C Using Advanced File Management Techniques continues on the next page)

10 In the **address bar**, click **Food_Beverage** to navigate up to this folder, and then in the **file list**, select the file **CO_FB_Menu_Presentation**. On the **Home tab**, in the **Open group**, click the **Open button arrow**, and then click **Choose another app**. What is the file extension for this file?

    A. .docx

    B. .ppt

    C. .pptx

To complete this project: Press Esc to close the list. In the **navigation pane**, under **Quick access**, right-click **Florida_Keys**, and then click **Unpin from Quick access**. In the upper right corner of the window, click **Restore Down** ⧉. Close any open windows to display the **desktop**, on the taskbar click the **Word** icon, and type your answers into the correct boxes. Save and close your Word document, and submit as directed by your instructor. **Close** any open windows.

END | You have completed Project 3C

<table>
<tr><td>

Apply 3B skills from these Objectives:

4 Use Search Tools in File Explorer

5 Use the Taskbar Search Box and Search with Cortana

</td></tr>
</table>

Skills Review Project 3D Using Advanced Search Techniques

 PROJECT FILES

For Project 3D, you will need the following files:

win03_3D_Bell_Orchid folder from the student data files that accompany this textbook

win03_3D_Answer_Sheet (Word document) from the student data files that accompany this textbook

You will save your results as:

Lastname_Firstname_3D_Answer_Sheet

1 Close any open apps and windows and display your desktop. On the taskbar, click **File Explorer**. From your **win10_03_Student_Data_Files**, copy the folder **win03_3D_Bell_Orchid** to your **Documents** folder on your hard drive.

From your **win10_03_Student_Data_Files**, open the Word document **win03_3D_Answer_Sheet**. Using your own name, save this document in your **Windows 10 Chapter 3** folder as **Lastname_Firstname_3D_Answer_Sheet** and then minimize the document to leave it open.

Close all File Explorer windows and display your desktop. As you complete each step in this Project, write the letter of your answer on a piece of paper; you will fill in your Answer Sheet after you complete all the steps in this Project.

Display your **Documents** folder, and then navigate to **win03_3D_Bell_Orchid > Corporate > Food_Beverage > Restaurants**. Maximize ☐ the **Restaurants** window, and then on the **View tab**, click **Details pane** to display the pane on the right. Hold down Ctrl, and then select the following group of files: **Breakfast_Continental**, **Breakfast_Menus**, **Brunch_Menus**, **Grill_Menu**, and **Refreshments**. In the **Details pane**, add the tag **Menu** and then at the bottom of the **Details pane**, click **Save**. At the top of the **Details pane**, what number of files are indicated as selected?

A. 5

B. 6

C. 7

2 With the **Restaurants** folder window still displayed, click in the search box to display the **Search Tools**, and then type **menu** How many files display?

A. 5

B. 6

C. 7

3 Clear the **search** box, and then type **costs** How many files display?

A. 2

B. 3

C. 4

(Project 3D Using Advanced Search Techniques continues on the next page)

4 **Clear** the **search** box. In the **Refine group**, click **Other properties**, click **Type**, and then in the search box, type **xlsx** How many files display?

A. 5

B. 10

C. 15

5 **Clear** the **search** box, and then type **costs NOT overtime** How many files display?

A. 3

B. 4

C. 7

6 **Clear** the **search** box, and then type **menu AND breakfast** How many files display?

A. 4

B. 3

C. 2

7 **Clear** the **search** box, and then type **menu OR breakfast** How many files display?

A. 3

B. 5

C. 7

8 **Clear** the **search** box. In the **Refine group**, click **Other properties**, click **Name**, and then type **kitchen** How many files display?

A. 3

B. 2

C. 1

9 On the ribbon, click **Close search**, click the **View tab**, and then click **Details pane** to close the pane. Click **Restore Down** 🗗, and then **Close** ✕ the folder window. Press 🪟 to display the Start menu and position the insertion point in the search box, and then type **minecraft** At the top of the search results, click **More**, and then click **Apps**. Which of the following is true?

A. Search results from the Web display.

B. Search results from the Windows Store display.

C. Search results from your Bell Orchid files display.

10 Press ⎋Esc to close the search pane. Press 🪟, and then type **orlando** At the top of the search pane, click **More**, click **Web**, and then click **orlando Search the web**. Which of the following is true?

A. All of the documents in the Bell Orchid Orland folder display.

B. The Bing search engine displays information about Orlando.

C. A list of airline flights to Orlando displays.

To complete this project: Close all windows and apps to display the **desktop**. On the taskbar click the **Word** icon, and type your answers into the correct boxes. Save and close your Word document, and submit as directed by your instructor.

END | You have completed Project 3D

Apply **3A** skills from these Objectives:

Apply 3A skills from these Objectives:

1 Navigate by Using the Address Bar and Quick Access List

2 Manage Folder Options and Views

3 Recognize File Types and Associate Files with Programs

Mastering Windows 10 | **Project 3E Using Advanced File Management Techniques**

In the following Mastering Windows 10 Project, you will change the way a folder displays. You will capture and save two screens in a PowerPoint presentation that will look similar to Figure 3.56.

 PROJECT FILES

For Project 3E, you will need the following files:

win03_3E_Bell_Orchid folder from the student data files that accompany this textbook

A new PowerPoint presentation

You will save your results in a PowerPoint presentation as:

Lastname_Firstname_3E_HR

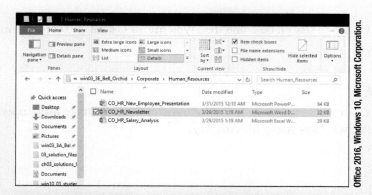

FIGURE 3.56

Office 2016, Windows 10, Microsoft Corporation.

(Project 3E Using Advanced File Management Techniques continues on the next page)

Mastering Windows 10 | **Project 3E Using Advanced File Management Techniques** (continued)

1 Close any open apps and windows and display your desktop. On the taskbar, click **File Explorer**. From your student data files, copy the folder **win03_3E_Bell_Orchid** to your **Documents** folder on your hard drive.

2 Navigate to **Documents** > **win03_3E_Bell_Orchid** > **Corporate** > **Human_Resources**. On the **View tab**, in the **Show/hide group**, be sure that **Item check boxes** is still selected, and then select the check box for the **CO_HR_Newsletter** file.

3 Open a new blank PowerPoint presentation, and then using your own name, save it in your **Windows 10 Chapter 3** folder as **Lastname_Firstname_3E_HR**

4 In PowerPoint, set the **Layout** to **Blank**, insert the **Screenshot** of your File Explorer window, and then click to deselect the image.

5 Navigate to **Corporate** > **Food_Beverage** > **Restaurants** and then sort by **Type**. **Maximize** the window.

6 Insert this screenshot as the second slide in your PowerPoint presentation.

7 **Close** the PowerPoint window; when prompted, click **Save**.

8 In your **Human_Resources** window, in the upper right corner click **Restore Down**. Close any open windows, and then submit your PowerPoint file as directed by your instructor.

END | You have completed Project 3E

Mastering Windows 10 | **Project 3F Using Advanced Search Techniques**

In the following Mastering Windows 10 project, you will change the way a folder displays. You will capture five screens in a PowerPoint presentation that will look similar to Figure 3.57.

 PROJECT FILES

For Project 3F, you will need the following files:

win03_3F_Bell_Orchid folder from the student data files that accompany this textbook
A new PowerPoint presentation

You will save your results in a PowerPoint presentation as:

Lastname_Firstname_3F_Search

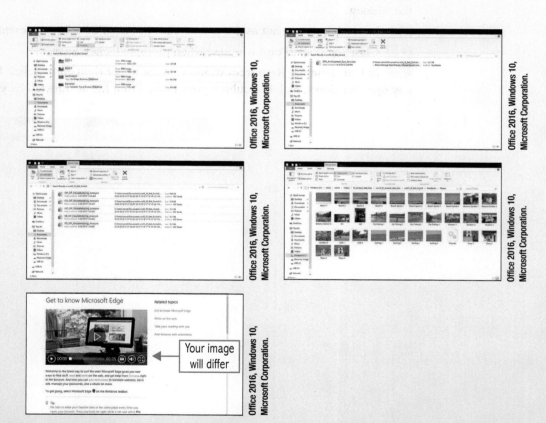

FIGURE 3.57

(Project 3F Using Advanced Search Techniques continues on the next page)

Mastering Windows 10 | **Project 3F Using Advanced Search Techniques** (continued)

1 Close any open apps and windows and display your desktop. On the taskbar, click **File Explorer**. From your student data files, copy the folder **win03_3F_Bell_Orchid** to your **Documents** folder on your hard drive.

2 Open a new blank PowerPoint presentation, and then using your own name, save it in your **Windows 10 Chapter 3** folder as **Lastname_Firstname_3F_Search Minimize** [–] the PowerPoint window.

3 Navigate to **This PC > Documents > win03_3F_Bell_Orchid** and **Maximize** [□] the window. Search for files that contain the word **golf** *OR* the word **water** and then refine the search by **Kind** using **Picture**. Be sure the **Layout** is set to **Content**.

4 Open your PowerPoint presentation, set the **Layout** to **Blank**, insert the **Screenshot** of your File Explorer window, and then click to deselect the image. **Minimize** [–] the PowerPoint window.

5 Clear the search. In the search box, search for **"infrared sauna"** and then insert a screenshot of your results as the second slide in your PowerPoint presentation. **Minimize** [–] the PowerPoint window.

6 Clear the search. Begin a new search by refining for **Other properties** by **Type**. In the search box, type **xlsx** Press Spacebar one time, type **housekeeping** Be sure the **View** is set to **Content**. Insert a screenshot of your results as the third slide in your PowerPoint presentation. **Minimize** [–] the PowerPoint window.

7 Close the **File Explorer** window. Press [■] and then type **montecito** and then at the top of the search pane, click **More**, and then click **Folders**. In the Search pane, click the folder name **Montecito - in win03_3F_Bell_Orchid**, and then open the **Photos** folder. On the **View tab**, set the **Layout** to **Large icons**. Insert a screenshot of your results as the fourth slide in your PowerPoint presentation. **Minimize** [–] the PowerPoint window.

8 Close the **File Explorer** window. Press [■], type **get started** and then open the **Get Started Trusted Windows Store** app. **Maximize** the window, on the left click **Browse**, and then click **Microsoft Edge**. Click **Get to know Microsoft Edge**. Insert a **Screen Clipping** of the white portion of the Get Started window as the fifth slide in your PowerPoint presentation.

9 **Close** the PowerPoint window; when prompted, click **Save**. Close the **Get Started** window and any other open windows, and then submit your PowerPoint file as directed by your instructor.

END | You have completed Project 3F

OUTCOMES-BASED ASSESSMENTS

RUBRIC

The following outcomes-based assessments are *open-ended assessments*. That is, there is no specific correct result; your result will depend on your approach to the information provided. Make *Professional Quality* your goal. Use the following scoring rubric to guide you in *how* to approach the problem, and then to evaluate *how well* your approach solves the problem.

The *criteria*—Software Mastery, Content, Format and Layout, and Process—represent the knowledge and skills you have gained that you can apply to solving the problem. The *levels of performance*—Professional Quality, Approaching Professional Quality, or Needs Quality Improvements—help you and your instructor evaluate your result.

	Your completed project is of Professional Quality if you:	Your completed project is Approaching Professional Quality if you:	Your completed project Needs Quality Improvements if you:
1-Software Mastery	Choose and apply the most appropriate skills, tools, and features and identify efficient methods to solve the problem.	Choose and apply some appropriate skills, tools, and features, but not in the most efficient manner.	Choose inappropriate skills, tools, or features, or are inefficient in solving the problem.
2-Content	Construct a solution that is clear and well organized, contains content that is accurate, appropriate to the audience and purpose, and is complete. Provide a solution that contains no errors of spelling, grammar, or style.	Construct a solution in which some components are unclear, poorly organized, inconsistent, or incomplete. Misjudge the needs of the audience. Have some errors in spelling, grammar, or style, but the errors do not detract from comprehension.	Construct a solution that is unclear, incomplete, or poorly organized, containing some inaccurate or inappropriate content, and contains many errors of spelling, grammar, or style. Do not solve the problem.
3-Format and Layout	Format and arrange all elements to communicate information and ideas, clarify function, illustrate relationships, and indicate relative importance.	Apply appropriate format and layout features to some elements, but not others. Overuse features, causing minor distraction.	Apply format and layout that does not communicate information or ideas clearly. Do not use format and layout features to clarify function, illustrate relationships, or indicate relative importance. Use available features excessively, causing distraction.
4-Process	Use an organized approach that integrates planning, development, self-assessment, revision, and reflection.	Demonstrate an organized approach in some areas, but not others; or, use an insufficient process of organization throughout.	Do not use an organized approach to solve the problem.

Problem Solving   Project 3G Help Desk

In this Project, you will construct a solution by applying any combination of the skills you practiced from the Objectives in Projects 3A and 3B.

For Project 3G, you will need the following file:

win03_3G_Help_Desk

You will save your document as:

Lastname_Firstname_3G_Help_Desk

From the student files that accompany this textbook, locate and open the Word document **win03_3G_Help_Desk**. Save the document in your chapter folder as **Lastname_Firstname_3G_Help_Desk**

The following e-mail question has arrived at the Help Desk from an employee at the Bell Orchid Hotel's corporate office. In the Word form, construct a response based on your knowledge of Windows 10. Although an email response is not as formal as a letter, you should still use good grammar, good sentence structure, professional language, and a polite tone. Save your document and submit the response as directed by your instructor.

To: Help Desk

I can navigate all over the Internet without having to double-click to display what I want to look at. Is there a way to avoid double-clicking so often when I am navigating in Windows 10?

END | You have completed Project 3G

Problem Solving   Project 3H Help Desk

In this Project, you will construct a solution by applying any combination of the skills you practiced from the Objectives in Projects 3A and 3B.

For Project 3H, you will need the following file:

win03_3H_Help_Desk

You will save your document as:

Lastname_Firstname_3H_Help_Desk

From the student files that accompany this textbook, locate and open the Word document **win03_3H_Help_Desk**. Save the document in your chapter folder as **Lastname_Firstname_3H_Help_Desk**

The following e-mail question has arrived at the Help Desk from an employee at the Bell Orchid Hotel's corporate office. In the Word form, construct a response based on your knowledge of Windows 10. Although an email response is not as formal as a letter, you should still use good grammar, good sentence structure, professional language, and a polite tone. Save your document and submit the response as directed by your instructor.

To: Help Desk

I just received over one hundred new photo files of golf courses, restaurants, and scenic mountain views in Palm Springs, California, where we are considering opening a new resort hotel. First, I want the photos to open in the Paint program, but every time I open a photo, it opens with the Windows 10 Photo app. How can I change my system so that photos open in Paint? Second, I don't want to rename all the photos. Is there a way I could add identifying information so I could search for them by *golf* or by *restaurants*, and so on?

> **END | You have completed Project 3H**

Problem Solving Project 3I Help Desk

In this Project, you will construct a solution by applying any combination of the skills you practiced from the Objectives in Projects 3A and 3B.

For Project 3I, you will need the following file:

win03_3I_Help_Desk

You will save your document as:

Lastname_Firstname_3I_Help_Desk

From the student files that accompany this textbook, locate and open the Word document **win03_3I_Help_Desk**. Save the document in your chapter folder as **Lastname_Firstname_3I_Help_Desk**

The following e-mail question has arrived at the Help Desk from an employee at the Bell Orchid Hotel's corporate office. In the Word form, construct a response based on your knowledge of Windows 10. Although an email response is not as formal as a letter, you should still use good grammar, good sentence structure, professional language, and a polite tone. Save your document and submit the response as directed by your instructor.

To: Help Desk

I am the Corporate Director of Food and Beverage. I have hundreds of files from all of our different facilities that deal with various aspects of the Food and Beverage operation. I need to find files by location and also by type of menu. Is there a way I could find, for example, only files that pertain to brunch menus at our Orlando facility or only files that pertain to dinner menus at both the Honolulu and Montecito locations?

END | You have completed Project 3I

Searching the Web, Using Apps for Utility and Accessibility, and Securing Your Computer

4

WINDOWS 10

PROJECT **4A**

OUTCOMES
Search the Web in Microsoft Edge, use Windows 10 utilities for convenience, and use the Ease of Access apps for accessibility.

PROJECT **4B**

OUTCOMES
Secure your computer by using Windows Defender, Windows Firewall, and Privacy settings.

OBJECTIVES

1. Explore Web Browsers and Search Engines
2. Conduct Google Searches in Microsoft Edge
3. Use Windows 10 Utility Apps
4. Use Windows 10 Ease of Access Apps

OBJECTIVES

5. Understand Viruses and Spyware
6. Explore Windows Defender
7. Explore Windows Firewall
8. Explore Windows Update and Privacy Settings

Ra2 studio/Fotolia

In This Chapter

In this chapter, you will learn Internet search techniques that will enable you to find information easily and efficiently by using the Bing search engine with Microsoft's Edge browser. Organizations frequently conduct Web searches for business research related to new sales opportunities and for information related to their business operations. When using a search engine to conduct a search, you want only the search results that are pertinent to your search criteria, and you want to reduce the number of search results that are not useful to your search criteria. By using good search techniques, you will be able to get the results you need quickly.

When you secure your computer, you safeguard its programs and data so that it performs as intended.

To control computer security, you should use software that guards against malware. If you are a parent, you can control how your child uses the computer and the Internet.

The Projects in this chapter relate to the **Bell Orchid Hotels**, headquartered in Boston, and which own and operate resorts and business-oriented hotels. Resort properties are located in popular destinations, including Honolulu, Orlando, San Diego, and Santa Barbara. The resorts offer deluxe accommodations and a wide array of dining options. Other Bell Orchid Hotels are located in major business centers and offer the latest technology in their meeting facilities.

PROJECT 4A
Searching the Web and Using Utility and Accessibility Apps

PROJECT ACTIVITIES

In Activities 4.01 through 4.15, you will work with Barbara Hewitt and Steven Ramos, employees in the Information Technology Department at the headquarters office of Bell Orchid Hotels, as they explore how to efficiently perform research by searching the Web, to use the Windows 10 built-in apps for utility, and to use Windows Ease of Access apps to increase accessibility for staff and hotel guests. As you progress through the Project, you will insert screenshots of windows that you create into a PowerPoint presentation similar to Figure 4.1.

PROJECT FILES

For Project 4A, you will need the following file:

A new blank PowerPoint presentation

You will save your PowerPoint presentation as:

Lastname_Firstname_4A_Search_and_Utilities

PROJECT RESULTS

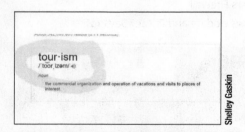

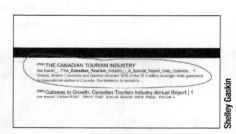

Office 2016, Windows 10, Microsoft Corporation.

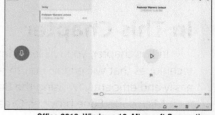
Office 2016, Windows 10, Microsoft Corporation.

FIGURE 4.1 Project 4A Using Edge and Bing to Search the Web

Objective 1 Explore Web Browsers and Search Engines

A *web browser* is a software program that displays webpages as you navigate the Internet. *Microsoft Edge* is the web browser software program developed by Microsoft Corporation and that is included with Windows 10.

Google Chrome is the web browser software program developed by Google Inc. and that you can download for free on any Windows-based system, Apple Mac system, and also on any system running the *Chrome OS*—for example on a PC known as a *Chromebook*. Chrome OS is an operating system conceived to run applications and store user data in the cloud. A PC or laptop that runs the Chrome OS is referred to as a Chromebook.

A *search engine* is a computer program that gathers information from the Web, indexes it, and puts it in a database that you can search based on specific words. The results of a search are a list of documents or websites in which the search term was found.

Bing is the search engine developed by Microsoft Corporation and that is included with Windows 10. When you search with Cortana, you are using Bing. When you use *Smart Lookup*—a feature that enables you to select text in a Word document and have a search conducted on the text and the results displayed in a pane on the right—the results are powered by Bing.

Google Search—also referred to as *Google Web Search* or simply *Google*—is the web search engine developed by Google Inc., and that you can use for free on any Windows-based computer, on an Apple Mac computer, or on any Chromebook.

Browsing is the term used to describe the process of using your computer to view webpages. *Surfing* refers to the process of navigating the Internet either for a particular item or for anything that is of interest, and quickly moving from one item to another.

Browsing the Web is one of the most common activities performed by individuals who use computers. Common tasks that you perform on the Internet might include looking at your favorite news sites, managing your finances with your bank, conducting research, shopping, sending email, and using social media sites such as Facebook or Twitter.

A *search expression* refers to the *keywords* and *syntax* that you type into a search engine to begin your search. Keywords are words you enter into the search expression that help to limit and focus your search results so that you find the information you want. Syntax refers to the arrangement of the keywords in your search expression.

Activity 4.01 | Exploring Bing

1 Close any open windows and display your Windows 10 desktop. If the **Microsoft Edge** browser [e] is pinned to your taskbar, go to Step 2. If it is not, click **Start** [⊞] to place the insertion point in the search box, type **Microsoft Edge** and then at the top of the search pane, under **Best match**, point to **Microsoft Edge** and right-click. Click **Pin to taskbar**.

2 On the taskbar, click **Microsoft Edge** [e], and if necessary, **Maximize** [□] the window. Compare your screen with Figure 4.2.

FIGURE 4.2

3 Under the text *Where to next?*, with the insertion point blinking, type **weather** and then compare your screen with Figure 4.3.

> The Microsoft Edge browser is powered by the Bing search engine, so a search begins immediately when you type. Here you will see the local weather and a list of sites that you might be looking for.

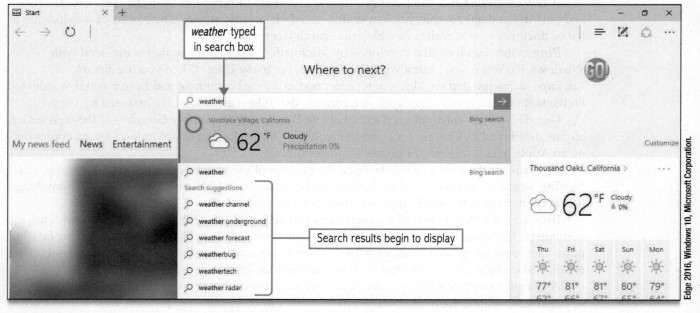

FIGURE 4.3

ALERT! **If You Do Not See *Where to next?***

If this is the first time you have opened the Edge browser, you may not see the text *Where to next?* and the Search box. Close Edge and open it again to display these elements. Or, in the upper right, click . . . , click Settings, at the top click the Open Microsoft Edge with arrow, and then click Start page.

---

4 Press [Esc] to clear the search box, type **bing.com** and then press [Enter]. If a message displays to show you new features, click Continue searching. Compare your screen with Figure 4.4, and then take a moment to study the table in Figure 4.5, which describes the parts of the Bing window.

> The Bing home page always displays a beautiful image, which changes daily. You can point to areas of the image to find hotspots with information about the subject and a link to find out more information about the subject of the image.

> In addition to being a search engine, the Bing site offers links to news, maps, and a wealth of other information.

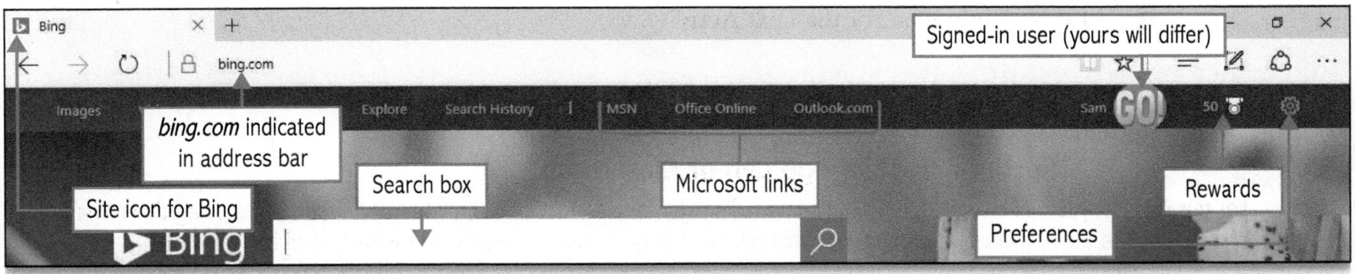

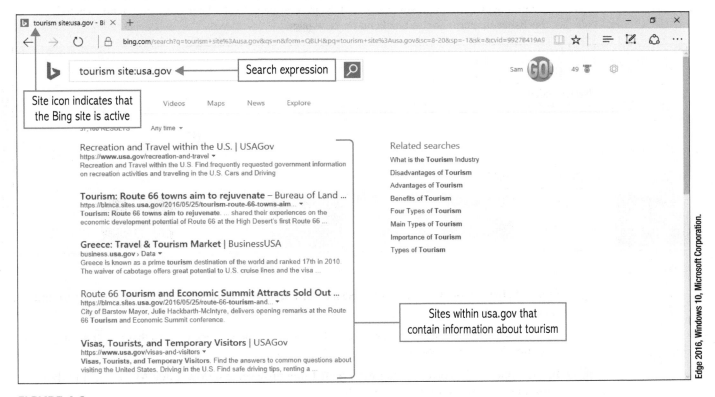

Edge 2016, Windows 10, Microsoft Corporation.

FIGURE 4.4

PARTS OF THE BING BROWSER WINDOW	
WINDOW PART	**DESCRIPTION**
Rewards	Information about a Microsoft program in which you can earn rewards.
Microsoft links	Provides links to MSN, Office Online programs, and to outlook.com
Preferences	Commands to help you personalize Bing, Cortana, and MSN to your specific interests and to change Bing's settings.
Search box	The area in which you can type your search.
Signed-in user	Picture and name of the signed-in user.
Site icon	Displays the icon of the website currently displayed in the browsing window.

Edge 2016, Windows 10, Microsoft Corporation.

FIGURE 4.5

5 In the **Bing search box**, type **tourism site:usa.gov** and press Enter. Compare your screen with Figure 4.6.

In a Bing search, the keyword ***site*** followed by a colon returns webpages that belong to the specified site. Here you narrowed the focus of your search to webpages on the topic of *tourism* at the site *usa.gov*.

Edge 2016, Windows 10, Microsoft Corporation.

FIGURE 4.6

6 Leave Bing open for the next Activity.

Activity 4.02 | Changing the Default Search Engine in Windows 10

ALERT!   **Settings in a College Lab or Classroom**

For this Activity, you will change settings, and in a college lab or classroom you may be prevented from making these changes. You can still complete the Activities that follow, but you will need to go to www.google.com for each search.

Bing is the default search engine in Windows 10, but Google is the more popular search engine for everyday use and for college research. When you type a search expression in the Microsoft Edge search box, the search is conducted using the default Bing search engine, but you can change the default to Google, or even some other search engine like DuckDuckGo.

1 In the upper left corner, click the **Microsoft Edge Back** button ← to redisplay the Bing homepage. Compare your screen with Figure 4.7.

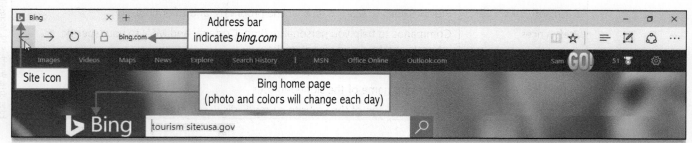

Edge 2016, Windows 10, Microsoft Corporation.

FIGURE 4.7

2 Above the **address bar**, click **New tab** ⊞, and then compare your screen with Figure 4.8.

Tabbed browsing is a feature that enables you to open multiple websites and then switch among them. When you click on the **New tab** button, a new page opens for you to perform your next search, while leaving open any other tabs to refer back to at a later time. Frequently visited websites display as thumbnails on the new page.

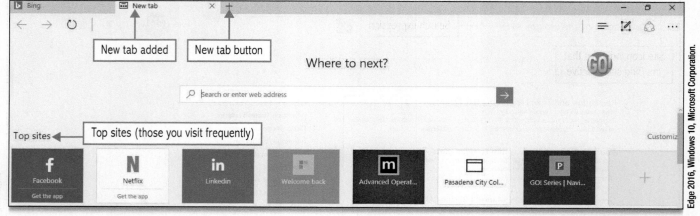

Edge 2016, Windows 10, Microsoft Corporation.

FIGURE 4.8

3 Under **Where to next?**, click in the **Search or enter web address** box, type **google.com** and then press Enter.

To change your default search engine to Google, visit the site one time so that it will display as an option for changing the default.

4 In the upper right corner of the **Microsoft Edge** browser window, click **More** ⋯, and then compare your screen with Figure 4.9.

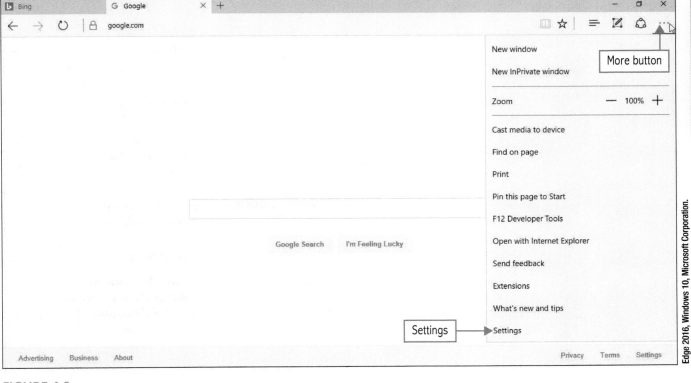

FIGURE 4.9

5 On the list of commands, click **Settings**, and then compare your screen with Figure 4.10.

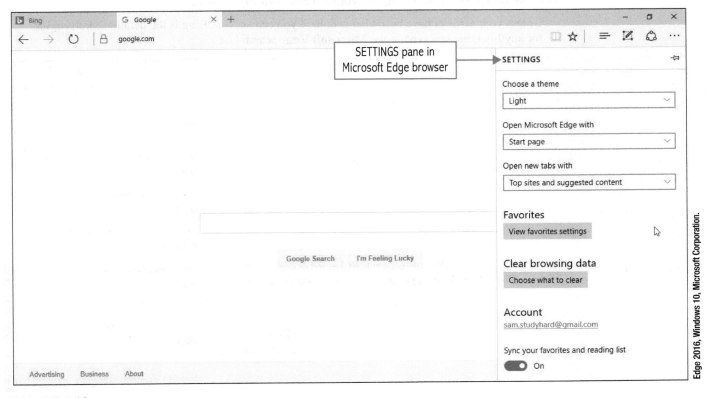

FIGURE 4.10

6 If necessary, move your mouse inside the **Settings** pane to display the scroll bar, and then scroll toward the bottom of the pane, as shown in Figure 4.11.

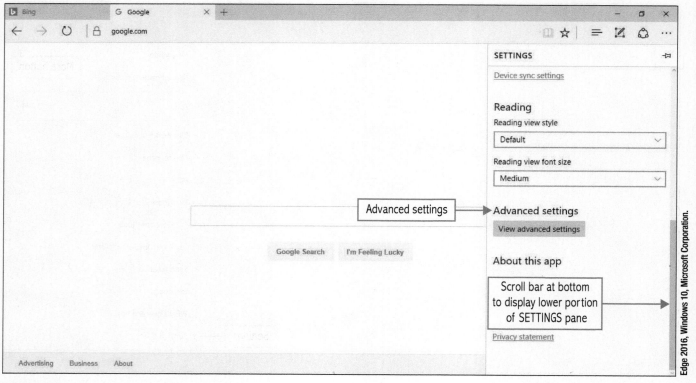

FIGURE 4.11

> 7 ▸ Under **Advanced settings**, click **View advanced settings**, and then scroll about two-thirds of the way down the pane. Compare your screen with Figure 4.12.
>
> Unless your settings have been changed, here you can see that Bing is the default search engine for anything that you type in the **Microsoft Edge** search box.

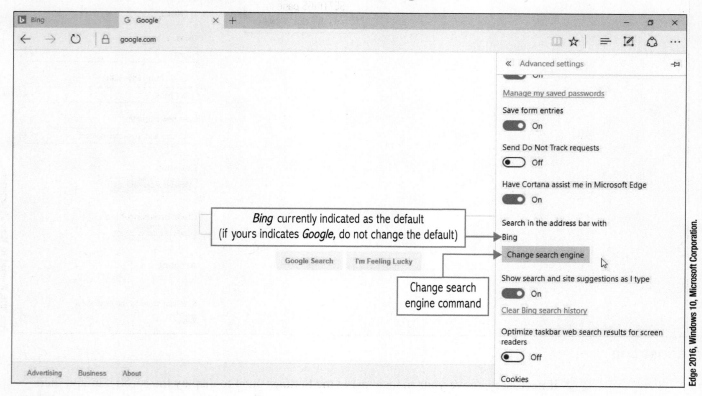

FIGURE 4.12

8 ▶ Above the **Change search engine** command, if Google is already set as the search engine, you can skip this step and also Step 9. If your screen indicates **Bing**, click **Change search engine**, and then on the list, click **Google Search (discovered)**. Compare your screen with Figure 4.13.

Because you have visited Google at least one time, Microsoft Edge sees it as a potential search engine. Here, other discovered search engines include Yahoo Search and Wikipedia.

A *wiki* is a website that permits anyone visiting the site to change its content by adding, removing, or editing the content. *Wikipedia* is the largest and most popular wiki on the Internet.

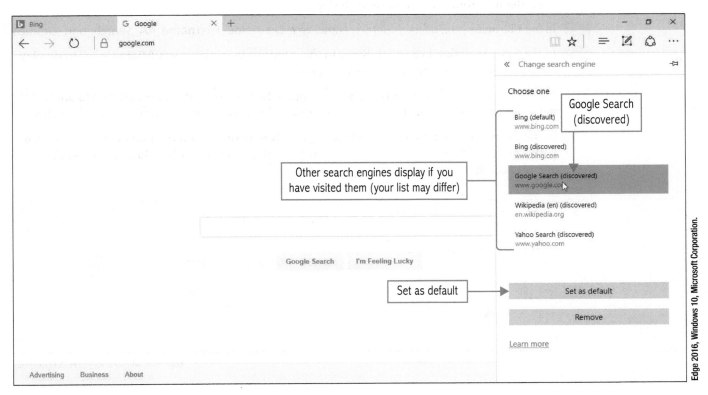

FIGURE 4.13

9 ▶ At the bottom of the pane, click **Set as default**, and then in the upper right corner, **Close** ☒ the **Microsoft Edge** browser. If necessary, in the displayed message, click **Close all**.

Objective 2 Conduct Google Searches in Microsoft Edge

The Edge browser is fast and secure—possibly more so than other browsers. Additionally, it has new and modern features that will make it useful for conducting searches and for everyday browsing. For example, you can grab a clip of a page and annotate it, save it, and share it. You can select a word on a webpage, right-click on the word, and then click Ask Cortana, which will display a pane on the right with information about the word. You can add extensions like those in the Chrome browser. And like other browsers, you can pin tabs, create bookmarks, store passwords, view a History list, and so on. Because you can use the Google search engine from within the Edge browser, you will find that combining these tools will make your Internet searches easy and useful.

Google refers to keywords as *operators*—words you can use in your search expression to get more specific search results. In this Activity, you will use the *define* operator to search for a definition.

1 From the taskbar, or by searching, open **PowerPoint**, and then click **Blank Presentation**. On the **Home tab**, in the **Slides group**, click **Layout**, and then click **Blank**.

2 Click the **File tab**, on the left click **Save As**, click **Browse**, and then in the **Save As** dialog box, navigate to the storage location where you will store your files for this chapter. Click **New folder**, as the folder name type **Windows 10 Chapter 4** and then press [Enter]. Click **Open** to open the new folder in the **Save As** dialog box.

3 In the **File name** box, using your own name, type **Lastname_Firstname_4A_Search_and_Utilities**

4 In the **Save As** dialog box, click **Save**. In the upper right corner, click **Minimize** [–] to display the desktop and leave the presentation open.

5 On the taskbar, click **Microsoft Edge** [e] to open the browser, and if necessary, **Maximize** [□] the window. If Microsoft Edge is not on your taskbar, you can search for it and pin it there.

6 In the **Search or enter web address** box, type **define:tourism** and then compare your screen with Figure 4.14. Notice that *Google search* is indicated because you have changed the default search engine.

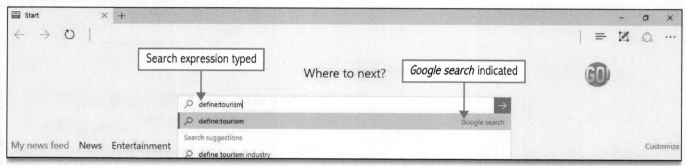

FIGURE 4.14　　　　　　　　　　　　　　　　　　Edge 2016, Windows 10, Microsoft Corporation.

7 Press [Enter]. With the results displayed, in the upper right corner, click **Make a Web Note** [☑]. Compare your screen with Figure 4.15.

Make a Web Note is a Microsoft Edge feature that enables you to take notes, write, and highlight directly on webpages and then save and share the note.

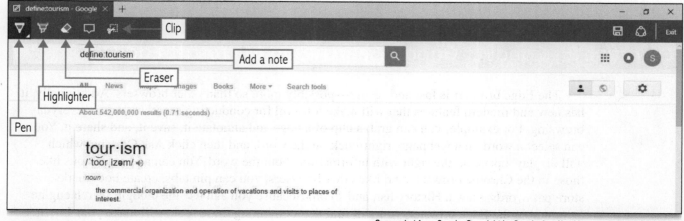

FIGURE 4.15　　　　　　　　　Screenshot from Google. Copyright by Google, Inc. Used by permission of Google, Inc.

8 In the upper left corner, click **Highlighter** 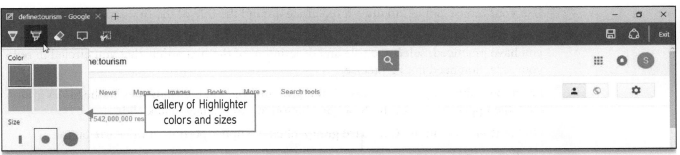, and then click the **small white triangle** on the Highlighter icon to display a gallery of Highlighter colors and sizes. Compare your screen with Figure 4.16.

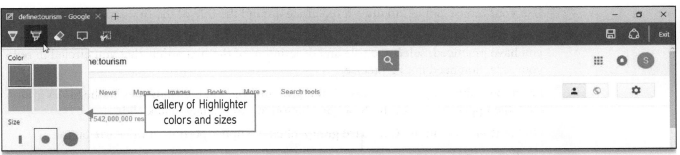

Gallery of Highlighter colors and sizes

FIGURE 4.16

Screenshot from Google. Copyright by Google, Inc. Used by permission of Google, Inc.

9 In the gallery, click the **Yellow** color, and notice that the icon becomes Yellow. On the **Highlighter** icon, if necessary, click the **small white triangle** again, and then in the gallery, under **Size**, click the largest size.

10 With your mouse pointer, draw a circle around the large definition for *tourism*, and notice that thick yellow highlighter marks display.

11 In the upper left corner, click **Clip**, and then using the + mouse pointer, point to the upper left corner of the large definition, hold down the left mouse button, and then drag down and to the right to capture the large definition and your yellow highlight in a manner similar to using the Screen Clipping feature in PowerPoint. Notice that the word *Copied!* displays briefly in the lower right corner of the portion that you clipped.

12 From the taskbar, open your PowerPoint presentation. On the **Home tab**, in the **Clipboard group**, click the upper portion of the **Paste** button.

13 Click in a white area to deselect the image. In the upper left corner, click **Save**, and then in the upper right corner, click **Minimize** .

14 In the upper right corner of the **Microsoft Edge** window, click **Exit**, and then in the **Save your changes** message, click **No**.

Activity 4.04 | Searching the Web by Using the *Filetype* and *Intitle* Operators

In this Activity, you will use the ***filetype*** operator, which finds files of a specific type; for example, a PDF file, which is commonly used for reports. You will also use the ***intitle*** operator to focus the results on a specific word in the title of a report.

1 At the top of the screen, click **New tab** . In the **Search or enter web address** box, type **filetype:pdf canada intitle:tourism** and then compare your screen with Figure 4.17.

The search expression will search for *pdf files* about *Canada* that have the word *tourism* in the title.

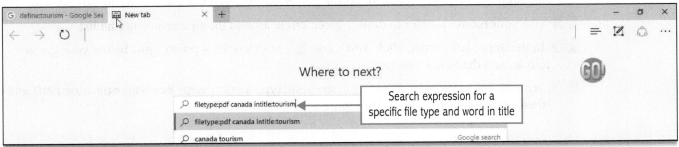

Search expression for a specific file type and word in title

FIGURE 4.17

Edge 2016, Windows 10, Microsoft Corporation.

2 Press Enter. Notice that your results consist of PDF files about Canadian tourism.

3 Click **Make a Web Note** 🖊, and then in the upper left corner, click the **Pen** ▽. By using the techniques you have practiced, set the pen color to **Red** and the size to the smallest size.

4 Use your mouse pointer to draw a red circle around the title of the first article.

5 In the upper left corner, click **Clip** ✂, and then using the + mouse pointer and the technique you have practiced, select the title and description of the first article that you circled in red; your selection need not be precise.

6 From the taskbar, open your PowerPoint presentation. On the **Home tab**, in the **Slides group**, click the upper portion of the **New Slide** button to insert a new blank slide.

7 On the **Home tab**, in the **Clipboard group**, click the upper portion of the **Paste** button.

8 Click in a white area to deselect the image. In the upper left corner, click **Save** 🖫, and then in the upper right corner, click **Minimize** ⊟.

9 In the upper right corner of the Edge window, click **Exit** Exit, and then in the **Save your changes** message, click **No**.

Activity 4.05 | Searching the Web by Using Boolean Operators

Recall that a statement using ***Boolean operators*** such as AND, OR, and NOT expresses a condition that is either true or false. In this Activity, you will use Boolean operators in a Google search.

1 At the top of the **Microsoft Edge** browser, click **New tab** ➕.

2 In the **Search or enter web address** box, type **site:usa.gov seattle AND restaurants** and then compare your screen with Figure 4.18.

The search expression will search only the usa.gov site and then display pages from that site that include both the words *seattle* and *restaurants*.

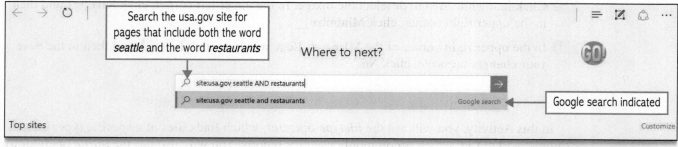

	Search the usa.gov site for pages that include both the word *seattle* and the word *restaurants*	Where to next?		GO
	site:usa.gov seattle AND restaurants			
	site:usa.gov seattle and restaurants	Google search	Google search indicated	
Top sites				Customize

FIGURE 4.18

Edge 2016, Windows 10, Microsoft Corporation.

3 Press Enter and notice the list of webpages from the usa.gov site.

4 Click **Make a Web Note** 🖊, and then in the upper left corner, click the **Pen** ▽. By using the techniques you have practiced, set the pen color to **Green** and the size to the largest size.

5 Use your mouse pointer to draw a green circle around the first article on the list.

6 In the upper left corner, click **Add a note** 💬, position the + pointer just below your green circle, and then click one time.

7 With the insertion point blinking in the note, type **Search with Boolean operator AND** and then compare your screen with Figure 4.19.

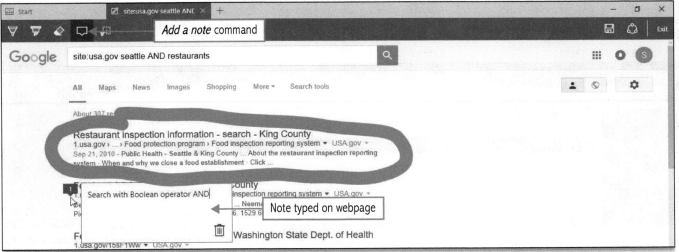

FIGURE 4.19

Edge 2016, Windows 10, Microsoft Corporation.

8 In the upper left corner, click **Clip** ⬚, and then using the + mouse pointer and the technique you have practiced, select the area of the screen that includes your green circle and your note; your selection need not be precise.

9 From the taskbar, open your PowerPoint presentation. On the **Home tab**, in the **Slides group**, click the upper portion of the **New Slide** button to insert a new blank slide.

10 On the **Home tab**, in the **Clipboard group**, click the upper portion of the **Paste** button.

11 Click in a white area to deselect the image. In the upper left corner, click **Save** 🖫, and then in the upper right corner, click **Minimize** ⊟.

12 In the upper right corner of the **Microsoft Edge** window, click **Exit** Exit, and then in the **Save your changes** message, click **No**.

Activity 4.06 │ Finding Items on a Webpage

After you have a webpage displayed, the next challenge might be to find the specific word or group of words on the page. In this Activity, you will use the ⌨Ctrl + ⌨F command to find information on a displayed webpage.

1 At the top of the **Microsoft Edge** browser, click **New tab** ⊞.

2 In the **Search or enter web address** box, type **travel.trade.gov/ttab** and then press ⏎Enter.

The webpage from the U.S. Travel and Tourism Advisory Board displays.

3 Hold down ⌨Ctrl and press ⌨F and then compare your screen with Figure 4.20.

The Find on page box displays in the upper left corner of the screen.

FIGURE 4.20

Screenshot from International Trade Administration, U.S. Department of Commerce.

4 With the insertion point blinking in the **Find on page** dialog box, type **secretary of commerce** and then click outside the white area of the webpage. Compare your screen with Figure 4.21.

The instances of *Secretary of Commerce* are highlighted. Use this technique to find a word or phrase on a webpage.

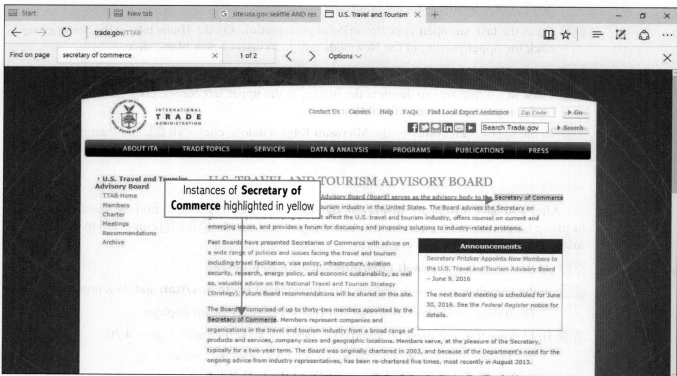

FIGURE 4.21

Screenshot from International Trade Administration, U.S. Department of Commerce.

5 Click **Make a Web Note** 📝, in the upper left corner, click **Clip** ✂️, and then using the + mouse pointer and the technique you have practiced, select the area of the screen that includes the highlighted selections; your selection need not be precise.

6 From the taskbar, open your PowerPoint presentation. On the **Home tab**, in the **Slides group**, click the upper portion of the **New Slide** button to insert a new blank slide.

7 On the **Home tab**, in the **Clipboard group**, click the upper portion of the **Paste** button.

8 Click in a white area to deselect the image. In the upper left corner, click **Save** 🖫, and then in the upper right corner, click **Minimize** ⊟.

9 In the upper right corner of the **Microsoft Edge** window, click **Exit** [Exit].

Activity 4.07 | Finding an Author's Work by Using Google Scholar

Google Scholar enables you to search for scholarly literature; for example, when you are creating a research paper for college or for work. From the Google Scholar site, a search expression that you enter will search articles, theses, online repositories, and abstracts of research studies.

1 At the top of the **Microsoft Edge** browser, click **New tab** ⊞.

2 In the **Search or enter web address** box, type **scholar.google.com** and then press [Enter].

3 With your insertion point blinking in the **Google Scholar** search box, type **author:pinker cognition** and press [Enter].

> Scholarly works by the cognitive scientist Steven Pinker display. Use Google Scholar when you need to find sources of information for your research papers.

Activity 4.08 | Converting Units and Making Calculations

You can quickly solve mathematical calculations and convert units, such as pounds to kilograms, by simply typing in the search box.

1 At the top of the **Microsoft Edge** browser, click **New tab** ⊞.

2 In the **Search or enter web address** box, type **14 gallons in liters** and then press [Enter].

3 Click **Make a Web Note** ✎, and then in the upper left corner, click **Clip** ✂.

4 By using the **+** mouse pointer and the technique you have practiced, select the area of the screen that shows the conversion; your selection need not be precise.

5 From the taskbar, open your PowerPoint presentation. On the **Home tab**, in the **Slides group**, click the upper portion of the **New Slide** button to insert a new blank slide.

6 On the **Home tab**, in the **Clipboard group**, click the upper portion of the **Paste** button. Click in a white area to deselect the image, and then compare your screen with Figure 4.22.

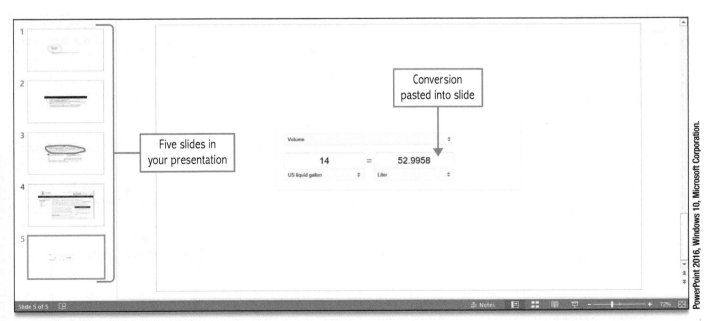

FIGURE 4.22

7 In the upper left corner, click **Save** 🖫, and then in the upper right corner, click **Minimize** ▭. In the upper right corner, click **Exit**.

8 At the top of the **Microsoft Edge** browser, click **New tab** ⊞.

9 In the **Search or enter web address** box, type **(5*20)/4** and then press Enter.

10 Notice your result, and then using the techniques you have practiced, make a **Clip** 🖾 of just the upper portion of the calculator with the result, and then paste it into a new slide in your PowerPoint presentation.

This becomes the sixth slide in your PowerPoint presentation.

11 In the upper left corner, click **Save** 🖫, and then in the upper right corner, click **Minimize** ▭.

12 In the upper right corner of the **Microsoft Edge** window, click **Exit** ⏻, **Close** ✕ the **Microsoft Edge** window, and then if necessary, click **Close all**.

Objective 3 | Use Windows 10 Utility Apps

Some of the Windows 10 built-in apps are simply small programs that provide a way to perform common tasks or find system information.

Activity 4.09 | Using Alarms & Clock

The **_Alarms & Clock_** app enables you to set alarms on your computer, and it also functions as a timer, a stopwatch, and a world clock.

1 In the lower left corner of your screen, click **Start** ⊞, and then in the group of apps that begin with the letter _A_, click **Alarms & Clock**. If necessary, **Maximize** ▢ the window, and at the top of the screen, if necessary click **Alarm**. Compare your screen with Figure 4.23.

By default, the alarm is set to off unless you have set the alarm. To turn on an alarm that you have set, you must click the Manage button in the lower right corner.

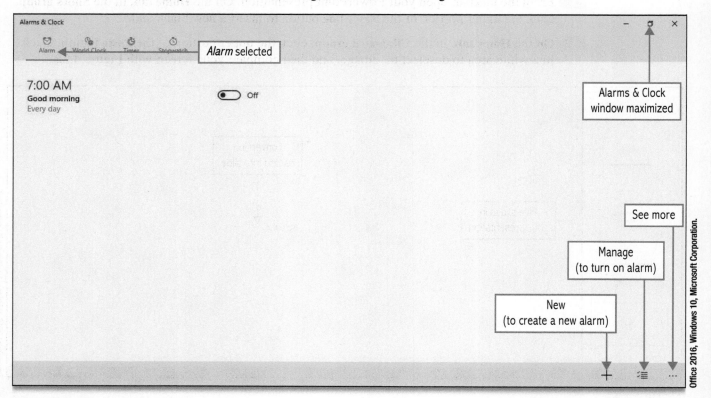

FIGURE 4.23

2 In the lower right corner, click **New** ➕, and then compare your screen with Figure 4.24.

Here you can set the time of the alarm, name the alarm, select how often the alarm repeats, select the alarm sound, and set a snooze time.

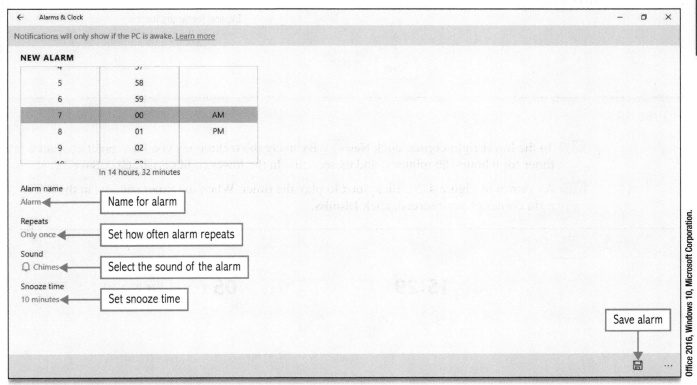

FIGURE 4.24

3 Under **NEW ALARM**, point to a number in the first column, and then either by clicking the **up scroll arrow** ▲ or the **down scroll arrow** ▼, or by rolling the wheel on your mouse, set the first column to **6**.

4 By using the same technique, set the middle column to **30** and set the third column to **AM**.

5 Under **Alarm name**, click **Alarm** (or whatever text is highlighted in blue) and then type **Wake Up**

6 Set the number of **Repeats** to **Monday** through **Friday** by clicking each day, set the **Sound** to **Jingle**, and set the **Snooze** time to **5 minutes**.

7 From the taskbar, open your PowerPoint presentation, add a new slide in the **Blank** layout, and then on the **Insert tab**, in the **Images group**, click **Screenshot**. Click **Screen Clipping**, and then by using the techniques you have practiced, drag to capture the entire screen but not the taskbar.

8 Deselect the image. In the upper left corner, click **Save** 🖫, and then in the upper right corner, click **Minimize** ➖.

Unless you want to do so, do not save this alarm.

9 In the upper left corner, click **Back** ← , and then at the top, click **Timer**. Compare your screen with Figure 4.25.

Here you can set a timer. For example, you could set the timer to remind yourself to make a phone call in 20 minutes.

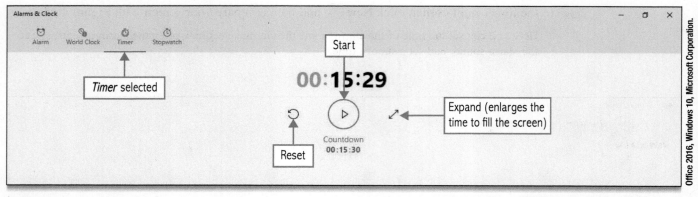

FIGURE 4.25

> **10** In the lower right corner, click **New** ⊞. By using the techniques you have practiced, set a timer for **0** hours, **00** minutes, and **05** seconds. In the lower right corner, click **Save** 🖫.

> **11** As shown in Figure 4.26, click **Start** to play the timer. When the timer sounds, in the lower right corner of your screen, click **Dismiss**.

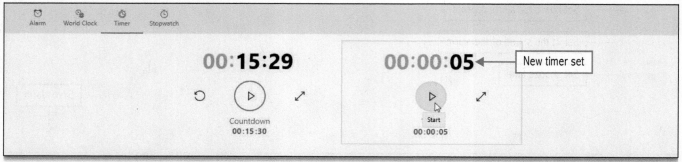

FIGURE 4.26

> **12** In the lower right corner, click **Manage** ≡, and then to the left of the timer you just set, click **Delete** 🗑.

> **13** In the lower right corner, click **Done** ✓ to reactivate the commands at the top of the screen.

> **14** At the top of the screen, click **World Clock**. In the lower right corner, click **New** ⊞. Type **Paris, France** and press Enter. In the lower right corner, click **Compare** ⅋, and then compare your screen with Figure 4.27.

Here you can see the time and date for your location and the time and date for Paris.

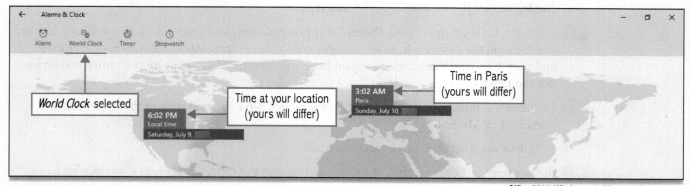

FIGURE 4.27

> **15** **Close** ☒ the **Alarms & Clock** window.

Activity 4.10 | Using Steps Recorder

The **Steps Recorder** captures the steps you perform on your computer, including a text description of where you clicked and a screenshot of the screen during each click. After you capture the steps, you can save them to a file, and then send the file in an email to your Help Desk or to someone else who can help you with a computer problem. Conversely, if you are helping a friend, colleague, or family member with a computer problem, they can send a file to you so that you can view the steps they performed.

1 In the lower left corner of your screen, click **Start** ⊞ , and then in the group of apps that begin with the letter *A*, click **A** to display the alphabet layout. Click **W**, click **Windows Accessories**, and then click **Steps Recorder**. Compare your screen with Figure 4.28.

The Steps Recorder window displays as a small window.

Office 2016, Windows 10, Microsoft Corporation.

FIGURE 4.28

2 Click **Start Record**.

Beginning now, your clicks and keystrokes are being recorded.

3 Click **Start** ⊞ , click **Settings** ⚙ , and then click **Devices**. On the left, click **Printers & scanners**. Compare your screen with Figure 4.29.

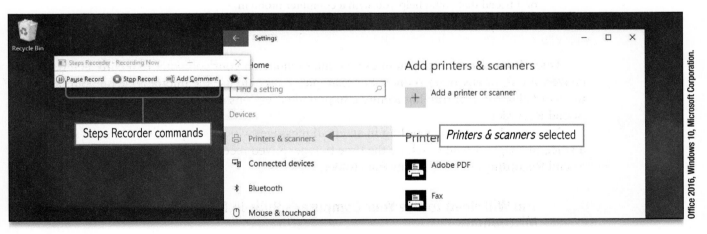

FIGURE 4.29

4 In the **Steps Recorder** window, click **Add Comment**, and then in the **Highlight Area and Comment** box that displays, type **I'm not sure which one to choose.** Then click **OK**.

5 In the **Steps Recorder** window, click **Stop Record**. Compare your screen with Figure 4.30.

The recording stops and a window displays your recorded steps. Here you can scroll down to view the steps and then save the recording.

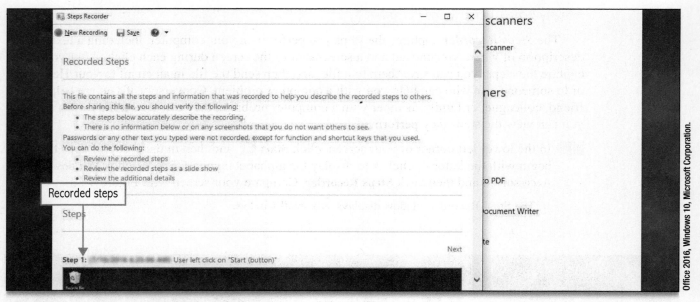

FIGURE 4.30

6 Scroll down to see your recorded steps and display the step where you typed *I'm not sure which one to choose.*

7 From the taskbar, open your PowerPoint presentation, add a new slide in the **Blank** layout, and then on the **Insert tab**, in the **Images group**, click **Screenshot**. Click **Screen Clipping**, and then by using the techniques you have practiced, drag to capture the entire screen but not the taskbar.

8 Deselect the image. In the upper left corner, click **Save** 🔲, and then in the upper right corner, click **Minimize** ⊟.

9 **Close** ☒ the **Steps Recorder** window without saving, and then **Close** ☒ the **Settings** window.

> If you wanted to do so, you could save the recording and send it to someone such as a Help Desk or a friend that could help you with a computer problem.

Activity 4.11 │ Using Voice Recorder

Voice Recorder enables you to use the microphone on your computer to record lectures, conversations, or any other sounds. For example, you could use the microphone on your laptop to record classroom or training lectures. In previous versions of Windows, this feature was named Sound Recorder.

You can also share a recording in an email message, which is a quick way to send someone a voice message instead of taking the time to type. Saved recordings are stored in a folder named Sound Recordings in your Documents folder.

ALERT! **You Will Need to Use Your Computer's Built-In Microphone or a Connected Microphone**

To complete this Activity, you will need to use your computer's built-in microphone or a connected microphone such as a headset with a microphone or the microphone on a webcam.

1 First, to be sure that your microphone is enabled for Voice Recorder, on the right end of your taskbar, click **Action Center** ▭, and then click **All settings**.

2 Click **Privacy**, and then on the left, click **Microphone**. On the right, scroll down to view all the apps that use your microphone, and then if necessary, set **Voice Recorder** to **On**, as shown in Figure 4.31.

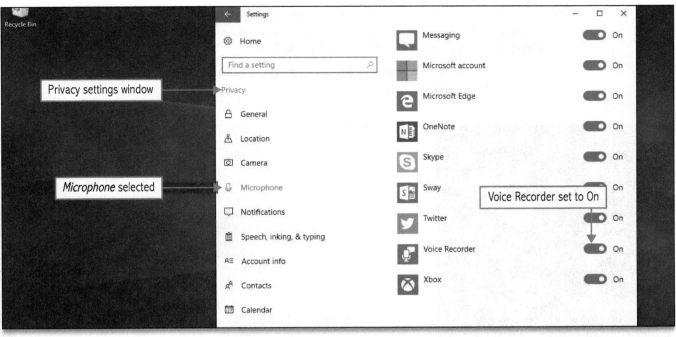

Privacy settings window

Microphone selected

Voice Recorder set to On

FIGURE 4.31

3 **Close** ☒ the **Settings** window.

4 In the lower left corner of your screen, click **Start** ⊞, and then in the group of apps that begin with the letter *A*, click **A** to display the alphabet layout. Click **V**, and then click **Voice Recorder**. Compare your screen with Figure 4.32.

The Voice Recorder window displays.

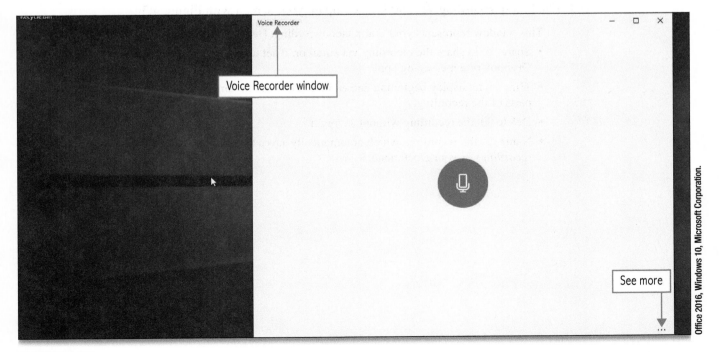

Voice Recorder window

See more

FIGURE 4.32

5 Click the large **Record** button ⦿ and begin speaking "I am using the Voice Recorder" (or just let the recorder run a few seconds, you need not actually record) and then click **Pause** ‖ . Compare your screen with Figure 4.33.

By clicking the Pause button, you can stop the recording. The Pause button turns blue and becomes the Resume recording button.

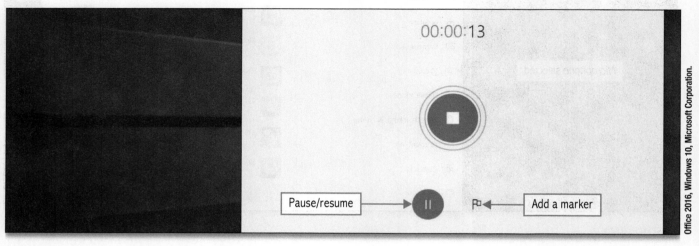

00:00:13

Pause/resume → ‖   ⚑ ← Add a marker

Office 2016, Windows 10, Microsoft Corporation.

FIGURE 4.33

6 Click **Resume recording** ⦿ , speak some words if you want to do so—or just let the recorder run—and as the recorder is running, click **Add a marker** ⚑ . Notice that a marker is placed at the number of seconds.

You can add a marker to mark specific points in the recording that you want to find later; for example, an important point that your professor made in a lecture.

7 Click **Stop recording** ⦿ , and then compare your screen with Figure 4.34.

This window represents your completed recording. Here you can click:

- Share ⌂ to share the recording via email or, if set up on your computer, you can share to Dropbox or a messaging app.
- Trim ⊶ to display beginning and ending marks on the timeline and then move the marks to trim parts of the recording.
- Delete ⌦ the recording without saving it.
- Name ⌀ the recording, which automatically saves the recording in a folder named *Sound recordings* in your Documents folder.

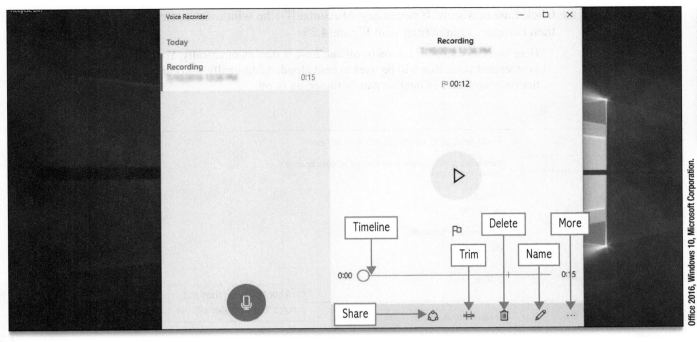

FIGURE 4.34

8 If necessary, **Maximize** □ the **Voice Recorder** window. Then, in the lower right corner of the **Voice Recorder** window, click **Name** ✎. In the **Rename** box, with the existing text highlighted, type **Professor Warren's Lecture** and then click **Rename**.

9 From the taskbar, open your PowerPoint presentation, add a new slide in the **Blank** layout, and then on the **Insert tab**, in the **Images group**, click **Screenshot**. Click **Screen Clipping**, and then by using the techniques you have practiced, drag to capture the window but without the taskbar.

10 Deselect the image. In the upper left corner, click **Save** 🖫, and then in the upper right corner, click **Minimize** ─.

11 **Close** ✕ the **Voice Recorder** window.

Objective 4 | Use Windows 10 Ease of Access Apps

In computing, *accessibility* refers to the design of hardware and software in a manner that helps individuals with disabilities use computing tools. Windows 10 includes *Windows Ease of Access*, which is a set of accessibility apps that you can access in a central location. Within Settings, you can click Ease of Access to locate and modify the app settings. For example, these apps make it easier to see your computer's screen, to use the mouse and keyboard, and to use other input devices.

Activity 4.12 | Using Narrator

Narrator is a program that reads text on your PC screen aloud and that serves as a basic *screen reader*—a computer program that converts text into speech. Narrator also describes events; for example, notifications for calendar appointments.

1 On the right end of your taskbar, click **Action Center** ▣, and then click **All settings**.

2 Click **Ease of Access**. If necessary, **Maximize** ▫ the window. On the left, click **Narrator**, and then compare your screen with Figure 4.35.

Here you can turn Narrator on or off and have it start automatically. You can also select the synthesized voice that will be used to read aloud. Additionally, you can set the speed and pitch of the voice and have intonation pauses turned on or off.

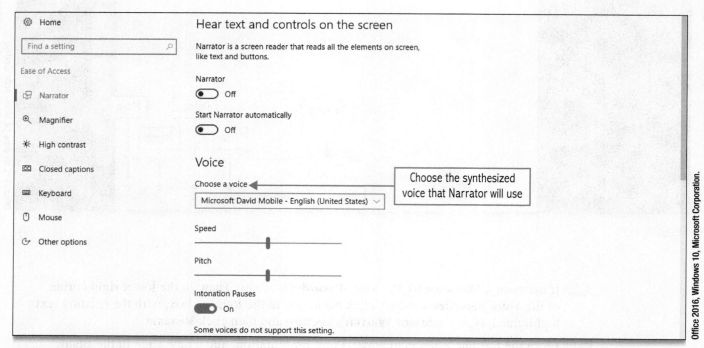

FIGURE 4.35

3 From the taskbar, open your PowerPoint presentation, add a new slide in the **Blank** layout, and then on the **Insert tab**, in the **Images group**, click **Screenshot**. Click **Screen Clipping**, and then by using the techniques you have practiced, drag to capture the entire window but without the taskbar.

4 Deselect the image. In the upper left corner, click **Save** ▫, and then in the upper right corner, click **Minimize** ▫.

5 **Close** ☒ the **Settings** window.

Activity 4.13 | Using Magnifier

Magnifier is a screen enlarger that magnifies a portion of the screen. This feature is helpful for computer users with impaired vision and for those who require occasional screen magnification for such tasks as editing art.

1 On the right end of your taskbar, click **Action Center** ▫, and then click **All settings**.

2 Click **Ease of Access**. If necessary, **Maximize** ▫ the window. On the left, click **Magnifier**, and then compare your screen with Figure 4.36.

Here you can turn Magnifier on or off or have it start automatically. You can also set tracking options.

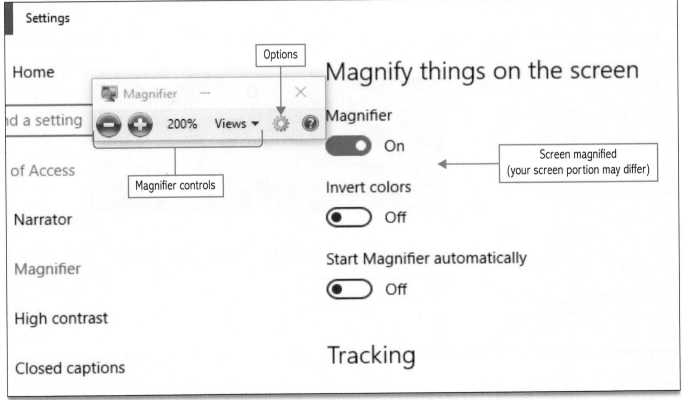

Office 2016, Windows 10, Microsoft Corporation.

FIGURE 4.36

3 ▶ Under **Magnify things on the screen**, click the **Magnifier** button to turn it on.

4 ▶ Move your mouse pointer into each corner of your screen, and notice that the window is magnified. Then, point to the **magnifying glass** and click **>>**. Compare your screen with Figure 4.37.

The small Magnifier window displays. Here you can select different views and change the percentage of magnification.

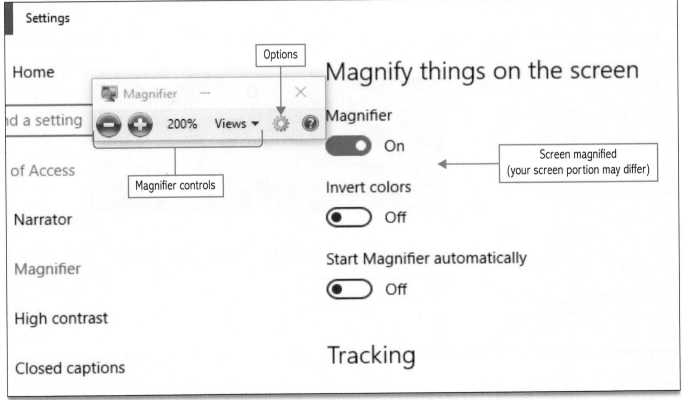

Office 2016, Windows 10, Microsoft Corporation.

FIGURE 4.37

5 **Close** ⊠ the **Magnifier** window to turn off the Magnifier.

6 **Close** ⊠ the **Settings** window.

Activity 4.14 | Using the On-Screen Keyboard

You can use the *On-Screen Keyboard*, sometimes referred to as *OSK*, instead of a physical keyboard to move around a PC's screen or type text. The OSK does not require a touchscreen computer. The On-Screen Keyboard displays a standard keyboard on the screen enabling you to use your mouse or other pointing device to select keys.

1 On the right end of your taskbar, click **Action Center** ▣, and then click **All settings**.

2 Click **Ease of Access**. If necessary, **Maximize** ▢ the window. On the left, click **Keyboard**.

3 On the right, at the top of the screen, under **Turns on the On-Screen Keyboard**, click to set the On-Screen Keyboard to **On**.

4 On the displayed keyboard, in the lower right portion, click **Options**, and then compare your screen with Figure 4.38.

Some of the options you can select here include:

- *Use click sound* to hear a sound when you press a key.
- *Show keys to make it easier to move around the screen* to have the keys light up as you type.
- *Turn on numeric key pad* to expand the keyboard to display a numeric key pad.
- *Click on keys* to click or tap the on-screen keys to enter text.
- *Hover over keys* to use a mouse to point to a key; the characters to which you point are entered automatically if you hover briefly.
- *Scan through keys* to have the OSK continually scan the keyboard; this mode highlights areas where you can type.
- *Use Text Prediction* to have the OSK suggest words for you as you type.

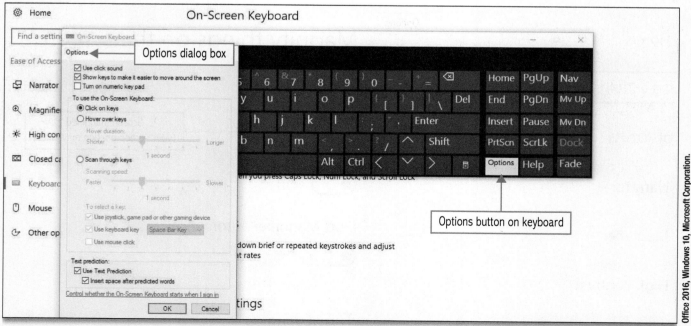

FIGURE 4.38

5 Close ☒ the **Options** dialog box. Close ☒ the **On-Screen Keyboard** window. Close ☒ the **Settings** window.

6 From the taskbar, redisplay your PowerPoint presentation. In the upper left corner, click **Save** 🖫, and then in the upper right corner, click **Close** ☒. Submit your completed PowerPoint presentation, which contains ten slides, as directed by your instructor.

ALERT! | **This Activity Is Optional**

Because you may not be able to complete this Activity in a college lab, or if you do not want to use speech recognition at this time, this Activity is optional.

Activity 4.15 | Using Windows Speech Recognition

Windows Speech Recognition enables you to control your computer by using your voice. Individuals who are unable to type, or anyone who would like to reduce the use of the keyboard and mouse, will find this feature to be both powerful and easy to use.

1 In the lower left corner of your screen, click **Start** ⊞, and then in the group of apps that begin with the letter *A*, click **A** to display the alphabet layout. Click **W**, click **Windows Ease of Access**, and then click **Windows Speech Recognition**. Compare your screen with Figure 4.39.

The Set up Speech Recognition welcome message displays. Here you begin the setup wizard that will enable the system to recognize your voice.

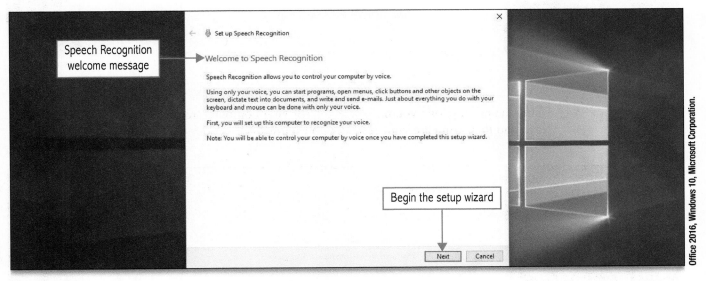

FIGURE 4.39

2 Click **Next**, and then compare your screen with Figure 4.40.

Here the system recognizes that a headset microphone is connected. You can use a headset microphone, a desktop microphone, or an array microphone that is built into your computer.

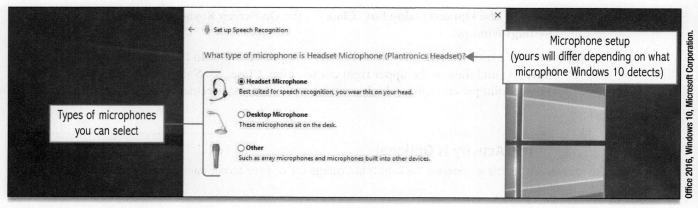

Types of microphones you can select

Microphone setup (yours will differ depending on what microphone Windows 10 detects)

FIGURE 4.40

3 ▶ Select the type of microphone you will use, and then click **Next**. (You may have to click Next one more time to see the screen shown in Figure 4.41.) Compare your screen with Figure 4.41.

Here you begin to train the system to recognize your voice by reading aloud into the microphone.

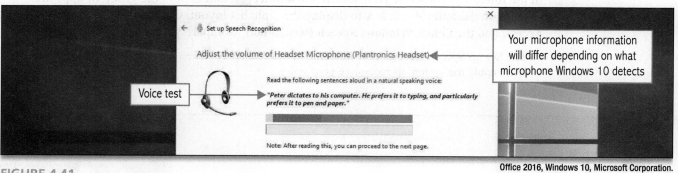

Voice test

Your microphone information will differ depending on what microphone Windows 10 detects

FIGURE 4.41

4 ▶ Using the microphone you have selected for your computer, read the sentence aloud, click **Next**, and then compare your screen with Figure 4.42.

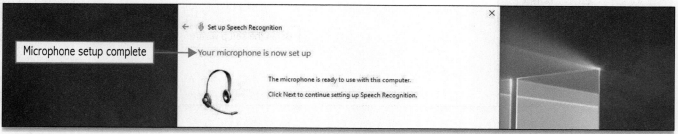

Microphone setup complete

FIGURE 4.42

5 ▶ Click **Next**, and then compare your screen with Figure 4.43.

Here you can agree to allow the system to look at the documents and email messages in your indexed locations so that the computer can learn words and phrases that distinguish the way you speak.

Help your computer learn how you speak and write

FIGURE 4.43

6 Click to select **Enable document review**, and then click **Next**.

Here you choose what happens when you say the "Stop Listening" command.

7 Select the **Use voice activation** mode option button so that you can activate speech recognition by voice by saying "Start listening," and then click **Next**. Compare your screen with Figure 4.44.

Here you can print the list of commands to which the computer will respond when you speak the commands.

View and print the list of commands

FIGURE 4.44

8 Click **Next**. In the **Run Speech Recognition every time I start the computer** screen, click **Next**.

Windows indicates that you are now able to control your computer with your voice, and recommends that you begin the tutorial. If you plan to use speech recognition on your own computer, be sure to go through the tutorial.

9 Close ⨯ the **Set up Speech Recognition** window.

> **NOTE** To Turn Off Windows Speech Recognition
>
> To turn off Windows Speech Recognition, right-click the Start button, click Control Panel, on the right click the View by arrow, click Small icons, click Speech Recognition, on the left click Text to Speech, in the Speech Properties dialog box, click the Speech Recognition tab, and then under User Settings, clear all the check boxes. Click Apply, click OK, and perform a restart on your computer.

END | You have completed Project 4A

Securing Your Computer

PROJECT ACTIVITIES

In Activities 4.16 through 4.20, you will work with Barbara Hewitt and Steven Ramos, employees in the Information Technology Department at the headquarters office of Bell Orchid Hotels, as they explore how Windows 10 helps to secure a computer. As you progress through the Project, you will insert screenshots of windows that you create into a PowerPoint presentation similar to Figure 4.45.

PROJECT FILES

For Project 4B, you will need the following file:

A new blank PowerPoint presentation

You will save your PowerPoint presentation as:

Lastname_Firstname_4B_Security

PROJECT RESULTS

1. Malicious software
2. Infect
3. Attachment
4. Trojan horse
5. Security holes

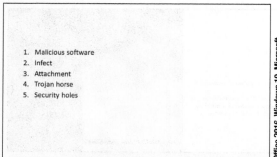

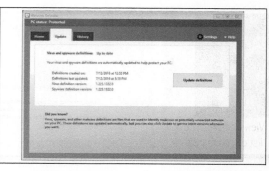

FIGURE 4.45   Project 4B Securing Your Computer

Malware—a shortened term for *malicious software*—is a computer program that intentionally harms your computer. If a malware program installs itself and then runs on your computer, your computer is said to be *infected*. *Anti-malware programs* protect your computer from a malware infection.

Anti-malware programs specialize in protecting your computer from either *viruses* or *spyware*. A virus is a type of malware designed specifically to replicate itself by spreading its infection from computer to computer; a virus can damage hardware, software, or data. Spyware is a type of malware that collects personal information or changes your browser settings. Spyware can infect your computer without your knowledge when you download a program or visit a website. Spyware is most commonly installed through free software, such as file sharing software or screen savers. *Keylogger spyware* is a type of spyware that records all of your keystrokes and then sends your typed data—including user names and passwords—to someone else. To protect your computer from both types of malware, you need to follow safe practices to keep malware from infecting your computer.

Activity 4.16 | Protecting Your Computer from Malware

A virus can delete files on your hard drive, format your hard drive, or take control of your computer so that it can attack other computers. A virus can look for sensitive information on your hard drive such as your list of e-mail addresses and credit card information. Some viruses have the capability to shut down or change your computer's security programs so that they no longer protect your computer. In this unprotected state, viruses can easily spread throughout many locations on your hard drive, or leave your computer vulnerable to an attack from another computer.

Viruses are commonly classified by the methods they use to infect other computers. A traditional virus infects your computer when you open a file on your computer. This type of virus is commonly hidden in files attached to e-mail messages or in files downloaded from websites. A *worm* is a self-replicating program—similar to a virus—that spreads on its own to every computer on a network. You do not have to open a file to spread this type of malware. After one computer on the network is infected, a worm spreads extremely fast, often before its presence is discovered.

A *Trojan horse* is a malicious software program that hides inside a legitimate program, such as a game or media player or screen saver. For example, a free game may work as you intended, but the software has hidden features that are initiated later. A Trojan horse might place code into the operating system that enables a hacker to take control of your computer.

A *boot-sector virus* replicates itself onto your hard drive's master boot record—the program that executes each time your computer boots up. Therefore, the virus will be loaded into memory before some virus protection programs on your computer start.

With the exception of worms, viruses infect the computer only after you take some action to allow it to do so, such as viewing an e-mail file attachment or visiting a non-reputable website. Virus authors make it difficult for you to know that such an action may be dangerous. For example, Trojan horse authors persuade individuals to download and install their malware by offering free or inexpensive software. Others send you e-mail attachments in hopes that you will open the attachment, and by doing so, install the virus. Determined virus authors have discovered ways to install a virus on your computer when you view a website designed to spread the virus. A website that spreads a virus is referred to as a *poisoned website*.

Viruses take advantage of *security holes*—vulnerabilities in an operating system or program that allow malware to infect a computer without your knowledge. As security holes are discovered, programmers work to write a *patch*—a small repair to an operating system or program that closes a security hole. Windows 10 automatically installs new updates whenever necessary to repair newly discovered security holes.

Be wary of all file attachments, even when they are from people that you know. Do not open any attachment that has the *.exe* file extension unless you are absolutely certain it is safe, because files with this extension can install programs on your computer. Also avoid files from ***peer-to-peer file sharing sites*** that let you share files such as music, videos, and software with others using the Internet. Virus authors often place infected files at these sites in hopes that you will download and thus install their virus.

NOTE User Rights May Vary in College Labs

The setup of user rights in a college lab varies among colleges; you may not have access to as many Windows 10 features in a college lab as you would have on your own computer.

---

1 From the taskbar, or by searching, open **PowerPoint**, and then click **Blank Presentation**. On the **Home tab**, in the **Slides group**, click **Layout**, and then click **Title and Content**.

2 Click the **File tab**, on the left click **Save As**, click **Browse**, and then in the **Save As** dialog box, navigate to and open your **Windows 10 Chapter 4** folder.

3 In the **File name** box, using your own name, type **Lastname_Firstname_4B_Security**

4 In the **Save As** dialog box, click **Save**. With the **Layout** set to **Title and Content**, click the text *Click to add text*.

5 On the **Home tab**, in the **Paragraph group**, click **Numbering** [≡ ▾]. Compare your screen with Figure 4.46.

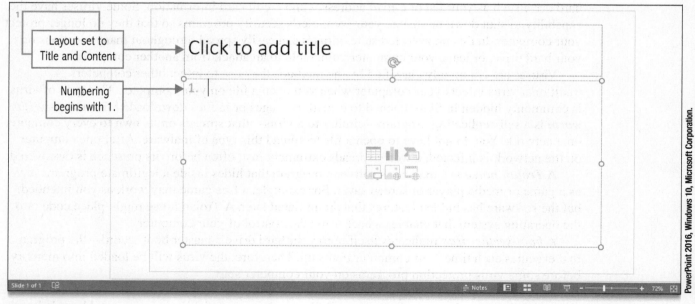

FIGURE 4.46

6 To check how well you understand protecting your computer from viruses, answer the following questions and type your answers into your PowerPoint slide; when you press [Enter], the next number will display automatically:

1. Malware is a shortened term for _____ _____.
2. Viruses are commonly classified by the method they use to _____ other computers.
3. One type of malware is an e-mail _____ that, when opened, installs a virus.
4. A malicious software program that hides inside legitimate programs, such as a game or media player or screen saver, is a _____ _____.
5. Vulnerabilities in an operating system or program that allow malware to infect a computer without your knowledge are referred to as _____ _____.

7 In the upper left corner, click **Save** [▣], and then in the upper right corner, click **Minimize** [−].

4
WINDOWS 10

Windows 10 provides strong security. In fact, with each version of Windows, the built-in security has gotten stronger. Threats to your computer all come from the Internet, so Windows 10 security features focus on Internet threats.

ALERT!   **Windows 10 Is an Evolving Operating System**

Like all modern operating systems, Windows 10 is constantly evolving with new features, updates, and security enhancements. Therefore, you may encounter occasional differences in techniques and screens as you progress through the Projects. You can often look at the screens in Windows 10 to determine how to complete steps, or you can search for information about new features.

Activity 4.17 │ Exploring Windows Defender

Windows Defender is the free and trusted antivirus program built in to Windows 10. It includes virus protection and removal, malware protection and removal, spyware detection and removal, and boot-time protection. For most consumer PC users, this is the only program you need—and it's free!

It's difficult to resist loading those trial versions of commercial antivirus programs that present themselves to you on a new PC. If you try to delete them or refuse the trial, messages may display indicating that your PC is unprotected. It is not; Windows Defender is protecting your PC automatically.

Ultimately, you will have to pay $50 or more per year for these programs that come on a new PC, and you don't need them. Your PC is protected with Windows Defender, and you do not need to pay for it. You can confidently uninstall any commercial antivirus programs that come with your PC and be assured that Windows Defender is protecting your PC.

Windows Defender is automatic, so you need do nothing to use it. It is always on, it is on by default, and it works in the background with no intervention on your part. Installing a full-featured commercial security suite—such as those that are offered to you on a new PC—may disable Windows Defender.

Although you can trust Windows Defender to protect your PC, some individuals want a second anti-malware solution. If you decide to use Windows Defender, and there is no reason not to do so, you can still augment Windows Defender with a free product that experts recommend and rely on, which is Malwarebytes Anti-Malware Free. You can download the free version at www.malwarebytes.com.

Windows Defender provides *real-time protection*, which means that the system is continuously monitoring your computer at all times for suspicious activity such as viruses and spyware. The free version of Malwarebytes does *not* provide real-time protection. Rather, if you suspect something is wrong, you can activate the program and have it scan all of your files. A *paid* version of Malwarebytes provides real-time monitoring.

So a secure and reliable solution to protect your computer is to use Windows 10 augmented by occasional scans of your computer with Malwarebytes Free. This combination is completely free and experts agree that it is secure.

1 In the lower left corner of your screen, click **Start** ⊞, and then in the group of apps that begin with the letter *A*, click **A** to display the alphabet layout. Click **W**, and then click **Windows System**. Compare your screen with Figure 4.47.

Windows Defender is included in the group of programs called Windows System.

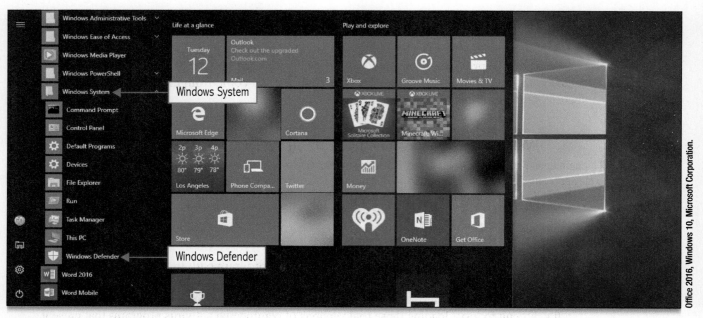

FIGURE 4.47

ANOTHER WAY   Display Settings, click Update & security, and then click Windows Defender; or, search for Windows Defender in the search box.

> **2** Click **Windows Defender**. As shown in Figure 4.48, you may see a *What's new in Windows Defender* message.

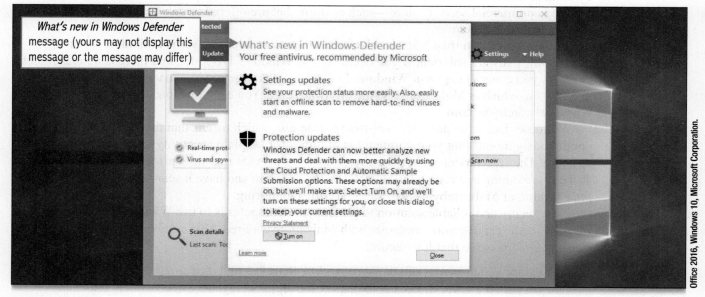

FIGURE 4.48

> **3** If the window shown in Figure 4.48 displays, click **Close**, and then compare your screen with Figure 4.49. If necessary, click the **Home tab**.

By default, every day Windows Defender downloads updated *definitions*—updates to Microsoft's database of potential viruses—and performs a quick scan of your computer. This definitions database is constantly updated as new threats are found that could potentially make their way into your PC.

Here you can see that your PC is being monitored and protected, that Real-time protection is On, and that the virus and spyware definitions are up to date.

Although Windows Defender is continuously monitoring your PC, if you notice something unusual, you can perform a scan of your files manually. A *quick scan* checks the areas on your hard drive where malware programs are most likely to reside. A *full scan* looks at everything on your hard drive; this can take a long time, but you can still use your computer while the scan is running. A *custom scan* searches only those drives or folders or files that you select; for example, an email attachment that was just sent to you.

In the event of unusual activity or a website that acts as *ransomware*—malware that blocks access to your PC until a sum of money is paid—you should immediately perform a full scan and perhaps another scan by Malwarebytes.

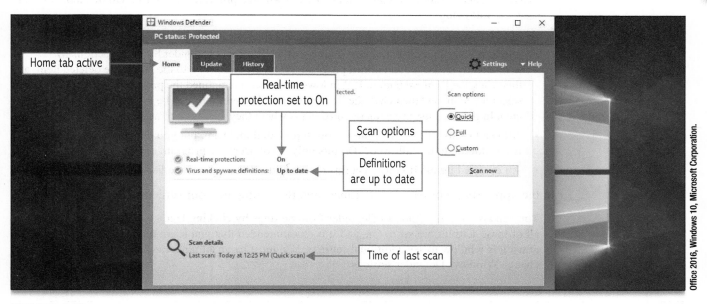

FIGURE 4.49

4 ▶ Click the **Update tab**, and then read the information at the bottom of the window under *Did you know?* Compare your screen with Figure 4.50.

Here you can see that your virus and spyware definitions are up to date, and you can also see the date and time that an update occurred. This is the power of Windows Defender. It is always working for you in the background protecting your system.

Here you can also click Update definitions to see if any new definitions have been added since the time of the last update.

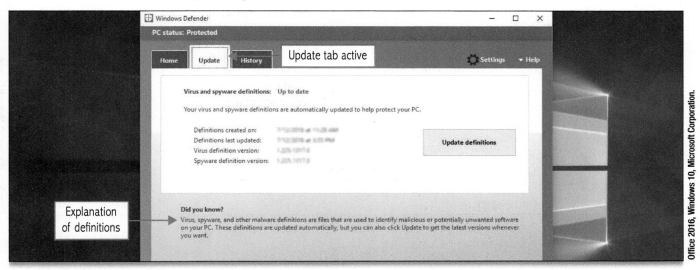

FIGURE 4.50

5 From the taskbar, open your PowerPoint presentation, add a new slide in the **Blank** layout, and then on the **Insert tab**, in the **Images group**, click **Screenshot**. Under **Available Windows**, click the **Windows Defender** window to insert it in the slide.

6 Deselect the image. In the upper left corner, click **Save** 🖫, and then in the upper right corner, click **Minimize** ⊟.

7 In the **Windows Defender** window, click the **History tab**.

If malware is detected, Windows Defender places the software in the *quarantine area*—an area in a designated location on your computer from which a program cannot run. On this tab, you can view the following:

- Quarantined items: If you select this option and then click View details at the bottom of the window, you can see a list of programs on which Windows Defender has taken action. To permanently delete a quarantined program, select the check box to the left of the deleted item, and then click the Remove button. If Windows Defender quarantined the program by mistake, you can select the item, and then click the Restore button. The program will be moved from the quarantine area. In general, just leave quarantined items where they are—in quarantine!

- Allowed items: If Defender alerts you to potential malware, but you decide to run it anyway, it is considered to be "allowed." Do this only if you trust the program completely.

- All detected items: If you select this option button, you can view a list any detected items.

8 In the upper right corner, click **Settings**, and then compare your screen with Figure 4.51.

You can also access Windows Defender from Settings by clicking Update & security. By default, all of these settings are set to On, and it is recommended that you leave them on. You can scroll down this window to see additional settings. You must be an administrator on the computer to change Windows Defender settings.

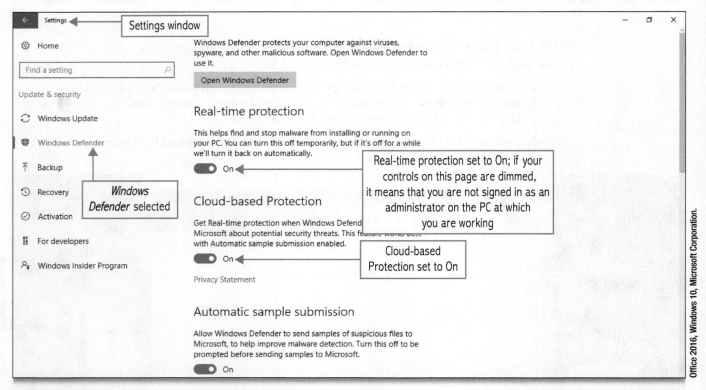

FIGURE 4.51

9 Close ✕ the **Settings** window, and then **Close** ✕ **Windows Defender**.

To protect an Internet-connected computer from malware, the computer should have a *firewall*, which is software or hardware that can help protect a computer from hackers, or prevent malicious software from gaining access to a computer through a network or over the Internet. It also helps prevent a computer from sending malicious software to other computers. *Hacker* is a term used to describe a person who uses computer expertise to gain access to computer systems often without permission. Companies have begun to hire *white hat hackers*, which are ethical security experts that test an organization's data and network security by attempting to hack into it. Windows 10 installs Windows Firewall and enables it by default. Several other publishers offer their own firewall software.

Activity 4.18 | Protecting Your Computer by Using Windows Firewall

In Windows 10, the Windows Firewall is always on. The firewall looks at all of your Internet traffic and permits only safe communications.

1 ▶ Press [⊞] to place the insertion point in the search box, and then type **firewall** With **Windows Firewall** displayed at the top of the search pane, press [Enter]. Compare your screen with Figure 4.52.

Here, you can disable all *incoming connections*—traffic sent from the Internet to your computer. If you suspect that your computer is currently threatened, you can block all outside access.

Think of the Windows Firewall window as a dashboard with information about whether or not your firewall is turned on, the name of your network, and what the settings are.

It is recommended that you use the default settings on your own computer.

FIGURE 4.52

2 ▶ From the taskbar, open your PowerPoint presentation, add a new slide in the **Blank** layout, and then on the **Insert tab**, in the **Images group**, click **Screenshot**. Under **Available Windows**, click the **Windows Firewall** window to insert it in the slide.

3 Deselect the image. In the upper left corner, click **Save** ⊟, and then in the upper right corner, click **Minimize** −.

4 **Close** ✕ the **Windows Firewall** window.

More **Knowledge** **Secure Your Router**

You cannot rely on a firewall to completely protect your network from outside threats. There are several other actions that you should take. Be sure to change your router's password. Malicious individuals know the default passwords assigned to routers, and can use them to change your router's security settings.

Objective 8 Explore Windows Update and Privacy Settings

You expect your smartphone and tablet to receive updates frequently, and now, too, you can expect frequent updates to your Windows 10 operating system. You no longer have to wait for a new version of Windows, or for what used to be called *service packs*, to get updates. Rather, Windows 10 is continuously and automatically updated over the Internet, and by doing so, you receive new features and new security updates. This feature is referred to as *Windows Update*.

Activity 4.19 │ Examining Windows Update

There will be different versions of Windows 10; for example, Windows 10 Home and other versions for large organizations. Larger organizations can manage the update process. On your own PC running Windows 10 Home, you cannot decline the updates. In an organization, updates can be managed to occur at specific times. As shown in Figure 4.53, Action Center will notify you when updates were installed.

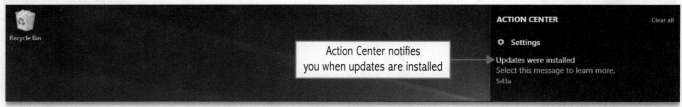

Office 2016, Windows 10, Microsoft Corporation.

FIGURE 4.53

1 On the right end of the taskbar, click **Action Center** ▱, click **All settings**, click **Update & security**, and then on the left, click **Windows Update**. If necessary, in the upper right corner of the **Settings** window, click **Restore Down** ⧉. Compare your screen with Figure 4.54.

Typically, you will see that no updates are available, because updates are installed automatically every day.

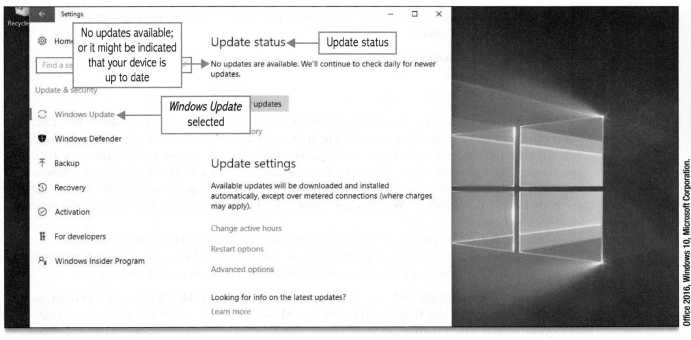

FIGURE 4.54

2 From the taskbar, open your PowerPoint presentation, add a new slide in the **Blank** layout, and then on the **Insert tab**, in the **Images group**, click **Screenshot**. Click **Screen Clipping**. Position the + pointer in the upper left corner of the **Settings** window, hold down the left mouse button, drag down and to the lower right corner of the window, and then release the mouse button to insert the clipping into your PowerPoint presentation. Click outside of the image to deselect it. Compare your screen with Figure 4.55.

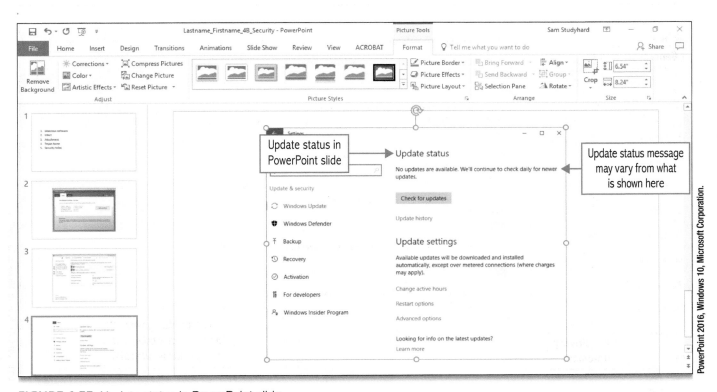

FIGURE 4.55 Update status in PowerPoint slide

3 Deselect the image. In the upper left corner, click **Save** ⊟, and then in the upper right corner, click **Minimize** ⊟.

4 **Close** ⊠ the **Settings** window.

Activity 4.20 | Exploring Privacy Settings

Now that your devices—phone, tablet, and PC—are connected to the Internet all the time, concerns about privacy are common. Letting apps and other devices access your information is, overall, valuable. For example, if you are traveling with your laptop computer, a movie listing app can supply information about movie times for your current location. Or, sharing your calendar information with Cortana will enable you to receive alerts about upcoming appointments. And certainly having the Windows Weather app know your location is useful for checking upcoming weather conditions.

There are numerous privacy settings that you can set within Windows 10. Some will differ depending on the type of hardware you have. Fortunately, Microsoft is clear about what information it collects and enables you to fine-tune privacy settings on your computer.

1 On the right end of the taskbar, click **Action Center** ▣, click **All settings**, click **Privacy**, and then on the left, click **General**. If necessary, **Maximize** ▢ the window, and then compare your screen with Figure 4.56.

Here you can set your General privacy options. Your computer will be most useful and relevant to you if you leave the default settings; however, set the options to your own comfort level.

The first setting in this General section—the advertising ID—relates to ads displayed within Windows apps or apps that you download from the Windows store. Ads that you see while visiting websites are controlled by the browser software.

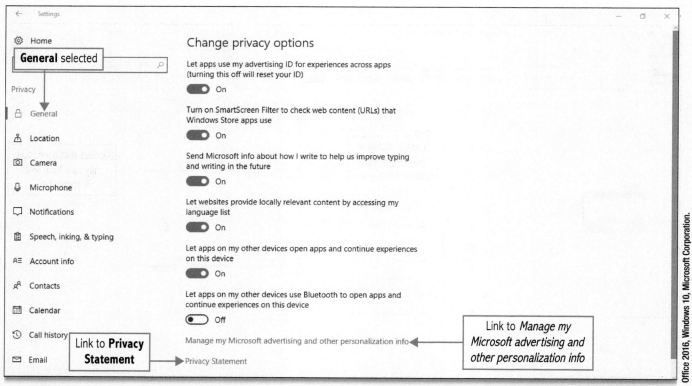

FIGURE 4.56

2 At the bottom of the window, click **Manage my Microsoft advertising and other personalization info**, and then compare your screen with Figure 4.57.

Here you can read about the information about ads. One thing to remember is that advertising pays much of the cost of bringing you free information, and you have the choice to see advertising that is interesting and relevant to your personal interests.

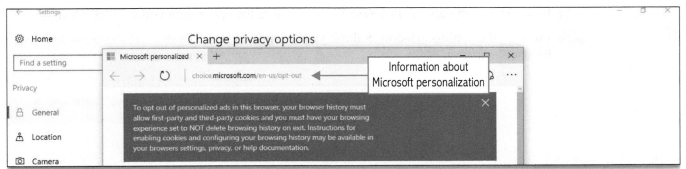

FIGURE 4.57

Office 2016, Windows 10, Microsoft Corporation.

3 **Close** ☒ the browser window.

4 On the left, scroll down to the bottom of the list, and then click **Background apps**. Compare your screen with Figure 4.58.

Here you can choose which apps can receive information and send you notifications. On a laptop computer, turning off some of these apps can help conserve power on your PC.

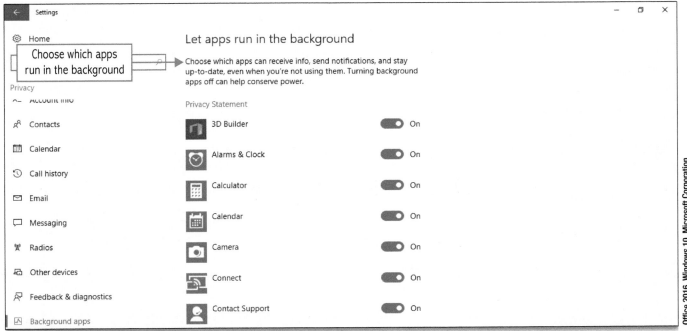

FIGURE 4.58

Office 2016, Windows 10, Microsoft Corporation.

5 From the taskbar, open your PowerPoint presentation, add a new slide in the **Blank** layout, and then on the **Insert tab**, in the **Images group**, click **Screenshot**. Click **Screen Clipping**. Position the + pointer in the upper left corner of the **Settings** window, hold down the left mouse button, drag down and to the lower right corner of the window but do not include the taskbar, and then release the mouse button to insert the clipping into your PowerPoint presentation. Click outside of the image to deselect it.

6 In the upper left corner, click **Save** 🖫, and then in the upper right corner, click **Close** ⊠.

7 **Close** ⊠ the **Settings** window. Submit your completed PowerPoint presentation as directed by your instructor.

> **END | You have completed Project 4B**

END OF CHAPTER

SUMMARY

The Microsoft Edge browser is a modern, secure, and fast browser with which you can conduct Google searches. When searching, use good research techniques such as Boolean operators and the Google Scholar site.

The Windows Ease of Access apps provide for accessibility features, such as having the computer read the screen, magnifying the size of the screen, displaying an on-screen keyboard, and being able to speak commands and text.

Rely on Windows Defender to protect your PC from malware. This program is free and is on by default. You can use the features in Windows Firewall to scan all or part of your computer if you suspect malicious activity.

Windows Update continuously and automatically updates your PC over the Internet so that you receive new features and new security updates to keep your system protected. You can control all of the privacy settings in Windows 10.

GO! LEARN IT ONLINE

Review the concepts and key terms in this chapter by completing these online challenges, which you can find in **MyITLab**:

Matching and Multiple Choice: Answer matching and multiple choice questions to test what you learned in this chapter.

Lessons on the GO!: Learn how to use all the new apps and features as they are introduced by Microsoft.

GO! FOR JOB SUCCESS

Discussion: Cyber Hacking

Your instructor may assign this discussion to your class, and then ask you to think about, or discuss with your classmates, these questions:

The US Homeland Security Department describes cyber incidents (hacking) as actions where there is an attempt to gain unauthorized access to a system or its data, unwanted disruption to service, unauthorized use of a system, or change to a system without the owner's permission. As companies store and process more and more data at centralized, offsite "cloud" data centers, the opportunities for criminals to hack data are growing. Cyber security is an important part of every organization's information systems protocols, and many companies now employ a senior executive with the title Chief Information Security Officer.

FotolEdhar/Fotolia

Question 1: What cyber incidents have you heard of in the news over the last year?

Question 2: What precautions have you taken with your personal data to prevent a hack?

Question 3: What would you do if you learned a company you do business with, such as your bank or college, had been the subject of a cyber incident?

	Review and Assessment Guide for Windows 10 Chapter 4		
Project	**Apply Skills from These Chapter Objectives**	**Project Type**	**Project Location**
4A	Objectives 1-4 from Project 4A	**4A Instructional Project (Scorecard Grading)** Guided instruction to learn the skills in Project 4A.	In text
4B	Objectives 5-8 from Project 4B	**4B Instructional Project (Scorecard Grading)** Guided instruction to learn the skills in Project 4B.	In text
4C	Objectives 1-4 from Project 4A	**4C Skills Review (Scorecard Grading)** A guided review of the skills from Project 4A.	In text
4D	Objectives 5-8 from Project 4B	**4D Skills Review (Scorecard Grading)** A guided review of the skills from Project 4B.	In text
4E	Objectives 1-4 from Project 4A	**4E Mastery (Scorecard Grading)** **Mastery and Transfer of Learning** A demonstration of your mastery of the skills in Project 4A with decision-making.	In text
4F	Objectives 5-8 from Project 4B	**4F Mastery (Scorecard Grading)** **Mastery and Transfer of Learning** A demonstration of your mastery of the skills in Project 4B with decision-making.	In text
4G	Combination of Objectives from Projects 4A and 4B	**4G GO! Think (Rubric Grading)** **Critical Thinking** A demonstration of your understanding of the Chapter concepts applied in a manner that you would outside of college. An analytic rubric helps you and your instructor grade the quality of your work by comparing it to the work an expert in the discipline would create.	In text
4H	Combination of Objectives from Projects 4A and 4B	**4H GO! Think (Rubric Grading)** **Critical Thinking** A demonstration of your understanding of the Chapter concepts applied in a manner that you would outside of college. An analytic rubric helps you and your instructor grade the quality of your work by comparing it to the work an expert in the discipline would create.	In text
4I	Combination of Objectives from Projects 4A and 4B	**4I GO! Think (Rubric Grading)** **Critical Thinking** A demonstration of your understanding of the Chapter concepts applied in a manner that you would outside of college. An analytic rubric helps you and your instructor grade the quality of your work by comparing it to the work an expert in the discipline would create.	In text

GLOSSARY

Accessibility A term that refers to the design of hardware and software in a manner that helps individuals with disabilities use computing tools.

Alarms & Clock A Windows 10 app that enables you to set alarms on your computer; the app also functions as a timer, a stopwatch, and a world clock.

Anti-malware programs Programs that protect your computer from a malware infection.

Bing The search engine developed by Microsoft Corporation and that is included with Windows 10.

Boolean operators Search operators such as AND, OR, and NOT that express a condition that is either true or false.

Boot-sector virus A virus that replicates itself onto your hard drive's master boot record—the program that executes each time your computer boots up.

Browsing The term used to describe the process of using your computer to view webpages.

Chrome OS An operating system conceived to run applications and store user data in the cloud.

Chromebook A PC or laptop that runs the Chrome OS.

Custom scan A type of scan that you can initiate in Windows Defender that searches only those drives or folders or files that you select; for example, an email attachment that was just sent to you.

Define A Google search operator that searches the Web for the definition of a word you specify.

Definitions Updates to Microsoft's database of potential viruses.

Filetype A Google search operator that finds files of a specific type; for example, a PDF file, which is commonly used for reports.

Firewall Software or hardware that can help protect a computer from hackers, or prevent malicious software from gaining access to a computer through a network or over the Internet.

Full scan A type of scan that you can initiate in Windows Defender that looks at everything on your hard drive.

Google A name used to refer to the Web search engine developed by Google Inc., and that you can use for free on any Windows-based computer, on an Apple Mac computer, or on any Chromebook; also referred to as *Google Search* or *Google Web Search*.

Google Chrome The Web browser software program developed by Google Inc. that you can download for free on any Windows-based system, Apple Mac system, and also on any system running the Chrome OS.

Google Scholar A Google site where you can search for scholarly literature; for example, when you are creating a research paper for college or for work.

Google Search The Web search engine developed by Google Inc., and that you can use for free on any Windows-based computer, on an Apple Mac computer, or on any Chromebook; also referred to as *Google Web Search* or simply *Google*.

Google Web Search The Web search engine developed by Google Inc., and that you can use for free on any Windows-based computer, on an Apple Mac computer, or on any Chromebook; also referred to as *Google Search* or simply *Google*.

Hacker A term used to describe a person who uses computer expertise to gain access to computer systems often without permission.

Incoming connections Traffic sent from the Internet to your computer.

Infected The term that describes a computer if a malware program installs itself and then runs.

Intitle A Google search operator that focuses search results on a specific word in the title of a report.

Keylogger spyware A type of spyware that records all of your keystrokes and then sends your typed data—including user names and passwords—to someone else.

Keywords Words you enter into a search expression that help to limit and focus your search results so that you find the information you want.

Magnifier A Windows 10 accessibility app that magnifies a portion of the screen.

Make a Web Note A Microsoft Edge feature that enables you to take notes, write, and highlight directly on webpages and then share the note.

Malware A shortened term for the words *malicious software*, which is a computer program that intentionally harms your computer.

Microsoft Edge The Web browser software program developed by Microsoft Corporation and that is included with Windows 10.

Narrator A Windows 10 accessibility app that reads text on your PC screen aloud and that serves as a basic screen reader.

On-Screen Keyboard A Windows 10 accessibility app that displays a keyboard on the screen that you can use instead of a physical keyboard; also referred to as *OSK*.

Operators Words you can use in your search expression to get more specific search results.

OSK The term used to refer to the On-Screen Keyboard.

Patch A small repair to an operating system or program that closes a security hole.

Peer-to-peer file sharing sites Websites that let you share files such as music, videos, and software with others using the Internet.

Poisoned website A website that spreads a virus.

Quarantine area An area in a designated location on your computer from which a program cannot run.

Quick scan A type of scan that you can initiate in Windows Defender that checks the areas on your hard drive where malware programs are most likely to reside.

Ransomware Malware that blocks access to your PC until a sum of money is paid.

Real-time protection Protection provided by Windows 10 in which the system is continuously monitoring your computer at all times for suspicious activity such as viruses and spyware.

Screen reader A computer program that converts text into speech.

Search engine A computer program that gathers information from the Web, indexes it, and puts it in a database that you can search based on specific words.

Search expression The keywords and syntax that you type into a search engine to begin your search.

Security holes Vulnerabilities in an operating system or program that allow malware to infect a computer without your knowledge.

Site A keyword in a search expression that returns webpages that belong to a specified site.

Smart Lookup A Bing-powered feature that enables you to select text in a Word document and have a search conducted on the text and the results displayed in a pane on the right.

Spyware A type of malware that collects personal information or changes your browser settings, which can infect your computer without your knowledge when you download a program or visit a website.

Steps Recorder A Windows 10 app that captures the steps you perform on your computer, including a text description of where you clicked and a screenshot of the screen during each click.

Surfing The process of navigating the Internet either for a particular item or for anything that is of interest, and quickly moving from one item to another.

Syntax The arrangement of the keywords in a search expression.

Tabbed browsing A feature that enables you to open multiple websites and then switch among them.

Trojan horse A malicious software program that hides inside legitimate programs, such as a game or media player or screen saver.

Virus A type of malware designed specifically to replicate itself by spreading its infection from computer to computer.

Voice Recorder A Windows 10 app that enables you to use the microphone on your computer to record lectures, conversations, or any other sounds.

Web browser A software program that displays webpages as you navigate the Internet.

White hat hacker An ethical security expert that tests an organization's data and network security by attempting to hack into it.

Wiki A website that permits anyone visiting the site to change its content by adding, removing, or editing the content.

Wikipedia The largest and most popular wiki on the Internet.

Windows Defender The free antivirus program built in to Windows 10; includes virus protection and removal, malware protection and removal, spyware detection and removal, and boot-time protection.

Windows Ease of Access A set of accessibility apps that you can access in a central location.

Windows Speech Recognition A Windows 10 accessibility app that enables you to control your computer by using your voice.

Windows Update The Windows 10 feature that continuously and automatically updates your PC over the Internet so that you receive new features and new security updates.

Worm A self-replicating program—similar to a virus—that spreads on its own to every computer on a network.

Apply 4A skills from these Objectives:

1 Explore Web Browsers and Search Engines

2 Conduct Google Searches in Microsoft Edge

3 Use Windows 10 Utility Apps

4 Use Windows 10 Ease of Access Apps

Skills Review Project 4C Searching the Web and Using Utility and Accessibility Apps

 PROJECT FILES

For Project 4C, you will need the following file:

win04_4C_Answer_Sheet (Word document) from the student data files that accompany this textbook

You will save your results as:

Lastname_Firstname_4C_Answer_Sheet

1 From your **win10_04_Student_Data_Files**, open the Word document **win04_4C_Answer_Sheet**. Using your own name, save it in your **Windows 10 Chapter 4** folder as **Lastname_Firstname_4C_Answer_Sheet** and then minimize the document to leave it open.

Close all windows and display your desktop. As you complete each step in this Project, write the letter of your answer on a piece of paper; you will fill in your Answer Sheet after you complete all the steps in this Project.

Open the **Microsoft Edge** browser. In the **Search or enter web address** box, type **define:rack rate** and be sure that Google search is indicated as the search engine. Press [Enter]. This term refers to the price of what?

A. Clothing in a department store

B. A hotel room

C. Servers in a data center

2 At the top of the **Microsoft Edge** browser window, click **New tab** [+]. In the **Search or enter web address** box, type **usa.gov/elected-officials** Press [Enter], and then press [Ctrl] + [F]. In the upper left corner, in the **Find on page** box, type **elected officials** What is your result?

A. Pictures of recently elected officials display.

B. A new webpage displays a list of elected officials.

C. Every instance of the text *elected officials* is highlighted on the page.

3 At the top of the **Microsoft Edge** browser window, click **New tab** [+]. In the **Search or enter a web address** box, type **filetype:pdf Miami intitle:construction** Press [Enter], and then scroll down below the list of sites. What is your result?

A. Links to information about construction in Miami in the form of PDF reports display.

B. The site for Miami City Hall displays.

C. Links to city maps display.

4 At the top of the **Microsoft Edge** browser window, click **New tab** [+]. In the **Search or enter web address** box, type **www.wikipedia.org** and press [Enter]. In the search box in the lower portion of the screen, type **lawrence lessig** and press [Enter]. Mr. Lessig is known for founding what organization?

A. AmeriCorps

B. Creative Commons

C. The Red Cross

(Project 4C Searching the Web and Using Utility and Accessibility Apps continues on the next page)

5 At the top of the **Microsoft Edge** browser window, click **New tab** +. In the **Search or enter web address** box, type **35 liters in gallons** and press Enter. What is the result of the calculation?

A. 35

B. 62

C. 9.24602

6 At the top of the **Microsoft Edge** browser window, click **New tab** +. By searching at **www.wikipedia.org** which of the following is the name of a famous book by Tim Wu?

A. The Cluetrain Manifesto

B. The Master Switch

C. The Innovator's Dilemma

7 **Close** Microsoft Edge and display the desktop. Search for and display the **Alarms & Clock** app, and if necessary, at the top, click **Alarm**. Add a new alarm and display the list of possible sounds. Which of the following is *not* the name of a sound you can use for an alarm?

A. Xylophone

B. Bounce

C. Percussion

8 **Close** the **Alarms & Clock** window, and then display **Settings**. Click **Ease of Access**, and if necessary, **Maximize** the window. On the left click **Narrator**. Which of the following is a voice you can select?

A. Microsoft Olympia

B. Microsoft Zira

C. Microsoft Michael

9 On the left click **Magnifier**. Which of the following is a tracking option you can select for Magnifier?

A. Follow the mouse cursor

B. Follow the stylus

C. Follow the magnifying glass

10 On the left click **Other options**. Which of the following is a visual notification you can select for sound?

A. Flash Start button

B. Flash taskbar

C. Flash active title bar

To complete this project: Close any open windows to display the **desktop**, on the taskbar click the **Word** button, type your answers into the correct boxes. Save and close your Word document, and submit as directed by your instructor. **Close** ☒ any open windows.

> **END | You have completed Project 4C**

Apply 4B skills from these Objectives:

5 Understand Viruses and Spyware
6 Explore Windows Defender
7 Explore Windows Firewall
8 Explore Windows Update and Privacy Settings

Skills Review Project 4D Securing Your Computer

 PROJECT FILES

For Project 4D, you will need the following file:

win04_4D_Answer_Sheet (Word document) from the student data files that accompany this textbook

You will save your results as:

Lastname_Firstname_4D_Answer_Sheet

1 From your **win10_04_Student_Data_Files**, open the Word document **win04_4D_Answer_Sheet**. Using your own name, save it in your **Windows 10 Chapter 4** folder as **Lastname_Firstname_4D_Answer_Sheet** and then minimize the document to leave it open.

Close all windows and display your desktop. As you complete each step in this Project, write the letter of your answer on a piece of paper; you will fill in your Answer Sheet after you complete all the steps in this Project.

At the right end of the taskbar, click **Action Center**, click **All settings**, click **Update & security**, and then on the left, click **Windows Defender**. What is your result?

A. The Windows Defender window displays.

B. Settings that are set to On and Off display.

C. New security definitions display.

2 According to the information on this screen, what is **automatic sample submission**?

A. The ability to have your computer exclude some files from protection.

B. The ability to have your computer back up infected files.

C. The ability to have your computer send samples of suspicious files to Microsoft.

3 According to the information on this screen, which of the following describes the **Enhanced notifications** feature?

A. Notifications about your PC will flash on the taskbar.

B. Windows Defender notifies Microsoft if your PC crashes.

C. Windows Defender sends you notifications about the health of your PC.

4 **Close** the **Settings** window. Click **Start**, display apps that begin with letter **W**, and then click **Windows System**. Which of the following is *not* a Windows System program?

A. Resource Monitor

B. Control Panel

C. Windows Defender

(Project 4D Securing Your Computer continues on the next page)

Skills Review | **Project 4D Securing Your Computer** (continued)

5 ▶ Display **Settings**, click **Update & security**, click **Windows Defender**, and then click **Open Windows Defender**. How many tabs are contained in the **Windows Defender** window?

A. One

B. Two

C. Three

6 ▶ In the upper right corner of the **Windows Defender** window, click **Help**. Which of the following is true?

A. Here you can view the list of the latest virus and spyware definitions.

B. Here you can submit a malicious software sample.

C. Here you can send an inquiry to Microsoft.

7 ▶ **Close** all open windows, and then display **Settings**. In the search box at the top, type **firewall** and then click **Allow an app through Windows Firewall**. Which of the following is true?

A. A list of allowed apps and features displays.

B. The Windows Firewall window opens.

C. Here you can disable the firewall.

8 ▶ Scroll toward the bottom of the list, locate and click on the text *Windows Firewall Remote Management*, and then click **Details**. What is your result?

A. The Ports window displays.

B. The Control Panel displays.

C. A description of the feature displays.

9 ▶ **Close** all open windows, display **Settings**, click **Privacy**, and then on the left, click **Speech, inking, & typing**. Which of the following is true?

A. The system can collect speech patterns to make better suggestions for you.

B. The system provides ink colors for you to use on a touchscreen.

C. An on-screen keyboard displays.

10 ▶ On the left, click **Location**, and scroll to the bottom of the right pane. According to this information, what is the meaning of **geofencing**?

A. Using your location to find a lost device.

B. Using your location to see when you cross in or out of a boundary drawn around a place of interest.

C. Using your location to provide traffic information.

To complete this project: Close any open windows to display the **desktop**, on the taskbar click the **Word** button, type your answers into the correct boxes. Save and close your Word document, and submit as directed by your instructor. **Close** ⊠ any open windows.

> **END | You have completed Project 4D**

Mastering Windows 10 | **Project 4E Searching the Web and Using Utility and Accessibility Apps**

In the following Mastering Windows 10 Project, you will conduct Internet searches and use Windows 10 apps for utility and accessibility. You will insert screenshots of windows that you create into a PowerPoint presentation similar to Figure 4.59.

 PROJECT FILES

For Project 4E, you will need the following file:

A new PowerPoint presentation

You will save your results in a PowerPoint presentation as:

Lastname_Firstname_4E_Search_Apps

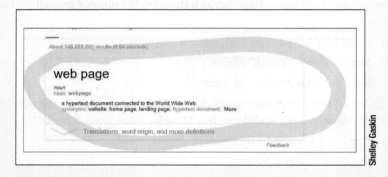

FIGURE 4.59

1 Open a new blank PowerPoint presentation. On the **Home tab**, in the **Slides group**, click **Layout**, and then click **Blank**. Using your own name, save the presentation in your **Windows 10 Chapter 4** folder as **Lastname_Firstname_4E_Search_Apps** **Minimize** the PowerPoint window.

2 Open **Microsoft Edge**. By using the **define** operator, search for the definition of **webpage** and then with the results displayed, in the upper right corner, click **Make a Web Note**. Use the large orange highlighter to circle the definition.

3 In the upper left corner, click **Clip**, and then using the + mouse pointer, point to the upper left corner of the large definition, hold down the left mouse button, and then drag down and to the right to capture the large definition and your orange highlight.

4 From the taskbar, open your PowerPoint presentation, and then paste the clip in the first slide. Click in a white area to deselect the image. **Save** your presentation and then **Minimize** the PowerPoint window.

5 Open a new tab, and then by using the Boolean operator AND, conduct a search of the **usa.gov site** for both *illinois* and *officials*. Make a web note, use the small red pen to circle the first two results, and then add a note below the circle with the text **Links for research.**

6 Make a **Clip** of the circled results and the note, and paste it into the second slide of your presentation. **Save** your presentation and then **Minimize** the PowerPoint window. Close the browser window; if asked, do not save any changes.

7 Display **Settings** and then display the **Privacy** settings. On the left, click **Microphone**. Display your PowerPoint presentation, and then by using PowerPoint's **Screen Clipping** command, capture this entire window not including the taskbar and paste it as the third slide.

8 **Save** and close your PowerPoint presentation. **Close** all open windows, and then submit your PowerPoint file as directed by your instructor.

END | You have completed Project 4E

Mastering Windows 10 Project 4F Secure Your Computer

In the following Mastering Windows 10 project, you will find use Windows Defender and Privacy settings. You will insert screenshots of windows that you create into a PowerPoint presentation similar to Figure 4.60.

 PROJECT FILES

For Project 4F, you will need the following file:

A new PowerPoint presentation

You will save your results in a PowerPoint presentation as:

Lastname_Firstname_4F_Windows_Security

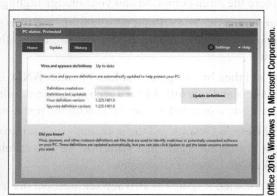

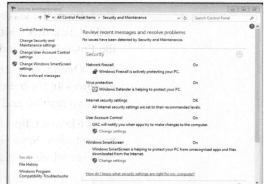

FIGURE 4.60

(Project 4F Secure Your Computer continues on the next page)

Mastering Windows 10 | **Project 4F Secure Your Computer** (continued)

1 ▸ Open a new blank PowerPoint presentation. On the **Home tab**, in the **Slides group**, click **Layout**, and then click **Blank**. Using your own name, save the presentation in your **Windows 10 Chapter 4** folder as **Lastname_Firstname_4F_Windows_Security Minimize** the PowerPoint window.

2 ▸ From the **Windows Defender** window, display the **Update tab**. Click **Update definitions**, and then when the update is complete, insert a screenshot of this window as the first slide in your PowerPoint presentation.

3 ▸ Display **Settings**, in the search box at the top, type **security and maintenance** and press [Enter]. On the left, click **Security and Maintenance**. In the center of the screen, click **Security**. Insert a screenshot of this window as the second slide in your PowerPoint presentation.

4 ▸ Open the **Microsoft Edge** browser and conduct a **Google Scholar** search for the term **spyware** Make a web note and circle the first three results with the red pen. Create a clip of your circled entries and paste the clip into the third slide of your PowerPoint presentation.

5 ▸ **Save** and close your PowerPoint presentation. **Close** all open windows, and then submit your PowerPoint file as directed by your instructor.

END | You have completed Project 4F

RUBRIC

The following outcomes-based assessments are *open-ended assessments*. That is, there is no specific correct result; your result will depend on your approach to the information provided. Make *Professional Quality* your goal. Use the following scoring rubric to guide you in *how* to approach the problem, and then to evaluate *how well* your approach solves the problem.

The *criteria*—Software Mastery, Content, Format and Layout, and Process—represent the knowledge and skills you have gained that you can apply to solving the problem. The *levels of performance*—Professional Quality, Approaching Professional Quality, or Needs Quality Improvements—help you and your instructor evaluate your result.

	Your completed project is of Professional Quality if you:	Your completed project is Approaching Professional Quality if you:	Your completed project Needs Quality Improvements if you:
1-Software Mastery	Choose and apply the most appropriate skills, tools, and features and identify efficient methods to solve the problem.	Choose and apply some appropriate skills, tools, and features, but not in the most efficient manner.	Choose inappropriate skills, tools, or features, or are inefficient in solving the problem.
2-Content	Construct a solution that is clear and well organized, contains content that is accurate, appropriate to the audience and purpose, and is complete. Provide a solution that contains no errors of spelling, grammar, or style.	Construct a solution in which some components are unclear, poorly organized, inconsistent, or incomplete. Misjudge the needs of the audience. Have some errors in spelling, grammar, or style, but the errors do not detract from comprehension.	Construct a solution that is unclear, incomplete, or poorly organized, containing some inaccurate or inappropriate content, and contains many errors of spelling, grammar, or style. Do not solve the problem.
3-Format and Layout	Format and arrange all elements to communicate information and ideas, clarify function, illustrate relationships, and indicate relative importance.	Apply appropriate format and layout features to some elements, but not others. Overuse features, causing minor distraction.	Apply format and layout that does not communicate information or ideas clearly. Do not use format and layout features to clarify function, illustrate relationships, or indicate relative importance. Use available features excessively, causing distraction.
4-Process	Use an organized approach that integrates planning, development, self-assessment, revision, and reflection.	Demonstrate an organized approach in some areas, but not others; or, use an insufficient process of organization throughout.	Do not use an organized approach to solve the problem.

Problem Solving   Project 4G Help Desk

In this project, you will construct a solution by applying any combination of the skills you practiced from the Objectives in Projects 4A and 4B.

For Project 4G, you will need the following file:

win04_4G_Help_Desk

You will save your document as:

Lastname_Firstname_4G_Help_Desk

From the student files that accompany this textbook, locate and open the Word document **win04_4G_Help_Desk**. Save the document in your chapter folder as **Lastname_Firstname_4G_Help_Desk**

The following e-mail question has arrived at the Help Desk from an employee at the Bell Orchid Hotel's corporate office. In the Word form, construct a response based on your knowledge of Windows 10. Although an email response is not as formal as a letter, you should still use good grammar, good sentence structure, professional language, and a polite tone. Save your document and submit the response as directed by your instructor.

To: Help Desk

I am the Manager of the Bell Orchid Hotel in Miami. We would like to build a convention center on property that we have acquired across the street from the hotel. How would we conduct an Internet search to get information about City of Miami requirements for building such a facility?

END | You have completed Project 4G

Problem Solving   Project 4H Help Desk

In this project, you will construct a solution by applying any combination of the skills you practiced from the Objectives in Projects 4A and 4B.

For Project 4H, you will need the following file:

win04_4H_Help_Desk

You will save your document as:

Lastname_Firstname_4H_Help_Desk

From the student files that accompany this textbook, locate and open the Word document **win04_4H_Help_Desk**. Save the document in your chapter folder as **Lastname_Firstname_4H_Help_Desk**

The following e-mail question has arrived at the Help Desk from an employee at the Bell Orchid Hotel's corporate office. In the Word form, construct a response based on your knowledge of Windows 10. Although an email response is not as formal as a letter, you should still use good grammar, good sentence structure, professional language, and a polite tone. Save your document and submit the response as directed by your instructor.

To: Help Desk

I am the Manager of the Help Desk for the corporate IT office in Boston. Many of our employees who call the Help Desk for assistance are not always able to describe their computer problem succinctly. Is there a tool that would enable them to document, step by step, exactly what their problem is so that we could provide better answers?

END | You have completed Project 4H

Problem Solving   Project 4I Help Desk

In this project, you will construct a solution by applying any combination of the skills you practiced from the Objectives in Projects 4A and 4B.

For Project 4I, you will need the following file:

win04_4I_Help_Desk

You will save your document as:

Lastname_Firstname_4I_Help_Desk

From the student files that accompany this textbook, locate and open the Word document **win04_4I_Help_Desk**. Save the document in your chapter folder as **Lastname_Firstname_4I_Help_Desk**

The following e-mail question has arrived at the Help Desk from an employee at the Bell Orchid Hotel's corporate office. In the Word document, construct a response based on your knowledge of Windows 10. Although an email response is not as formal as a letter, you should still use good grammar, good sentence structure, professional language, and a polite tone. Save your document and submit the response as directed by your instructor.

To: Help Desk

I am the Corporate Director of Food and Beverage. Frequently I use my own laptop at meetings and conventions. What is the best malware protection to use on my own computer?

END | You have completed Project 4I

Monitoring and Tracking System Performance

PROJECT 5A

OUTCOMES
Use Task Manager to manage applications, manage processes, view services, and monitor system performance.

PROJECT 5B

OUTCOMES
Track performance with Performance and Resource Monitors, and manage services by using the Services console.

OBJECTIVES

1. View Applications and Manage Processes by Using Task Manager
2. View Performance and App History in Task Manager
3. View Startup Programs and Users in Task Manager
4. View Details and Services in Task Manager

OBJECTIVES

5. Track Performance by Using the Resource and Performance Monitors
6. Create a System Diagnostics Report
7. Manage Services by Using the Services Console

Shock/Fotolia

In This Chapter

Nearly everyone experiences times when his or her computer seems to slow down or stops responding completely. When this happens frequently, you may need to find out what could be causing the slowdown. Task Manager, Performance Monitor, and Resource Monitor track various system resources as you work on your computer. These tools display information that helps you discover the cause of performance slowdowns. After the problem is located, you—or a computer technician—will be able to find solutions to have your computer performing well again. In this chapter, you will use Task Manager, Performance Monitor, and Resource Monitor to monitor and track your computer's performance.

The projects in this chapter relate to the **Bell Orchid Hotels**, headquartered in Boston, and which own and operate resorts and business-oriented hotels. Resort properties are located in popular destinations, including Honolulu, Orlando, San Diego, and Santa Barbara. The resorts offer deluxe accommodations and a wide array of dining options. Other Bell Orchid hotels are located in major business centers and offer the latest technology in their meeting facilities. The company plans to open new properties and update existing properties over the next ten years.

Using Task Manager

PROJECT ACTIVITIES

In Activities 5.01 through 5.06, you will participate in training along with Steven Ramos and Barbara Hewitt, both of whom work for the Information Technology Department at the headquarters office of the Bell Orchid Hotels. After completing this part of the training, you will be able to stop unresponsive applications, identify applications that run at system startup, find out which background processes and services consume the most computer resources, and view charts displaying computer performance over time. As you progress through the project, you will insert screenshots of windows that you create into a PowerPoint presentation similar to Figure 5.1.

PROJECT FILES

For Project 5A, you will need the following files:

win05_5A_Bell_Orchid folder from the student data files that accompany this textbook

A new blank PowerPoint presentation

You will save your results in a PowerPoint file as:

Lastname_Firstname_5A_Task_Manager

PROJECT RESULTS

Word 2016, Windows 10, Microsoft Corporation.

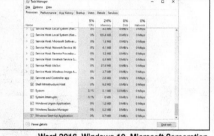

Word 2016, Windows 10, Microsoft Corporation.

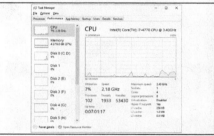

Word 2016, Windows 10, Microsoft Corporation.

Word 2016, Windows 10, Microsoft Corporation.

Word 2016, Windows 10, Microsoft Corporation.

Word 2016, Windows 10, Microsoft Corporation.

FIGURE 5.1 Project 5A Using Task Manager

Task Manager is a Windows 10 tool that shows you information about the programs, processes, and services that are currently running on your computer. A *process* is a file that is part of a running program and performs a specific task such as starting the program. For example, a file with a file name extension of *.exe* is a process file that your computer uses to start a program or to start other services. *Services* are computer programs or processes that run in the background and provide support to other programs.

There are two reasons that you will want to use Task Manager:

- To monitor your computer's performance.

- To close a program that is not responding—referred to as a *nonresponsive program*.

A nonresponsive program is a program that is open but has stopped responding to your commands, which means it has stopped communicating with Windows 10. In this nonresponsive state, the program cannot respond to your actions or update any of its windows; nor can the program be closed by using any of the program's commands.

The two main functions of Task Manager are to provide a place to close a program that is not responding and to monitor the performance of your computer by looking at what programs and processes are running at any given time.

The programs that you run on your computer have one or more processes associated with them. Recall that a process is a part of a running program that performs a specific task such as starting the program. For example, if you open Microsoft Word, the *WINWORD.EXE* process runs until you close the program. Likewise, the Microsoft Edge browser runs processes named *MicrosoftEdge.exe* and *MicrosoftEdgeCP.exe*.

Activity 5.01 | Viewing Applications in Task Manager

Task Manager displays a list of currently running programs—also called *applications*. When a program you are using enters a nonresponsive state and you are unable to close it, display the Task Manager, from which you can close a nonresponsive program.

A program may become nonresponsive when it performs a task that has no way of ending, or when the program cannot access the correct instructions that it had stored in memory. Closing a nonresponsive program stops all tasks that the program is performing and removes the program's instructions from computer memory. So closing a nonresponsive program and then reopening it usually corrects the problem.

NOTE | **User Rights May Vary in College Labs and Windows 10 Changes Frequently**

The setup of user rights in a college lab varies among colleges; you may not have access to as many Windows 10 features in a college lab as you would have on your own computer. Also, Microsoft updates Windows 10 frequently, so you may encounter some differences as you complete this Project.

---

1. Sign in to your computer to display the **desktop**. Close any open windows.

2. From the taskbar, or by searching, open **PowerPoint**, and then click **Blank Presentation**. On the **Home tab**, in the **Slides group**, click **Layout**, and then click **Blank**.

3. Click the **File tab**, on the left click **Save As**, click **Browse**, and then in the **Save As** dialog box, navigate to the storage location where you will store your files for this chapter. Click **New folder**, as the folder name type **Windows 10 Chapter 5** and then press Enter. Click **Open** to open the new folder in the **Save As** dialog box.

4. In the **File name** box, using your own name, type **Lastname_Firstname_5A_Task_Manager**

5 In the **Save As** dialog box, click **Save**. In the upper right corner of the PowerPoint window, click **Minimize** $\boxed{-}$ to display the desktop and leave the presentation open.

6 By using **File Explorer**, from the student data files for Chapter 5—**win10_05_Student_Data_Files**— that you downloaded from www.pearsonhighered.com/go or obtained from your instructor, copy the folder **win05_5A_Bell_Orchid** to your **Documents** folder.

7 Navigate to **This PC › Documents › win05_5A_Bell_Orchid › San_Diego › Operations** to display the contents of this folder in the **file list**. If necessary, set the **View** to **Details**, and then compare your screen with Figure 5.2.

   In the file list, three files display: a PowerPoint presentation, an Excel workbook, and a Word document.

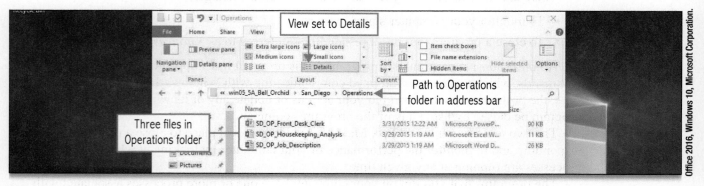

FIGURE 5.2

8 In the **file list**, double-click the PowerPoint file **SD_OP_Front_Desk_Clerk** to open the presentation. If necessary, when opening student data files, at the top of the screen, click Enable Editing.

9 On the taskbar, click **File Explorer** to switch to this window, and then double-click to open the Excel file **SD_OP_Housekeeping_Analysis**.

10 On the taskbar, click **File Explorer** to switch to this window, and then double-click the Word file **SD_OP_Job_Description**.

11 On the taskbar, right-click in an empty area to display the shortcut menu as shown in Figure 5.3.

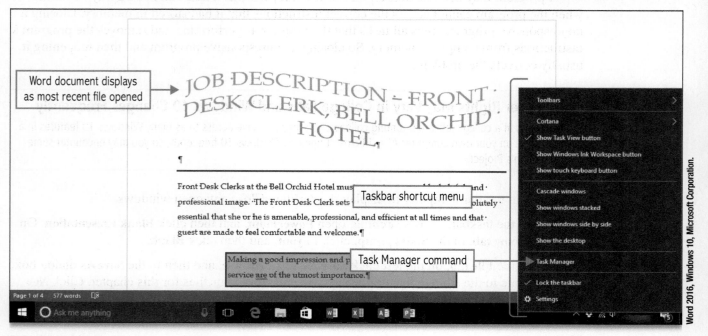

FIGURE 5.3

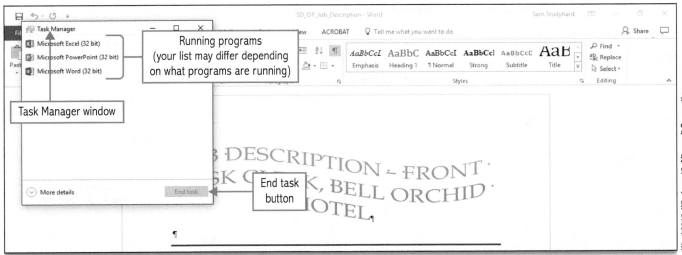

12 On the displayed menu, click **Task Manager**. Notice the **Task Manager icon** on your taskbar, and then compare your screen with Figure 5.4.

The Task Manager window displays running programs. In this view of Task Manager, there are two things you can do:

- If a program on your computer indicates *Not responding* or otherwise freezes, you can select the program, and then click End task.

- You can double-click the name of a program to switch to it. However, if you need to switch to another program, simply clicking its icon on the taskbar is probably faster, or use the Task View ⬚ button on the taskbar to switch to another open program.

Terminating a program by clicking End task in Task Manager will close the program without giving you the opportunity to save any open files in that program. The Microsoft Office programs will typically try to recover your files when you reopen the program, but not all programs will do this.

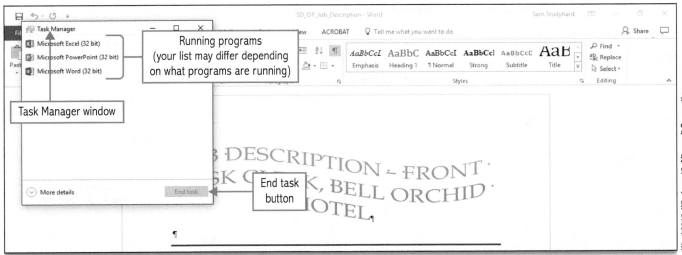

FIGURE 5.4

13 In the lower left corner of your keyboard, hold down ⊞ and then in the upper right corner of your keyboard, quickly press [PrintScrn] (your key may be labeled as *Print Screen*) and then release the two keys. Notice that the screen briefly dims.

This action causes the screen to dim briefly during which time an image of your screen is placed on the Clipboard and also captured in the Screenshots folder of your Pictures folder.

14 On the taskbar, point to the **PowerPoint icon** to display thumbnail images of the two open PowerPoint files. Compare your screen with Figure 5.5.

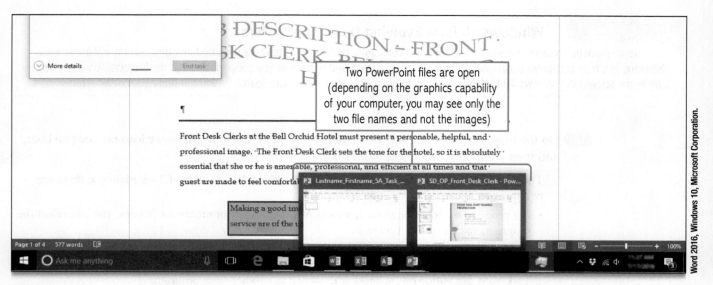

Word 2016, Windows 10, Microsoft Corporation.

FIGURE 5.5

15 Click the image of your **5A_Task_Manager** presentation to display it on the screen, and then in the **Clipboard group**, click the upper portion of the **Paste** button to paste the image of your screen into your PowerPoint slide. Compare your screen with Figure 5.6.

The image of your screen fills the PowerPoint slide.

PowerPoint 2016, Windows 10, Microsoft Corporation.

FIGURE 5.6

ANOTHER WAY   To capture just an active window—not the entire screen—press **Alt** + **PrintScrn**.

16 Click in a white area to deselect the image. In the upper left corner, click **Save**, and then in the upper right corner, click **Minimize** −.

Allow a Program Some Time to Respond Before Ending It

A program can seem nonresponsive if it is performing a complex task or is competing with other programs or system tasks for the computer's resources. Before ending the program in the Task Manager, give the program a little time to complete the task. If the task is one that normally completes in a few seconds, wait a minute or so. If the task is a large one, for example searching a large database, and you can hear disk activity or see the disk activity light flickering, consider waiting several minutes before ending the program.

Using Task Manager to end a program might be faster than waiting, but recall that any unsaved changes will be lost.

Activity 5.02 | Managing Processes by Using Task Manager

The *Processes tab* shows how Apps, Background processes, and Windows processes are using the system resources. Every program on the Processes tab will have at least one corresponding process on the Details tab of the Task Manager window. Most processes run in the background and you never see them unless you view them with a tool like Task Manager.

From a security standpoint, this list of processes is especially valuable, because most malware running on your computer will show up in this list. By performing an Internet search on the names of processes that you cannot identify as being associated with one of your installed programs, you can usually identify the name of a malware program and delete it. Managing processes with Task Manager enables you to find out what these processes are, see how they affect your computer's performance, and end or delete the process file if necessary.

1 From the taskbar, open **Microsoft Edge** , and then **Minimize** the window. If enabled on your computer, also open the Google Chrome browser and minimize its window.

2 In the lower left corner of the **Task Manager** window, click **More details**. If necessary, click the **Processes tab**, and then compare your screen with Figure 5.7.

Processes that are currently running display on the Processes tab. By default, the processes on the Processes tab are grouped by type—Apps, Background processes, and Windows processes. Apps include any programs that are currently open and that display active buttons on the taskbar.

The Name column displays the title from each application's title bar. The ^ arrow at the upper edge of the Name column heading indicates that the column can be sorted. Below the Apps, a list of Background processes displays, and if you scroll down, Windows processes display.

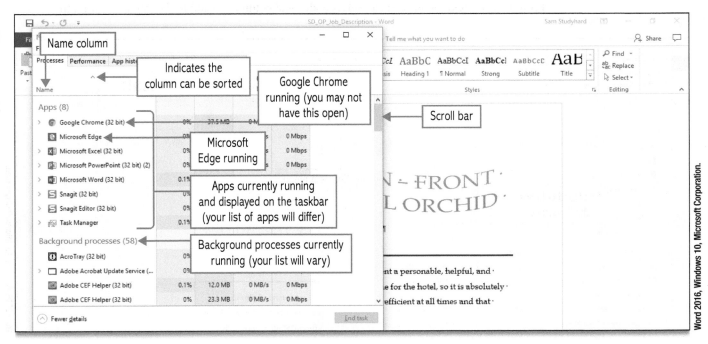

FIGURE 5.7

The Processes tab displays as a *heat map*—a graphical representation of data displayed as a matrix in which the individual statistical values are represented as colors. In this instance, pale yellow indicates low resource utilization, darker shades represent higher resource utilization, and red (not shown here) represents utilization at a critical level. When your computer slows down dramatically, it might be because a program is using an unusually large amount of system resources. Here you can see what program that might be, and close it if necessary.

The columns on the Processes tab include CPU, Memory, Disk, and Network, each displaying statistics about process usage.

3 In the upper left corner of the **Task Manager** window, on the menu bar, click **View**, and then compare your screen with Figure 5.8.

Here you can deselect Group by type if you prefer to see all the processes in simple alphabetic order.

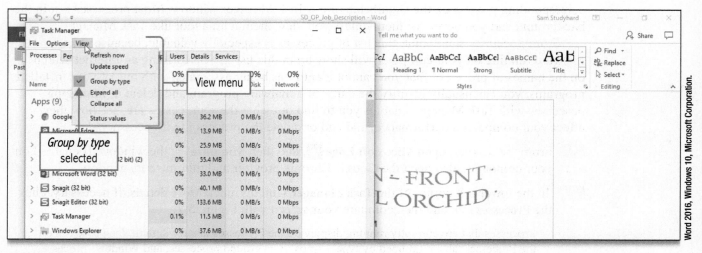

FIGURE 5.8

4 Press Esc to cancel the menu. Point to the column heading **Memory**, right-click, and then compare your screen with Figure 5.9.

From this shortcut menu, you can select additional columns to add to the tab if you want to do so.

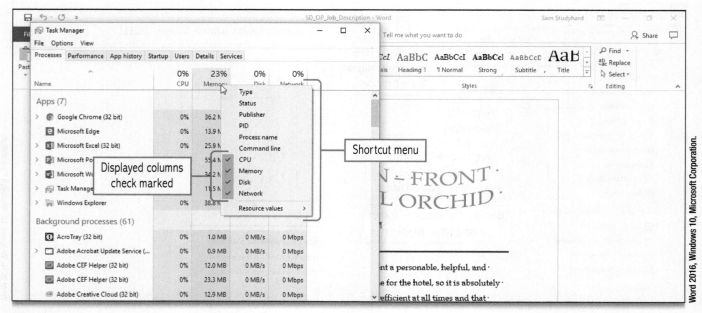

FIGURE 5.9

5 Press [Esc] to cancel the shortcut menu. By using the scroll bar on the right side of the **Task Manager** window, scroll down until you see Windows processes. Compare your screen with Figure 5.10.

As you scroll, you might be surprised at how many Background processes and Windows processes are running.

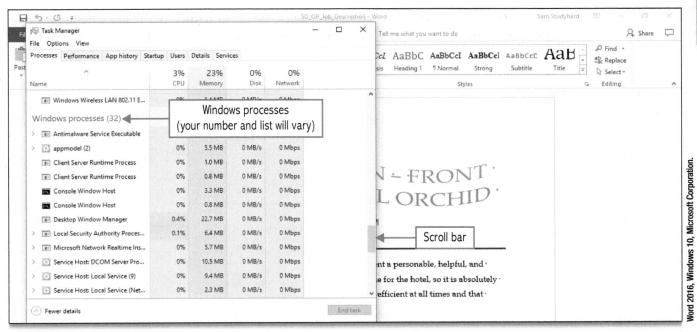

FIGURE 5.10

6 Scroll to the bottom of the list, point to the last process—in this instance *Windows Start-Up Application*—and then right-click. Compare your screen with Figure 5.11.

Here you can end the process, get more details by jumping to the Details tab, open the file's location, and most interestingly, search for information about the process online. This is useful if you are unsure about what the process does.

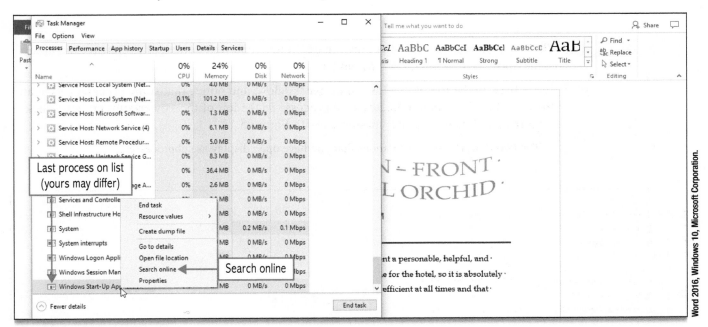

FIGURE 5.11

7 Press **Esc** to close the shortcut menu. Hold down **Alt** and press **PrintScrn**—you will not see the screen dim.

This action copies the active window—not the entire screen—to the Clipboard.

8 From the taskbar, open your PowerPoint presentation. On the **Home tab**, in the **Slides group**, click the upper portion of the **New Slide** button to insert a new slide in the **Blank** layout.

9 On the **Home tab**, in the **Clipboard group**, click the upper portion of the **Paste** button to copy the active window—the **Task Manager** window—to the new slide. Compare your screen with Figure 5.12.

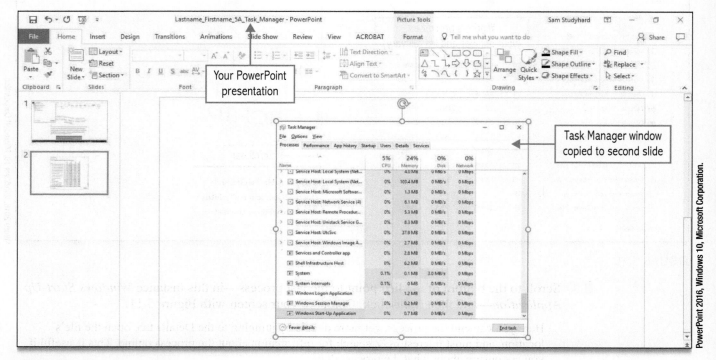

FIGURE 5.12

10 Click in a white area to deselect the image. In the upper left corner, click **Save** ⊟, and then in the upper right corner, click **Minimize** −.

11 Scroll back to the top of the **Task Manager** window, and notice that some processes have an arrow to the left, which indicates a subprocess. To the left of the PowerPoint process, click the arrow, and then compare you screen with Figure 5.13.

The two PowerPoint presentations that you have open display as subprocesses.

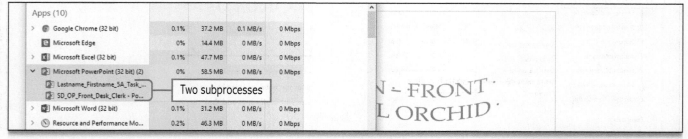

FIGURE 5.13

The *Performance tab* provides both data and graphs about the current activity of your CPU, Memory, Disks, and Network. In the first column you can click an item, and then see graphical information and data about the selected item. This information is useful to understand your computer hardware.

The *App history tab* provides information about how Windows apps are using the system resources—in a manner similar to the Processes tab. Desktop apps are not included here. The information here is accumulated over a period of time, which is why it includes the term *history*. The information can give you an idea of how you are using your computer. If you never delete the usage history, the information will begin with the installation of Windows 10 or the purchase of your computer.

Activity 5.03 | Viewing Performance and App History in Task Manager

1 In the **Task Manager** window, click the **Performance tab**. On the left, if necessary, click **CPU**. Compare your screen with Figure 5.14.

> The Performance tab displays a navigation pane on the left side. The *CPU* tab is active and a CPU % Utilization pane displays on the right, which provides a *real time* graphical representation of the *CPU % Utilization* over time at one-second intervals. Real time is the actual time during which something takes place. Advanced, real time performance statistics display below the graph.
>
> This continuous stream of data can assist you in recognizing irregular spikes in the use of a resource. Computer performance is often measured by CPU usage and Memory (RAM) usage. The Performance tab in Task Manager provides several graphs that chart these two important indicators. Such charts provide a view of your computer's CPU usage and Memory usage over a period of time.

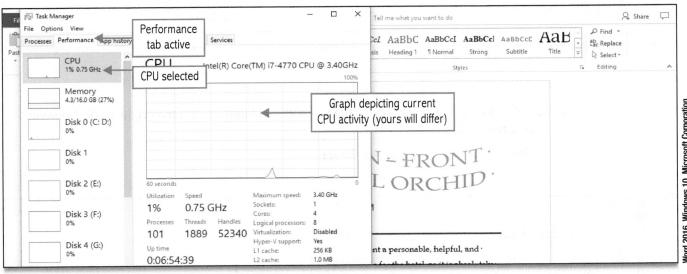

FIGURE 5.14

2 Hold down `Alt` and press `PrintScrn`.

> This action copies the active window—not the entire screen—to the Clipboard.

3 From the taskbar, open your PowerPoint presentation. On the **Home tab**, in the **Slides group**, click the upper portion of the **New Slide** button to insert a new slide in the **Blank** layout.

4 On the **Home tab**, in the **Clipboard group**, click the upper portion of the **Paste** button to copy the active window—the **Task Manager** window—to the new slide.

5 Click in a white area to deselect the image. In the upper left corner, click **Save** 🖫, and then in the upper right corner, click **Minimize** ⊟.

6 In the **Task Manager** window, click the **App history tab**. Compare your screen with Figure 5.15.

Information about Windows app usage displays. If you have a metered Internet connection—meaning a cellular connection—you can see if you are spending money using specific apps. This table could also tell you if someone using your computer is spending a lot of time using a specific app; for example, if a child is spending time playing a specific game that he or she downloaded from the Windows store.

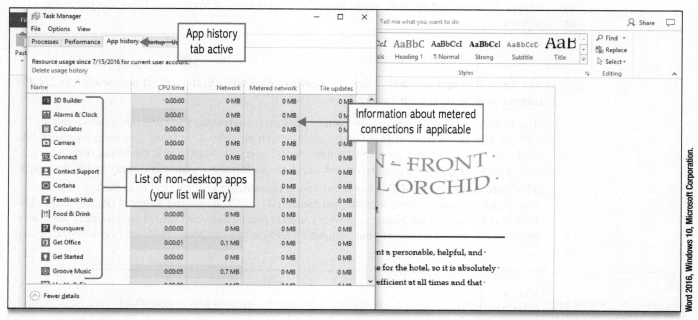

FIGURE 5.15

7 Scroll down the list as necessary, point to **Contact Support**, and then right-click. Compare your screen with Figure 5.16.

Here you can open—switch to—the app.

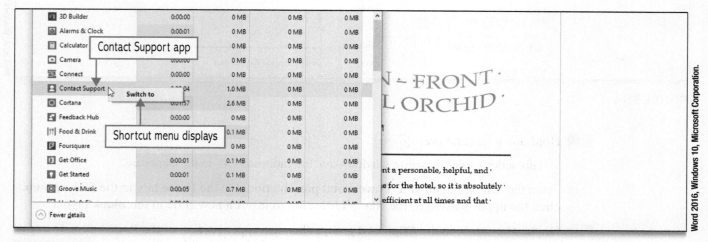

FIGURE 5.16

8 Click **Switch to,** and then compare your screen with Figure 5.17.

The Contact Support app opens.

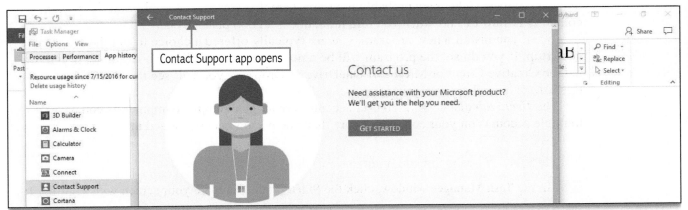

FIGURE 5.17

9 Hold down ⊞ and press PrintScrn, notice that the screen dims for a moment, and then from the taskbar, display your PowerPoint presentation.

10 On the **Home tab,** click the upper portion of the **New Slide** button to insert a fourth slide in the **Blank** layout, and then in the **Clipboard group,** click the upper portion of the **Paste** button. Compare your screen with Figure 5.18.

FIGURE 5.18

11 Click in a white area to deselect the image. In the upper left corner, click **Save** ⊟, and then in the upper right corner, click **Minimize** ⎯.

12 **Close** ☒ the **Contact Support** window.

The **Startup tab** displays the programs that are starting up automatically when you turn on your computer. There are probably programs here that you are not even aware of. If your computer is slow to start when you turn it on, this is a good place to check.

When you install a new program, you are typically offered a choice to run the program at startup. If you do so, the program will be among those on this list. For example, if you use Adobe Creative Cloud or Microsoft OneDrive or Dropbox, you will see those programs on this list.

The **Users tab** displays which user accounts are logged in to the computer. If you have multiple accounts on your computer, more than one person may be logged in.

Activity 5.04 | Viewing Startup Programs and Users in Task Manager

1 In the **Task Manager** window, click the **Startup tab**. Compare your screen with Figure 5.19.

Information about startup programs displays. Here you can disable programs from starting when you turn on or restart your computer. To do so, right-click the program name and click Disable. Reducing the number of programs that run at startup can save memory space on your computer.

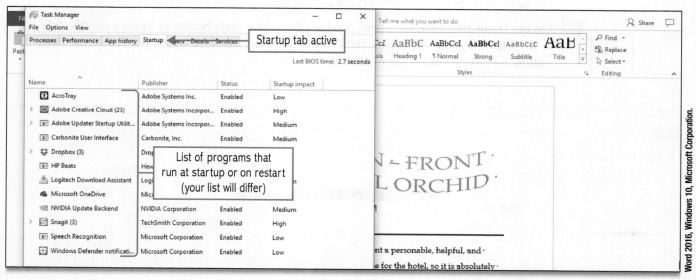

FIGURE 5.19

2 Hold down Alt and press PrintScrn—you will not see the screen dim.

This action copies the active window—not the entire screen—to the Clipboard.

3 From the taskbar, open your PowerPoint presentation. On the **Home tab**, in the **Slides group**, click the upper portion of the **New Slide** button to insert a new slide in the **Blank** layout.

4 On the **Home tab**, in the **Clipboard group**, click the upper portion of the **Paste** button to copy the active window—the **Task Manager** window—to the new slide. Compare your screen with Figure 5.20.

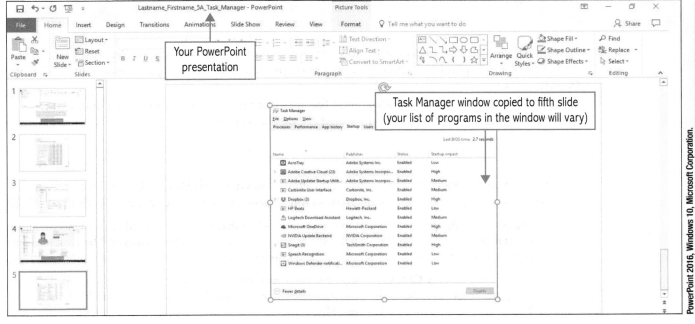

FIGURE 5.20

PowerPoint 2016, Windows 10, Microsoft Corporation.

5 Click in a white area to deselect the image. In the upper left corner, click **Save** ⊟, and then in the upper right corner, click **Minimize** −.

6 In the **Task Manager** window, click the **Users tab**. Compare your screen with Figure 5.21.

FIGURE 5.21

Word 2016, Windows 10, Microsoft Corporation.

7 Hold down Alt and press PrintScrn—you will not see the screen dim.

This action copies the active window—not the entire screen—to the Clipboard.

8 From the taskbar, open your PowerPoint presentation. On the **Home tab**, in the **Slides group**, click the upper portion of the **New Slide** button to insert a new slide in the **Blank** layout.

9 On the **Home tab**, in the **Clipboard group**, click the upper portion of the **Paste** button to copy the active window—the **Task Manager** window—to the new slide.

This is the sixth slide in your PowerPoint presentation.

10 Click in a white area to deselect the image. In the upper left corner, click **Save** ⊟, and then in the upper right corner, click **Minimize** −.

The **Details tab** displays detailed information about the processes on the Processes tab. The Details tab displays the actual process names instead of the names you see on the Processes tab.

The **Services tab** displays background features that are always running; for example, the indexing of your hard drive that you learned about is a service.

Activity 5.05 | Viewing Details in Task Manager

1 ▶ In the **Task Manager** window, click the **Details tab**. On the right, use the scroll bar as necessary to scroll down to view **System Idle Process**. Compare your screen with Figure 5.22.

The **System Idle Process** indicates the amount of CPU that is *not* being used. This number changes constantly as the CPU works with the various processes listed in Task Manager. The Task Manager program itself is running through the *Taskmgr.exe* process.

You can see that the CPU percentage for Taskmgr.exe changes as Task Manager monitors your computer. With this knowledge, you can determine how much of your CPU capability would become available if you closed Task Manager.

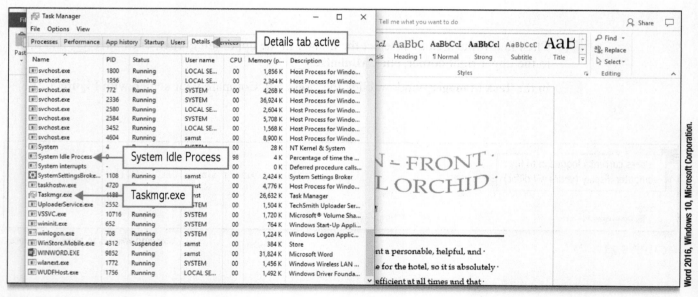

FIGURE 5.22

2 ▶ Point to the column heading that begins *Memory*, and notice the ScreenTip that displays, as shown in Figure 5.23.

Memory (*Private Working Set*) refers to the amount of memory that must be *reserved* by each process, which is not necessarily the amount of memory currently being *used* by that process. Programs reserve blocks of memory to prevent other programs from using memory that it may need as you work. This prevents the program from performing too slowly.

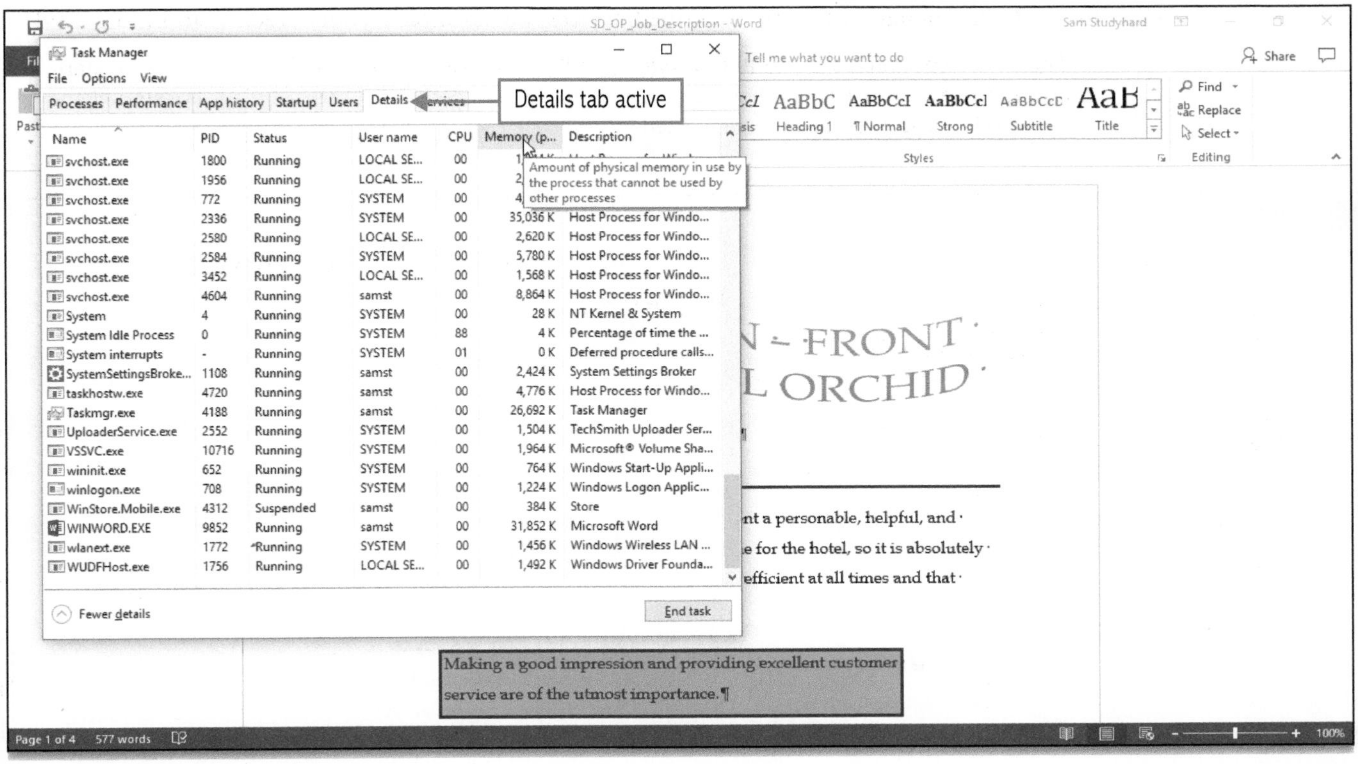

Word 2016, Windows 10, Microsoft Corporation.

FIGURE 5.23

3 Hold down Alt and press PrintScrn—you will not see the screen dim.

This action copies the active window—not the entire screen—to the Clipboard.

4 From the taskbar, open your PowerPoint presentation. On the **Home tab**, in the **Slides group**, click the upper portion of the **New Slide** button to insert a new slide in the **Blank** layout.

5 On the **Home tab**, in the **Clipboard group**, click the upper portion of the **Paste** button to copy the active window—the **Task Manager** window—to the new slide.

This is the seventh slide in your PowerPoint presentation.

6 Click in a white area to deselect the image. In the upper left corner, click **Save**, and then in the upper right corner, click **Minimize**.

Activity 5.06 | Viewing Services in Task Manager

Recall that a service is a computer program or process that runs in the background and that provides support to other programs. Many services operate at a low level; that is, the service interacts directly with a hardware device. Most of the services that are essential to running your computer are set to start automatically when you start your computer and stop when you shut down your computer.

On rare occasions, you might need to stop a service if directed to do so by a computer technician or another IT professional. For example, if too many print requests have caused your printer to become nonresponsive, one remedy might be to stop and then restart a service named *Spooler*.

1 In the **Task Manager** window, click the **Services tab**. Compare your screen with Figure 5.24.

The Status column displays either *Running* or *Stopped*. Most of the running services were started during the boot process or when you logged on to your computer. Other services are started and stopped by processes as they are needed.

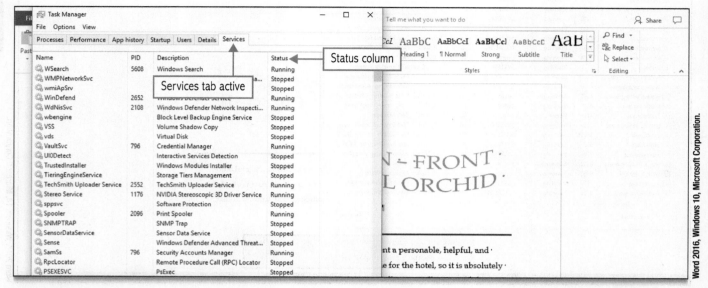

FIGURE 5.24

2 Click the **PID** column heading as necessary to sort the column in *descending* order, and then scroll to the top of the list. Compare your screen with Figure 5.25.

Here, five services are used by the process with **PID 4604**—yours may vary. A PID, or **Process Identifier**, is a number assigned to each process while it runs. A single process may use several services. This enables each service to focus on small, specific tasks.

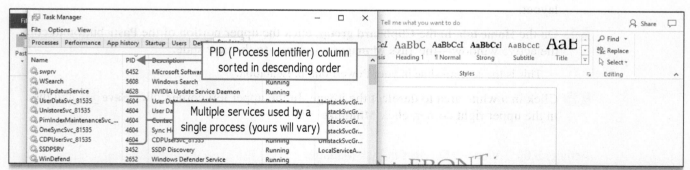

FIGURE 5.25

Word 2016, Windows 10, Microsoft Corporation.

3 Click the **Name** column heading as necessary to sort the column in alphabetical order. Scroll down as necessary, locate and point to the **Spooler** service, and then right-click. Compare your screen with Figure 5.26.

When you experience printing problems, such as not being able to add a printer or your printer stops printing, stopping and restarting this service often fixes the problem.

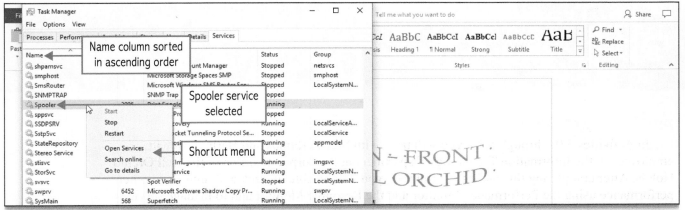

FIGURE 5.26

Word 2016, Windows 10, Microsoft Corporation.

4 Hold down [⊞] and press [PrintScrn]—the screen will dim for a moment.

This action copies the entire screen, including the displayed shortcut menu, to the Clipboard.

5 From the taskbar, open your PowerPoint presentation. On the **Home tab**, in the **Slides group**, click the upper portion of the **New Slide** button to insert a new slide in the **Blank** layout.

6 On the **Home tab**, in the **Clipboard group**, click the upper portion of the **Paste** button to copy the captured screen to the new slide.

This is the eighth slide in your PowerPoint presentation.

7 Click in a white area to deselect the image. In the upper left corner, click **Save** 🖫. In the upper right corner, click **Close** ☒. Submit your completed PowerPoint presentation, which contains eight slides, as directed by your instructor. Close all open windows.

More Knowledge   **Stopping Services**

To stop a service, right-click the service, and then click *Stop*. To start a service, right-click, and then click *Start*. Unless you are working with an IT professional or you are familiar with the purpose for a service, you should not stop or start services.

◄ **END | You have completed Project 5A**

Tracking System Performance

PROJECT ACTIVITIES

In Activities 5.07 through 5.10, you will train with Steven Ramos and Barbara Hewitt, employees in the Information Technology Department at the corporate office of the Bell Orchid Hotels. After completing this part of the training, you will be able to track and report computer performance using the Performance Monitor and the Resource Monitor and to manage services using the Services console. As you progress through the Project, you will insert screenshots of windows that you create into a PowerPoint presentation similar to Figure 5.27.

PROJECT FILES

For Project 5B, you will need the following file:

A new blank PowerPoint presentation

You will save your results in a PowerPoint file as:

Lastname_Firstname_5B_Resource_Manager

PROJECT RESULTS

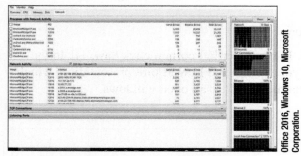
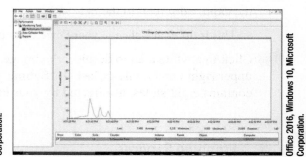
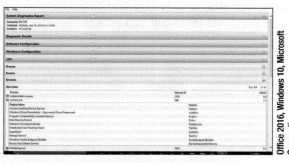

FIGURE 5.27 Project 5B Tracking System Performance

Objective 5 | Track Performance by Using the Resource and Performance Monitors

The Performance and Resource Monitors are Windows 10 tools that combine system information, performance tests, and data collected over time to monitor computer performance.

Each tool contains real time graphs and detailed descriptions. Each component can be saved as an HTML webpage so that you can save your performance data for later reference or share the information with others—a computer service technician for example. You can also customize the Performance Monitor to monitor various system-related data.

Activity 5.07 | Tracking Performance by Using Resource Monitor

The **Resource Monitor** area of the Performance Monitor provides both instantaneous and recent-history (45- or 60 second) readouts of your computer's four key performance measurements—CPU usage, hard disk drive usage, network usage, and memory usage.

This tool is similar to the Task Manager, but Resource Monitor has more graphs of computer resources. This visual representation makes it faster to get an overall view of your computer's performance. One advantage is that the monitor lists each process only when it is using a computer resource.

If your computer is having performance problems, use the Resource Monitor for a fast and informative view to see which area is slowing performance. In this Activity, you will use the Resource Monitor to track your computer's performance.

NOTE | **It Is Assumed That You Have an Administrator Account**

Learning to customize and control your computer by using Windows 10 as an administrator is the best way to learn Windows 10, because many features are available only to an individual who has an administrator account. For this Project, it is assumed that you are logging on with an administrator account.

---

1 Sign in to your computer to display the **desktop**. Close any open windows.

2 From the taskbar, or by searching, open **PowerPoint**, and then click **Blank Presentation**. On the **Home tab**, in the **Slides group**, click **Layout**, and then click **Blank**.

3 Click the **File tab**, on the left click **Save As**, click **Browse**, and then in the **Save As** dialog box, navigate to and open your **Windows 10 Chapter 5** folder.

4 In the **File name** box, using your own name, type **Lastname_Firstname_5B_Resource_Manager**

5 In the **Save As** dialog box, click **Save**. In the upper right corner of the PowerPoint window, click **Minimize** ⎯ to display the desktop and leave the presentation open.

6 On the taskbar, right-click in an empty area to display the shortcut menu, and then click **Task Manager**. If necessary, in the lower left corner, click **More details**.

7 Click the **Performance tab**, and then near the bottom left corner of the **Task Manager** window, click **Open Resource Monitor**. If necessary, sign in as the Administrator. Click the **Overview tab**, and then **Maximize** ☐ the window. As shown in Figure 5.28, be sure the **CPU** section is expanded and the other sections are collapsed.

The Overview tab displays information and real time graphs for four key performance areas: CPU, Disk, Network, and Memory. Graphs display on the right and summary information for each resource that is being monitored displays on the left. You can expand or collapse the section header arrows to view the performance areas. Within each section, the columns can be resized and sorted, and like Task Manager, columns can be added or removed from the summary area.

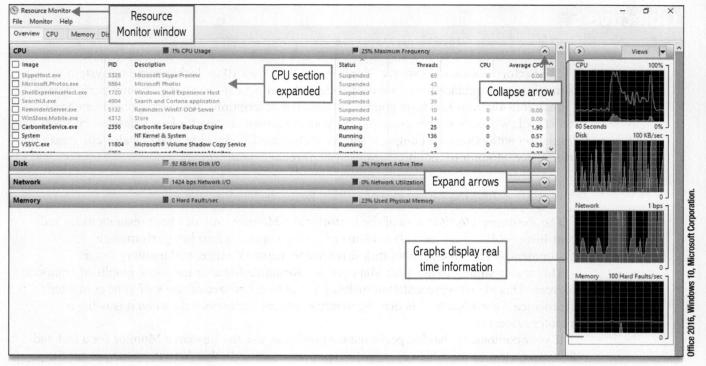

FIGURE 5.28

> 8 ▶ Click the **CPU tab** to display the CPU resources that are currently running. Point to the lower edge of the **Processes section** to display the 🔲 pointer, as shown in Figure 5.29, and then drag down several inches to expand the section about halfway down the screen.

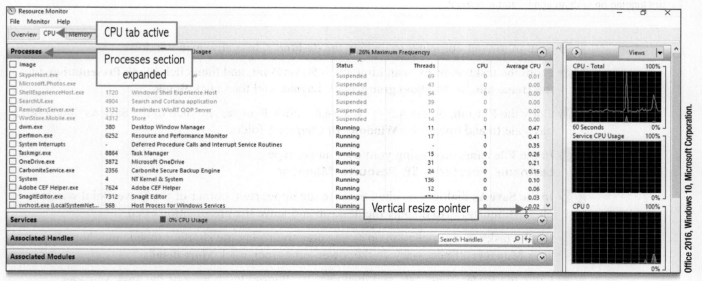

FIGURE 5.29

> 9 ▶ Click slightly to the right of the column heading *Image* and then click as necessary to sort the column in *ascending* (A to Z) alphabetical order.

In the summary information for the CPU, only those processes that are currently using the CPU resources display. Because processes consume computer resources for only brief periods of time, the list changes frequently. In the CPU resources list, the areas can be resized, columns can be resized and sorted, and like Task Manager, columns can be added or removed from the summary data area.

The CPU graphs and summary information report your processor's activity. Your processor could reach 100% usage, but it will typically have considerable idle time.

10 Scroll down the list as necessary to locate **POWERPNT.EXE** on the list, and then compare your screen with Figure 5.30.

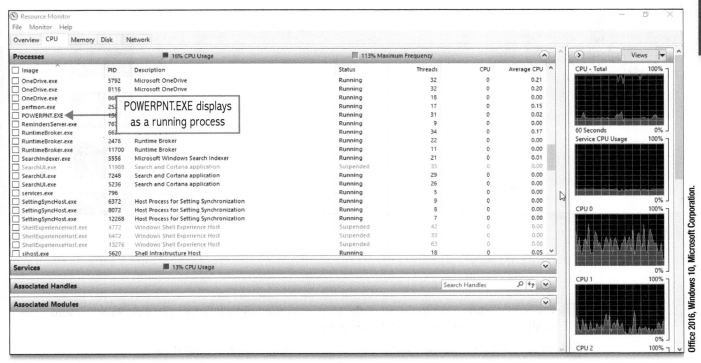

FIGURE 5.30

11 Near the top of the **Resource Monitor**, click the **Network tab,** and then as necessary, expand the **Processes with Network Activity** section and the **Network Activity** section.

The network summary information displays network activity including Internet traffic.

12 From the taskbar, start the **Microsoft Edge** browser and then navigate to the site **www.usa.gov** While the webpage is loading, on the taskbar, quickly click the **Resource Monitor** icon , and then compare your screen with Figure 5.31.

While the page loads, the *MicrosoftEdgeCP.exe* process uses network resources. The Network Activity text shows the IP addresses of the web servers being used and the speed, in bytes per second, with which the page is loading.

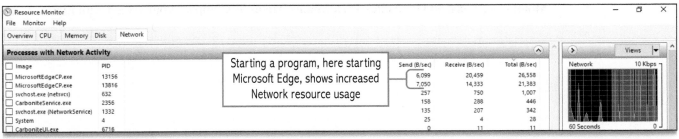

FIGURE 5.31

Office 2016, Windows 10, Microsoft Corporation.

13 Press + , display your PowerPoint presentation, and then paste the captured window as the first slide. Compare your screen with Figure 5.32.

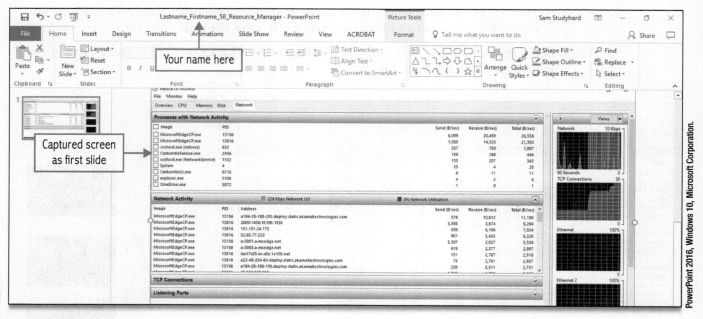

FIGURE 5.32

14 ▶ Click in a white area to deselect the image. In the upper left corner, click **Save** ⊟, and then in the upper right corner, click **Minimize** −.

15 ▶ **Close** ✕ the **Resource Monitor**, **Close** ✕ the **Edge** window, and then **Close** ✕ **Task Manager**.

Activity 5.08 │ Using the Performance Monitor

Performance Monitor is a tool that focuses on computer performance. Performance Monitor creates charts with more detail than the charts you have viewed in Task Manager and the Resource Monitor. Performance Monitor charts can also be modified and saved as image files, so that you can store them for later reference or share them with others—for example, with a computer support technician. In this Activity, you will use the Performance Monitor to chart CPU usage while you open two programs.

1 ▶ In the taskbar search box, type **performance monitor** and then with **Performance Monitor Desktop app** selected at the top of the search pane, press Enter.

2 ▶ **Maximize** ▢ the **Performance Monitor** window. In the left pane, if necessary expand **Monitoring Tools**, and then click **Performance Monitor**. Compare your screen with Figure 5.33.

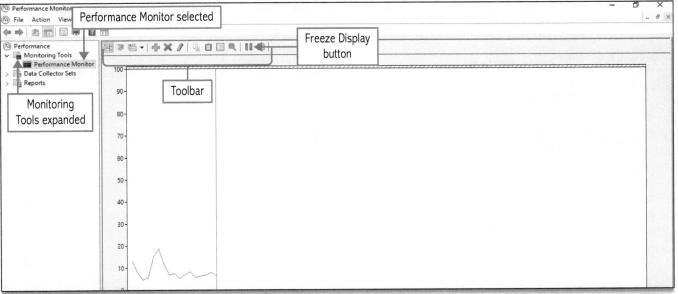

FIGURE 5.33

3 From the taskbar, open the **Microsoft Edge** browser and then open **Microsoft Word**. Then on the taskbar, click the **Performance Monitor** icon.

4 On the toolbar directly above the graph, click **Freeze Display** ⏸, and then compare your screen with Figure 5.34.

> With the Performance Monitor paused, you will be able to work with the chart without it collecting more CPU usage data. The Performance Monitor displays a graph that shows CPU usage while you opened Edge and Microsoft Word.

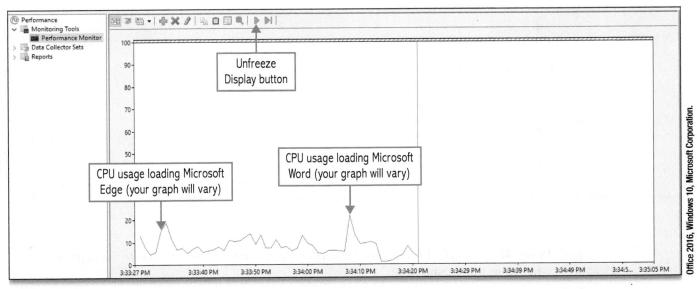

FIGURE 5.34

5 On the menu bar, click **Action**, and then click **Properties**. In the **Performance Monitor Properties** dialog box, click the **Graph tab**.

6 On the **Graph tab**, click in the **Title** box, and then, using your own name, type **CPU Usage Captured by Firstname Lastname**

7 Click in the **Vertical axis** box, type **Percent Used** and then compare your screen with Figure 5.35.

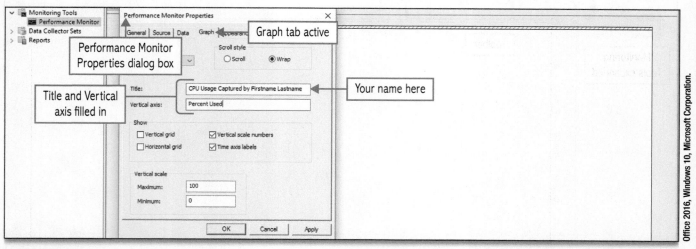

FIGURE 5.35

8 Click **OK**, and then compare your screen with Figure 5.36.

The chart displays a title that includes your name, and the vertical axis label describes what the chart is measuring.

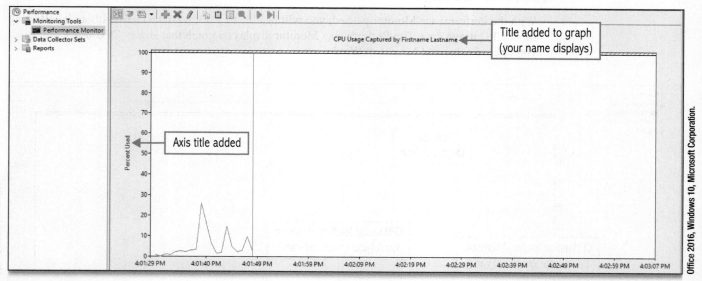

FIGURE 5.36

9 Press ⊞ + PrintScrn, display your PowerPoint presentation, and then paste the captured window as the second slide.

10 Click in a white area to deselect the image. In the upper left corner, click **Save** 🔲, and then in the upper right corner, click **Minimize** –.

11 On the taskbar, point to the **Word icon** 📘, right-click, and then click **Close window**. Point to the **Microsoft Edge icon** 🅴, right-click, and then click **Close window**.

12 In the **Performance Monitor** window, on the toolbar above the graph, click **Unfreeze Display** ▶, and then **Close** ✖ the **Performance Monitor**.

Objective 6 Create a System Diagnostics Report

The **System Diagnostics Report** is a pre-built report that contains an easy to understand summary of your computer's overall performance. Additionally, the report provides detailed information areas that you can expand or collapse for easy viewing. You can save this report as an HTML webpage, which makes the report easy to share with others. Additionally, you can use this report while the problem is occurring to gather information.

Activity 5.09 | Creating a System Diagnostics Report

In this Activity, you will create a System Diagnostics Report and view different areas of the report.

1 Point to **Start** , right-click, and then click **Command Prompt (Admin)**. If necessary, in the **User Account Control** message, click **Yes** or sign in as the Administrator. At the command prompt **C:\WINDOWS\system32>** type **perfmon/report** and then compare your screen with Figure 5.37.

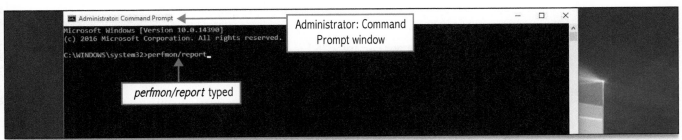

Office 2016, Windows 10, Microsoft Corporation.

FIGURE 5.37

2 Press Enter, and then compare your screen with Figure 5.38.

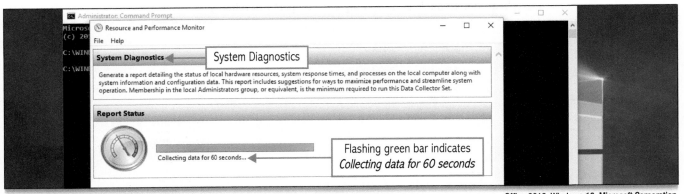

Office 2016, Windows 10, Microsoft Corporation.

FIGURE 5.38

3 While the green bar is still flashing, from the taskbar open **Microsoft Edge** , and then navigate to **http://www.ed.gov** Wait for the page to display, and then **Close** ☒ the browser window.

As you performed this step, the Performance Monitor collected performance data for your CPU, Network, Disk, and Memory.

4 **Maximize** ☐ the **Resource and Performance Monitor** window, if necessary wait a few seconds for the report to complete, and then compare your screen with Figure 5.39.

Some *Warnings* may display a problem. In Figure 5.39, the warning is merely informational. Under *Basic System Checks*, five tests display as *Passed*. Under *Performance*, the *Resource Overview* section interprets the data and displays a green circle if the component is healthy, yellow if the component came close to being overused, and red if the component has been overused.

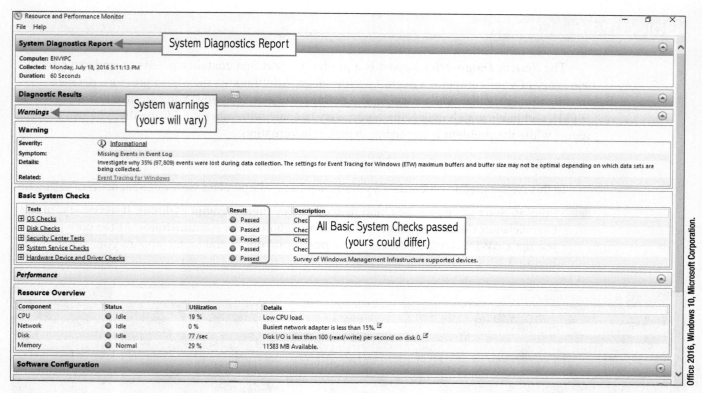

FIGURE 5.39

5 Under **Basic System Checks, expand** ⊞ **Hardware Device and Driver Checks**, and then scroll through the list. Compare your screen with Figure 5.40.

The Performance Monitor tests all of the computer's essential hardware. You can see that even the computer's cooling system is checked. Cooling information is important because a computer that overheats due to inadequate cooling will not perform reliably.

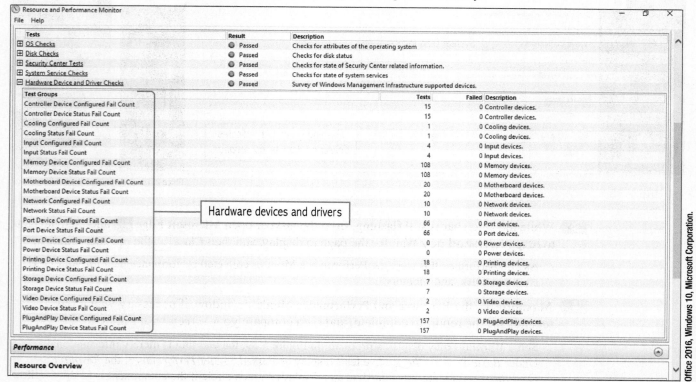

FIGURE 5.40

6 Scroll to the top of the report window, and then click the **Diagnostic Results arrow** to collapse the section. Click the **CPU arrow**, and then click the **Services** arrow. Under **Services**, expand ⊞ one of the first few processes listed.

> By expanding each process, the services that the process uses display.

7 Press ⊞ + PrintScrn, display your PowerPoint presentation, and then paste the captured window as the third slide.

8 Click in a white area to deselect the image. In the upper left corner, click **Save** ⊟, and then in the upper right corner, click **Minimize** ⊟.

9 **Close** ☒ all open windows.

NOTE	Saving Your System Diagnostics Report as a Webpage

You can save your System Diagnostics Report as a webpage. From the File menu, click Save As, and then navigate to your storage location. The file will be saved as an HTML document. The System Diagnostics Report webpage can be viewed on any computer. On your own computer, you may want to create a System Diagnostics Report every quarter, and save it as a webpage. Your report collection will provide an accessible and thorough history of your computer's performance.

Objective 7 Manage Services by Using the Services Console

Recall that services are low level programs that typically run in the background waiting to be called on by processes. A service typically supports other programs. The *Services desktop app*—sometimes referred to as the *Services console*—is a Windows 10 tool that lists all services and provides a way to change their settings. Disabling unnecessary services increases computer performance. For example, if you never use your computer as a fax machine, you could disable the Fax service. Boot time can be shortened by setting a service to start after Windows 10 finishes the boot process. If you seldom use your computer as a fax, as soon as you turn on your computer, you could set the Fax service to start after Windows 10 boots. Some problems, such as printing problems, can be solved by restarting a service. You can make all of these changes in the Services console.

Activity 5.10 | Managing Services by Using the Services Console

In this Activity, you will use the Services console to change two services—Print Spooler and Fax.

1 Click in the taskbar search box, type **services** and then with **Services Desktop app** selected at the top of the search pane, press Enter.

> The Services window displays.

2 If necessary, **Maximize** ☐ the **Services** window. Compare your screen with Figure 5.41.

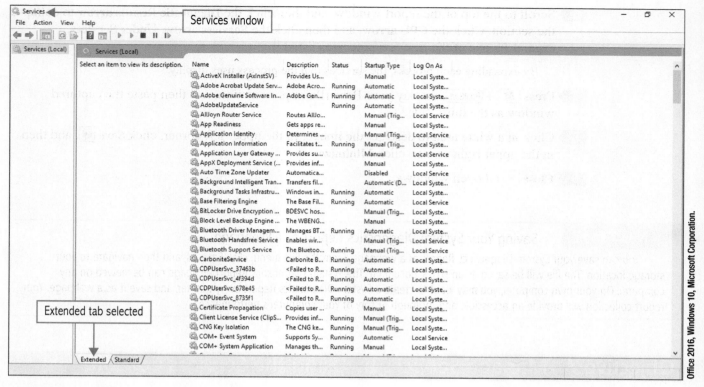

FIGURE 5.41

3 Point to the column separator between the **Name** column and the **Description** column to display the ⊞ pointer, and then double-click to widen the column. In the lower portion of the window, be sure that the **Extended tab** is selected.

4 In the **Name** column, click **App Readiness**. If **App Readiness** is not displayed, click another service, and then compare your screen with Figure 5.42.

The Services toolbar displays four buttons that control a service: Start Service, Stop Service, Pause Service, Restart Service. When the Extended tab is selected, a column displays to the left of the Name column, which includes a *Description* of the service and a link to *Start*, *Stop*, and/or *Restart* the selected service—the links vary depending on the current status of the service.

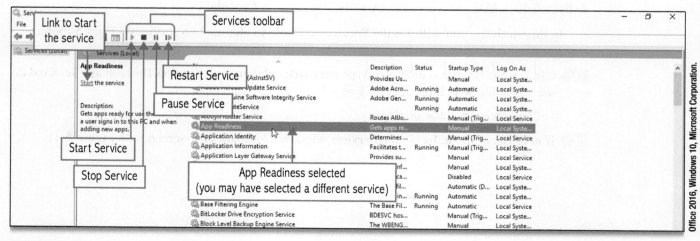

FIGURE 5.42

5 Scroll down the list of services, and then locate and click **Print Spooler**. Compare your screen with Figure 5.43.

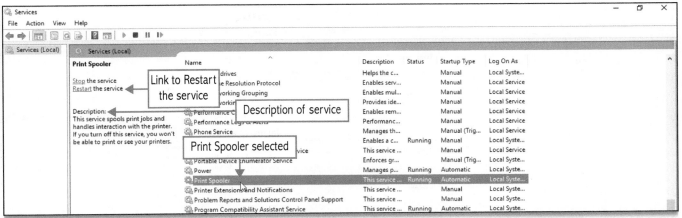

FIGURE 5.43

Office 2016, Windows 10, Microsoft Corporation.

6 In the column to the left of the **Name** column, click the **Restart** link.

The Service Control message briefly displays as the Print Spooler service is stopped and then restarted. Recall that the Print Spooler handles print requests so that you can continue using your computer for other tasks while your document is printing. When printing problems occur, restarting the print spooler service often solves the problem.

7 Scroll as necessary in the list of services, and then right-click **Fax**. Compare your screen with Figure 5.44.

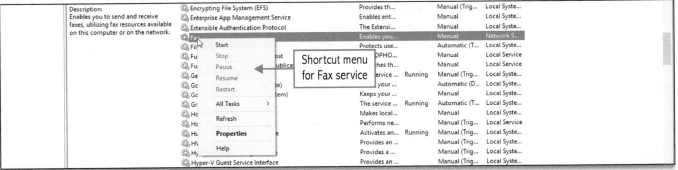

FIGURE 5.44

Office 2016, Windows 10, Microsoft Corporation.

8 From the shortcut menu, click **Properties**. On the **General tab**, click the **Startup type arrow**, and then compare your screen with Figure 5.45.

The Fax service enables you to send and receive faxes on your computer. Services can be assigned one of four service startup types. By default, the *Fax* service is assigned the *Manual* startup type, which means the service is started by the logged on user or by a program only when it is needed.

A service assigned the *Automatic* startup type means the service will start during the Windows 10 boot process. A service assigned the *Automatic (Delayed Start)* startup type will wait for Windows 10 to boot before it is started. With fewer services to start, Windows 10 will boot faster and you can start working sooner. The delayed services will start while you work on other tasks.

A service set to the *Disabled* startup type cannot be started until its startup type is changed to one of the other types. Disabling unused services improves performance. However, you should always be aware of what a service does before you disable it.

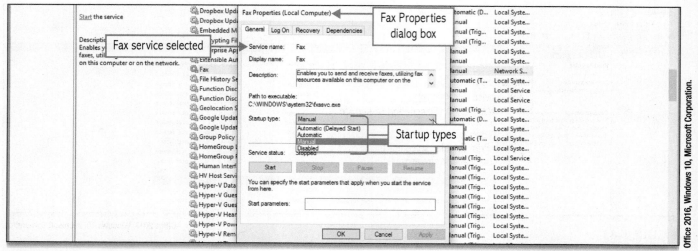

FIGURE 5.45

9 ▶ Click **Automatic (Delayed Start)**, and then click **Apply**.

Changing a service from *Manual* to *Automatic (Delayed Start)* makes the service always available, but does not increase the time needed for Windows 10 to boot. The Fax service will wait until after Windows finishes its boot process before it is started.

10 ▶ At the top of the dialog box, click the **Dependencies tab**, and then compare your screen with Figure 5.46.

Before disabling or delaying when a service is started, it is good practice to check that no other services depend on that service.

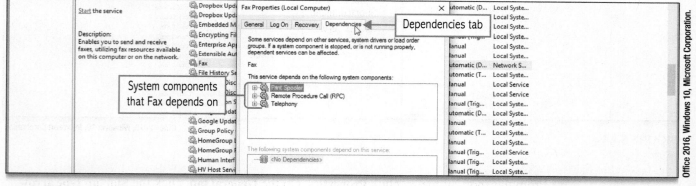

FIGURE 5.46

11 ▶ Click **OK**. At the bottom of the **Services** pane, click the **Standard tab**. Point to the column divider to the right of the **Startup Type** column to display the ⊞ pointer, and then double-click so that all of the column information displays. Compare your screen with Figure 5.47.

The Standard display is similar to the Extended display except that it does *not* display the column to the left of the Name column, which includes the *Description*, link to *Start*, *Stop*, and/or *Restart the selected service*.

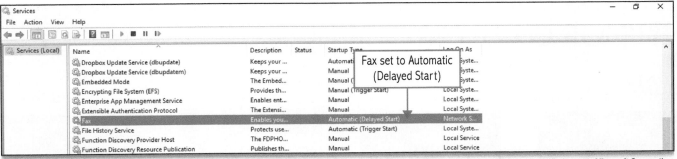

Office 2016, Windows 10, Microsoft Corporation.

FIGURE 5.47

12 ▶ Press **⊞** + **PrintScrn**, display your PowerPoint presentation, and then paste the captured window as the fourth slide.

13 ▶ Click in a white area to deselect the image. In the upper left corner, click **Save** 🖫, and then in the upper right corner, click **Minimize** ⊟.

14 ▶ Right-click **Fax**, and then on the shortcut menu, click **Properties**. Click the **Startup type arrow**, click **Manual**, and then click **OK**.

On your own computer, you may want to use the Services window to view and manage the services running on your computer. Generally, the settings used by Windows 10 are ideal, so consult with an IT professional before making any changes.

15 ▶ In the upper right corner of the **Services** window, click **Restore Down** 🗗.

16 ▶ **Close** ☒ the **Services** window. Display and save your PowerPoint presentation, **Close** ☒ PowerPoint, and then submit your completed PowerPoint presentation as directed by your instructor.

END | You have completed Project 5B

END OF CHAPTER

SUMMARY

Rely on Task Manager to show the programs, processes, and services that are currently running on your computer. Use Task Manager to monitor your system's performance and close nonresponsive programs.

A program on your computer may become nonresponsive when it performs a task that has no way of ending, or when the program cannot access the correct instructions that it had stored in memory.

The Resource Monitor provides both instantaneous and recent-history (45 or 60 seconds) readouts of your computer's four key performance measurements— CPU, hard disk drive, network, and memory usage.

Performance Monitor creates charts with more detail than the charts created in Task Manager. Additionally, the charts can be modified and saved as image files to share with a computer support professional.

GO! LEARN IT ONLINE

Review the concepts and key terms in this chapter by completing these online challenges, which you can find in **MyITLab**:

Matching and Multiple Choice: Answer matching and multiple choice questions to test what you learned in this chapter.

Lessons on the GO!: Learn how to use all the new apps and features as they are introduced by Microsoft.

GO! FOR JOB SUCCESS

Discussion: Wearable Technology

Your instructor may assign these questions to your class, and then ask you to think about them or discuss them with your classmates.

Personal technology has evolved beyond smartphones and now includes wearable devices like watches and fitness bands that enable you check emails and calendars on your wrist and to track health data such as heart rate.

Wearables also provide opportunities for businesses to provide better service and safer workplaces. In a manufacturing environment, smart goggles or badges and sensors in clothing can detect unsafe conditions or provide real-time information to improve productivity. At a retail store, associates with wearables can access up-to-date inventory data and customer information to provide better service and streamline operations.

Wearable technology also gives employers greater ability to track and monitor employees. In an open office environment, requiring employees to scan a badge every time they enter a cube or conference room is efficient if employees need to be contacted or there is an emergency. Movement and location information of field employees like sales staff or delivery drivers is vital business data. On the other hand, wearables allow employers to also monitor personal data like heart rate, physical activity, and sleep patterns.

FotolEdhar/Fotolia

Question 1: How could employees with hands-free, wearable devices improve efficiency in a restaurant or enhance care in a hospital?

Question 2: What are some disadvantages for employees of wearable tracking technology?

Question 3: Could there be advantages to employees if their stress and fatigue levels were monitored?

	Review and Assessment Guide for Windows 10 Chapter 5		
Project	**Apply Skills from These Chapter Objectives**	**Project Type**	**Project Location**
5A	Objectives 1-4 from Project 5A	**5A Instructional Project (Scorecard Grading)** Guided instruction to learn the skills in Project 5A.	In text
5B	Objectives 5-7 from Project 5B	**5B Instructional Project (Scorecard Grading)** Guided instruction to learn the skills in Project 5B.	In text
5C	Objectives 1-4 from Project 5A	**5C Skills Review (Scorecard Grading)** A guided review of the skills from Project 5A.	In text
5D	Objectives 5-7 from Project 5B	**5D Skills Review (Scorecard Grading)** A guided review of the skills from Project 5B.	In text
5E	Objectives 1-4 from Project 5A	**5E Mastery (Scorecard Grading)** **Mastery and Transfer of Learning** A demonstration of your mastery of the skills in Project 5A with decision-making.	In text
5F	Objectives 5-7 from Project 5B	**5F Mastery (Scorecard Grading)** **Mastery and Transfer of Learning** A demonstration of your mastery of the skills in Project 5B with decision-making.	In text
5G	Combination of Objectives from Projects 5A and 5B	**5G GO! Think (Rubric Grading)** **Critical Thinking** A demonstration of your understanding of the Chapter concepts applied in a manner that you would outside of college. An analytic rubric helps you and your instructor grade the quality of your work by comparing it to the work an expert in the discipline would create.	In text
5H	Combination of Objectives from Projects 5A and 5B	**5H GO! Think (Rubric Grading)** **Critical Thinking** A demonstration of your understanding of the Chapter concepts applied in a manner that you would outside of college. An analytic rubric helps you and your instructor grade the quality of your work by comparing it to the work an expert in the discipline would create.	In text
5I	Combination of Objectives from Projects 5A and 5B	**5I GO! Think (Rubric Grading)** **Critical Thinking** A demonstration of your understanding of the Chapter concepts applied in a manner that you would outside of college. An analytic rubric helps you and your instructor grade the quality of your work by comparing it to the work an expert in the discipline would create.	In text

GLOSSARY

App history tab In Task Manager, the tab that provides information about how Windows apps are using the system resources in a manner similar to the Processes tab.

Details tab In Task Manager, the tab that displays detailed information about the processes on the Processes tab.

Heat map A graphical representation of data displayed as a matrix in which the individual statistical values are represented as colors.

Memory (Private Working Set) The amount of memory that must be reserved by each process.

Nonresponsive program A program that is open but has stopped responding to your commands, which means it has stopped communicating with Windows 10.

Performance Monitor A tool that focuses on computer performance; Performance Monitor creates charts with more detail than the charts in Task Manager and in the Resource Monitor.

Performance tab In Task Manager, the tab that provides both data and graphs about the current activity of your CPU, Memory, Disks, and Network.

PID The acronym for *Process Identifier*, which is a number assigned to each process while it runs.

Process A file that is part of a running program and performs a specific task such as starting the program.

Process Identifier A number assigned to each process while it runs.

Processes tab In Task Manager, the tab that shows how Apps, Background processes, and Windows processes are using the system resources.

Real time The actual time during which something takes place.

Resource Monitor An area of the Performance Monitor that provides both instantaneous and recent-history (45 seconds) readouts of your computer's four key performance measurements—CPU usage, hard disk drive usage, network usage, and memory usage.

Services Computer programs or processes that run in the background and provide support to other programs.

Services console A Windows 10 tool that lists all services and provides a way to change their settings; also referred to as the Services desktop app.

Services desktop app A Windows 10 tool that lists all services and provides a way to change their settings; also referred to as the Services console.

Services tab In Task Manager, the tab that displays background features that are always running.

Startup tab In Task Manager, the tab that displays the programs that are starting up automatically when you turn on your computer.

System Diagnostics Report A pre-built report that contains an easy to understand summary of your computer's overall performance.

System Idle Process A process that indicates the amount of CPU that is *not* being used.

Task Manager A Windows 10 tool that shows you information about the programs, processes, and services that are currently running on your computer.

Users tab In Task Manager, the tab that displays which user accounts are logged in to the computer.

Skills Review · Project 5C Using Task Manager

 PROJECT FILES

For Project 5C, you will need the following file:

win05_5C_Answer_Sheet (Word document) from the student data files that accompany this textbook

You will save your results as:

Lastname_Firstname_5C_Answer_Sheet

1 From your **win10_05_Student_Data_Files**, open the Word document **win05_5C_Answer_Sheet**. Using your own name, save it in your **Windows 10 Chapter 5** folder as **Lastname_Firstname_5C_Answer_Sheet** and then minimize the document to leave it open.

Close all windows and display your desktop. As you complete each step in this Project, write the letter of your answer on a piece of paper; you will fill in your Answer Sheet after you complete all the steps in this Project.

On the taskbar, right-click in an empty area, and then on the menu that displays, click **Task Manager**. If necessary, at the bottom click More details. Do *not* maximize the window. Which of the following is *not* a tab in the Task Manager window?

A. Performance

B. Network

C. Services

2 Display the **Processes tab**. Which of the following statements is true?

A. There are fewer applications running than processes.

B. The number of applications running is equal to the number of processes running.

C. There are more applications running than processes.

3 Click **Start** ⊞, and then by using the techniques you have practiced, locate and open the **Photos app**. Then, **Minimize** ⌐ the **Photos** window. On the **Processes tab** of **Task Manager**, under **Apps**, point to **Photos**, right-click, and then click **Go to details**. On the displayed **Details tab**, what is the name of process selected?

A. Photos

B. Photos.exe

C. Microsoft.Photos.exe

4 Click **Start** ⊞ and then by using the techniques you have practiced, locate and open the **Store app**. Then minimize the window. On the **Details tab** of the **Task Manager**, scroll as necessary to locate the name **WinStore.Mobile.exe** in the first column. In the **Description** column, what is the name for this process?

A. App Store

B. Store

C. Windows 10 Store

(Project 5C Using Task Manager continues on the next page)

Apply **5A** skills from these Objectives:

1 View Applications and Manage Processes by Using Task Manager

2 View Performance and App History in Task Manager

3 View Startup Programs and Users in Task Manager

4 View Details and Services in Task Manager

5 In the **Task Manager** window, click the **Performance tab**, and then on the left, click **CPU**. Which of the following is *not* displayed in the statistics below the chart?

A. Minimum speed

B. Utilization

C. Processes

6 In the **Task Manager** window, click the **App history tab**. Which of the following is *not* listed as an app on this list?

A. Get Started

B. Microsoft Word

C. Maps

7 In the list of apps, point to **Groove Music**, right-click, and then click **Switch to**. What is your result?

A. Music plays from your computer's speakers.

B. The Groove Music app opens.

C. A list of movies that you can rent displays.

8 **Close** the **Groove Music** window. In the **Task Manager** window, click the **Startup tab**. Which of the following is *not* a column heading?

A. Publisher

B. Startup impact

C. Startup speed

9 In the **Task Manager** window, click the **Users tab**, and then on the menu bar, click **Options**. Which of the following is true?

A. From this menu, you can display the password for any signed-in users.

B. From this menu, you can show the full account name of a user.

C. From this menu, you can set a user to Administrator status.

10 Press Esc to close the menu. In the **Task Manager** window, click the **Services tab**. How is the **Status** of services indicated?

A. On or Off

B. Services that are running display in green letters

C. Running or Stopped

To complete this project: Close any open windows to display the **desktop**, on the taskbar click the **Word** button, type your answers into the correct boxes. Save and close your Word document, and submit as directed by your instructor. **Close** ⊠ Photos and any other open programs or windows.

END | You have completed Project 5C

Skills Review **Project 5D Tracking System Performance**

<table>
<tr><td>

Apply 5B skills from these Objectives:

5 Track Performance by Using the Resource and Performance Monitors

6 Create a System Diagnostics Report

7 Manage Services by Using the Services Console

</td></tr>
</table>

PROJECT FILES

For Project 5D, you will need the following file:

win05_5D_Answer_Sheet (Word document) from the student data files that accompany this textbook

You will save your results as:

Lastname_Firstname_5D_Answer_Sheet

1 From your **win10_05_Student_Data_Files**, open the Word document **win05_5D_Answer_Sheet**. Using your own name, save it in your **Windows 10 Chapter 5** folder as **Lastname_Firstname_5D_Answer_Sheet** and then minimize the document to leave it open.

Close all windows and display your desktop. As you complete each step in this Project, write the letter of your answer on a piece of paper; you will fill in your Answer Sheet after you complete all the steps in this Project.

On the taskbar, right-click in an empty area, and then on the menu that displays, click **Task Manager**. If necessary, at the bottom click More details. Click the **Performance tab**, and then near the bottom left corner of the **Task Manager** window, click **Open Resource Monitor**. If necessary, enter the admin user name and password. **Maximize** □ the **Resource Monitor** window. In the **Resource Monitor** window, how many tabs display?

A. Three

B. Four

C. Five

2 If necessary, click the **Overview tab**. Below the row of tabs, what are the names of the four sections that can be expanded or collapsed?

A. CPU, Disk, Security, Network

B. CPU, Disk, Memory, Hard Drive

C. CPU, Disk, Network, Memory

3 On the right, how many graphs display?

A. Four

B. Three

C. Two

4 Expand each section. What column title is shown in each of the four sections?

A. Description

B. PID

C. Threads

5 Click the **CPU tab**. Which of the following is *not* a section on this tab?

A. Associated Processes

B. Associated Handles

C. Associated Modules

(Project 5D Tracking System Performance continues on the next page)

6 ▶ **Close** the **Resource Monitor** window and the **Task Manager** window. In the search box, search for **performance monitor** and then display the **Performance Monitor Desktop app**. **Maximize** ☐ the window. On the left, if necessary expand **Monitoring Tools**, and then click **Performance Monitor**. What is your result?

    A. A report regarding performance displays.

    B. A chart for each disk drive displays

    C. A graph line displays and moves across the window.

7 ▶ On the menu bar, click **Action**, and then click **Properties**. In the dialog box, click the **Graph tab**. Which of the following is true?

    A. Here you can change the name of a disk drive.

    B. Here you can place a title on the graph.

    C. Here you can change the color of the line in the graph.

8 ▶ **Close** the **Properties** dialog box. In the toolbar, click **Freeze Display** ❚❚. What is your result?

    A. The graph line stops moving.

    B. The Freeze Display button is replaced with the Unfreeze Display button ▶.

    C. Both A. and B.

9 ▶ **Close** the **Performance Monitor** window. In the taskbar search box, type **services** and then with **Services Desktop app** selected at the top of the search pane, press Enter. **Maximize** ☐ the window. At the bottom, if necessary, click the **Extended tab**. Scroll as necessary, and then click to select **Windows Defender Service**. According to the description, what does this service do?

    A. Prevents users from changing their password.

    B. Protects users from malware.

    C. Enables users to delete Web cookies.

10 ▶ Scroll as necessary, and then click to select **Windows Firewall**. According to the description, what does this service do?

    A. Prevents starting processes under alternate sign-ins.

    B. Provides Windows Backup and Restore capabilities.

    C. Prevents unauthorized users from gaining access to your computer through the Internet or a network.

To complete this project: Close any open windows to display the **desktop**, on the taskbar click the **Word** button, type your answers into the correct boxes. Save and close your Word document, and submit as directed by your instructor. **Close** ☒ any open windows.

END | You have completed Project 5D

Apply 5A skills from these Objectives:

1 View Applications and Manage Processes by Using Task Manager

2 View Performance and App History in Task Manager

3 View Startup Programs and Users in Task Manager

4 View Details and Services in Task Manager

Mastering Windows 10 Project 5E Using Task Manager

In the following Mastering Windows 10 Project, you will locate information by using Task Manager. You will capture screens and insert them into a PowerPoint presentation that will look similar to Figure 5.48.

📁 PROJECT FILES

For Project 5E, you will need the following file:

A new PowerPoint presentation

You will save your results in a PowerPoint presentation as:

Lastname_Firstname_5E_Task_Manager

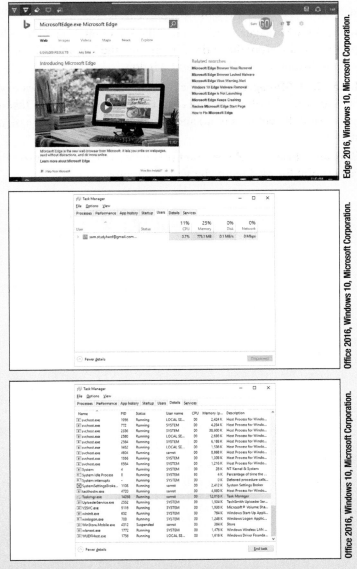

FIGURE 5.48

(Project 5E Using Task Manager continues on the next page)

Mastering Windows 10 **Project 5E Using Task Manager** (continued)

1 Open a new blank PowerPoint presentation. On the **Home tab**, in the **Slides group**, click **Layout**, and then click **Blank**. Using your own name, save the presentation in your **Windows 10 Chapter 5** folder as **Lastname_Firstname_5E_Task_Manager** **Minimize** the PowerPoint window.

2 From the taskbar, open **Microsoft Edge**, and then minimize the Edge window. Display **Task Manager**, do *not* maximize the window, and then click the **Processes tab**. Under **Apps**, point to **Microsoft Edge**, right-click, and then click **Search online**. In the displayed window from Bing, click **Make a Web Note**, and then use the large yellow highlighter to circle your user name shown in the upper right corner of the window.

3 Press [⊞] + [PrintScrn] to copy the window, from the taskbar display your PowerPoint presentation, and then paste the screen into the first slide. Minimize the PowerPoint window and close Microsoft Edge without saving any changes.

4 In the **Task Manager** window, click the **Users tab**. Press [Alt] + [PrintScrn], and then paste the captured window (not the entire screen) into the second slide of your PowerPoint presentation. Minimize the PowerPoint window.

5 In the **Task Manager** window, click the **Details tab**. If necessary, sort the **Name** column in ascending order. Scroll down and click one time to select the **Taskmgr.exe** service. Capture the window (not the entire screen) and paste it into the third slide of your PowerPoint presentation.

6 **Save** and close your PowerPoint presentation. **Close** all open windows, and then submit your PowerPoint file as directed by your instructor.

END | You have completed Project 5E

5

WINDOWS 10

Apply 5B skills from these Objectives:

5 Track Performance by Using the Resource and Performance Monitors

6 Create a System Diagnostics Report

7 Manage Services by Using the Services Console

Mastering Windows 10 | **Project 5F Tracking System Performance**

In the following Mastering Windows 10 Project, you will use the Resource Monitor and Performance Monitor. You will capture screens and insert them into a PowerPoint presentation that will look similar to Figure 5.49.

 PROJECT FILES

For Project 5F, you will need the following file:

A new PowerPoint presentation

You will save your results in a PowerPoint presentation as:

Lastname_Firstname_5F_System_Performance

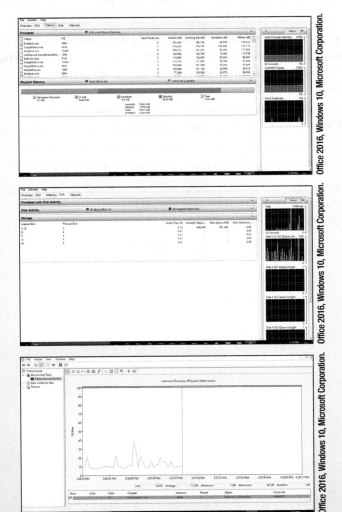

FIGURE 5.49

(Project 5F Tracking System Performance continues on the next page)

1 Open a new blank PowerPoint presentation. On the **Home tab**, in the **Slides group**, click **Layout**, and then click **Blank**. Using your own name, save the presentation in your **Windows 10 Chapter 5** folder as **Lastname_Firstname_5F_System_Performance** **Minimize** the PowerPoint window.

2 In the taskbar search box, type **resource monitor** and then with the **Resource Monitor Desktop app** selected at the top of the search pane, press [Enter]. **Maximize** the window. If necessary, sign in with your admin user name and password. Click the **Memory tab** and expand both sections, if necessary.

3 Press [⊞] + [PrintScrn] to copy the screen, from the taskbar display your PowerPoint presentation, and then paste the screen into the first slide. **Minimize** the PowerPoint window.

4 Click the **Disk tab**. Expand only the **Storage** section; collapse the other two sections. Capture the window, from the taskbar display your PowerPoint presentation, and then paste the window into the second slide. **Minimize** the PowerPoint window.

5 **Close** the **Resource Monitor**. Search for **performance monitor** and open the desktop app. **Maximize** the window, and then in the left pane, expand **Monitoring Tools** and click **Performance Monitor**. Wait until the vertical bar on the graph reaches the middle of the white area, and then freeze the display.

6 Display the **Properties** dialog box. Using your own name, title the graph **Lastname Firstname 5F System Performance** and title the axis **5F Data**

7 Close the **Properties** dialog box. Capture the window, from the taskbar display your PowerPoint presentation, and then paste the window into the third slide.

8 **Save** and close your PowerPoint presentation. **Close** all open windows, and then submit your PowerPoint file as directed by your instructor.

END | You have completed Project 5F

OUTCOMES-BASED ASSESSMENTS

RUBRIC

The following outcomes-based assessments are *open-ended assessments*. That is, there is no specific correct result; your result will depend on your approach to the information provided. Make *Professional Quality* your goal. Use the following scoring rubric to guide you in *how* to approach the problem, and then to evaluate *how well* your approach solves the problem.

The *criteria*—Software Mastery, Content, Format and Layout, and Process—represent the knowledge and skills you have gained that you can apply to solving the problem. The *levels of performance*—Professional Quality, Approaching Professional Quality, or Needs Quality Improvements—help you and your instructor evaluate your result.

	Your completed project is of Professional Quality if you:	Your completed project is Approaching Professional Quality if you:	Your completed project Needs Quality Improvements if you:
1-Software Mastery	Choose and apply the most appropriate skills, tools, and features and identify efficient methods to solve the problem.	Choose and apply some appropriate skills, tools, and features, but not in the most efficient manner.	Choose inappropriate skills, tools, or features, or are inefficient in solving the problem.
2-Content	Construct a solution that is clear and well organized, contains content that is accurate, appropriate to the audience and purpose, and is complete. Provide a solution that contains no errors of spelling, grammar, or style.	Construct a solution in which some components are unclear, poorly organized, inconsistent, or incomplete. Misjudge the needs of the audience. Have some errors in spelling, grammar, or style, but the errors do not detract from comprehension.	Construct a solution that is unclear, incomplete, or poorly organized, containing some inaccurate or inappropriate content, and contains many errors of spelling, grammar, or style. Do not solve the problem.
3-Format and Layout	Format and arrange all elements to communicate information and ideas, clarify function, illustrate relationships, and indicate relative importance.	Apply appropriate format and layout features to some elements, but not others. Overuse features, causing minor distraction.	Apply format and layout that does not communicate information or ideas clearly. Do not use format and layout features to clarify function, illustrate relationships, or indicate relative importance. Use available features excessively, causing distraction.
4-Process	Use an organized approach that integrates planning, development, self-assessment, revision, and reflection.	Demonstrate an organized approach in some areas, but not others; or, use an insufficient process of organization throughout.	Do not use an organized approach to solve the problem.

Problem Solving   Project 5G Help Desk

In this Project, you will construct a solution by applying any combination of the skills you practiced from the Objectives in Projects 5A and 5B.

For Project 5G, you will need the following file:

win05_5G_Help_Desk

You will save your document as:

Lastname_Firstname_5G_Help_Desk

From the student files that accompany this textbook, locate and open the Word document **win05_5G_Help_Desk**. Save the document in your chapter folder as **Lastname_Firstname_5G_Help_Desk**

The following e-mail question has arrived at the Help Desk from an employee at the Bell Orchid Hotel's corporate office. In the Word form, construct a response based on your knowledge of Windows 10. Although an e-mail response is not as formal as a letter, you should still use good grammar, good sentence structure, professional language, and a polite tone. Save your document and submit the response as directed by your instructor.

To: Help Desk

I read somewhere that stopping and then restarting the print spooler can often clear up a printer problem. How can I do this?

END | You have completed Project 5G

Problem Solving   Project 5H Help Desk

In this Project, you will construct a solution by applying any combination of the skills you practiced from the Objectives in Projects 5A and 5B.

For Project 5H, you will need the following file:

win05_5H_Help_Desk

You will save your document as:

Lastname_Firstname_5H_Help_Desk

From the student files that accompany this textbook, locate and open the Word document **win05_5H_Help_Desk**. Save the document in your chapter folder as **Lastname_Firstname_5H_Help_Desk**

The following e-mail question has arrived at the Help Desk from an employee at the Bell Orchid Hotel's corporate office. In the Word form, construct a response based on your knowledge of Windows 10. Although an e-mail response is not as formal as a letter, you should still use good grammar, good sentence structure, professional language, and a polite tone. Save your document and submit the response as directed by your instructor.

To: Help Desk

How can I display and print a graph of my computer's CPU performance? The system seems to have slowed down considerably in the past two weeks.

END | You have completed Project 5H

Problem Solving   Project 5I Help Desk

In this Project, you will construct a solution by applying any combination of the skills you practiced from the Objectives in Projects 5A and 5B.

For Project 5I, you will need the following file:

win05_5I_Help_Desk

You will save your document as:

Lastname_Firstname_5I_Help_Desk

From the student files that accompany this textbook, locate and open the Word document **win05_5I_Help_Desk**. Save the document in your chapter folder as **Lastname_Firstname_5I_Help_Desk**

The following e-mail question has arrived at the Help Desk from an employee at the Bell Orchid Hotel's corporate office. In the Word form, construct a response based on your knowledge of Windows 10. Although an e-mail response is not as formal as a letter, you should still use good grammar, good sentence structure, professional language, and a polite tone. Save your document and submit the response as directed by your instructor.

To: Help Desk

My computer has been crashing at least once a day for the past two weeks. I understand that in Windows 10 I can see a report that documents computer crashes and other failures. What is this report and what steps do I need to take to create it? Finally, how can I save this report so that I can send it to you?

> **END | You have completed Project 5I**

Glossary Key Terms

.png An image file format, commonly pronounced *PING*, that stands for Portable Network Graphic; this is an image file type that can be transferred over the Internet.

.txt file A simple file consisting of lines of text with no formatting that almost any computer can open and display.

2 in 1 PC A laptop or notebook computer that can function as both a traditional laptop and as a tablet by either detaching the keyboard or by rotating the keyboard 360 degrees on hinges to look like a tablet.

Access work or school A Windows 10 feature with which you can connect to your work or school system based on established policies.

Accessibility A term that refers to the design of hardware and software in a manner that helps individuals with disabilities use computing tools.

Action Center A vertical panel that displays on the right side of your screen when you click the icon in the notifications area of the taskbar; the upper portion displays notifications you have elected to receive such as mail and social network updates and the lower portion displays buttons for frequently used system commands.

Address bar (File Explorer) The area at the top of a File Explorer window that displays your current location in the folder structure as a series of links separated by arrows.

Administrator account A user account that lets you make changes that will affect other users of the computer; the most powerful of the two account types, because it permits the most control over the computer.

Alarms & Clock A Windows 10 app that enables you to set alarms on your computer; the app also functions as a timer, a stopwatch, and a world clock.

AND filter When used in a search, finds files that contain both search terms even if those terms are not next to each other.

Anti-malware programs Programs that protect your computer from a malware infection.

App The shortened version of the term *application*, and which typically refers to a smaller application designed for a single purpose.

App bar A term used to describe a horizontal or vertical array of command icons in a Windows app.

App developer An individual who makes money by developing and selling apps on the Windows Store, or more generically that develops apps for any computing platform, especially for mobile computing platforms.

App history tab In Task Manager, the tab that provides information about how Windows apps are using the system resources in a manner similar to the Processes tab.

Application A set of instructions that a computer uses to accomplish a task; also called a program.

Application developer An individual who writes computer applications.

Backing up The process of creating a copy of your files somewhere other than on your computer.

Badge An icon that displays on the Lock screen for lock screen apps that you have selected.

Base locations Locations that you frequently need to access to manage your computer; includes your OneDrive folder, your personal folder, This PC, your Homegroup if you have one, Control Panel, and Recycle Bin.

Bing The search engine developed by Microsoft Corporation and that is included with Windows 10. It also powers Cortana.

Boolean operators The terms AND, OR, and NOT that govern the logical functions and express a condition that is either true or false.

Booting the computer The process of turning on a computer when the computer has been completely shut down.

Boot-sector virus A virus that replicates itself onto your hard drive's master boot record—the program that executes each time your computer boots up.

Browsing The term used to describe the process of using your computer to view webpages.

Check box feature A folder option that, when applied, displays a check box to the left of folders and files.

Chrome OS An operating system conceived to run applications and store user data in the cloud.

Chromebook A PC or laptop that runs the Chrome OS.

Click The action of pressing the left mouse button.

Clipboard A temporary storage area for information that you have copied or moved from one place and plan to use somewhere else.

Cloud storage Storage space on an Internet site that may also display as a drive on your computer.

Compressed file A file that has been reduced in size and that takes up less storage space and can be transferred to other computers faster than uncompressed files.

Compressed Folder Tools File Explorer tools, available on the ribbon, to assist you in extracting compressed files.

Contact Support A Windows 10 app that can link you to many useful help sites.

Content pane Another term for *file list*.

Contextual tab A tab that is added to the ribbon automatically when a specific object, such as a zipped file, is selected and that contains commands relevant to the selected object.

Control Panel An area of Windows 10 where you can manipulate some of the Windows 10 basic system settings and customize the appearance and functionality of your computer. You can add or remove programs, set up network connections, and manage user accounts—a carryover from previous versions of Windows.

Cortana Microsoft's intelligent personal assistant that is part of the Windows 10 operating system.

Custom scan A type of scan that you can initiate in Windows Defender that searches only those drives or folders or files that you select; for example, an email attachment that was just sent to you.

Dashboard A descriptive term for the Windows 10 Start menu because it provides a one-screen view of links to information and programs that matter most to the signed-in user.

Data All the files—documents, spreadsheets, pictures, songs, and so on—that you create and store during the day-to-day use of your computer.

Data management The process of managing your files and folders in an organized manner so that you can find information when you need it.

Define A Google search operator that searches the Web for the definition of a word you specify.

Definitions Updates to Microsoft's database of potential viruses.

Desktop The main Windows 10 screen that serves as a starting point and surface for your work, like the top of an actual desk.

Desktop app A computer program that is installed on the hard drive of a personal computer and that requires a computer operating system like Microsoft Windows or macOS to run.

Desktop background Displays the colors and graphics of your desktop; you can change the desktop background to look the way you want.

Desktop shortcuts Desktop icons that link to any item accessible on your computer or on a network, such as a program, file, folder, disk drive, printer, or another computer.

Details pane Displays the most common properties associated with the selected file in File Explorer.

Details tab In Task Manager, the tab that displays detailed information about the processes on the Processes tab.

Details view A view in File Explorer that displays a list of files or folders and their most common properties.

Dialog box A small window that displays options for completing a task.

Directory A file folder on a disk in which you store files; also called a *path*.

Double-click The action of pressing the left mouse button twice in rapid succession while holding the mouse still.

Download The action of transferring or copying a file from another location—such as a cloud storage location or from an Internet site—to your computer.

Downloads folder A folder that holds items that you have downloaded from the Internet.

Drag The action of moving something from one location on the screen to another while holding down the left mouse button; the action of dragging includes releasing the mouse button at the desired time or location.

Drive An area of storage that is formatted with a file system compatible with your operating system and is identified by a drive letter.

Driver Software that enables hardware or devices such as a printer, mouse, or keyboard to work with your computer.

Email client A program that enables you to view and manage your email from multiple email providers; for example, Microsoft Outlook or Mail for Windows 10.

Enter selection mode In Mail for Windows 10, a command that displays selection boxes to the left of messages, similar to Item check boxes in File Explorer.

External hard drive A disk drive that plugs into an external port on your computer, typically into a USB port; also referred to as a portable hard drive.

Extract The action of decompressing—pulling out—files from a compressed form.

File A collection of information that is stored on a computer under a single name, for example, a text document, a picture, or a program.

File association The association between a file and the program that created the file.

File Explorer window A window that displays the contents of the current location and contains helpful parts so that you can navigate within the file organizing structure of Windows.

File History A backup and recovery tool in Windows 10 that automatically backs up your files to a separate location. It also enables you to restore those files if the originals are lost, damaged, or deleted.

File list Displays the contents of the current folder or location; if you type text into the Search box, only the folders and files that match your search will display here—including files in subfolders; also referred to as the *content pane*.

File name extension A set of characters at the end of a file name that helps Windows 10 understand what kind of information is in a file and what program should open it.

File properties Information about a file such as its author, the date the file was last changed, and any descriptive tags.

Filetype A Google search operator that finds files of a specific type; for example, a PDF file, which is commonly used for reports.

Filtered list A display of files that is limited based on specified criteria.

Firewall Software or hardware that can help protect a computer from hackers, or prevent malicious software from gaining access to a computer through a network or over the Internet.

Folder A container in which you store files.

Folder structure The hierarchy of folders in Windows 10.

Folder window Another name for the window that displays the contents of the current folder or location.

Free-form snip When using Snipping Tool, the type of snip that lets you draw an irregular line, such as a circle, around an area of the screen.

Full scan A type of scan that you can initiate in Windows Defender that looks at everything on your hard drive.

Full-screen snip When using Snipping Tool, the type of snip that captures the entire screen.

Get Started A Windows 10 app that contains information and videos to explain how to do things; for example, how to use Cortana.

Google A name used to refer to the Web search engine developed by Google Inc., and that you can use for free on any Windows-based computer, on an Apple Mac computer, or on any Chromebook; also referred to as *Google Search* or *Google Web Search*.

Google Chrome The Web browser software program developed by Google Inc. that you can download for free on any Windows-based system, Apple Mac system, and also on any system running the Chrome OS.

Google Drive Google's cloud storage.

Google Scholar A Google site where you can search for scholarly literature; for example, when you are creating a research paper for college or for work.

Google Search The Web search engine developed by Google Inc., and that you can use for free on any Windows-based computer, on an Apple Mac computer, or on any Chromebook; also referred to as *Google Web Search* or simply *Google*.

Google Web Search The Web search engine developed by Google Inc., and that you can use for free on any Windows-based computer, on an Apple Mac computer, or on any Chromebook; also referred to as *Google Search* or simply *Google*.

Graphical user interface The system by which you interact with your computer and that uses graphics such as an image of a file folder or wastebasket that you click to activate the item represented.

Groove Music A Windows 10 app that enables you to play the music from a collection that exists on your PC.

Group by In a folder window, a feature that enables you to group the items by Name, Date modified, Type, Size, Date created, Authors, Tags, and Title, in Ascending or Descending order.

GUI The acronym for a graphical user interface, pronounced *GOO-ee*.

Hacker A term used to describe a person who uses computer expertise to gain access to computer systems often without permission.

Hamburger Another name for the hamburger menu.

Hamburger menu An icon made up of three lines that evoke a hamburger on a bun.

Hard disk drive The primary storage device located inside your computer and where most of your files and programs are typically stored; usually labeled as drive C.

Heat map A graphical representation of data displayed as a matrix in which the individual statistical values are represented as colors.

Hierarchy An arrangement where items are ranked and where each level is lower in rank than the item above it.

HoloLens A see-through holographic computer developed by Microsoft.

Hub A feature in Microsoft Edge where you can save favorite websites and create reading lists.

iCloud Apple's cloud storage that is integrated into its Mac and iOS operating systems.

Icons Small images that represent commands, files, or other windows.

Incoming connections Traffic sent from the Internet to your computer.

Index A collection of detailed information about the files on your computer that Windows 10 maintains for the purpose of conducting fast searches; when you begin a search, Windows 10 searches this summary information rather than searching file by file on your hard disk drive.

Indexed locations All of the folders in your personal folder (Documents, Pictures, and so on) and offline files, if any, that Windows 10 includes in a search.

Infected The term that describes a computer if a malware program installs itself and then runs.

Insertion point A blinking vertical line that indicates where text or graphics will be inserted.

Internet of Things A growing network of physical objects that will have sensors connected to the Internet.

Intitle A Google search operator that focuses search results on a specific word in the title of a report.

IoT The common acronym for the Internet of Things.

JPEG An acronym for Joint Photographic Experts Group, and that is a common file type used by digital cameras and computers to store digital pictures; JPEG is popular because it can store a high-quality picture in a relatively small file.

Jump list A list that displays when you right-click a button on the taskbar, and that displays locations (in the upper portion) and tasks (in the lower portion) from a program's taskbar button.

Keyboard shortcut A combination of two or more keyboard keys, used to perform a task that would otherwise require a mouse.

Keylogger spyware A type of spyware that records all of your keystrokes and then sends your typed data—including user names and passwords—to someone else.

Keywords Words you enter into a search expression that help to limit and focus your search results so that you find the information you want.

Live tiles Tiles on the Windows 10 Start menu that are constantly updated with fresh information relevant to the signed-in user; for example, the number of new email messages, new sports scores of interest, or new updates to social networks such as Facebook or Twitter.

Location Any disk drive, folder, or other place in which you can store files and folders.

Location icon An icon on the address bar that depicts the location—disk drive, folder, and so on—you are accessing.

Lock screen The first screen that displays after turning on a Windows 10 device and that displays the time, day, and date, and one or more icons representing the status of the device's Internet connection, battery status on a tablet or laptop, and any lock screen apps that are installed such as email notifications.

Lock screen apps Apps that display on a Windows 10 lock screen and that show quick status and notifications, even if the screen is locked.

Magnifier A Windows 10 accessibility app that magnifies a portion of the screen.

Mail for Windows 10 A Windows 10 app with which you can efficiently read and respond to messages from multiple email accounts from a single user interface.

Make a Web Note A Microsoft Edge feature that enables you to take notes, write, and highlight directly on webpages and then share the note.

Malware A shortened term for the words *malicious software*, which is a computer program that intentionally harms your computer.

Managed backup service A service that provides a system for backing up your computer files over the Internet on a scheduled basis and then storing the data securely on their computers; also referred to as remote backup or online backup service.

Maps A Windows 10 app that provides maps and directions.

Maximize The command to display a window in full-screen view.

Memory (Private Working Set) The amount of memory that must be reserved by each process.

Menu A list of commands within a category.

Menu bar A group of menus at the top of a program window.

Menu icon Another name for the hamburger menu.

Messages pane In Mail for Windows 10, an area that displays the messages for the selected folder, such as the Inbox folder.

Metadata The data that describes other data; for example, the collective group of a file's properties, such as its title, subject, author, and file size.

Microsoft account A single login account for Microsoft systems and services.

Microsoft Edge The Web browser software program developed by Microsoft Corporation and that is included with Windows 10.

Microsoft Garage A group at Microsoft that develops experimental projects.

Microsoft Outlook A program in the Microsoft Office suite of programs that enables you to view and manage your email from multiple email providers.

Mobile device platform The hardware and software environment for smaller-screen devices such as tablets and smartphones.

Money A Windows 10 app that provides financial news and information such as stock market quotes.

Mouse pointer Any symbol that displays on your screen in response to moving your mouse.

Movies & TV A Windows 10 app where you can either buy or rent movies and episodes of TV shows and that also acts as a video player so you can play videos from your own files.

Narrator A Windows 10 accessibility app that reads text on your PC screen aloud and that serves as a basic screen reader.

Navigate Explore within the file organizing structure of Windows 10.

Navigation pane The area on the left side of a folder window in File Explorer that displays the Quick access area and an expandable list of drives and folders.

Network and Sharing Center A Windows 10 feature in the Control Panel where you can view your basic network information.

News A Windows 10 app that provides world and national news and that you can customize to your interests.

Node The locations on the Quick access list that indicate a central point of connections or a place where things come together.

Nonresponsive program A program that is open but has stopped responding to your commands, which means it has stopped communicating with Windows 10.

NOT filter When used in a search, finds files that contain the first word but that do not contain the second word.

Notepad A basic text-editing program included with Windows 10 that you can use to create simple documents.

OneDrive A free file storage and file sharing service provided by Microsoft when you sign up for a free Microsoft account.

Online backup services A service that provides a system for backing up your computer files over the Internet on a scheduled basis and then storing the data securely on their computers; also referred to as remote backup or managed backup service.

On-Screen Keyboard A Windows 10 accessibility app that displays a keyboard on the screen that you can use instead of a physical keyboard; also referred to as *OSK*.

Operating system A specific type of computer program that manages the other programs on a computer—including computer devices such as desktop computers, laptop computers, smartphones, tablet computers, and game consoles.

Operators Words you can use in your search expression to get more specific search results.

OR filter When used in a search, finds files that contain either search term.

OSK The term used to refer to the On-Screen Keyboard.

Outlook.com A free web-based email system from Microsoft similar to Gmail and Yahoo mail.

Parent folder In the file organizing structure of File Explorer, the location where the folder you are viewing is saved—one level up in the hierarchy.

Partial matching A technique employed by the Windows 10 search feature that matches your search criteria to part of a word or phrase rather than to whole words.

Patch A small repair to an operating system or program that closes a security hole.

Path A sequence of folders (directories) that leads to a specific file or folder.

PC Reset A set of Windows 10 tools that you can use to bring your PC back to its original factory settings.

Peer-to-peer file sharing sites Websites that let you share files such as music, videos, and software with others using the Internet.

Pen A pen-shaped stylus that you tap on a computer screen.

Performance Monitor A tool that focuses on computer performance; Performance Monitor creates charts with more detail than the charts in Task Manager and in the Resource Monitor.

Performance tab In Task Manager, the tab that provides both data and graphs about the current activity of your CPU, Memory, Disks, and Network.

Personal folder A folder created for each user account on a Windows 10 computer, labeled with the account holder's name, and that contains the subfolders *Documents*, *Pictures*, *Music*, and *Videos*.

Phone Companion A Windows 10 app from the Store that assists you in adding Microsoft services to an iPhone, iPad, or Android phone.

Photos A Windows 10 app that will display photo albums from your Pictures folder, from your OneDrive, and from other connected devices and then display them all in one place.

PID The acronym for *Process Identifier*, which is a number assigned to each process while it runs.

PIN Acronym for personal identification number; in Windows 10 Settings, you can create a PIN to use in place of a password.

Platform An underlying computer system on which application programs can run.

Point to The action of moving the mouse pointer over a specific area.

Pointer Any symbol that displays on your screen in response to moving your mouse and with which you can select objects and commands.

Pointing device A mouse, touchpad, or other device that controls the pointer position on the screen.

Poisoned website A website that spreads a virus.

Portable hard drive A disk drive that plugs into an external port on your computer, typically into a USB port; also referred to as an external hard drive.

Process A file that is part of a running program and performs a specific task such as starting the program.

Process Identifier A number assigned to each process while it runs.

Processes tab In Task Manager, the tab that shows how Apps, Background processes, and Windows processes are using the system resources.

Program A set of instructions that a computer uses to accomplish a task; also called an application.

Progress bar In a dialog box or taskbar button, a bar that indicates visually the progress of a task such as a download or file transfer.

Quarantine area An area in a designated location on your computer from which a program cannot run.

Quick access list The first node in the navigation pane, which contains links to folders and files that Windows determines you access frequently and links that you add yourself.

Quick Access toolbar (File Explorer) The small row of buttons in the upper left corner of a File Explorer window from which you can perform frequently used commands.

Quick scan A type of scan that you can initiate in Windows Defender that checks the areas on your hard drive where malware programs are most likely to reside.

Quotes filter When used in a search, finds files that contain the exact phrase placed within the quotes.

Ransomware Malware that blocks access to your PC until a sum of money is paid.

Reading pane In Mail for Windows 10, an area that displays the contents of a message when it is selected.

Real time The actual time during which something takes place.

Real-time protection Protection provided by Windows 10 in which the system is continuously monitoring your computer at all times for suspicious activity such as viruses and spyware.

Recent locations A button on the address bar that displays a list of recently accessed locations; the current location is indicated by a check mark.

Recently added On the Start menu, a section that displays apps that you have recently downloaded and installed.

Rectangular snip When using Snipping Tool, the type of snip that lets you draw a precise box by dragging the mouse pointer around an area of the screen to form a rectangle.

Recycle Bin A folder that stores anything that you delete from your computer, and from which anything stored there can be retrieved until the contents are permanently deleted by activating the Empty Recycle Bin command.

Remote backup service A service that provides a system for backing up your computer files over the Internet on a scheduled basis and then storing the data securely on their computers; also referred to as online backup or managed backup service.

Removable storage device A portable device on which you can store files, such as a USB flash drive, a flash memory card, or an external hard drive, commonly used to transfer information from one computer to another.

Resource Monitor An area of the Performance Monitor that provides both instantaneous and recent-history (45 seconds) readouts of your computer's four key performance measurements—CPU usage, hard disk drive usage, network usage, and memory usage.

Resources A term used to refer collectively to the parts of your computer such as the central processing unit (CPU), memory, and any attached devices such as a printer.

Restore Down A command to restore a window to its previous size before it was maximized.

Restore point A snapshot of your computer's settings created by the System Restore tool.

Ribbon The area at the top of a folder window in File Explorer that groups common tasks such as copying and moving, creating new folders, emailing and zipping items, and changing views on related tabs.

Right-click The action of clicking the right mouse button.

Screen Clipping A snapshot of all or part of your screen that you can add to a document.

Screen reader A computer program that converts text into speech.

Screenshot Another name for a screen capture.

ScreenTip Useful information that displays in a small box on the screen when you perform various mouse actions, such as pointing to screen elements.

Scroll arrow An arrow at the top, bottom, left, or right, of a scroll bar that when clicked, moves the window in small increments.

Scroll bar A bar that displays on the bottom or right side of a window when the contents of a window are not completely visible; used to move the window up, down, left, or right to bring the contents into view.

Scroll box The box in a vertical or horizontal scroll bar that you drag to reposition the document on the screen.

Search engine A computer program that gathers information from the Web, indexes it, and puts it in a database that you can search based on specific words.

Search expression The keywords and syntax that you type into a search engine to begin your search.

Security holes Vulnerabilities in an operating system or program that allow malware to infect a computer without your knowledge.

Select To specify, by highlighting, a block of data or text on the screen with the intent of performing some action on the selection.

Services Computer programs or processes that run in the background and provide support to other programs.

Services console A Windows 10 tool that lists all services and provides a way to change their settings; also referred to as the Services desktop app.

Services desktop app A Windows 10 tool that lists all services and provides a way to change their settings; also referred to as the Services console.

Services tab In Task Manager, the tab that displays background features that are always running.

SharePoint A Microsoft technology that enables employees in an organization to access information across organizational and geographic boundaries.

Shortcut menu A context-sensitive menu that displays commands and options relevant to the active object.

Shut down Turning off your computer in a manner that closes all open programs and files, closes your network connections, stops the hard disk, and discontinues the use of electrical power.

Site A keyword in a search expression that returns webpages that belong to a specified site.

Sleep Turning off your computer in a manner that automatically saves your work, stops the fan, and uses a small amount of electrical power to maintain your work in memory.

Smart Lookup A Bing-powered feature that enables you to select text in a Word document and have a search conducted on the text and the results displayed in a pane on the right.

Snap Assist The ability to drag windows to the edges or corners of your screen, and then having Task View display thumbnails of other open windows so that you can select what other windows you want to snap into place.

Snip (from Microsoft Garage) A Microsoft Garage project that enables you to capture a screenshot, photo, or whiteboard drawing, annotate it with voice and ink, and share it.

Snip (Snipping Tool) The name for an image captured with Snipping Tool.

Snipping Tool A program included with Windows 10 with which you can capture an image of all or part of a computer screen, and then annotate, save, copy, or share the image via email.

Sort by In a folder window, a feature that enables you to sort the items by Name, Date modified, Type, Size, Date created, Authors, Tags, and Title, in Ascending or Descending order.

Split button A button that has two parts—a button and an arrow; clicking the main part of the button performs a command and clicking the arrow opens a menu with choices.

Sports A Windows 10 app that provides sports news and that can be viewed by individual sport type.

Spyware A type of malware that collects personal information or changes your browser settings, which can infect your computer without your knowledge when you download a program or visit a website.

Start menu The menu that displays when you click the Start button, which consists of a list of installed programs on the left and a customizable group of app tiles on the right.

Startup tab In Task Manager, the tab that displays the programs that are starting up automatically when you turn on your computer.

Steps Recorder A Windows 10 app that captures the steps you perform on your computer, including a text description of where you clicked and a screenshot of the screen during each click.

Subfolder A folder within another folder.

Surfing The process of navigating the Internet either for a particular item or for anything that is of interest, and quickly moving from one item to another.

Sync this view In Mail for Windows 10, a command that syncs all of your configured accounts to display.

Syntax The arrangement of the keywords in a search expression.

System Diagnostics Report A pre-built report that contains an easy to understand summary of your computer's overall performance.

System Idle Process A process that indicates the amount of CPU that is *not* being used.

System Image A Windows 10 tool that makes an exact copy of your hard drive and that you can use to completely restore your computer in the event of a hard drive failure.

System image backup A backup and recovery tool that creates a full system image backup from which you can restore your entire PC.

System Restore A Windows 10 tool that enables you to take your computer back to a previous point in time.

System tray Another name for the notification area on the taskbar.

Tabbed browsing A feature that enables you to open multiple websites and then switch among them.

Tags Properties that you create and add to a file to help you find and organize your files.

Task Manager A Windows 10 tool that shows you information about the programs, processes, and services that are currently running on your computer.

Task View A button on the taskbar that displays thumbnail images of all open apps enabling you to switch quickly between open apps.

Taskbar The area of the desktop that contains program buttons, and buttons for all open programs; by default, it is located at the bottom of the desktop, but you can move it.

This PC An area on the navigation pane that provides navigation to your internal storage and attached storage devices including optical media such as a DVD drive.

Thumbnail A reduced image of a graphic.

Tiles Square and rectangular boxes on the Windows 10 Start menu from which you can access apps, websites, programs, and tools for using the computer by simply clicking or tapping them.

Title bar The bar across the top of the window that displays the program name.

Trojan horse A malicious software program that hides inside legitimate programs, such as a game or media player or screen saver.

Universal apps Windows apps that use a common code base to deliver the app to any Windows device.

Unzip Extract files.

User account A collection of information that tells Windows 10 what files and folders the account holder can access, what changes the account holder can make to the computer system, and what the account holder's personal preferences are.

Users tab In Task Manager, the tab that displays which user accounts are logged in to the computer.

Virtual desktop An additional desktop display to organize and quickly access groups of windows.

Virtual folder A folder that does not represent a physical location.

Virus A type of malware designed specifically to replicate itself by spreading its infection from computer to computer.

Voice Recorder A Windows 10 app that enables you to use the microphone on your computer to record lectures, conversations, or any other sounds.

Wallpaper Another term for the desktop background.

Weather A Windows 10 app that provides a visually appealing and informative view of your weather or of the weather in a location that you designate.

Web browser A software program that displays webpages as you navigate the Internet.

White hat hacker An ethical security expert that tests an organization's data and network security by attempting to hack into it.

Wiki A website that permits anyone visiting the site to change its content by adding, removing, or editing the content.

Wikipedia The largest and most popular wiki on the Internet.

Window snip When using Snipping Tool, the type of snip that captures the entire displayed window.

Windows 10 An operating system developed by Microsoft Corporation designed to work with mobile computing devices of all types and also with traditional PCs.

Windows Accessories A group of system tools in Windows 10 that includes programs like Snipping Tool, WordPad, and Paint.

Windows apps Apps that run not only on a Windows phone and a Windows tablet, but also on your Windows desktop PC or laptop PC.

Windows Defender The free antivirus program built in to Windows 10; includes virus protection and removal, malware protection and removal, spyware detection and removal, and boot-time protection.

Windows Ease of Access A set of accessibility apps that you can access in a central location.

Windows Firewall Protection built into Windows 10 that can prevent hackers or malicious software from gaining access to your computer through a network or the Internet.

Windows Speech Recognition A Windows 10 accessibility app that enables you to control your computer by using your voice.

Windows Store The program where you can find and download Windows apps.

Windows Update The Windows 10 feature that continuously and automatically updates your PC over the Internet so that you receive new features and new security updates.

WordPad A simple word processing program that comes with Windows 10.

Worm A self-replicating program—similar to a virus—that spreads on its own to every computer on a network.

Zip Compress files.

Index